D0323302

Eighty Years and More

Elizabeth Cady Stanton

EIGHTY YEARS AND MORE

REMINISCENCES 1815–1897

ELIZABETH CADY STANTON

Introduction by Ellen Carol DuBois
Afterword by Ann D. Gordon

"Social science affirms that woman's place in society marks the
level of civilization."

Northeastern University Press
BOSTON

Northeastern University Press 1993

Introduction copyright 1993 by Ellen Carol DuBois
Afterword copyright 1993 by Ann D. Gordon

First published in 1898

Library of Congress Cataloging-in-Publication Data

Stanton, Elizabeth Cady, 1815–1902.
Eighty years and more : reminiscences, 1815–1897 / Elizabeth Cady
Stanton ; introduction by Ellen Carol DuBois ; afterword by Ann D.
Gordon
p. cm.
Originally published: T. Fisher Unwin, 1898.
Includes index.
ISBN 1-55553-136-9 — ISBN 1-55553-137-7 (pbk.)
1. Stanton, Elizabeth Cady, 1815–1902. 2. Suffragists—United
States—Biography. 3. Suffrage—United States—History—19th
century. 4. Feminism—United States—History—19th century.
I. Title. II. Title: 80 years and more.
JK1899.S7A3   1993
324.6′23′092—dc20
[B]   92-36249

Printed and bound by Edwards Brothers, Inc., Ann Arbor,
Michigan. The paper is Glatfelter Offset, an acid-free sheet.

MANUFACTURED IN THE UNITED STATES OF AMERICA
98   97   96   95   94   93   5   4   3   2   1

INTRODUCTION TO THE 1993 EDITION

Eighty Years and More is Elizabeth Cady Stanton's account of her life as one of the leading thinkers and activists of American feminism; it is also an important source for the history of the women's rights movement in the nineteenth century. But, like all great autobiographies, it is also much more. In these reminiscences, Stanton summarized a lifetime's exploration of America, both the place and the principle. Like other representative figures of nineteenth-century America, Stanton was deeply committed to unlimited expansion of America's mission and of her own vistas. She made her first trip when she was eleven, journeying by stagecoach from her hometown of Johnstown, New York, seventy miles east to her grandmother's home. Forty years later, soon after the transcontinental railroad was completed, she and her companion Susan B. Anthony were riding the rails to California. She spent the 1870s and early 1880s crisscrossing the United States and the next decade traveling back and forth across the Atlantic; even her trips to France and England in those years can be seen as a way of further exploring America through contrast.

Stanton's search for America was not only physical; it was philosophical. From her earliest years in her father's law office, she was trying to understand America not just as a place but as a political principle. Living in a town in which the memory of the Revolution was still fresh, growing up at a time in which the notions of natural rights and human freedom were gaining new vigor, she began to grapple with the concept of "liberty" — what did it mean and to whom did it apply? "In gathering up the threads of history in the last century, . . . one can trace the liberal social ideas," she wrote in 1881, and their "tendency to substitute for the divine right of kings, priests, and orders of nobility, the higher and broader one of individual conscience and judgment. . . ."[1] In her memoirs, Stanton investigated this grand battle of individual liberty versus unjust authority and asked how it explained her own life and place in history.

Liberalism is a term that American politics and political thinkers endlessly redefine, but never find they can do without. Elizabeth Cady Stanton was always and thoroughly a liberal but what this meant to her — and what therefore she means to the readers of her memoirs — has many dimensions. As a young woman, she was a passionate advocate of abolitionism; indeed, she argued that she learned the meaning of liberty in the recognition of how the slaves were deprived of it. By the end of her life, she was a believer in America's imperial mission, in the necessity of civilizing and uplifting the world's "inferior" peoples. She came from one of America's great landed families, loved to surround herself with wealth and elegance, and yet just as strongly appreciated the spare life of the western pioneer and contended that socialism was the highest expression of the American principle of equal rights for all.

Through all these changes and contradictions, one thing was consistent. Stanton steadily and brilliantly assessed the possibility of America and of its liberal legacy from the unexplored perspective of women. For the free white men of her father's generation, the American Revolution stood unambiguously for the principles of personal freedom and individual liberty. Throughout her account of her life, Stanton posed the question: how could the Revolution's daughters make these principles their own? She was not content with the political role that patriotic and aspiring women before her had occupied, the compromise historians have labeled "republican motherhood," by which women devoted to liberty agreed to realize it at a distance, through their sons. Instead, she longed for the time when the steady progress of liberal ideals would reach women themselves, bringing them under the emancipating light of individual conscience, personal independence, rational thought, and remunerative labor.

Yet Stanton also understood that much of the case for liberty as men had made it did not apply to women. Women did not generally acquire, own, or bestow property; they only bore and raised their husbands' heirs. They were not educated or renowned for their inventive genius, and were regarded as traditional and conservative in their convictions, rather than liberal and rational. Above all, women enjoyed no private realm of independence and self-governance that they sought to shield from the intrusion of government; rather, their private life was marked by dependence, and they were the permanent subjects of a form of government operating within the family and not just outside it. For women to enjoy the blessings of liberty and freedom, therefore, required radical alterations in all these extremely fundamental and seemingly natural relations of the sexes and it was to this that Stanton devoted her powerful and visionary intelligence.

Eighty Years and More begins with memories of the natural beauty and playfulness of childhood, a kind of personal state of nature from which each individual emerges. Children of different classes, races, and above all sexes mix in happy community, as yet unaware of the invidious distinctions that await them as adults. Stanton skillfully contrasted recollections of her youthful pleasures and instinctual independence with the dark and gloomy constraints of traditional Protestant culture and patriarchal family life as practiced in Johnstown in the 1820s. "Our parents were as kind, indulgent, and considerate as the Puritan ideas of those days permitted," she wrote, "but fear, rather than love, of God and parents alike, predominated" (4). Here, in the child's natural rebellion at the obligations of obedience and humility, she found the roots of her lifelong repudiation of arbitrary authority. Young Elizabeth's angry response to a nursemaid who objected to the shadow of a mischievous thought as it passed over the child's face became her lifelong manifesto: "I am so tired of that everlasting no! no! no!" (10).

Against this portrait of free and happy childhood, Stanton posed the patriarchal figure of her father, Daniel Cady, whom she both loved and challenged in ways that are almost impossible to separate. Her relationship with her father can be seen as symbolizing a larger tension — between her filial devotion to the principles of liberalism and republican citizenship for which he stood, and her use of these principles to challenge the basis of his and all other established authority. Judge Cady, a distant but imposing figure, presided over a world from which Elizabeth found herself barred and which she vowed to enter:

the world of free and rational individuals, the world of
law and politics, the world of men. Nothing she could
do, she sadly realized, could turn her into her father's
son, his rightful heir. But rather than breaking her spirit,
this discovery of what she called "the problem of boyhood" (21) became a challenge to meet. She recalled her
youth as a meditation on these dilemmas: how could a
woman secure a man's privileges? how could daughters
enjoy a place in the family of liberty equal to that
of sons?

The world of masculine privilege as Stanton remembered it from her growing-up rested on two major foun-
dations. One was the law, her father's special domain.
In his office she learned how the law enforced women's
subordination and what it would take to challenge and
change it. She recalled the story of her own naive belief
that she could eliminate women's legal subordination by
cutting all the "odious laws" out of her father's law books
and her father's suggestion that instead she "go down to
Albany and talk to the legislators" to change them (32).
Thus she felt herself both excluded by her father from
the world of the law and indebted to him for the knowledge she needed to challenge that exclusion. In an emotional as well as a philosophical sense, Stanton's lifelong
course was marked by the two sides of this relationship
to her father and to legal authority: armed with his/its
powerful resources, she revolted against the limits that
they imposed on her sex. In just this way, she deeply
identified with and radically challenged American society. She spent her life calling for "radical changes in . . .
the whole system of American jurisprudence," and yet
insisting that "these claims were but the logical outgrowth
of the fundamental theories of our republic" (162).

Along with law, religion was the other great force that deprived women of their freedom and independence. Stanton's understanding of the deep cultural roots of sexual inequality, which she attributed to religious superstition, complemented and deepened her focus on the power of law to shape women's status. Her basic anticlerical and secular convictions were formed in her youth. One of the most powerful stories in *Eighty Years and More* is Stanton's account of her futile struggle to accept religious authority and her inability to experience conversion at the hand of America's greatest antebellum evangelical, Charles Grandison Finney. She brilliantly captured the intense struggles of her generation of Americans to achieve conversion, because she had some critical distance on what she had come to regard as an ancient, atavistic ritual. "From our present standpoint," she wrote in retrospect, "nothing could be more puzzling and harrowing to the young mind" than insistence on "the total depravity of human nature and the sinner's awful danger of everlasting punishment" unless conversion was achieved (41).

In her memoirs, Stanton recalled her discovery that rational thought was the alternative to religious superstition and scientific truth was the antidote to the depression that she had suffered in subordinating herself to religion's dictates. "Science" for Stanton included things that late twentieth-century readers will regard as old-fashioned cultural fads, such as phrenology, the study of cranial bumps as an index to personality, and homeopathy, a nineteenth-century medical regimen. More generally, science signified independent inquiry, the experimental method, and individual evaluation of the evidence, not deference to some other external authority.

Thus, as a young mother Stanton rejected the advice of physicians in favor of her own best observations about how to care for infants. Finally, "science" was identified with the spirit of the modern age, the source of progress, and the foundation of industry, all of which she celebrated throughout *Eighty Years and More*.

Though Stanton worshiped progress, she had no faith in its automatic triumph. Challenging the subordinate position for which she was destined by her sex, she determined to array herself as an activist against the injustices and irrationalities of her imperfect society. While still a young woman she chose a secular vocation for herself, the role of reformer. Her memoirs document the many manifestations of the optimistic and activist spirit of social perfection — from dress reform to the abolition of slavery — which flourished in the second quarter of the nineteenth century. The antebellum advocates of fundamental social change, known somewhat modestly as "reformers," sought to raise up to the highest levels of human possibility both practices of the law and matters of the spirit, a combination that deeply appealed to Stanton. So too did the call to take active responsibility for and offer leadership to a post-revolutionary society seeking a way to live out its inspiriting principles. Fortified by this very belief in social perfection, Elizabeth Stanton and other antebellum women insisted on their right to take up the role of reformer in the same way and with the same fervor as men.

In her reminiscences, Stanton described her first exposure to "reform" in the elegant, liberal home of her older cousin, Gerrit Smith, and recalled her determination to become a part of this fascinating world. Smith was one of the richest landowners in western New York, his family fortune derived from beneficial land "bargains" struck with the Oneida tribe (454). Under his capacious roof, displaced Indians and runaway slaves were welcomed with gracious hospitality, and young Elizabeth also found there a kind of escape from the gloom of her parents' home. Here Elizabeth met the man she chose to marry, Henry Brewster Stanton, a prominent antislavery orator. After a period of doubt and conflict reminiscent of her religious struggles, she threw her lot in, not just with Henry Stanton but with the world of reform of which he was a part.

In its desire for perfection, antebellum reform addressed all aspects of the society, but one call for change rose above the others: the immediate, unconditional abolition of slavery. Abolitionism spoke to and elaborated Stanton's natural liberal impulses. She credited the abolitionist indictment of the major Protestant denominations for their refusal to condemn slavery with freeing her completely and forever from deference to established religious authority. Abolitionism also taught reformers the necessity of challenging unjust secular rule, providing what Stanton characterized as "the best school the American people ever had on which to learn republican principles and ethics" (59). By this she meant that abolitionists alone carried liberal principles through to their ultimate expression, which was the equal claims of all to enjoy personal freedom and individual development.

Modern readers concerned with Stanton's attitudes toward the place of Africans in America and the impact of abolitionism on her social thought may find contradictory indications in these memoirs. In the very first chapter, she described her deep attachment to the "black as coal" manservant (not slave) named Peter, who helped care for her when she was a child (14). Dependent himself, womanly in both his nurturant love for his charges and his subordinate place in her father's household, Peter was a companion and a solace to her in childhood and a dignified example of how to respond to social prejudice. The first actual slave whom she met was a young runaway named Harriet, who was hiding in Gerrit Smith's house on her way to freedom in Canada; Harriet's tale of sexual exploitation and enslavement deeply moved Elizabeth, who included it in her memoirs immediately after the story of her own difficult decision to marry. However, when Black men finally "walked through the constitutional door" to full citizenship in the late 1860s, without white women like herself on their arms, Stanton felt deserted and deeply offended, and she never fully cast off the tone of outraged racial superiority that she assumed in these years. Unlike other ex-abolitionists, who were sensitive to the racialism that underlay America's imperialist policies in the late nineteenth century, Stanton enthusiastically embraced the notion that her country had a mission to civilize the world's "backward" peoples.

The relation between Stanton's position in the class structure and her understanding and vision of American democracy is also complex. On the one hand, she took for granted a large measure of material comfort and relative leisure in assuming her liberal ideals. Liberty as she understood it had to do with personal choice and independent judgment, the right to do things "to suit one's own fancy." This is much closer to what late twentieth-century readers mean by "freedom" than is the classical liberal emphasis on the right to own and sell property, which as a woman she did not especially possess; nonetheless, the modest wealth and privilege of the

antebellum middle class was implicit even in her emphasis on self-expression. The years before marriage, during
which her sense of personal liberty and freedom from the
dictates of her parents became so intense, were carefree
precisely because she and her companions were not required to earn wages or even to perform any significant
unpaid labor to maintain the household. No wonder this
was a period of untrammeled personal expression, the
memory of which she treasured for the rest of her life.
Even so, she was early on drawn to the utopian socialist
vision of cooperative households and community collab-
oration, rather than the bourgeois household with its
numerous servants as the ideal way of life. By the end of
the nineteenth century, she was inclined to socialism and
a partisan of labor in its battles against capital. Had she
been able to see more of the twentieth century, socialism
might have provided her with the kind of overarching,
critical framework for evaluating America's democratic
claims that abolitionism once had.

So far we have considered *Eighty Years and More* with
respect to the world of men, from which its author had
been barred, and to which she longed for admission. But
what about the world of women, into which she had been
born and for which she was destined? The traditional
practices and relations of her sex, which contemporary
historians have labeled (and romanticized) as "woman's
sphere," were no solace for her dissatisfaction at being
denied the liberties men enjoyed. In comparison with
Judge Cady, the "queenly looking" Margaret Livingston
Cady plays only a minor role in *Eighty Years and More*.
Like fathers, mothers reprimanded children and interrupted their fun, but mothers had no future of freedom

or legacy of authority to will to their daughters. Nor did the exclusive company of young Elizabeth's female peers offer her relief from the discriminations she suffered as a girl in a world ruled by men. In her reminiscences of her time at Emma Willard's Female Academy, where she went for the final stages of her education, she highlighted an incident in which a deceitful classmate exposed her to a false charge of plagiarism, a story that seems intended to refute notions of women's superior morality.

Frustrated by the limited possibilities of "woman's sphere," Stanton eventually turned to the philosophy of women's rights as an alternative way to live out her woman's life. Portentously, she was first exposed to the advocates and ideas of women's rights on her honeymoon! She described her meeting, on her wedding journey, with Lucretia Mott, the leading woman abolitionist in America and a stalwart advocate of moral and intellectual equality for women. "These were the first women I had ever met who believed in the equality of the sexes and who did not believe in the popular orthodox religion" (83). Previously, Stanton had hated men's condescension to women and repudiated widespread notions of women's inferiority, but women themselves had seemed to her not much more than the low expectations the world had of them. To find that other women shared her discontent, her longing for some larger way to be a woman, changed her life. Mott showed her that it was possible to combine hatred of women's subordination with loyalty to her sex.

For the time being, however, she did not follow the path of women's rights, preferring instead the expanded scope that middle-class marriage, motherhood, and homemaking offered. In her own home, a woman might have an arena to exercise her talents, taste, and judgment

— at least for a while. "It is a proud moment in a woman's life to reign supreme within four walls," Stanton wrote (136). She recalled in detail her first home as a married woman, in Boston, in the midst of many literary and reform excitements, with her husband nearby, few children, and enough servants. Under such conditions, her domestic responsibilities were relatively light and compatible with continued public activities. At first, motherhood was also a challenge, a testing ground for just those traits of rational thought, individual judgment, and self-reliance that she insisted women possessed equally with men. Stanton's descriptions of her initial pleasure at homemaking and motherhood are among the most timeless in the book, especially as they contrast with her later descent into isolation, futility, and deep discontent at her limited domestic vistas. Eventually, she and her family moved to the small, central New York town of Seneca Falls, far from the thrills of the Boston literary and reform scene. Now "Mr. Stanton was frequently from home, I had poor servants, and an increasing number of children. . . . Then, too, the novelty of housekeeping had passed away" (145).

This is the point in her autobiography, when "woman's sphere" and the "isolated home" began to close in on her, that Stanton chose to introduce the theme of women's rights at length. Beginning with her role in convening the Seneca Falls Convention of 1848, Stanton expressed her frustration with woman's portion by turning back to her sex rather than away from it. She found the remedy for her discontent with "woman's sphere" in challenging its prescriptions on behalf and in the company of other women. With their help, she recalled, her "petty domestic annoyances gradually took a subordinate place" (151–52) and her life took on a larger purpose, the realization of liberty's promise for her sex. Domestic cloisters dissolved and new vistas — activities, associates, purpose — suddenly appeared, even in the previously limited society of Seneca Falls.

At the core of Stanton's account of her turn to women's rights activism is a long essay on Susan B. Anthony, her political partner for a half-century. The three years between the 1848 convention and their first meeting dissolve entirely in the pages of *Eighty Years and More*. In shifting the focus of her memoirs temporarily to Anthony, Stanton demonstrated the lesson she was learning, that the emancipation of any one woman involves the emancipation of all. Here was one of the most curious aspects of her ambition to extend liberalism to women: individual freedom could be won only by collective effort. Just as Stanton liberated her new friend from an inclination to accept arbitrary religious authority into "the holy of holies of her own self" (160), Anthony freed Stanton from her domestic confines and from the temptations of "narrow family selfishness" (165). (Stanton recalled that when they first met, the only liberty she was engaged in cultivating was that of her three rambunctious boy children.) "I do believe that I have developed into much more of a woman under her jurisdiction, fed on statute laws and constitutional amendments," Stanton credited her friend many years later, "than if left to myself reading novels in an easy chair. . . ."[2]

As Stanton inherited it, the politics of women's rights identified the institution of marriage — its legal conventions and economic underpinnings — as the fundamental barrier to women's equality. Here, in the very bosom of the family, were the obstacles to the universal triumph of individual rights. All of the venerable rights of Americans "to person, children, property, wages, life, liberty, and the pursuit of happiness" (224) were placed beyond the reach of woman once she became wife — this was the fundamental injustice that women's rights challenged. At the time of the Seneca Falls Convention, Stanton had already apprenticed on the campaign for New York's first married women's property act, which undid the traditional disability that marriage brought to women and secured for wives the rights to own and sell property. Later, with Anthony, she demanded the right of wives to contract for their own labor and to retain custody of their children after divorce, which began to be established in New York in 1860 with a second married women's property act. Radical change in the laws and practices of marriage continued to be a major concern for Stanton for the rest of her life. Once she was reasonably certain that wives would be awarded their basic economic rights, she concentrated on liberalizing divorce laws; even her advocacy of reproductive and sexual self-determination for women can best be understood in the larger context of defending women's individuality within marriage. Speaking to all-female audiences on the subject of what she called "Marriage and Maternity," she took the venerable principle of individual liberty in a radical new direction, using it to insist on wives' rights to reject their husbands' sexual claims; indeed, she believed that such rights were even more important than economic rights for wives, "by just so much as the rights of persons are more sacred than the rights of property" (425).

To the women's rights commitment to bring the arbitrary authority of husbands under the rule of law, Stanton added her own distinctive vision of the equality of women with men: the importance of winning equal political rights for women. If reform in the laws and customs of marriage and divorce were necessary to bring down the barriers to women's development as independent persons, access to the challenges of republican citizenship was crucial to cultivating women's individual judgment, consciousness, and sense of public responsibility. Anger at the inequality of women's disfranchisement was the stick that drove her to advocate woman suffrage, but the excitements and possibilities of politics were the carrot. Woman suffrage was for Stanton the link between her women's rights commitment and her larger political intentions: her driving hope was that political rights would signify women's equality with men and simultaneously strengthen the cause of reform, by adding the power of women's voices to those of men.

In her memoirs, Stanton's deeply political understanding of women's equality comes into focus in the chapters that chronicle the national upheaval and crisis of Civil War and Reconstruction. When the future of the nation and the meanings of democracy were being debated "at every fireside," Stanton wrote (241), women longed for a field grander than that provided by their traditional charitable labors. They were as deeply affected as men by the crisis of southern secession and as eager "to labor for a principle" to resolve it (235–36). Indeed, with men occupied on the battlefield, Stanton felt that it was left to the women of the north to fight the political war, to insist that there was an "'irrepressible conflict' between slavery and freedom, [and] . . . that freedom for the slaves was the only way to victory" (235). She proudly recalled the National Woman's Loyal League that she and Anthony organized in 1863, which gathered hundreds of thousands of petitions on behalf of the constitutional abolition of slavery. "When every hour is big with destiny, . . ." Stanton wrote in the call to this organization, "it is high time for the daughters of the Revolution . . . to unseal the last will and testaments of the fathers, lay hold of their birthright of freedom, and keep it a sacred trust for all coming generations" (237).

While women's dedication to the political principle of freedom is the major theme of Stanton's account of the Civil War crisis, the unwillingness of Republicans, "claiming to be the liberal party" (244), to include women in its blessings is the corollary. At this crucial moment in history, as Stanton saw it, the men charged with the historic mission of defending and extending American liberalism failed to meet their historic obligations. They could have written the fundamental principle of equal rights for all, regardless of condition, into the Constitution, but held back because they were unwilling to bestow political power on women along with the freedmen. Instead of making an absolute statement about equality, congressional Republicans wrote women's disfranchisement into the Constitution by including what she disdainfully called "the word 'male'" in the Fourteenth Amendment (242).

Stanton deeply understood the significance of this failed opportunity: the establishment of women's political equality, which formerly would have been a matter for the states to resolve, now shifted to the federal, indeed constitutional, arena. In a variety of ways — through congressional petition, constitutional argument, court cases, and ultimately a campaign for another constitutional amendment — Stanton led the woman suffrage movement in pursuit of this goal: constitutional establishment of the principle that "women, as citizens of the United States, cannot be governed by laws in the making of which they have no part" (425). As far as Stanton was concerned, Reconstruction was still unfinished business for women thirty years later, at century's end.

Of all the political lessons contained within *Eighty Years and More*, none is more important than those of the Civil War epoch. While the Reconstruction crisis revealed, in Stanton's memorable words, "that it is impossible for the best of men to understand women's feelings or the humiliation of their position" (254), this unfortunate truth was something she had long before learned from her father's stubborn indifference to her youthful aspirations for recognition. Rather, the new lesson that the historic challenge of the 1860s taught her, and what she wanted her readers to take from her account of it, was that women must establish freedom and equality for themselves by their own exertions. In the political visions and disappointments of Reconstruction, Stanton wrote, "women generally awoke to their duty to themselves" (255) and self-reliance became the standard, not only for their individual emancipation but for their collective political involvement.

In making this ringing call for political autonomy, Stanton could not quite acknowledge that there might be a tension between women's collective pursuit of freedom and equality, and other aspects of the struggle for the triumph of liberal principles. Yet this was precisely the result when the political circumstances surrounding the enactment of the Fourteenth and Fifteenth amendments combined with Stanton's own sense of outraged entitlement that men she considered her social inferiors were enfranchised, while women like herself, "daughters of the Revolution," were not. In searching for allies to challenge Republicans for their refusal to take up woman suffrage, she and Anthony turned in 1867 to the flamboyant and racist Democrat George Francis Train. In her account of this period, written decades later, Stanton was still defensive regarding charges that Train had tainted the woman suffrage movement with his Negrophobia. Yet readers will see plenty of evidence of racial bias in her suspicion of male comradeship: it was the ex-slaves she expected to betray women's rights, while she treated the bombastic Train warmly, as a true ally.

Despite what *Eighty Years and More* reveals about Stanton's profound disappointment at Reconstruction Republicans' refusal to embrace women's equality, it also indicates how hopeful she was about women's prospects in America in the aftermath of the Civil War. Just as she had urged, women were establishing broader fields and higher standards for themselves and not waiting for men to grant them equality. In addition to the spread of the demand for woman suffrage, to which she was so deeply committed, Stanton documented other aspects of women's enlarged vistas, notably women's successful efforts to gain admission into previously all-male universities. The development of the post–Civil War women's movement is the unstated backdrop for the later chapters of *Eighty Years and More*. In her memoirs, Stanton portrayed herself primarily as an observer of these changes in American womanhood and slighted her role as a leader in bringing them about. Throughout the 1870s and early 1880s, Stanton counseled younger suffrage activists, encouraged local suffrage movements, and campaigned for woman suffrage in a series of state voter referenda.

Stanton offered her observations about the new possibilities for women in post–Civil War America in the
context of her travels back and forth across the United
States from the late 1860s through the early 1880s. During
these years she was a busy and successful lecturer on the
newly established "lyceum circuit," which brought culture and political controversy to the far-flung American
population. Stanton constructed her account of her dozen
years on the road as if it were one trip, from east to west,
following the westward move of Yankee pioneers across
the American continent. From Pennsylvania and Michigan, her reminiscences move through the plains states,
with their barren and unyielding physical conditions,
eventually emerging into the bounteous natural beauty
of the Pacific Coast. The women — and men — of whom
she wrote were the audiences at her lectures, her hosts
on her travels, and fellow passengers in innumerable
railroad cars. These chapters in *Eighty Years and More*
can also be read as a typical platform performance, pre-
served for generations of readers in the pages of her
memoirs. Stanton organized her reminiscences as she did
her speeches, around elaborate and amusing incidents,
often drawn from her travels, into which she inserted
serious political commentary and observations about the
capacities and equality of women.

This section of her memoirs can be read as a woman's
meditation on American liberalism in the age of manifest
destiny. There are two portraits of the expansion of
America here, in unacknowledged tension with each
other, which together capture some of Stanton's ambiv-
alence about American democracy in the post–Civil War
era. Stanton evoked the brutal physical and economic
conditions faced by the western pioneers, especially by

the women whose "courage and endurance . . . surpassed all description" (253). Her own experience with such conditions gave her great respect for these sturdy people and for herself as well. "Heretofore my idea had been that pioneer life was a period of romantic freedom," she wrote, "but a few months of pioneer life permanently darkened my rosy ideal" (250–51). On the other hand, there is also a much more complacent version of American expansion in *Eighty Years and More*, the triumphant establishment of Yankee civilization in what was until then a wilderness. She praised the charming homes, visited the charitable institutions, named the leading citizens, and celebrated the social order being established throughout the cities and towns of the west. Absent for the most part from this celebration of the progress of Yankee civilization were Native Americans, who appear briefly as a disembodied threat but never a besieged people; Mexicans, whose battles with the U.S. Army on the Texas border Stanton barely noticed; European immigrants, who seemed at best victims of centuries of ignorance, to be reborn in the pure air and new life to be found in the west; and Asian immigrants, whose presence in the west she did not even notice.

In both visions of the west — the pioneering and the settled — Stanton focused on the Yankee women who seemed to her a new breed, strong, accomplished, a promise of the eventual triumph of freedom among women. In her travels through post–Civil War America, she virtually announced the disestablishment of "woman's sphere." "While the lords of creation have been debating her sphere and drawing their chalk marks here and there," she wrote, "woman has quietly stepped out-

side the barren fields where she was compelled to graze
for centuries, . . . a power in the world of thought" (265).
In more than one of Stanton's western anecdotes, "stately
wom[e]n" are inappropriately bound to "puny men"
whose claims to masculine superiority appear so ludicrous as to be occasions for amusement rather than outrage (295).

The tension in Stanton's portrait of freedom in the west
— freedom as the pioneer's struggle versus freedom as
the settler's order — has its equivalent in her portrait of
the emancipated woman of the west. On the one hand,
Stanton portrayed the power of woman as an elemental
force, eternally present if too often ignored. On the other
hand, she rendered the emancipation of women as a
process, constantly taking place, marked by struggle,
growth, and change. She expressed her complex understanding of western women and their strength appropri-
ately enough through an extended geological metaphor.
Contemplating the majestic bluffs rising above the Mississippi River, "the Great Mother of Waters," Stanton
imagined that "these bluffs and the sons of Adam, too"
had been raised up by the very flowing power they dis-
dained to recognize. Yet she also wrote that women's
freedom was like an earthquake, and urged "those who
have ears to hear [to] discern low, rumbling noises that
foretell convulsions in our social world that may, perchance, . . . bring woman up to the surface" (273).

Stanton's account of the 1876 Centennial celebration
resolves this tension in her approach to American democracy in the direction of protest, rebellion, and critical
challenge. Offered the opportunity to assess the degree
to which America had met the promise of its Revolution,

Stanton found it wanting. While some were celebrating America's grand destiny, she and other women's rights leaders offered "an impeachment" — the word carefully chosen — "of the Fathers . . . and their male descendants for their injustice and oppression" (310). Women's unmet claims were here linked rather than opposed to the insurgencies of other oppressed groups, notably the former slaves; and Gilded Age America's arrogant belief in its superiority to "Hindoo" and Chinese civilization was lampooned. American patriotism, *Eighty Years and More* argues, is better expressed through protest than through parades. Stanton the instinctual oppositionist, the perpetual rebel, was reasserting herself over Stanton the privileged and entitled daughter of a powerful man. Entering the last decades of her life, she was still objecting to "that everlasting no! no! no!"

In the final chapters of *Eighty Years and More*, which treat the late 1880s and the 1890s, Stanton had far less time to work over her material and refine her themes than she had in earlier sections of the book. She used these chapters primarily to chronicle her activities and list — often in exhausting profusion — the names of literary and political figures with whom she was associating in her later decades. After 1882 she gave up the rigors of the lyceum circuit and her travels through America in favor of a series of trips to France and England. Two of her seven children, Theodore and Harriot, had married Europeans and lived abroad; Stanton was an eager and enthusiastic "Queenmother" to her European grandchildren. While in England, she also began to organize an international network of woman suffragists and

reformers, which culminated in the 1888 International
Council of Women, and this is also the subject of one of
the later chapters of her memoirs.

Stanton's several trips to Europe offered her one final
pespective for assessing America, through comparison
with the ways of more settled societies. For the most part,
her travels confirmed what she already knew: that the
New World was superior to the Old, that rational thought
and scientific skepticism met humanity's needs better
than religion, and that she was lucky to live in the modern
world. "Glorious Nineteenth Century," she exclaimed,
"what conquests are thine!" (341). On one crucial issue,
however, the prospects for liberalism were greater in
England than in America. In England, secularism was a
flourishing philosophy and religious establishmentari-
anism was on the wane. Back home, by contrast, an
aggressive, politically ambitious strand of Protestantism
was gaining influence in many spheres, including the
rapidly expanding women's movement, in which Stanton
had placed so much faith.

The role of religion in the continuing subordination of
women is thus an emerging theme in the final chapters
of *Eighty Years and More*. Stanton was frustrated with
the lack of progress being made in women's demand for
political equality and looking for insights into the stubborn persistence of ideas of male superiority through the
ages. But she was also responding to historical develop-
ments, in particular the accelerating numbers of European immigrants to America, most of them Jews and
Catholics. However, instead of calling for the quasi-
official establishment of Protestant standards of morality
and culture, as other thinkers and reformers of her gen-

eration were doing, Stanton developed a critical perspective on all religious thought, Protestantism included. She used these memoirs to argue that American Protestanism was as illiberal, backward, and contemptuous of women as the Old World faiths.

Stanton concluded her memoirs with a brief account of her eightieth birthday. Sponsored by the National Council of Women, her birthday celebration was heralded by a large group of "representative women" as a symbol of women's triumphant ascension into equality and social power. While Stanton no doubt appreciated this "recognition of the debt the present generation owes to the pioneers of the past" (459), the celebratory mode disturbed her: being made the symbol of the history of women's emancipation, a process understood by her admirers virtually to have reached its triumphant end, was uncomfortably close to being declared dead and buried. Most of this chapter is offered in the words of others, and not until the final pages does Stanton allow herself a few words of her own and a dissenting perspective on the significance of her own life. Everything for which she had worked and that was regarded in the 1890s as "a step in progress" was, she reminded her readers, criticized as "a grave mistake" when she first advocated it (466); of this she was very proud. Rather than be "revered . . . as a queen among women" (459), she wanted to be entered in history as a perpetual rebel, a continuing iconoclast.

By extension, here too is Stanton's ultimate perspective on the principle to which she dedicated her life. Freedom for women, *Eighty Years and More* teaches its readers, is less a condition than a process, a horizon that recedes just as fast as we approach it; its history is one of continual struggle, opposition, and change. "To be as good as our fathers," Wendell Phillips had declared in his Phi Beta Kappa speech of 1881, "we must be better" (333–34). Stanton recorded this message in her memoirs because she believed it; *Eighty Years and More* is the record of how she lived these words, with the added challenge of having been born "a daughter of the Revolution," determined to expand its promise to include her sex.

ELLEN CAROL DUBOIS

Notes

1. *History of Woman Suffrage*, Vol. 1, ed. Elizabeth Cady Stanton, Susan B. Anthony, and Matilda Joslyn Gage (Rochester, N.Y.: Susan B. Anthony, 1881), 50.

2. Stanton's remarks at Anthony's seventieth birthday, quoted in Ida Husted Harper, *The Life and Work of Susan B. Anthony*, Vol. 2 (Indianapolis and Kansas City: Bowen-Merrill, 1898), 667.

PREFACE.

THE interest my family and friends have always manifested in the narration of my early and varied experiences, and their earnest desire to have them in permanent form for the amusement of another generation, moved me to publish this volume. I am fully aware that its contents have no especial artistic merit, being composed partly of extracts from my diary, a few hasty sketches of my travels and people I have met, and of my opinions on many social questions.

The story of my private life as the wife of an earnest reformer, as an enthusiastic housekeeper, proud of my skill in every department of domestic economy, and as the mother of seven children, may amuse and benefit the reader.

The incidents of my public career as a leader in the most momentous reform yet launched upon the world—the emancipation of woman—will be found in " The History of Woman Suffrage."

ELIZABETH CADY STANTON.

NEW YORK CITY, *September*, 1897.

I DEDICATE THIS VOLUME TO

SUSAN B. ANTHONY,

MY STEADFAST FRIEND FOR HALF A CENTURY.

CONTENTS.

LIST OF PORTRAITS.

EIGHTY YEARS AND MORE.

CHAPTER I.

CHILDHOOD.

THE psychical growth of a child is not influenced by days and years, but by the impressions passing events make on its mind. What may prove a sudden awakening to one, giving an impulse in a certain direction that may last for years, may make no impression on another. People wonder why the children of the same family differ so widely, though they have had the same domestic discipline, the same school and church teaching, and have grown up under the same influences and with the same environments. As well wonder why lilies and lilacs in the same latitude are not all alike in color and equally fragrant. Children differ as widely as these in the primal elements of their physical and psychical life.

Who can estimate the power of antenatal influences, or the child's surroundings in its earliest years, the effect of some passing word or sight on one, that makes no impression on another? The unhappiness of one child under a certain home discipline is not inconsistent with the content of another under this same discipline. One, yearning for broader freedom, is in a chronic condition of rebellion; the other, more easily satisfied, quietly accepts the situation. Everything is seen from a different standpoint; everything takes its color from the mind of the beholder.

I am moved to recall what I can of my early days, what I thought and felt, that grown people may have a better understanding of children and do more for their happiness and development. I see so much tyranny exercised over children, even by well-disposed parents, and in so many varied forms,—a tyranny to which these parents are themselves insensible,—that I desire to paint my joys and sorrows in as vivid colors as possible, in the hope that I may do something to defend the weak from the strong. People never dream of all that is going on in the little heads of the young, for few adults are given to introspection, and those who are incapable of recalling their own feelings under restraint and disappointment can have no appreciation of the sufferings of children who can neither describe nor analyze what they feel. In defending themselves against injustice they are as helpless as dumb animals. What is insignificant to their elders is often to them a source of great joy or sorrow.

With several generations of vigorous, enterprising ancestors behind me, I commenced the struggle of life under favorable circumstances on the 12th day of November, 1815, the same year that my father, Daniel Cady, a distinguished lawyer and judge in the State of New York, was elected to Congress. Perhaps the excitement of a political campaign, in which my mother took the deepest interest, may have had an influence on my prenatal life and given me the strong desire that I have always felt to participate in the rights and duties of government.

My father was a man of firm character and unimpeachable integrity, and yet sensitive and modest to a painful degree. There were but two places in which he felt at ease—in the courthouse and at his own fireside. Though gentle and tender, he had such a dignified repose and reserve of manner that, as children, we regarded him with fear rather than affection.

My mother, Margaret Livingston, a tall, queenly looking woman, was courageous, self-reliant, and at her ease under all circumstances and in all places. She was the daughter of Colonel James Livingston, who took an active part in the War of the Revolution.

Colonel Livingston was stationed at West Point when Arnold made the attempt to betray that stronghold into the hands of the enemy. In the absence of General Washington and his superior officer, he took the responsibility of firing into the *Vulture*, a suspicious looking British vessel that lay at anchor near the opposite bank of the Hudson River. It was a fatal shot for André, the British spy, with whom Arnold was then consummating his treason. Hit between wind and water, the vessel spread her sails and hastened down the river, leaving André, with his papers, to be captured while Arnold made his escape through the lines, before his treason was suspected.

On General Washington's return to West Point, he sent for my grandfather and reprimanded him for acting in so important a matter without orders, thereby making himself liable to court-martial; but, after fully impressing the young officer with the danger of such self-sufficiency on ordinary occasions, he admitted that a most fortunate shot had been sent into the *Vulture*, " for," he said, " we are in no condition just now to defend ourselves against the British forces in New York, and the capture of this spy has saved us."

My mother had the military idea of government, but her children, like their grandfather, were disposed to assume the responsibility of their own actions; thus the ancestral traits in mother and children modified, in a measure, the dangerous tendencies in each.

Our parents were as kind, indulgent, and considerate as the Puritan ideas of those days permitted, but fear, rather than love, of God and parents alike, predominated. Add to this our timidity in our intercourse with servants and teachers, our dread of the ever present devil, and the reader will see that, under such conditions, nothing but strong self-will and a good share of hope and mirthfulness could have saved an ordinary child from becoming a mere nullity.

The first event engraved on my memory was the birth of a sister when I was four years old. It was a cold morning in January when the brawny Scotch nurse carried me to see the little stranger, whose advent was a matter of intense interest to me for many weeks after. The large, pleasant room with the white curtains and bright wood fire on the hearth, where panada, catnip, and all kinds of little messes which we were allowed to taste were kept warm, was the center of attraction for the older children. I heard so many friends remark, " What a pity it is she's a girl! " that I felt a kind of compassion for the little baby. True, our family consisted of five girls and only one boy, but I did not understand at that time that girls were considered an inferior order of beings.

To form some idea of my surroundings at this time, imagine a two-story white frame house with a hall through the middle, rooms on either side, and a large back building with grounds on the side and rear, which joined the garden of our good Presbyterian minister, the Rev. Simon Hosack, of whom I shall have more to say in another chapter. Our favorite resorts in the house were the garret and cellar. In the former were barrels of hickory nuts, and, on a long shelf, large cakes of maple sugar and all kinds of dried herbs and sweet flag; spinning wheels, a number of small white cotton bags filled with bundles, marked in ink, " silk," " cotton," " flannel," " calico," etc., as well as ancient masculine and feminine costumes. Here we would crack the nuts, nibble the sharp edges of the maple sugar, chew some favorite herb, play ball with the bags, whirl the old spinning wheels, dress up in our ancestors' clothes, and take a bird's-eye view of the surrounding country from an enticing scuttle hole. This was forbidden ground; but, nevertheless, we often went there on the sly, which only made the little escapades more enjoyable.

The cellar of our house was filled, in winter, with barrels of apples, vegetables, salt meats, cider, butter, pounding barrels, washtubs, etc., offering admirable nooks for playing hide and seek. Two tallow candles threw a faint light over the scene on certain occasions. This cellar was on a level with a large kitchen where we played blind man's buff and other games when the day's work was done. These two rooms are the center of many of the merriest memories of my childhood days.

I can recall three colored men, Abraham, Peter, and Jacob, who acted as menservants in our youth. In turn they would sometimes play on the banjo for us to dance, taking real enjoyment in our games. They are all at rest now with " Old Uncle Ned in the place where the good niggers go." Our nurses, Lockey Danford, Polly Bell, Mary Dunn, and Cornelia Nickeloy—peace to their ashes—were the only shadows on the gayety of these winter evenings; for their chief delight was to hurry us off to bed, that they might receive their beaux or make short calls in the neighborhood. My memory of them is mingled with no sentiment of gratitude or affection. In expressing their opinion of us in after years, they said we were a very troublesome, obstinate, disobedient set of children. I have no doubt we were in constant rebellion against their petty tyranny. Abraham, Peter, and Jacob viewed us in a different light, and I have the most pleasant recollections of their kind services.

In the winter, outside the house, we had the snow with which to build statues and make forts, and huge piles of wood covered with ice, which we called the Alps, so difficult were they of ascent and descent. There we would climb up and down by the hour, if not interrupted, which, however, was generally the case. It always seemed to me that, in the height of our enthusiasm, we were invariably summoned to some disagreeable duty, which would appear to show that thus early I keenly enjoyed outdoor life. Theodore Tilton has thus described the place where I was born: " Birthplace is secondary parentage, and transmits character. Johnstown was more famous half a century ago than since; for then, though small, it was a marked intellectual center; and now, though large, it is an unmarked manufacturing town. Before the birth of Elizabeth Cady it was the vice-ducal seat of Sir William Johnson, the famous English negotiator with the Indians. During her girlhood it was an arena for the intellectual wrestlings of Kent, Tompkins, Spencer, Elisha Williams, and Abraham Van Vechten, who, as lawyers, were among the chiefest of their time. It is now devoted mainly to the fabrication of steel springs and buckskin gloves. So, like Wordsworth's early star, it has faded into the light of common day. But Johnstown retains one of its ancient splendors—a glory still fresh as at the foundation of the world. Standing on its hills, one looks off upon a country of enameled meadow lands, that melt away southward toward the Mohawk, and northward to the base of those grand mountains which are ' God's monument over the grave of John Brown.' "

Harold Frederic's novel, " In the Valley," contains many descriptions of this region that are true to nature, as I remember the Mohawk Valley, for I first knew it not so many years after the scenes which he lays there. Before I was old enough to take in the glory of this scenery and its classic associations, Johnstown was to me a gloomy-looking town. The middle of the streets was paved with large cobblestones, over which the farmer's wagons rattled from morning till night, while the sidewalks were paved with very small cobblestones, over which we carefully picked our way, so that free and graceful walking was out of the question. The streets were lined with solemn poplar trees, from which small yellow worms were continually dangling down. Next to the Prince of Darkness, I feared these worms. They were harmless, but the sight of one made me tremble. So many people shared in this feeling that the poplars were all cut down and elms planted in their stead. The Johnstown academy and churches were large square buildings, painted white, surrounded by these same

sombre poplars, each edifice having a doleful bell which
seemed to be ever tolling for school, funerals, church,
or prayer meetings. Next to the worms, those clang-
ing bells filled me with the utmost dread; they seemed
like so many warnings of an eternal future. Visions of
the Inferno were strongly impressed on my childish
imagination. It was thought, in those days, that firm
faith in hell and the devil was the greatest help to virtue. It certainly made me very unhappy whenever my
mind dwelt on such teachings, and I have always had
my doubts of the virtue that is based on the fear of
punishment.

Perhaps I may be pardoned a word devoted to my
appearance in those days. I have been told that I was
a plump little girl, with very fair skin, rosy cheeks, good
features, dark-brown hair, and laughing blue eyes. A
student in my father's office, the late Henry Bayard of
Delaware (an uncle of our recent Ambassador to the
Court of St. James's, Thomas F. Bayard), told me one
day, after conning my features carefully, that I had one
defect which he could remedy. "Your eyebrows
should be darker and heavier," said he, "and if you will
let me shave them once or twice, you will be much improved." I consented, and, slight as my eyebrows
were, they seemed to have had some expression, for the
loss of them had a most singular effect on my appearance. Everybody, including even the operator, laughed
at my odd-looking face, and I was in the depths of
humiliation during the period while my eyebrows
were growing out again. It is scarcely necessary for
me to add that I never allowed the young man
to repeat the experiment, although strongly urged to
do so.

I cannot recall how or when I conquered the alphabet, words in three letters, the multiplication table, the points of the compass, the chicken pox, whooping cough, measles, and scarlet fever. All these unhappy incidents of childhood left but little impression on my mind. I have, however, most pleasant memories of the good spinster, Maria Yost, who patiently taught three generations of children the rudiments of the English language, and introduced us to the pictures in "Murray's Spelling-book," where Old Father Time, with his scythe, and the farmer stoning the boys in his apple trees, gave rise in my mind to many serious reflections. Miss Yost was plump and rosy, with fair hair, and had a merry twinkle in her blue eyes, and she took us by very easy stages through the old-fashioned schoolbooks. The interesting Readers children now have were unknown sixty years ago. We did not reach the temple of knowledge by the flowery paths of ease in which our descendants now walk.

I still have a perfect vision of myself and sisters, as we stood up in the classes, with our toes at the cracks in the floor, all dressed alike in bright red flannel, black alpaca aprons, and, around the neck, a starched ruffle that, through a lack of skill on the part of either the laundress or the nurse who sewed them in, proved a constant source of discomfort to us. I have since seen full-grown men, under slighter provocation than we endured, jerk off a collar, tear it in two, and throw it to the winds, chased by the most soul-harrowing expletives. But we were sternly rebuked for complaining, and if we ventured to introduce our little fingers between the delicate skin and the irritating linen, our hands were slapped and the ruffle readjusted a degree closer. Our Sunday dresses were relieved with a black sprig and white aprons. We had red cloaks, red hoods, red mittens, and red stockings. For one's self to be all in red six months of the year was bad enough, but to have this costume multiplied by three was indeed monotonous. I had such an aversion to that color that I used to rebel regularly at the beginning of each season when new dresses were purchased, until we finally passed into an exquisite shade of blue. No words could do justice to my dislike of those red dresses. My grandfather's detestation of the British redcoats must have descended to me. My childhood's antipathy to wearing red enabled me later to comprehend the feelings of a little niece, who hated everything pea green, because she had once heard the saying, " neat but not gaudy, as the devil said when he painted his tail pea green." So when a friend brought her a cravat of that color she threw it on the floor and burst into tears, saying, " I could not wear that, for it is the color of the devil's tail." I sympathized with the child and had it changed for the hue she liked. Although we cannot always understand the ground for children's preferences, it is often well to heed them.

I am told that I was pensively looking out of the nursery window one day, when Mary Dunn, the Scotch nurse, who was something of a philosopher, and a stern Presbyterian, said: " Child, what are you thinking about; are you planning some new form of mischief? " " No, Mary," I replied, " I was wondering why it was that everything we like to do is a sin, and that everything we dislike is commanded by God or someone on earth. I am so tired of that everlasting no! no! no! At school, at home, everywhere it is *no!* Even at

church all the commandments begin ' Thou shalt not.'
I suppose God will say ' no ' to all we like in the next
world, just as you do here." Mary was dreadfully
shocked at my dissatisfaction with the things of time
and prospective eternity, and exhorted me to cultivate
the virtues of obedience and humility.

I well remember the despair I felt in those years, as I
took in the whole situation, over the constant cribbing
and crippling of a child's life. I suppose I found fit
language in which to express my thoughts, for Mary
Dunn told me, years after, how our discussion roused
my sister Margaret, who was an attentive listener. I
must have set forth our wrongs in clear, unmistakable
terms; for Margaret exclaimed one day, " I tell you
what to do. Hereafter let us act as we choose, without
asking." " Then," said I, " we shall be punished."
" Suppose we are," said she, " we shall have had our
fun at any rate, and that is better than to mind the
everlasting ' no ' and not have any fun at all." Her
logic seemed unanswerable, so together we gradually
acted on her suggestions. Having less imagination
than I, she took a common-sense view of life and suffered nothing from anticipation of troubles, while my
sorrows were intensified fourfold by innumerable apprehensions of possible exigencies.

Our nursery, a large room over a back building, had
three barred windows reaching nearly to the floor.
Two of these opened on a gently slanting roof over a
veranda. In our night robes, on warm summer evenings we could, by dint of skillful twisting and compress-
ing, get out between the bars, and there, snugly braced
against the house, we would sit and enjoy the moon
and stars and what sounds might reach us from the

streets, while the nurse, gossiping at the back door, imagined we were safely asleep.

I have a confused memory of being often under punishment for what, in those days, were called " tantrums." I suppose they were really justifiable acts of rebellion against the tyranny of those in authority. I have often listened since, with real satisfaction, to what some of our friends had to say of the high-handed manner in which sister Margaret and I defied all the transient orders and strict rules laid down for our guidance. If we had observed them we might as well have been embalmed as mummies, for all the pleasure and freedom we should have had in our childhood. As very little was then done for the amusement of children, happy were those who *conscientiously* took the liberty of amusing themselves.

One charming feature of our village was a stream of water, called the Cayadutta, which ran through the north end, in which it was our delight to walk on the broad slate stones when the water was low, in order to pick up pretty pebbles. These joys were also forbidden, though indulged in as opportunity afforded, especially as sister Margaret's philosophy was found to work successfully and we had finally risen above our infantile fear of punishment.

Much of my freedom at this time was due to this sister, who afterward became the wife of Colonel Duncan McMartin of Iowa. I can see her now, hat in hand, her long curls flying in the wind, her nose slightly retroussé, her large dark eyes flashing with glee, and her small straight mouth so expressive of determination. Though two years my junior, she was larger and stronger than I and more fearless and self-reliant. She was always ready to start when any pleasure offered, and, if I hesitated, she would give me a jerk and say, emphatically: " Oh, come along! " and away we went.

About this time we entered the Johnstown Academy, where we made the acquaintance of the daughters of the hotel keeper and the county sheriff. They were a few years my senior, but, as I was ahead of them in all my studies, the difference of age was somewhat equalized and we became fast friends. This acquaintance opened to us two new sources of enjoyment—the freedom of the hotel during " court week " (a great event in village life) and the exploration of the county jail. Our Scotch nurse had told us so many thrilling tales of castles, prisons, and dungeons in the Old World that, to see the great keys and iron doors, the handcuffs and chains, and the prisoners in their cells seemed like a veritable visit to Mary's native land. We made frequent visits to the jail and became deeply concerned about the fate of the prisoners, who were greatly pleased with our expressions of sympathy and our gifts of cake and candy. In time we became interested in the trials and sentences of prisoners, and would go to the court-house and listen to the proceedings. Sometimes we would slip into the hotel where the judges and lawyers dined, and help our little friend wait on table. The rushing of servants to and fro, the calling of guests, the scolding of servants in the kitchen, the banging of doors, the general hubbub, the noise and clatter, were all idealized by me into one of those royal festivals Mary so often described. To be allowed to carry plates of bread and butter, pie and cheese I counted a high privilege. But more especially I enjoyed listening to the conversations in regard to the probable fate of our friends the prisoners in the jail. On one occasion I projected a few remarks into a conversation between two lawyers, when one of them turned abruptly to me and said, " Child, you'd better attend to your business; bring me a glass of water." I replied indignantly, " I am not a servant; I am here for fun."

In all these escapades we were followed by Peter, black as coal and six feet in height. It seems to me now that his chief business was to discover our whereabouts, get us home to dinner, and take us back to school. Fortunately he was overflowing with curiosity and not averse to lingering a while where anything of interest was to be seen or heard, and, as we were deemed perfectly safe under his care, no questions were asked when we got to the house, if we had been with him. He had a long head and, through his diplomacy, we escaped much disagreeable surveillance. Peter was very fond of attending court. All the lawyers knew him, and wherever Peter went, the three little girls in his charge went, too. Thus, with constant visits to the jail, courthouse, and my father's office, I gleaned some idea of the danger of violating the law.

The great events of the year were the Christmas holidays, the Fourth of July, and " general training," as the review of the county militia was then called. The winter gala days are associated, in my memory, with hanging up stockings and with turkeys, mince pies, sweet cider, and sleighrides by moonlight. My earliest recollections of those happy days, when schools were closed, books laid aside, and unusual liberties allowed, center in that large cellar kitchen to which I have already referred. There we spent many winter evenings in uninterrupted enjoyment. A large fire-place with huge logs shed warmth and cheerfulness around. In one corner sat Peter sawing his violin, while our youthful neighbors danced with us and played blindman's buff almost every evening during the vacation. The most interesting character in this game was a black boy called Jacob (Peter's lieutenant), who made things lively for us by always keeping one eye open—a wise precaution to guard himself from danger, and to keep us on the jump. Hickory nuts, sweet cider, and *olie-koeks* (a Dutch name for a fried cake with raisins inside) were our refreshments when there came a lull in the fun.

As St. Nicholas was supposed to come down the chimney, our stockings were pinned on a broomstick, laid across two chairs in front of the fireplace. We retired on Christmas Eve with the most pleasing anticipations of what would be in our stockings next morning. The thermometer in that latitude was often twenty degrees below zero, yet, bright and early, we would run downstairs in our bare feet over the cold floors to carry stockings, broom, etc., to the nursery. The gorgeous presents that St. Nicholas now distributes show that he, too, has been growing up with the country. The boys and girls of 1897 will laugh when they hear of the contents of our stockings in 1823. There was a little paper of candy, one of raisins, another of nuts, a red apple, an *olie-koek*, and a bright silver quarter of a dollar in the toe. If a child had been guilty of any erratic performances during the year, which was often my case, a long stick would protrude from the stocking; if particularly good, an illustrated catechism or the New Testament would appear, showing that the St. Nicholas of that time held decided views on discipline and ethics.

During the day we would take a drive over the snow-clad hills and valleys in a long red lumber sleigh. All the children it could hold made the forests echo with their songs and laughter. The sleigh bells and Peter's fine tenor voice added to the chorus seemed to chant, as we passed, " Merry Christmas " to the farmers' children and to all we met on the highway.

Returning home, we were allowed, as a great Christmas treat, to watch all Peter's preparations for dinner. Attired in a white apron and turban, holding in his hand a tin candlestick the size of a dinner plate, containing a tallow candle, with stately step he marched into the spacious cellar, with Jacob and three little girls dressed in red flannel at his heels. As the farmers paid the interest on their mortgages in barrels of pork, headcheese, poultry, eggs, and cider, the cellars were well crowded for the winter, making the master of an establishment quite indifferent to all questions of finance. We heard nothing in those days of greenbacks, silver coinage, or a gold basis. Laden with vegetables, butter, eggs, and a magnificent turkey, Peter and his followers returned to the kitchen. There, seated on a big ironing table, we watched the dressing and roasting of the bird in a tin oven in front of the fire. Jacob peeled the vegetables, we all sang, and Peter told us marvelous stories. For tea he made flapjacks, baked in a pan with a long handle, which he turned by throwing the cake up and skillfully catching it descending.

Peter was a devout Episcopalian and took great pleasure in helping the young people decorate the church. He would take us with him and show us how to make evergreen wreaths. Like Mary's lamb, where'er he went we were sure to go. His love for us was unbounded and fully returned. He was the only being, visible or invisible, of whom we had no fear. We would go to divine service with Peter, Christmas morning and sit with him by the door, in what was called " the negro pew." He was the only colored member of the church and, after all the other communicants had taken the sacrament, he went alone to the altar. Dressed in a new suit of blue with gilt buttons, he looked like a prince, as, with head erect, he walked up the aisle, the grandest specimen of manhood in the whole congregation; and yet so strong was prejudice against color in 1823 that no one would kneel beside him. On leaving us, on one of these occasions, Peter told us all to sit still until he returned; but, no sooner had he started, than the youngest of us slowly followed after him and seated herself close beside him. As he came back, holding the child by the hand, what a lesson it must have been to that prejudiced congregation! The first time we entered the church together the sexton opened a white man's pew for us, telling Peter to leave the Judge's children there. " Oh," he said, " they will not stay there without me." But, as he could not enter, we instinctively followed him to the negro pew.

Our next great fête was on the anniversary of the birthday of our Republic. The festivities were numerous and protracted, beginning then, as now, at midnight with bonfires and cannon; while the day was ushered in with the ringing of bells, tremendous cannonading, and a continuous popping of fire-crackers and torpedoes. Then a procession of soldiers and citizens

marched through the town, an oration was delivered,
the Declaration of Independence read, and a great dinner given in the open air under the trees in the grounds
of the old courthouse. Each toast was announced with
the booming of cannon. On these occasions Peter
was in his element, and showed us whatever he considered worth seeing; but I cannot say that I enjoyed
very much either " general training " or the Fourth of
July, for, in addition to my fear of cannon and torpedoes, my sympathies were deeply touched by the sadness of our cook, whose drunken father always cut antics in the streets on gala days, the central figure in all
the sports of the boys, much to the mortification of his
worthy daughter. She wept bitterly over her father's
public exhibition of himself, and told me in what a condition he would come home to his family at night. I
would gladly have stayed in with her all day, but the fear
of being called a coward compelled me to go through
those trying ordeals. As my nerves were all on the
surface, no words can describe what I suffered with
those explosions, great and small, and my fears lest
King George and his minions should reappear among
us. I thought that, if he had done all the dreadful
things stated in the Declaration of '76, he might come
again, burn our houses, and drive us all into the street.
Sir William Johnson's mansion of solid masonry,
gloomy and threatening, still stood in our neighborhood. I had seen the marks of the Indian's toma-
hawk on the balustrades and heard of the bloody
deeds there enacted. For all the calamities of the
nation I believed King George responsible. At home
and at school we were educated to hate the English.
When we remember that, every Fourth of July, the
Declaration was read with emphasis, and the orator of

the day rounded all his glowing periods with denunciations of the mother country, we need not wonder at the national hatred of everything English. Our patriotism in those early days was measured by our dislike of Great Britain.

In September occurred the great event, the review of the county militia, popularly called " Training Day." Then everybody went to the race course to see the troops and buy what the farmers had brought in their wagons. There was a peculiar kind of gingerbread and molasses candy to which we were treated on those occasions, associated in my mind to this day with military reviews and standing armies.

Other pleasures were, roaming in the forests and sailing on the mill pond. One day, when there were no boys at hand and several girls were impatiently waiting for a sail on a raft, my sister and I volunteered to man the expedition. We always acted on the assumption that what we had seen done, we could do. Accordingly we all jumped on the raft, loosened it from its moorings, and away we went with the current. Navigation on that mill pond was performed with long poles, but, unfortunately, we could not lift the poles, and we soon saw we were drifting toward the dam. But we had the presence of mind to sit down and hold fast to the raft. Fortunately, we went over right side up and gracefully glided down the stream, until rescued by the ever watchful Peter. I did not hear the last of that voyage for a long time. I was called the captain of the expedition, and one of the boys wrote a composition, which he read in school, describing the adventure and emphasizing the ignorance of the laws of navigation shown by the officers in command. I shed tears many times over that performance.

CHAPTER II.

SCHOOL DAYS.

WHEN I was eleven years old, two events occurred which changed considerably the current of my life. My only brother, who had just graduated from Union College, came home to die. A young man of great talent and promise, he was the pride of my father's heart. We early felt that this son filled a larger place in our father's affections and future plans than the five daughters together. Well do I remember how tenderly he watched my brother in his last illness, the sighs and tears he gave vent to as he slowly walked up and down the hall, and, when the last sad moment came, and we were all assembled to say farewell in the silent chamber of death, how broken were his utterances as he knelt and prayed for comfort and support. I still recall, too, going into the large darkened parlor to see my brother, and finding the casket, mirrors, and pictures all draped in white, and my father seated by his side, pale and immovable. As he took no notice of me, after standing a long while, I climbed upon his knee, when he mechanically put his arm about me and, with my head resting against his beating heart, we both sat in silence, he thinking of the wreck of all his hopes in the loss of a dear son, and I wondering what could be said or done to fill the void in his breast. At length he heaved a deep sigh and said: " Oh, my daughter, I wish you were a boy! "

MARGARET LIVINGSTON CADY.

JUDGE DANIEL CADY.

Throwing my arms about his neck, I replied: " I will try to be all my brother was."

Then and there I resolved that I would not give so much time as heretofore to play, but would study and strive to be at the head of all my classes and thus delight my father's heart. All that day and far into the night I pondered the problem of boyhood. I thought that the chief thing to be done in order to equal boys was to be learned and courageous. So I decided to study Greek and learn to manage a horse. Having formed this conclusion I fell asleep. My resolutions, unlike many such made at night, did not vanish with the coming light. I arose early and hastened to put them into execution. They were resolutions never to be forgotten—destined to mold my character anew. As soon as I was dressed I hastened to our good pastor, Rev. Simon Hosack, who was always early at work in his garden.

" Doctor," said I, " which do you like best, boys or girls?"

" Why, girls, to be sure; I would not give you for all the boys in Christendom."

" My father," I replied, " prefers boys; he wishes I was one, and I intend to be as near like one as possible. I am going to ride on horseback and study Greek. Will you give me a Greek lesson now, doctor? I want to begin at once."

" Yes, child," said he, throwing down his hoe, " come into my library and we will begin without delay."

He entered fully into the feeling of suffering and sorrow which took possession of me when I discovered that a girl weighed less in the scale of being than a boy, and he praised my determination to prove the con-

trary.   The old grammar which he had studied in the
University of Glasgow was soon in my hands, and the
Greek article was learned before breakfast.

Then came the sad pageantry of death, the weeping
of friends, the dark rooms, the ghostly stillness, the
exhortation to the living to prepare for death, the
solemn prayer, the mournful chant, the funeral cortège,
the solemn, tolling bell, the burial.   How I suffered during those sad days!   What strange undefined fears of
the unknown took possession of me!   For months
afterward, at the twilight hour, I went with my father
to the new-made grave.   Near it stood two tall poplar
trees, against one of which I leaned, while my father
threw himself on the grave, with outstretched arms, as
if to embrace his child.   At last the frosts and storms of
November came and threw a chilling barrier between
the living and the dead, and we went there no more.

During all this time I kept up my lessons at the parsonage and made rapid progress.   I surprised even my
teacher, who thought me capable of doing anything.   I
learned to drive, and to leap a fence and ditch on horseback.   I taxed every power, hoping some day to hear
my father say: " Well, a girl is as good as a boy, after
all."   But he never said it.   When the doctor came
over to spend the evening with us, I would whisper in
his ear: " Tell my father how fast I get on," and he
would tell him, and was lavish in his praises.   But my
father only paced the room, sighed, and showed that
he wished I were a boy; and I, not knowing why he
felt thus, would hide my tears of vexation on the doctor's shoulder.

Soon after this I began to study Latin, Greek, and
mathematics with a class of boys in the Academy, many

of whom were much older than I. For three years one boy kept his place at the head of the class, and I always stood next. Two prizes were offered in Greek. I strove for one and took the second. How well I remember my joy in receiving that prize. There was no sentiment of ambition, rivalry, or triumph over my companions, nor feeling of satisfaction in receiving this honor in the presence of those assembled on the day of the exhibition. One thought alone filled my mind. "Now," said I, "my father will be satisfied with me." So, as soon as we were dismissed, I ran down the hill, rushed breathless into his office, laid the new Greek Testament, which was my prize, on his table and exclaimed: "There, I got it!" He took up the book, asked me some questions about the class, the teachers, the spectators, and, evidently pleased, handed it back to me. Then, while I stood looking and waiting for him to say something which would show that he recognized the equality of the daughter with the son, he kissed me on the forehead and exclaimed, with a sigh, "Ah, you should have been a boy!"

My joy was turned to sadness. I ran to my good doctor. He chased my bitter tears away, and soothed me with unbounded praises and visions of future success. He was then confined to the house with his last illness. He asked me that day if I would like to have, when he was gone, the old lexicon, Testament, and grammar that we had so often thumbed together. "Yes, but I would rather have you stay," I replied, "for what can I do when you are gone?" "Oh," said he tenderly, "I shall not be gone; my spirit will still be with you, watching you in all life's struggles." Noble, generous friend! He had but little on earth to be-

queath to anyone, but when the last scene in his life
was ended, and his will was opened, sure enough there
was a clause saying: "My Greek lexicon, Testament, and
grammar, and four volumes of Scott's commentaries,
I will to Elizabeth Cady." I never look at these books
without a feeling of thankfulness that in childhood I
was blessed with such a friend and teacher.

I can truly say, after an experience of seventy years,
that all the cares and anxieties, the trials and disappointments of my whole life, are light, when balanced
with my sufferings in childhood and youth from the
theological dogmas which I sincerely believed, and
the gloom connected with everything associated with
the name of religion, the church, the parsonage, the
graveyard, and the solemn, tolling bell. Everything
connected with death was then rendered inexpressibly
dolorous. The body, covered with a black pall, was
borne on the shoulders of men; the mourners were in
crape and walked with bowed heads, while the neighbors who had tears to shed, did so copiously and summoned up their saddest facial expressions. At the
grave came the sober warnings to the living and sometimes frightful prophesies as to the state of the dead.
All this pageantry of woe and visions of the unknown
land beyond the tomb, often haunted my midnight
dreams and shadowed the sunshine of my days. The
parsonage, with its bare walls and floors, its shriveled
mistress and her blind sister, more like ghostly shadows
than human flesh and blood; the two black servants,
racked with rheumatism and odoriferous with a pun-
gent oil they used in the vain hope of making their
weary limbs more supple; the aged parson buried in his
library in the midst of musty books and papers—all this

only added to the gloom of my surroundings. The church, which was bare, with no furnace to warm us, no organ to gladden our hearts, no choir to lead our songs of praise in harmony, was sadly lacking in all attractions for the youthful mind. The preacher, shut up in an octagonal box high above our heads, gave us sermons over an hour long, and the chorister, in a similar box below him, intoned line after line of David's Psalms, while, like a flock of sheep at the heels of their shepherd, the congregation, without regard to time or tune, straggled after their leader.

Years later, the introduction of stoves, a violoncello, Wesley's hymns, and a choir split the church in twain. These old Scotch Presbyterians were opposed to all innovations that would afford their people paths of flowery ease on the road to Heaven. So, when the thermometer was twenty degrees below zero on the Johnstown Hills, four hundred feet above the Mohawk Valley, we trudged along through the snow, foot-stoves in hand, to the cold hospitalities of the " Lord's House," there to be chilled to the very core by listening to sermons on " predestination," " justification by faith," and " eternal damnation."

To be restless, or to fall asleep under such solemn circumstances was a sure evidence of total depravity, and of the machinations of the devil striving to turn one's heart from God and his ordinances. As I was guilty of these shortcomings and many more, I early believed myself a veritable child of the Evil One, and suffered endless fears lest he should come some night and claim me as his own. To me he was a personal, ever-present reality, crouching in a dark corner of the nursery. Ah! how many times I have stolen out of bed, and sat shivering on the stairs, where the hall lamp and the sound of voices from the parlor would, in a measure, mitigate my terror. Thanks to a vigorous constitution and overflowing animal spirits, I was able to endure for years the strain of these depressing influences, until my reasoning powers and common sense triumphed at last over my imagination. The memory of my own suffering has prevented me from ever shadowing one young soul with any of the superstitions of the Christian religion. But there have been many changes, even in my native town, since those dark days. Our old church was turned into a mitten factory, and the pleasant hum of machinery and the glad faces of men and women have chased the evil spirits to their hiding places. One finds at Johnstown now, beautiful churches, ornamented cemeteries, and cheerful men and women, quite emancipated from the nonsense and terrors of the old theologies.

An important event in our family circle was the marriage of my oldest sister, Tryphena, to Edward Bayard of Wilmington, Delaware. He was a graduate of Union College, a classmate of my brother, and frequently visited at my father's house. At the end of his college course, he came with his brother Henry to study law in Johnstown. A quiet, retired little village was thought to be a good place in which to sequester young men bent on completing their education, as they were there safe from the temptations and distracting influences of large cities. In addition to this consideration, my father's reputation made his office a desirable resort for students, who, furthermore, not only improved their opportunities by reading Blackstone, Kent, and Story, but also by making love to the Judge's daughters. We thus had the advantage of many pleasant acquaintances from the leading families in the country, and, in this way, it was that four of the sisters eventually selected most worthy husbands.

Though only twenty-one years of age when married, Edward Bayard was a tall, fully developed man, remarkably fine looking, with cultivated literary taste and a profound knowledge of human nature. Warm and affectionate, generous to a fault in giving and serving, he was soon a great favorite in the family, and gradually filled the void made in all our hearts by the loss of the brother and son.

My father was so fully occupied with the duties of his profession, which often called him from home, and my mother so weary with the cares of a large family, having had ten children, though only five survived at this time, that they were quite willing to shift their burdens to younger shoulders. Our eldest sister and her husband, therefore, soon became our counselors and advisers. They selected our clothing, books, schools, acquaintances, and directed our reading and amusements. Thus the reins of domestic government, little by little, passed into their hands, and the family arrangements were in a manner greatly improved in favor of greater liberty for the children.

The advent of Edward and Henry Bayard was an inestimable blessing to us. With them came an era of picnics, birthday parties, and endless amusements; the buying of pictures, fairy books, musical instruments and ponies, and frequent excursions with parties on horseback. Fresh from college, they made our lessons in Latin, Greek, and mathematics so easy that we studied with real pleasure and had more leisure for play.

Henry Bayard's chief pleasures were walking, riding, and playing all manner of games, from jack-straws to chess, with the three younger sisters, and we have often said that the three years he passed in Johnstown were the most delightful of our girlhood.

Immediately after the death of my brother, a journey was planned to visit our grandmother Cady, who lived in Canaan, Columbia County, about twenty miles from Albany. My two younger sisters and myself had never been outside of our own county before, and the very thought of a journey roused our enthusiasm to the highest pitch. On a bright day in September we started, packed in two carriages. We were wild with delight as we drove down the Mohawk Valley, with its beautiful river and its many bridges and ferryboats. When we reached Schenectady, the first city we had ever seen, we stopped to dine at the old Given's Hotel, where we broke loose from all the moorings of propriety on beholding the paper on the dining-room wall, illustrating in brilliant colors the great events in sacred history. There were the Patriarchs, with flowing beards and in gorgeous attire; Abraham, offering up Isaac; Joseph, with his coat of many colors, thrown into a pit by his brethren; Noah's ark on an ocean of waters; Pharaoh and his host in the Red Sea; Rebecca at the well, and Moses in the bulrushes. All these distinguished personages were familiar to us, and to see them here for the first time in living colors, made silence and eating impossible. We dashed around the room, calling to each other: "Oh, Kate, look here!" "Oh, Madge, look there!" "See little Moses!" "See the angels on Jacob's ladder!" Our exclamations could not be kept within bounds. The guests were amused beyond description, while my mother and elder sisters were equally mortified; but Mr. Bayard, who appreciated our childish surprise and delight, smiled and said: " I'll take them around and show them the pictures, and then they will be able to dine," which we finally did.

On our way to Albany we were forced to listen to no end of dissertations on manners, and severe criticisms on our behavior at the hotel, but we were too happy and astonished with all we saw to take a subjective view of ourselves. Even Peter in his new livery, who had not seen much more than we had, while looking out of the corners of his eyes, maintained a quiet dignity and conjured us " not to act as if we had just come out of the woods and had never seen anything before." However, there are conditions in the child soul in which repression is impossible, when the mind takes in nothing but its own enjoyment, and when even the sense of hearing is lost in that of sight. The whole party awoke to that fact at last. Children are not actors. We never had experienced anything like this journey, and how could we help being surprised and delighted?

When we drove into Albany, the first large city we had ever visited, we exclaimed, " Why, it's general training, here!" We had acquired our ideas of crowds from our country militia reviews. Fortunately, there was no pictorial wall paper in the old City Hotel. But the decree had gone forth that, on the remainder of the journey, our meals would be served in a private room, with Peter to wait on us. This seemed like going back to the nursery days and was very humiliating. But eating, even there, was difficult, as we could hear the band from the old museum, and, as our

windows opened on the street, the continual panorama
of people and carriages passing by was quite as enticing
as the Bible scenes in Schenectady. In the evening we
walked around to see the city lighted, to look into the
shop windows, and to visit the museum. The next
morning we started for Canaan, our enthusiasm still
unabated, though strong hopes were expressed that we
would be toned down with the fatigues of the first day's
journey.

The large farm with its cattle, sheep, hens, ducks,
turkeys, and geese; its creamery, looms, and spinning
wheel; its fruits and vegetables; the drives among the
grand old hills; the blessed old grandmother, and the
many aunts, uncles, and cousins to kiss, all this kept
us still in a whirlpool of excitement. Our joy bubbled
over of itself; it was beyond our control. After spending a delightful week at Canaan, we departed, with an
addition to our party, much to Peter's disgust, of a
bright, coal-black boy of fifteen summers. Peter kept
grumbling that he had children enough to look after
already, but, as the boy was handsome and intelligent,
could read, write, play on the jewsharp and banjo, sing,
dance, and stand on his head, we were charmed with
this new-found treasure, who proved later to be a great
family blessing. We were less vivacious on the return
trip. Whether this was due to Peter's untiring efforts
to keep us within bounds, or whether the novelty of
the journey was in a measure gone, it is difficult to de-
termine, but we evidently were not so buoyant and
were duly complimented on our good behavior.

When we reached home and told our village companions what we had seen in our extensive travels (just
seventy miles from home) they were filled with wonder,

and we became heroines in their estimation. After this we took frequent journeys to Saratoga, the Northern Lakes, Utica, and Peterboro, but were never again so entirely swept from our feet as with the biblical illustrations in the dining room of the old Given's Hotel.

As my father's office joined the house, I spent there much of my time, when out of school, listening to the clients stating their cases, talking with the students, and reading the laws in regard to woman. In our Scotch neighborhood many men still retained the old feudal ideas of women and property. Fathers, at their death, would will the bulk of their property to the eldest son, with the proviso that the mother was to have a home with him. Hence it was not unusual for the mother, who had brought all the property into the family, to be made an unhappy dependent on the bounty of an uncongenial daughter-in-law and a dissipated son. The tears and complaints of the women who came to my father for legal advice touched my heart and early drew my attention to the injustice and cruelty of the laws. As the practice of the law was my father's business, I could not exactly understand why he could not alleviate the sufferings of these women. So, in order to enlighten me, he would take down his books and show me the inexorable statutes. The students, observing my interest, would amuse themselves by reading to me all the worst laws they could find, over which I would laugh and cry by turns. One Christmas morning I went into the office to show them, among other of my presents, a new coral necklace and bracelets. They all admired the jewelry and then began to tease me with hypothetical cases of future ownership. " Now," said Henry Bayard, " if in due time you should be my wife, those ornaments would be mine; I could take them and lock them up, and you could never wear them except with my permission. I could even exchange them for a box of cigars, and you could watch them evaporate in smoke."

With this constant bantering from students and the sad complaints of the women, my mind was sorely perplexed. So when, from time to time, my attention was called to these odious laws, I would mark them with a pencil, and becoming more and more convinced of the necessity of taking some active measures against these unjust provisions, I resolved to seize the first opportunity, when alone in the office, to cut every one of them out of the books; supposing my father and his library were the beginning and the end of the law. However, this mutilation of his volumes was never accomplished, for dear old Flora Campbell, to whom I confided my plan for the amelioration of the wrongs of my unhappy sex, warned my father of what I proposed to do. Without letting me know that he had discovered my secret, he explained to me one evening how laws were made, the large number of lawyers and libraries there were all over the State, and that if his library should burn up it would make no difference in woman's condition. " When you are grown up, and able to prepare a speech," said he, " you must go down to Albany and talk to the legislators; tell them all you have seen in this office—the sufferings of these Scotchwomen, robbed of their inheritance and left dependent on their unworthy sons, and, if you can persuade them to pass new laws, the old ones will be a dead letter." Thus was the future object of my life foreshadowed and my duty plainly outlined by him who was most opposed to my public career when, in due time, I entered upon it.

Until I was sixteen years old, I was a faithful student in the Johnstown Academy with a class of boys. Though I was the only girl in the higher classes of mathematics and the languages, yet, in our plays, all the girls and boys mingled freely together. In running races, sliding downhill, and snowballing, we made no distinction of sex. True, the boys would carry the school books and pull the sleighs up hill for their favorite girls, but equality was the general basis of our school relations. I dare say the boys did not make their snowballs quite so hard when pelting the girls, nor wash their faces with the same vehemence as they did each other's, but there was no public evidence of partiality. However, if any boy was too rough or took advantage of a girl smaller than himself, he was promptly thrashed by his fellows. There was an unwritten law and public sentiment in that little Academy world that enabled us to study and play together with the greatest freedom and harmony.

From the academy the boys of my class went to Union College at Schenectady. When those with whom I had studied and contended for prizes for five years came to bid me good-by, and I learned of the barrier that prevented me from following in their footsteps —" no girls admitted here "—my vexation and mortification knew no bounds. I remember, now, how proud and handsome the boys looked in their new clothes, as they jumped into the old stage coach and drove off, and how lonely I felt when they were gone and I had nothing to do, for the plans for my future were yet undetermined. Again I felt more keenly than ever the humiliation of the distinctions made on the ground of sex.

My time was now occupied with riding on horseback, studying the game of chess, and continually squabbling with the law students over the rights of women. Something was always coming up in the experiences of everyday life, or in the books we were reading, to give us fresh topics for argument. They would read passages from the British classics quite as aggravating as the laws. They delighted in extracts from Shakespeare, especially from " The Taming of the Shrew," an admirable satire in itself on the old common law of England. I hated Petruchio as if he were a real man. Young Bayard would recite with unction the famous reply of Milton's ideal woman to Adam: " God thy law, thou mine." The Bible, too, was brought into requisition. In fact it seemed to me that every book taught the " divinely ordained " headship of man; but my mind never yielded to this popular heresy.

CHAPTER III.

GIRLHOOD.

MRS. WILLARD'S Seminary at Troy was the fashionable school in my girlhood, and in the winter of 1830,
with upward of a hundred other girls, I found myself
an active participant in all the joys and sorrows of that
institution.   When in family council it was decided to
send me to that intellectual Mecca, I did not receive
the announcement with unmixed satisfaction, as I had
fixed my mind on Union College.   The thought of a
school without boys, who had been to me such a stimulus both in study and play, seemed to my imagination
dreary and profitless.

The one remarkable feature of my journey to Troy
was the railroad from Schenectady to Albany, the first
ever laid in this country.   The manner of ascending a
high hill going out of the city would now strike engi-
neers as stupid to the last degree.   The passenger cars
were pulled up by a train, loaded with stones, descending
the hill.   The more rational way of tunneling through
the hill or going around it had not yet dawned on our
Dutch ancestors.   At every step of my journey to Troy
I felt that I was treading on my pride, and thus in a
hopeless frame of mind I began my boarding-school
career.   I had already studied everything that was
taught there except French, music, and dancing, so I
devoted myself to these accomplishments.   As I had

a good voice I enjoyed singing, with a guitar accompaniment, and, having a good ear for time, I appreciated the harmony in music and motion and took great delight in dancing. The large house, the society of so many girls, the walks about the city, the novelty of everything made the new life more enjoyable than I had anticipated. To be sure I missed the boys, with whom I had grown up, played with for years, and later measured my intellectual powers with, but, as they became a novelty, there was new zest in occasionally seeing them. After I had been there a short time, I heard a call one day: " Heads out! " I ran with the rest and exclaimed, " What is it? " expecting to see a giraffe or some other wonder from Barnum's Museum. " Why, don't you see those boys? " said one. " Oh," I replied, " is that all? I have seen boys all my life." When visiting family friends in the city, we were in the way of making the acquaintance of their sons, and as all social relations were strictly forbidden, there was a new interest in seeing them. As they were not allowed to call upon us or write notes, unless they were brothers or cousins, we had, in time, a large number of kinsmen.

There was an intense interest to me now in writing notes, receiving calls, and joining the young men in the streets for a walk, such as I had never known when in constant association with them at school and in our daily amusements. Shut up with girls, most of them older than myself, I heard many subjects discussed of which I had never thought before, and in a manner it were better I had never heard. The healthful restraint always existing between boys and girls in conversation is apt to be relaxed with either sex alone. In all my intimate association with boys up to that period, I cannot recall one word or act for criticism, but I cannot say the same of the girls during the three years I passed at the seminary in Troy. My own experience proves to me that it is a grave mistake to send boys and girls to separate institutions of learning, especially at the most impressible age. The stimulus of sex promotes alike a healthy condition of the intellectual and the moral faculties and gives to both a development they never can acquire alone.

Mrs. Willard, having spent several months in Europe, did not return until I had been at the seminary some time. I well remember her arrival, and the joy with which she was greeted by the teachers and pupils who had known her before. She was a splendid-looking woman, then in her prime, and fully realized my idea of a queen. I doubt whether any royal personage in the Old World could have received her worshipers with more grace and dignity than did this far-famed daughter of the Republic. She was one of the remarkable women of that period, and did a great educational work for her sex. She gave free scholarships to a large number of promising girls, fitting them for teachers, with a proviso that, when the opportunity arose, they should, in turn, educate others.

I shall never forget one incident that occasioned me much unhappiness. I had written a very amusing composition, describing my room. A friend came in to see me just as I had finished it, and, as she asked me to read it to her, I did so. She enjoyed it very much and proposed an exchange. She said the rooms were all so nearly alike that, with a little alteration, she could use it. Being very susceptible to flattery, her praise of my production won a ready assent; but when I read her platitudes I was sorry I had changed, and still more so in the *denouement.*

Those selected to prepare compositions read them before the whole school. My friend's was received with great laughter and applause. The one I read not only fell flat, but nearly prostrated me also. As soon as I had finished, one of the young ladies left the room and, returning in a few moments with her composition book, laid it before the teacher who presided that day, showing her the same composition I had just read. I was called up at once to explain, but was so amazed and confounded that I could not speak, and I looked the personification of guilt. I saw at a glance the contemptible position I occupied and felt as if the last day had come, that I stood before the judgment seat and had heard the awful sentence pronounced, " Depart ye wicked into everlasting punishment." How I escaped from that scene to my own room I do not know. I was too wretched for tears. I sat alone for a long time when a gentle tap announced my betrayer. She put her arms around me affectionately and kissed me again and again.

"Oh!" she said, "you are a hero. You went through that trying ordeal like a soldier. I was so afraid, when you were pressed with questions, that the whole truth would come out and I be forced to stand in your place. I am not so brave as you; I could not endure it. Now that you are through it and know how bitter a trial it is, promise that you will save me from the same experience. You are so good and noble I know you will not betray me."

In this supreme moment of misery and disgrace, her loving words and warm embrace were like balm to my bruised soul and I readily promised all she asked. The girl had penetrated the weak point in my character. I loved flattery. Through that means she got my composition in the first place, pledged me to silence in the second place, and so confused my moral perceptions that I really thought it praiseworthy to shelter her from what I had suffered. However, without betrayal on my part, the trick came to light through the very means she took to make concealment sure. After compositions were read they were handed over to a certain teacher for criticism. Miss —— had copied mine, and returned to me the original. I had not copied hers, so the two were in the same handwriting—one with my name outside and one with Miss ——'s.

As I stood well in school, both for scholarship and behavior, my sudden fall from grace occasioned no end of discussion. So, as soon as the teacher discovered the two compositions in Miss ——'s writing, she came to me to inquire how I got one of Miss ——'s compositions. She said, " Where is yours that you wrote for that day? "

Taking it from my portfolio, I replied, " Here it is."

She then asked, " Did you copy it from her book? "

I replied, " No; I wrote it myself."

" Then why did you not read your own? "

" We agreed to change," said I.

" Did you know that Miss —— had copied that from the book of another young lady? "

" No, not until I was accused of doing it myself before the whole school."

" Why did you not defend yourself on the spot? "

" I could not speak, neither did I know what to say."

"Why have you allowed yourself to remain in such a false position for a whole week?"

"I do not know."

"Suppose I had not found this out, did you intend to keep silent?"

"Yes," I replied.

"Did Miss —— ask you to do so?"

"Yes."

I had been a great favorite with this teacher, but she was so disgusted with my stupidity, as she called my timidity, that she said:

"Really, my child, you have not acted in this matter as if you had ordinary common sense."

So little do grown people, in familiar surroundings, appreciate the confusion of a child's faculties, under new and trying experiences. When poor Miss ——'s turn came to stand up before the whole school and take the burden on her own shoulders she had so cunningly laid on mine, I readily shed the tears for her I could not summon for myself. This was my first sad lesson in human duplicity.

This episode, unfortunately, destroyed in a measure my confidence in my companions and made me suspicious even of those who came to me with appreciative words. Up to this time I had accepted all things as they seemed on the surface. Now I began to wonder what lay behind the visible conditions about me. Perhaps the experience was beneficial, as it is quite necessary for a young girl, thrown wholly on herself for the first time among strangers, to learn caution in all she says and does. The atmosphere of home life, where all disguises and pretensions are thrown off, is quite different from a large school of girls, with the petty jealousies and antagonisms that arise in daily competition in their dress, studies, accomplishments, and amusements.

The next happening in Troy that seriously influenced my character was the advent of the Rev. Charles G. Finney, a pulpit orator, who, as a terrifier of human souls, proved himself the equal of Savonarola. He held a protracted meeting in the Rev. Dr. Beaman's church, which many of my schoolmates attended. The result of six weeks of untiring effort on the part of Mr. Finney and his confreres was one of those intense revival seasons that swept over the city and through the seminary like an epidemic, attacking in its worst form the most susceptible. Owing to my gloomy Calvinistic training in the old Scotch Presbyterian church, and my vivid imagination, I was one of the first victims. We attended all the public services, beside the daily prayer and experience meetings held in the seminary. Our studies, for the time, held a subordinate place to the more important duty of saving our souls.

To state the idea of conversion and salvation as then understood, one can readily see from our present standpoint that nothing could be more puzzling and harrowing to the young mind. The revival fairly started, the most excitable were soon on the anxious seat. There we learned the total depravity of human nature and the sinner's awful danger of everlasting punishment. This was enlarged upon until the most innocent girl believed herself a monster of iniquity and felt certain of eternal damnation. Then God's hatred of sin was emphasized and his irreconcilable position toward the sinner so justified that one felt like a miserable, helpless, forsaken worm of the dust in trying to approach him, even in prayer.

Having brought you into a condition of profound humility, the only cardinal virtue for one under conviction, in the depths of your despair you were told that it required no herculean effort on your part to be transformed into an angel, to be reconciled to God, to escape endless perdition. The way to salvation was short and simple. We had naught to do but to repent and believe and give our hearts to Jesus, who was ever ready to receive them. How to do all this was the puzzling question. Talking with Dr. Finney one day, I said:

"I cannot understand what I am to do. If you should tell me to go to the top of the church steeple and jump off, I would readily do it, if thereby I could save my soul; but I do not know how to go to Jesus."

"Repent and believe," said he, "that is all you have to do to be happy here and hereafter."

"I am very sorry," I replied, "for all the evil I have done, and I believe all you tell me, and the more sincerely I believe, the more unhappy I am."

With the natural reaction from despair to hope many of us imagined ourselves converted, prayed and gave our experiences in the meetings, and at times rejoiced in the thought that we were Christians—chosen children of God—rather than sinners and outcasts.

But Dr. Finney's terrible anathemas on the depravity and deceitfulness of the human heart soon shortened our newborn hopes. His appearance in the pulpit on these memorable occasions is indelibly impressed on my mind. I can see him now, his great eyes rolling around the congregation and his arms flying about in the air like those of a windmill. One evening he described hell and the devil and the long procession of sinners being swept down the rapids, about to make the awful plunge into the burning depths of liquid fire below, and the rejoicing hosts in the inferno coming up to meet them with the shouts of the devils echoing through the vaulted arches. He suddenly halted, and, pointing his index finger at the supposed procession, he exclaimed:

" There, do you not see them! "

I was wrought up to such a pitch that I actually jumped up and gazed in the direction to which he pointed, while the picture glowed before my eyes and remained with me for months afterward. I cannot forbear saying that, although high respect is due to the intellectual, moral, and spiritual gifts of the venerable ex-president of Oberlin College, such preaching worked incalculable harm to the very souls he sought to save. Fear of the judgment seized my soul. Visions of the lost haunted my dreams. Mental anguish prostrated my health. Dethronement of my reason was apprehended by friends. But he was sincere, so peace to his ashes! Returning home, I often at night roused my father from his slumbers to pray for me, lest I should be cast into the bottomless pit before morning.

To change the current of my thoughts, a trip was planned to Niagara, and it was decided that the subject of religion was to be tabooed altogether. Accordingly our party, consisting of my sister, her husband, my father and myself, started in our private carriage, and for six weeks I heard nothing on the subject. About this time Gall and Spurzheim published their works on phrenology, followed by Combe's " Constitution of Man," his " Moral Philosophy," and many other liberal works, all so rational and opposed to the old theologies that they produced a profound impression on my brother-in-law's mind. As we had these books with us, reading and discussing by the way, we all became deeply interested in the new ideas. Thus, after many months of weary wandering in the intellectual labyrinth of " The Fall of Man," " Original Sin," " Total Depravity," " God's Wrath," " Satan's Triumph," " The Crucifixion," " The Atonement," and " Salvation by Faith," I found my way out of the darkness into the clear sunlight of Truth. My religious superstitions gave place to rational ideas based on scientific facts, and in proportion, as I looked at everything from a new standpoint, I grew more and more happy, day by day. Thus, with a delightful journey in the month of June, an entire change in my course of reading and the current of my thoughts, my mind was restored to its normal condition. I view it as one of the greatest crimes to shadow the minds of the young with these gloomy superstitions; and with fears of the unknown and the unknowable to poison all their joy in life.

After the restraints of childhood at home and in school, what a period of irrepressible joy and freedom comes to us in girlhood with the first taste of liberty. Then is our individuality in a measure recognized and our feelings and opinions consulted; then we decide where and when we will come and go, what we will eat, drink, wear, and do. To suit one's own fancy in clothes, to buy what one likes, and wear what one chooses is a great privilege to most young people. To go out at pleasure, to walk, to ride, to drive, with no one to say us nay or question our right to liberty, this is indeed like a birth into a new world of happiness and freedom. This is the period, too, when the emotions rule us, and we idealize everything in life; when love and hope make the present an ecstasy and the future bright with anticipation.

Then comes that dream of bliss that for weeks and months throws a halo of glory round the most ordinary characters in every-day life, holding the strongest and most common-sense young men and women in a thraldom from which few mortals escape. The period when love, in soft silver tones, whispers his first words of adoration, painting our graces and virtues day by day in living colors in poetry and prose, stealthily punctuated ever and anon with a kiss or fond embrace. What dignity it adds to a young girl's estimate of herself when some strong man makes her feel that in her hands rest his future peace and happiness! Though these seasons of intoxication may come once to all, yet they are seldom repeated. How often in after life we long for one more such rapturous dream of bliss, one more season of supreme human love and passion!

After leaving school, until my marriage, I had the most pleasant years of my girlhood. With frequent visits to a large circle of friends and relatives in various towns and cities, the monotony of home life was sufficiently broken to make our simple country pleasures always delightful and enjoyable. An entirely new life now opened to me. The old bondage of fear of the visible and the invisible was broken and, no longer subject to absolute authority, I rejoiced in the dawn of a new day of freedom in thought and action.

My brother-in-law, Edward Bayard, ten years my senior, was an inestimable blessing to me at this time, especially as my mind was just then opening to the consideration of all the varied problems of life. To me and my sisters he was a companion in all our amusements, a teacher in the higher departments of knowledge, and a counselor in all our youthful trials and disappointments. He was of a metaphysical turn of mind, and in the pursuit of truth was in no way trammeled by popular superstitions. He took nothing for granted and, like Socrates, went about asking questions. Nothing pleased him more than to get a bevy of bright young girls about him and teach them how to think clearly and reason logically.

One great advantage of the years my sisters and myself spent at the Troy Seminary was the large number of pleasant acquaintances we made there, many of which ripened into lifelong friendships. From time to time many of our classmates visited us, and all alike enjoyed the intellectual fencing in which my brother-in-law drilled them. He discoursed with us on law, philosophy, political economy, history, and poetry, and together we read novels without number. The long winter evenings thus passed pleasantly, Mr. Bayard alternately talking and reading aloud Scott, Bulwer, James, Cooper, and Dickens, whose works were just then coming out in numbers from week to week, always leaving us in suspense at the most critical point of the story. Our readings were varied with recitations, music, dancing, and games.

As we all enjoyed brisk exercise, even with the thermometer below zero, we took long walks and sleighrides during the day, and thus the winter months glided quickly by, while the glorious summer on those blue hills was a period of unmixed enjoyment. At this season we arose at five in the morning for a long ride on horseback through the beautiful Mohawk Valley and over the surrounding hills. Every road and lane in that region was as familiar to us and our ponies, as were the trees to the squirrels we frightened as we cantered by their favorite resorts.

Part of the time Margaret Christie, a young girl of Scotch descent, was a member of our family circle. She taught us French, music, and dancing. Our days were too short for all we had to do, for our time was not wholly given to pleasure. We were required to keep our rooms in order, mend and make our clothes, and do our own ironing. The latter was one of my mother's politic requirements, to make our laundry lists as short as possible.

Ironing on hot days in summer was a sore trial to all of us; but Miss Christie, being of an inventive turn of mind, soon taught us a short way out of it. She folded and smoothed her undergarments with her hands and then sat on them for a specified time. We all followed her example and thus utilized the hours devoted to our French lessons and, while reading " Corinne " and " Télémaque," in this primitive style we ironed our clothes. But for dresses, collars and cuffs, and pocket handkerchiefs, we were compelled to wield the hot iron, hence with these articles we used all due economy, and my mother's object was thus accomplished.

As I had become sufficiently philosophical to talk over my religious experiences calmly with my classmates who had been with me through the Finney revival meetings, we all came to the same conclusion—that we had passed through no remarkable change and that we had not been born again, as they say, for we found our tastes and enjoyments the same as ever. My brother-in-law explained to us the nature of the delusion we had all experienced, the physical conditions, the mental processes, the church machinery by which such excitements are worked up, and the impositions to which credulous minds are necessarily subjected. As we had all been through that period of depression and humiliation, and had been oppressed at times with the feeling that all our professions were arrant hypocrisy and that our last state was worse than our first, he helped us to understand these workings of the human mind and reconciled us to the more rational condition in which we now found ourselves. He never grew weary of expounding principles to us and dissipating the fogs and mists that gather over young minds educated in an atmosphere of superstition.

We had a constant source of amusement and vexation in the students in my father's office. A succession of them was always coming fresh from college and full of conceit. Aching to try their powers of debate on graduates from the Troy Seminary, they politely questioned all our theories and assertions. However, with my brother-in-law's training in analysis and logic, we were a match for any of them. Nothing pleased me better than a long argument with them on woman's equality, which I tried to prove by a diligent study of the books they read and the games they played. I confess that I did not study so much for a love of the truth or my own development, in these days, as to make those young men recognize my equality. I soon noticed that, after losing a few games of chess, my opponent talked less of masculine superiority. Sister Madge would occasionally rush to the defense with an emphatic " Fudge for these laws, all made by men! I'll never obey one of them. And as to the students with their impertinent talk of superiority, all they need is such a shaking up as I gave the most disagreeable one yesterday. I invited him to take a ride on horseback. He accepted promptly, and said he would be most happy to go. Accordingly I told Peter to saddle the toughest-mouthed, hardest-trotting carriage horse in the stable. Mounted on my swift pony, I took a ten-mile canter as fast as I could go, with that superior being at my heels calling, as he found breath, for me to stop, which I did at last and left him in the hands of Peter, half dead at his hotel, where he will be laid out, with all his marvelous masculine virtues, for a week at least. Now do not waste your arguments on these prigs from Union College. Take each, in turn, the ten-miles' circuit on ' Old Boney ' and they'll have no breath left to prate of woman's inferiority. You might argue with them all day, and you could not make them feel so small as I made that popinjay feel in one hour. I knew ' Old Boney ' would keep up with me, if he died for it, and that my escort could neither stop nor dismount, except by throwing himself from the saddle."

"Oh, Madge!" I exclaimed; " what will you say when he meets you again? "

" If he complains, I will say ' the next time you ride see that you have a curb bit before starting.' Surely, a man ought to know what is necessary to manage a horse, and not expect a woman to tell him."

Our lives were still further varied and intensified by the usual number of flirtations, so called, more or less lasting or evanescent, from all of which I emerged, as from my religious experiences, in a more rational frame of mind. We had been too much in the society of boys and young gentlemen, and knew too well their real character, to idealize the sex in general. In addition to our own observations, we had the advantage of our brother-in-law's wisdom.   Wishing to save us as long as possible from all matrimonial entanglements, he was continually unveiling those with whom he associated, and so critically portraying their intellectual and moral condition that it was quite impossible, in our most worshipful moods, to make gods of any of the sons of Adam.

However, in spite of all our own experiences and of all the warning words of wisdom from those who had seen life in its many phases, we entered the charmed circle at last, all but one marrying into the legal profession, with its odious statute laws and infamous decisions.   And this, after reading Blackstone, Kent, and Story, and thoroughly understanding the status of the wife under the old common law of England, which was in force at that time in most of the States of the Union.

CHAPTER IV.

LIFE AT PETERBORO.

THE year, with us, was never considered complete without a visit to Peterboro, N. Y., the home of Gerrit Smith. Though he was a reformer and was very radical in many of his ideas, yet, being a man of broad sympathies, culture, wealth, and position, he drew around him many friends of the most conservative opinions. He was a man of fine presence, rare physical beauty, most affable and courteous in manner, and his hospitalities were generous to an extreme, and dispensed to all classes of society.

Every year representatives from the Oneida tribe of Indians visited him. His father had early purchased of them large tracts of land, and there was a tradition among them that, as an equivalent for the good bargains of the father, they had a right to the son's hospitality, with annual gifts of clothing and provisions. The slaves, too, had heard of Gerrit Smith, the abolitionist, and of Peterboro as one of the safe points *en route* for Canada. His mansion was, in fact, one of the stations on the "underground railroad" for slaves escaping from bondage. Hence they, too, felt that they had a right to a place under his protecting roof. On such occasions the barn and the kitchen floor were utilized as chambers for the black man from the southern plantation and the red man from his home in the forest.

The spacious home was always enlivened with choice society from every part of the country. There one would meet members of the families of the old Dutch aristocracy, the Van Rensselaers, the Van Vechtens, the Schuylers, the Livingstons, the Bleeckers, the Brinkerhoffs, the Ten Eycks, the Millers, the Seymours, the Cochranes, the Biddles, the Barclays, the Wendells, and many others.

As the lady of the house, Ann Carroll Fitzhugh, was the daughter of a wealthy slaveholder of Maryland, many agreeable Southerners were often among the guests. Our immediate family relatives were well represented by General John Cochrane and his sisters, General Baird and his wife from West Point, the Fitzhughs from Oswego and Geneseo, the Backuses and Tallmans from Rochester, and the Swifts from Geneva. Here one was sure to meet scholars, philosophers, philanthropists, judges, bishops, clergymen, and statesmen.

Judge Alfred Conkling, the father of Roscoe Conkling, was, in his late years, frequently seen at Peterboro. Tall and stately, after all life's troubled scenes, financial losses and domestic sorrows, he used to say there was no spot on earth that seemed so like his idea of Paradise. The proud, reserved judge was unaccustomed to manifestations of affection and tender interest in his behalf, and when Gerrit, taking him by both hands would, in his softest tones say, " Good-morning," and inquire how he had slept and what he would like to do that day, and Nancy would greet him with equal warmth and pin a little bunch of roses in his buttonhole, I have seen the tears in his eyes. Their warm sympathies and sweet simplicity of manner melted the sternest natures and made the most reserved amiable. There never was such an atmosphere of love and peace, of freedom and good cheer, in any other home I visited. And this was the universal testimony of those who were guests at Peterboro. To go anywhere else, after a visit there, was like coming down from the divine heights into the valley of humiliation.

How changed from the early days when, as strict Presbyterians, they believed in all the doctrines of Calvin! Then, an indefinite gloom pervaded their home. Their consciences were diseased. They attached such undue importance to forms that they went through three kinds of baptism. At one time Nancy would read nothing but the Bible, sing nothing but hymns, and play only sacred music. She felt guilty if she talked on any subject except religion. She was, in all respects, a fitting mate for her attractive husband. Exquisitely refined in feeling and manner, beautiful in face and form, earnest and sincere, she sympathized with him in all his ideas of religion and reform. Together they passed through every stage of theological experience, from the uncertain ground of superstition and speculation to the solid foundation of science and reason. The position of the Church in the anti-slavery conflict, opening as it did all questions of ecclesiastical authority, Bible interpretation, and church discipline, awakened them to new thought and broader views on religious subjects, and eventually emancipated them entirely from the old dogmas and formalities of their faith, and lifted them into the cheerful atmosphere in which they passed the remainder of their lives. Their only daughter, Elizabeth, added greatly to the attractions of the home circle, as she drew many young people round her. Beside her personal charm she was the heiress of a vast estate and

had many admirers. The favored one was Charles
Dudley Miller of Utica, nephew of Mrs. Blandina
Bleecker Dudley, founder of the Albany Observatory.
At the close of his college life Mr. Miller had not only
mastered the languages, mathematics, rhetoric, and
logic, but had learned the secret windings of the human
heart. He understood the art of pleasing.

These were the times when the anti-slavery question
was up for hot discussion. In all the neighboring
towns conventions were held in which James G.
Birney, a Southern gentleman who had emancipated his
slaves, Charles Stuart of Scotland, and George Thompson of England, Garrison, Phillips, May, Beriah Greene,
Foster, Abby Kelly, Lucretia Mott, Douglass, and
others took part. Here, too, John Brown, Sanborn,
Morton, and Frederick Douglass met to talk over that
fatal movement on Harper's Ferry. On the question
of temperance, also, the people were in a ferment. Dr.
Cheever's pamphlet, " Deacon Giles' Distillery," was
scattered far and wide, and, as he was sued for libel, the
question was discussed in the courts as well as at every
fireside. Then came the Father Matthew and Wash-
ingtonian movements, and the position of the Church
on these questions intensified and embittered the conflict. This brought the Cheevers, the Pierponts, the
Delevans, the Nortons, and their charming wives to
Peterboro. It was with such company and varied discussions on every possible phase of political, religious,
and social life that I spent weeks every year. Gerrit
Smith was cool and calm in debate, and, as he was
armed at all points on these subjects, he could afford
to be patient and fair with an opponent, whether on
the platform or at the fireside. These rousing argu-

ments at Peterboro made social life seem tame and profitless elsewhere, and the youngest of us felt that the conclusions reached in this school of philosophy were not to be questioned. The sisters of General Cochrane, in disputes with their Dutch cousins in Schenectady and Albany, would end all controversy by saying, "This question was fully discussed at Peterboro, and settled."

The youngsters frequently put the lessons of freedom and individual rights they heard so much of into practice, and relieved their brains from the constant strain of argument on first principles, by the wildest hilarity in dancing, all kinds of games, and practical jokes carried beyond all bounds of propriety. These romps generally took place at Mr. Miller's. He used to say facetiously, that they talked a good deal about liberty over the way, but he kept the goddess under his roof. One memorable occasion in which our enthusiasm was kept at white heat for two hours I must try to describe, though words cannot do it justice, as it was pre-eminently a spectacular performance. The imagination even cannot do justice to the limp, woe-begone appearance of the actors in the closing scene. These romps were conducted on a purely democratic basis, without regard to color, sex, or previous condition of servitude.

It was rather a cold day in the month of March, when "Cousin Charley," as we called Mr. Miller, was superintending some men who were laying a plank walk in the rear of his premises. Some half dozen of us were invited to an early tea at good Deacon Huntington's. Immediately after dinner, Miss Fitzhugh and Miss Van Schaack decided to take a nap, that they might appear as brilliant as possible during the evening. That they

might not be late, as they invariably were, Cousin Lizzie
and I decided to rouse them in good season with a
generous sprinkling of cold water.   In vain they struggled to keep the blankets around them; with equal force
we pulled them away, and, whenever a stray finger or
toe appeared, we brought fresh batteries to bear, until
they saw that passive resistance must give place to active hostility.   We were armed with two watering pots.
They armed themselves with two large-sized syringes
used for showering potato bugs.   With these weapons
they gave us chase downstairs.   We ran into a closet
and held the door shut.   They quietly waited our forth-
coming.   As soon as we opened the door to peep out,
Miss Fitzhugh, who was large and strong, pulled it
wide open and showered us with a vengeance.   Then
they fled into a large pantry where stood several pans
of milk.

At this stage Cousin Charley, hearing the rumpus,
came to our assistance.   He locked them in the pantry
and returned to his work, whereupon they opened the
window and showered him with milk, while he, in turn,
pelted them with wet clothes, soaking in tubs near by.
As they were thinly clad, wet to the skin, and the cold
March wind blew round them (we were all in fatigue
costume in starting) they implored us to let them out,
which we did, and, in return for our kindness, they gave
us a broadside of milk in our faces.   Cousin Lizzie and
I fled to the dark closet, where they locked us in.
After long, weary waiting they came to offer us terms of
capitulation.   Lizzie agreed to fill their guns with milk,
and give them our watering pots full of water, and I
agreed to call Cousin Charley under my window until
they emptied the contents of guns and pots on his

head. My room was on the first floor, and Miss Fitzhugh's immediately overhead. On these terms we accepted our freedom. Accordingly, I gently raised the
window and called Charley confidentially within whis-
pering distance, when down came a shower of water. As
he stepped back to look up and see whence it came, and
who made the attack, a stream of milk hit him on the
forehead, his heels struck a plank, and he fell backward,
to all appearance knocked down with a stream of milk.
His humiliation was received with shouts of derisive
laughter, and even the carpenters at work laid down
their hammers and joined in the chorus; but his re-
venge was swift and capped the climax. Cold and wet
as we all were, and completely tired out, we commenced
to disrobe and get ready for the tea party. Unfortunately I had forgotten to lock my door, and in walked
Cousin Charley with a quart bottle of liquid blacking,
which he prepared to empty on my devoted head. I
begged so eloquently and trembled so at the idea of being dyed black, that he said he would let me off on one
condition, and that was to get him, by some means,
into Miss Fitzhugh's room. So I ran screaming up the
stairs, as if hotly pursued by the enemy, and begged her
to let me in. She cautiously opened the door, but when
she saw Charley behind me she tried to force it shut.
However, he was too quick for her. He had one leg
and arm in; but, at that stage of her toilet, to let him
in was impossible, and there they stood, equally strong,
firmly braced, she on one side of the door and he on the
other. But the blacking he was determined she should
have; so, gauging her probable position, with one desperate effort he squeezed in a little farther and, raising
the bottle, he poured the contents on her head. The

blacking went streaming down over her face, white robe, and person, and left her looking more like a bronze fury than one of Eve's most charming daughters. A yard or more of the carpet was ruined, the wallpaper and bedclothes spattered, and the poor victim was unfit to be seen for a week at least. Charley had a good excuse for his extreme measures, for, as we all by turn played our tricks on him, it was necessary to keep us in some fear of punishment. This was but one of the many outrageous pranks we perpetrated on each other. To see us a few hours later, all absorbed in an anti-slavery or temperance convention, or dressed in our best, in high discourse with the philosophers, one would never think we could have been guilty of such consummate follies. It was, however, but the natural reaction from the general serious trend of our thoughts.

It was in Peterboro, too, that I first met one who was then considered the most eloquent and impassioned orator on the anti-slavery platform, Henry B. Stanton. He had come over from Utica with Alvin Stewart's beautiful daughter, to whom report said he was engaged; but, as she soon after married Luther R. Marsh, there was a mistake somewhere. However, the rumor had its advantages. Regarding him as not in the matrimonial market, we were all much more free and easy in our manners with him than we would otherwise have been. A series of anti-slavery conventions was being held in Madison County, and there I had the pleasure of hearing him for the first time. As I had a passion for oratory, I was deeply impressed with his power. He was not so smooth and eloquent as Phillips, but he could make his audience both laugh and cry; the latter, Phillips himself said he never could do.

Mr. Stanton was then in his prime, a fine-looking, affable young man, with remarkable conversational talent, and was ten years my senior, with the advantage that that number of years necessarily gives.

Two carriage-loads of ladies and gentlemen drove off every morning, sometimes ten miles, to one of these conventions, returning late at night. I shall never forget those charming drives over the hills in Madison County, the bright autumnal days, and the bewitching moonlight nights. The enthusiasm of the people in these great meetings, the thrilling oratory, and lucid arguments of the speakers, all conspired to make these days memorable as among the most charming in my life. It seemed to me that I never had so much happiness crowded into one short month. I had become interested in the anti-slavery and temperance questions, and was deeply impressed with the appeals and arguments. I felt a new inspiration in life and was enthused with new ideas of individual rights and the basic principles of government, for the anti-slavery platform was the best school the American people ever had on which to learn republican principles and ethics. These conventions and the discussions at my cousin's fireside I count among the great blessings of my life.

One morning, as we came out from breakfast, Mr. Stanton joined me on the piazza, where I was walking up and down enjoying the balmy air and the beauty of the foliage. "As we have no conventions," said he, " on hand, what do you say to a ride on horseback this morning? " I readily accepted the suggestion, ordered the horses, put on my habit, and away we went. The roads were fine and we took a long ride. As we were returning home we stopped often to admire the scenery and, perchance, each other. When walking slowly through a beautiful grove, he laid his hand on the horn of the saddle and, to my surprise, made one of those charming revelations of human feeling which brave knights have always found eloquent words to utter, and to which fair ladies have always listened with mingled emotions of pleasure and astonishment.

One outcome of those glorious days of October, 1839, was a marriage, in Johnstown, the 10th day of May, 1840, and a voyage to the Old World.

Six weeks of that charming autumn, ending in the Indian summer with its peculiarly hazy atmosphere, I lingered in Peterboro. It seems in retrospect like a beautiful dream. A succession of guests was constantly coming and going, and I still remember the daily drives over those grand old hills crowned with trees now gorgeous in rich colors, the more charming because we knew the time was short before the cold winds of November would change all.

The early setting sun warned us that the shortening days must soon end our twilight drives, and the moonlight nights were too chilly to linger long in the rustic arbors or shady nooks outside. With the peculiar charm of this season of the year there is always a touch of sadness in nature, and it seemed doubly so to me, as my engagement was not one of unmixed joy and satisfaction. Among all conservative families there was a strong aversion to abolitionists and the whole antislavery movement. Alone with Cousin Gerrit in his library he warned me, in deep, solemn tones, while strongly eulogizing my lover, that my father would never consent to my marriage with an abolitionist. He felt in duty bound, as my engagement had occurred under his roof, to free himself from all responsibility by giving me a long dissertation on love, friendship, marriage, and all the pitfalls for the unwary, who, without due consideration, formed matrimonial relations. The general principles laid down in this interview did not strike my youthful mind so forcibly as the suggestion that it was better to announce my engagement by letter than to wait until I returned home, as thus I might draw the hottest fire while still in safe harbor, where Cousin Gerrit could help me defend the weak points in my position. So I lingered at Peterboro to prolong the dream of happiness and postpone the conflict I feared to meet.

But the Judge understood the advantage of our position as well as we did, and wasted no ammunition on us. Being even more indignant at my cousin than at me, he quietly waited until I returned home, when I passed through the ordeal of another interview, with another dissertation on domestic relations from a financial standpoint. These were two of the mc t bewildering interviews I ever had. They succeeded in making me feel that the step I proposed to take was the most momentous and far-reaching in its consequences of any in this mortal life. Heretofore my apprehensions had all been of death and eternity; now life itself was filled with fears and anxiety as to the possibilities of the future. Thus these two noble men, who would have done anything for my happiness, actually overweighted my conscience and turned the sweetest dream of my life into a tragedy. How little strong men, with their logic, sophistry, and hypothetical examples, appreciate the violence they inflict on the tender sensibilities of a woman's heart, in trying to subjugate her to their will!

The love of protecting too often degenerates into downright tyranny. Fortunately all these sombre pictures of a possible future were thrown into the background by the tender missives every post brought me, in which the brilliant word-painting of one of the most eloquent pens of this generation made the future for us both, as bright and beautiful as Spring with her verdure and blossoms of promise.

However, many things were always transpiring at Peterboro to turn one's thoughts and rouse new interest in humanity at large. One day, as a bevy of us girls were singing and chattering in the parlor, Cousin Gerrit entered and, in mysterious tones, said: " I have a most important secret to tell you, which you must keep to yourselves religiously for twenty-four hours."

We readily pledged ourselves in the most solemn manner, individually and collectively.

" Now," said he, " follow me to the third story."

This we did, wondering what the secret could be. At last, opening a door, he ushered us into a large room, in the center of which sat a beautiful quadroon girl, about eighteen years of age. Addressing her, he said:

" Harriet, I have brought all my young cousins to see you. I want you to make good abolitionists of them by telling them the history of your life—what you have seen and suffered in slavery."

Turning to us he said:

" Harriet has just escaped from her master, who is visiting in Syracuse, and is on her way to Canada. She will start this evening and you may never have another opportunity of seeing a slave girl face to face, so ask her all you care to know of the system of slavery."

For two hours we listened to the sad story of her

childhood and youth, separated from all her family and sold for her beauty in a New Orleans market when but fourteen years of age. The details of her story I need not repeat. The fate of such girls is too well known to need rehearsal. We all wept together as she talked, and, when Cousin Gerrit returned to summon us away, we needed no further education to make us earnest abolitionists.

Dressed as a Quakeress, Harriet started at twilight with one of Mr. Smith's faithful clerks in a carriage for Oswego, there to cross the lake to Canada. The next day her master and the marshals from Syracuse were on her track in Peterboro, and traced her to Mr. Smith's premises. He was quite gracious in receiving them, and, while assuring them that there was no slave there, he said that they were at liberty to make a thorough search of the house and grounds. He invited them to stay and dine and kept them talking as long as possible, as every hour helped Harriet to get beyond their reach; for, although she had eighteen hours the start of them, yet we feared some accident might have delayed her. The master was evidently a gentleman, for, on Mr. Smith's assurance that Harriet was not there, he made no search, feeling that they could not do so without appearing to doubt his word. He was evidently surprised to find an abolitionist so courteous and affable, and it was interesting to hear them in conversation, at dinner, calmly discussing the problem of slavery, while public sentiment was at white heat on the question. They shook hands warmly at parting and expressed an equal interest in the final adjustment of that national difficulty.

In due time the clerk returned with the good news

that Harriet was safe with friends in a good situation in Canada. Mr. Smith then published an open letter to the master in the New York _Tribune_, saying " that he would no doubt rejoice to know that his slave Harriet, in whose fate he felt so deep an interest, was now a free woman, safe under the shadow of the British throne. I had the honor of entertaining her under my roof, sending her in my carriage to Lake Ontario, just eighteen hours before your arrival; hence my willingness to have you search my premises."

Like the varied combinations of the kaleidoscope, the scenes in our social life at Peterboro were continually changing from grave to gay. Some years later we had a most hilarious occasion at the marriage of Mary Cochrane, sister of General John Cochrane, to Chapman Biddle, of Philadelphia. The festivities, which were kept up for three days, involved most elaborate preparations for breakfasts, dinners, etc., there being no Delmonico's in that remote part of the country. It was decided in family council that we had sufficient culinary talent under the roof to prepare the entire _menu_ of substantials and delicacies, from soup and salmon to cakes and creams. So, gifted ladies and gentlemen were impressed into the service. The Fitzhughs all had a natural talent for cooking, and chief among them was Isabella, wife of a naval officer,—Lieutenant Swift of Geneva,—who had made a profound study of all the authorities from Archestratus, a poet in Syracuse, the most famous cook among the Greeks, down to our own Miss Leslie. Accordingly she was elected manager of the occasion, and to each one was assigned the specialty in which she claimed to excel. Those who had no specialty were assistants to those who had. In this humble office—"assistant at large"—I labored throughout.

Cooking is a high art. A wise Egyptian said, long ago: "The degree of taste and skill manifested by a nation in the preparation of food may be regarded as to a very considerable extent proportioned to its culture and refinement." In early times men, only, were deemed capable of handling fire, whether at the altar or the hearthstone. We read in the Scriptures that Abraham prepared cakes of fine meal and a calf tender and good, which, with butter and milk, he set before the three angels in the plains of Mamre. We are told, too, of the chief butler and chief baker as officers in the household of King Pharaoh. I would like to call the attention of my readers to the dignity of this profession, which some young women affect to despise. The fact that angels eat, shows that we may be called upon in the next sphere to cook even for cherubim and seraphim. How important, then, to cultivate one's gifts in that direction!

With such facts before us, we stirred and pounded, whipped and ground, coaxed the delicate meats from crabs and lobsters and the succulent peas from the pods, and grated corn and cocoanut with the same cheerfulness and devotion that we played Mendelssohn's "Songs Without Words" on the piano, the Spanish Fandango on our guitars, or danced the minuet, polka, lancers, or Virginia reel.

During the day of the wedding, every stage coach was crowded with guests from the North, South, East, and West, and, as the twilight deepened, carriages began to roll in with neighbors and friends living at short distances, until the house and grounds were full. A son of Bishop Coxe, who married the tall and stately sister of Roscoe Conkling, performed the ceremony. The beautiful young bride was given away by her Uncle Gerrit. The congratulations, the feast, and all went off with fitting decorum in the usual way. The best proof of the excellence of our viands was that they were all speedily swept from mortal view, and every housewife wanted a recipe for something.

As the grand dinner was to come off the next day, our thoughts now turned in that direction. The responsibility rested heavily on the heads of the chief actors, and they reported troubled dreams and unduly early rising. Dear Belle Swift was up in season and her white soup stood serenely in a tin pan, on an upper shelf, before the town clock struck seven. If it had not taken that position so early, it might have been incorporated with higher forms of life than that into which it eventually fell. Another artist was also on the wing early, and in pursuit of a tin pan in which to hide her precious compound, she unwittingly seized this one, and the rich white soup rolled down her raven locks like the oil on Aaron's beard, and enveloped her in a veil of filmy whiteness. I heard the splash and the exclamation of surprise and entered the butler's pantry just in time to see the heiress of the Smith estate standing like a statue, tin pan in hand, soup in her curls, her eyebrows and eyelashes,—collar, cuffs, and morning dress saturated,—and Belle, at a little distance, looking at her and the soup on the floor with surprise and disgust depicted on every feature. The tableau was inexpressibly comical, and I could not help laughing outright; whereupon Belle turned on me, and, with indignant tones, said, " If you had been up since four o'clock making that soup you would not stand there like a laughing monkey, without the least feeling of pity!" Poor Lizzie was very sorry, and would have shed tears, but they could not penetrate that film of soup. I tried to apologize, but could only laugh the more when I saw Belle crying and Lizzie standing as if hoping that the soup might be scraped off her and gathered from the floor and made to do duty on the occasion.

After breakfast, ladies and gentlemen, alike in white aprons, crowded into the dining room and kitchen, each to perform the allotted task. George Biddle of Philadelphia and John B. Miller of Utica, in holiday spirits, were irrepressible—everywhere at the same moment, helping or hindering as the case might be. Dear Belle, having only partially recovered from the white-soup catastrophe, called Mr. Biddle to hold the ice-cream freezer while she poured in the luscious compound she had just prepared. He held it up without resting it on anything, while Belle slowly poured in the cream. As the freezer had no indentations round the top or rim to brace the thumbs and fingers, when it grew suddenly heavier his hands slipped and down went the whole thing, spattering poor Belle and spoiling a beautiful pair of gaiters in which, as she had very pretty feet, she took a laudable pride. In another corner sat Wealthea Backus, grating some cocoanut. While struggling in that operation, John Miller, feeling hilarious, was annoying her in divers ways; at length she drew the grater across his nose, gently, as she intended, but alas! she took the skin off, and John's beauty, for the remainder of the festivities, was marred with a black patch on that prominent feature. One can readily imagine the fun that must have transpired where so many amateur cooks were at work round one table, with all manner of culinary tools and ingredients.

As assistant-at-large I was summoned to the cellar, where Mrs. Cornelia Barclay of New York was evolving from a pan of flour and water that miracle in the pie department called puff paste. This, it seems, can only be accomplished where the thermometer is below forty, and near a refrigerator where the compound can be kept cold until ready to be popped into the oven. No jokes or nonsense here. With queenly dignity the flour and water were gently compressed. Here one hand must not know what the other doeth. Bits of butter must be so deftly introduced that even the rolling pin may be unconscious of its work. As the artist gave the last touch to an exquisite lemon pie, with a mingled expression of pride and satisfaction on her classic features, she ordered me to bear it to the oven. In the transit I met Madam Belle. "Don't let that fall," she said sneeringly. Fortunately I did not, and returned in triumph to transport another. I was then summoned to a consultation with the committee on toasts, consisting of James Cochrane, John Miller, and myself. Mr. Miller had one for each guest already written, all of which we accepted and pronounced very good.

Strange to say, a most excellent dinner emerged from all this uproar and confusion. The table, with its silver, china, flowers, and rich viands, the guests in satins, velvets, jewels, soft laces, and bright cravats, together reflecting all the colors of the prism, looked as beautiful as the rainbow after a thunderstorm.

Twenty years ago I made my last sad visit to that spot so rich with pleasant memories of bygone days. A few relatives and family friends gathered there to pay the last tokens of respect to our noble cousin. It was on one of the coldest days of gray December that we laid him in the frozen earth, to be seen no more. He died from a stroke of apoplexy in New York city, at the home of his niece, Mrs. Ellen Cochrane Walter, whose mother was Mr. Smith's only sister. The journey from New York to Peterboro was cold and dreary, and climbing the hills from Canastota in an open sleigh, nine hundred feet above the valley, with the thermometer below zero, before sunrise, made all nature look as sombre as the sad errand on which we came.

Outside the mansion everything in its wintry garb was cold and still, and all within was silent as the grave. The central figure, the light and joy of that home, had vanished forever. He who had welcomed us on that threshold for half a century would welcome us no more. We did what we could to dissipate the gloom that settled on us all. We did not intensify our grief by darkening the house and covering ourselves with black crape, but wore our accustomed dresses of chastened colors and opened all the blinds that the glad sunshine might stream in. We hung the apartment where the casket stood with wreaths of evergreens, and overhead we wove his favorite mottoes in living letters, " Equal rights for all! " " Rescue Cuba now! " The religious services were short and simple; the Unitarian clergyman from Syracuse made a few remarks, the children from the orphan asylum, in which he was deeply interested, sang an appropriate hymn, and around the grave stood representatives of the Biddles, the Dixwells, the Sedgwicks, the Barclays, and Stantons, and three generations of his immediate family. With a few appropriate words from General John

Cochrane we left our beloved kinsman alone in his last resting place. Two months later, on his birthday, his wife, Ann Carroll Fitzhugh, passed away and was laid by his side. Theirs was a remarkably happy union of over half a century, and they were soon reunited in the life eternal.

CHAPTER V.

MY engagement was a season of doubt and conflict —doubt as to the wisdom of changing a girlhood of freedom and enjoyment for I knew not what, and conflict because the step I proposed was in opposition to the wishes of all my family. Whereas, heretofore, friends were continually suggesting suitable matches for me and painting the marriage relation in the most dazzling colors, now that state was represented as beset with dangers and disappointments, and men, of all God's creatures as the most depraved and unreliable. Hard pressed, I broke my engagement, after months of anxiety and bewilderment; suddenly I decided to renew it, as Mr. Stanton was going to Europe as a delegate to the World's Anti-slavery Convention, and we did not wish the ocean to roll between us.

Thursday, May 10, 1840, I determined to take the fateful step, without the slightest preparation for a wedding or a voyage; but Mr. Stanton, coming up the North River, was detained on " Marcy's Overslaugh," a bar in the river where boats were frequently stranded for hours. This delay compelled us to be married on Friday, which is commonly supposed to be a most unlucky day. But as we lived together, without more than the usual matrimonial friction, for nearly a half a century, had seven children, all but one of whom are still living, and have been well sheltered, clothed, and

fed, enjoying sound minds in sound bodies, no one need
be afraid of going through the marriage ceremony on
Friday for fear of bad luck. The Scotch clergyman
who married us, being somewhat superstitious, begged
us to postpone it until Saturday; but, as we were to
sail early in the coming week, that was impossible.
That point settled, the next difficulty was to persuade
him to leave out the word " obey " in the marriage
ceremony. As I obstinately refused to obey one with
whom I supposed I was entering into an equal relation, that point, too, was conceded. A few friends were
invited to be present and, in a simple white evening
dress, I was married. But the good priest avenged
himself for the points he conceded, by keeping us on
the rack with a long prayer and dissertation on the
sacred institution for one mortal hour. The Rev.
Hugh Maire was a little stout fellow, vehement in manner and speech, who danced about the floor, as he laid
down the law, in the most original and comical manner. As Mr. Stanton had never seen him before, the
hour to him was one of constant struggle to maintain
his equilibrium. I had sat under his ministrations for
several years, and was accustomed to his rhetoric, accent, and gestures, and thus was able to go through
the ordeal in a calmer state of mind.

Sister Madge, who had stood by me bravely through
all my doubts and anxieties, went with us to New
York and saw us on board the vessel. My sister
Harriet and her husband, Daniel C. Eaton, a merchant
in New York city, were also there. He and I had had
for years a standing game of " tag " at all our partings,
and he had vowed to send me " tagged " to Europe.
I was equally determined that he should not. Accord-

H. B. Stanton

MRS. STANTON AND DAUGHTER, 1857.

ingly, I had a desperate chase after him all over the vessel, but in vain. He had the last "tag" and escaped. As I was compelled, under the circumstances, to conduct the pursuit with some degree of decorum, and he had the advantage of height, long limbs, and freedom from skirts, I really stood no chance whatever. However, as the chase kept us all laughing, it helped to soften the bitterness of parting.

Fairly at sea, I closed another chapter of my life, and my thoughts turned to what lay in the near future. James G. Birney, the anti-slavery nominee for the presidency of the United States, joined us in New York, and was a fellow-passenger on the *Montreal* for England. He and my husband were delegates to the World's Anti-slavery Convention, and both interested themselves in my anti-slavery education. They gave me books to read, and, as we paced the deck day by day, the question was the chief theme of our conversation.

Mr. Birney was a polished gentleman of the old school, and was excessively proper and punctilious in manner and conversation. I soon perceived that he thought I needed considerable toning down before reaching England. I was quick to see and understand that his criticisms of others in a general way and the drift of his discourses on manners and conversation had a nearer application than he intended I should discover, though he hoped I would profit by them. I was always grateful to anyone who took an interest in my improvement, so I laughingly told him, one day, that he need not make his criticisms any longer in that round-about way, but might take me squarely in hand and polish me up as speedily as possible. Sitting in the saloon at night after a game of chess, in which, perchance, I had been the victor, I felt complacent and would sometimes say:

"Well, what have I said or done to-day open to criticism?"

So, in the most gracious manner, he replied on one occasion:

"You went to the masthead in a chair, which I think very unladylike. I heard you call your husband 'Henry' in the presence of strangers, which is not permissible in polite society. You should always say 'Mr. Stanton.' You have taken three moves back in this game."

"Bless me!" I replied, "what a catalogue in one day! I fear my Mentor will despair of my ultimate perfection."

"I should have more hope," he replied, "if you seemed to feel my rebukes more deeply, but you evidently think them of too little consequence to be much disturbed by them."

As he found even more fault with my husband, we condoled with each other and decided that our friend was rather hypercritical and that we were as nearly perfect as mortals need be for the wear and tear of ordinary life. Being both endowed with a good degree of self-esteem, neither the praise nor the blame of mankind was overpowering to either of us. As the voyage lasted eighteen days—for we were on a sailing vessel—we had time to make some improvement, or, at least, to consider all friendly suggestions.

At this time Mr. Birney was very much in love with Miss Fitzhugh of Geneseo, to whom he was afterward married. He suffered at times great depression of spirits, but I could always rouse him to a sunny mood by introducing her name. That was a theme of which he never grew weary, and, while praising her, a halo of glory was to him visible around my head and I was faultless for the time being. There was nothing in our fellow-passengers to break the monotony of the voyage. They were all stolid, middle-class English people, returning from various parts of the world to visit their native land.

When out of their hearing, Mr. Birney used to ridicule them without mercy; so, one day, by way of making a point, I said with great solemnity, "Is it good breeding to make fun of the foibles of our fellow-men, who have not had our advantages of culture and education?" He felt the rebuke and blushed, and never again returned to that subject. I am sorry to say I was glad to find him once in fault.

Though some amusement, in whatever extraordinary way I could obtain it, was necessary to my existence, yet, as it was deemed important that I should thoroughly understand the status of the anti-slavery movement in my own country, I spent most of my time reading and talking on that question. Being the wife of a delegate to the World's Convention, we all felt it important that I should be able to answer whatever questions I might be asked in England on all phases of the slavery question.

The captain, a jolly fellow, was always ready to second me in my explorations into every nook and cranny of the vessel. He imagined that my reading was distasteful and enforced by the older gentlemen, so he was continually planning some diversion, and often invited me to sit with him and listen to his experiences of a sailor's life.

But all things must end in this mortal life, and our voyage was near its termination, when we were becalmed on the Southern coast of England and could not make more than one knot an hour. When within sight of the distant shore, a pilot boat came along and offered to take anyone ashore in six hours. I was so delighted at the thought of reaching land that, after much persuasion, Mr. Stanton and Mr. Birney consented to go. Accordingly we were lowered into the boat in an armchair, with a luncheon consisting of a cold chicken, a loaf of bread, and a bottle of wine, with just enough wind to carry our light craft toward our destination. But, instead of six hours, we were all day trying to reach the land, and, as the twilight deepened and the last breeze died away, the pilot said: "We are now two miles from shore, but the only way you can reach there to-night is by a rowboat."

As we had no provisions left and nowhere to sleep, we were glad to avail ourselves of the rowboat. It was a bright moonlight night, the air balmy, the waters smooth, and, with two stout oarsmen, we glided swiftly along. As Mr. Birney made the last descent and seated himself, doubtful as to our reaching shore, turning to me he said: "The woman tempted me and I did leave the good ship." However, we did reach the shore at midnight and landed at Torquay, one of the loveliest spots in that country, and our journey to Exeter the next day lay through the most beautiful scenery in England.

As we had no luggage with us, our detention by customs officers was brief, and we were soon conducted to a comfortable little hotel, which we found in the morning was a bower of roses. I had never imagined anything so beautiful as the drive up to Exeter on the top of a coach, with four stout horses, trotting at the rate of ten miles an hour. It was the first day of June, and the country was in all its glory. The foliage was of the softest green, the trees were covered with blossoms, and the shrubs with flowers. The roads were perfect; the large, fine-looking coachman, with his white gloves and reins, his rosy face and lofty bearing and the post-man in red, blowing his horn as we passed through every village, made the drive seem like a journey in fairyland. We had heard that England was like a garden of flowers, but we were wholly unprepared for such wealth of beauty.

In Exeter we had our first view of one of the great cathedrals in the Old World, and we were all deeply impressed with its grandeur. It was just at the twilight hour, when the last rays of the setting sun, streaming through the stained glass windows, deepened the shadows and threw a mysterious amber light over all. As the choir was practicing, the whole effect was heightened by the deep tones of the organ reverberating through the arched roof, and the sound of human voices as if vainly trying to fill the vast space above. The novelty and solemnity of the surroundings roused all our religious emotions and thrilled every nerve in our being. As if moved by the same impulse to linger there a while, we all sat down, silently waiting for something to break the spell that bound us. Can one wonder at the power of the Catholic religion for centuries, with such accessories to stimulate the imagination to a blind worship of the unknown?

Sitting in the hotel that evening and wanting something to read, we asked the waiter for the daily papers.

As there was no public table or drawing room for
guests, but each party had its own apartment, we
needed a little change from the society of each other.
Having been, as it were, shut from the outside world
for eighteen days, we had some curiosity to see whether
our planet was still revolving from west to east.   At
the mention of papers in the plural number, the attend-
ant gave us a look of surprise, and said he would get
"it."   He returned saying that the gentleman in No.
4 had "it," but he would be through in fifteen
minutes.   Accordingly, at the end of that time, he
brought the newspaper, and, after we had had it the
same length of time, he came to take it to another
party.   At our lodging house in London, a paper was
left for half an hour each morning, and then it was taken
to the next house, thus serving several families of
readers.

The next day brought us to London.   When I first
entered our lodging house in Queen Street, I thought
it the gloomiest abode I had ever seen.   The arrival of
a delegation of ladies, the next day, from Boston and
Philadelphia, changed the atmosphere of the establishment, and filled me with delightful anticipations of
some new and charming acquaintances, which I fully
realized in meeting Emily Winslow, Abby Southwick,
Elizabeth Neal, Mary Grew, Abby Kimber, Sarah
Pugh, and Lucretia Mott.   There had been a split in
the American anti-slavery ranks, and delegates came
from both branches, and, as they were equally represented at our lodgings, I became familiar with the whole
controversy.   The potent element which caused the
division was the woman question, and as the Garrisonian branch maintained the right of women to speak

and vote in the conventions, all my sympathies were with the Garrisonians, though Mr. Stanton and Mr. Birney belonged to the other branch, called political abolitionists. To me there was no question so important as the emancipation of women from the dogmas of the past, political, religious, and social. It struck me as very remarkable that abolitionists, who felt so keenly the wrongs of the slave, should be so oblivious to the equal wrongs of their own mothers, wives, and sisters, when, according to the common law, both classes occupied a similar legal status.

Our chief object in visiting England at this time was to attend the World's Anti-slavery Convention, to meet June 12, 1840, in Freemasons' Hall, London. Delegates from all the anti-slavery societies of civilized nations were invited, yet, when they arrived, those representing associations of women were rejected. Though women were members of the National Anti-slavery Society, accustomed to speak and vote in all its conventions, and to take an equally active part with men in the whole anti-slavery struggle, and were there as delegates from associations of men and women, as well as those distinctively of their own sex, yet all alike were rejected because they were women. Women, according to English prejudices at that time, were excluded by Scriptural texts from sharing equal dignity and authority with men in all reform associations; hence it was to English minds pre-eminently unfitting that women should be admitted as equal members to a World's Convention. The question was hotly debated through an entire day. My husband made a very eloquent speech in favor of admitting the women delegates.

When we consider that Lady Byron, Anna Jameson,
Mary Howitt, Mrs. Hugo Reid, Elizabeth Fry, Amelia
Opie, Ann Green Phillips, Lucretia Mott, and many
remarkable women, speakers and leaders in the Society
of Friends, were all compelled to listen in silence to the
masculine platitudes on woman's sphere, one may
form some idea of the indignation of unprejudiced
friends, and especially that of such women as
Lydia Maria Child, Maria Chapman, Deborah Weston, Angelina and Sarah Grimké, and Abby Kelly,
who were impatiently waiting and watching on
this side, in painful suspense, to hear how their
delegates were received. Judging from my own feelings, the women on both sides of the Atlantic must
have been humiliated and chagrined, except as these
feelings were outweighed by contempt for the shallow
reasoning of their opponents and their comical pose
and gestures in some of the intensely earnest flights of
their imagination.

The clerical portion of the convention was most violent in its opposition. The clergymen seemed to have
God and his angels especially in their care and keeping,
and were in agony lest the women should do or say
something to shock the heavenly hosts. Their all-sus-
taining conceit gave them abundant assurance that their
movements must necessarily be all-pleasing to the
celestials whose ears were open to the proceedings of
the World's Convention. Deborah, Huldah, Vashti,
and Esther might have questioned the propriety of
calling it a World's Convention, when only half of
humanity was represented there; but what were their
opinions worth compared with those of the Rev. A.
Harvey, the Rev. C. Stout, or the Rev. J. Burnet, who,

Bible in hand, argued woman's subjection, divinely de-
creed when Eve was created.

One of our champions in the convention, George
Bradburn, a tall thick-set man with a voice like thunder,
standing head and shoulders above the clerical representatives, swept all their arguments aside by declaring
with tremendous emphasis that, if they could prove
to him that the Bible taught the entire subjection of
one-half of the race to the other, he should consider
that the best thing he could do for humanity would be
to bring together every Bible in the universe and make
a grand bonfire of them.

It was really pitiful to hear narrow-minded bigots,
pretending to be teachers and leaders of men, so cruelly
remanding their own mothers, with the rest of womankind, to absolute subjection to the ordinary masculine
type of humanity. I always regretted that the women
themselves had not taken part in the debate before the
convention was fully organized and the question of
delegates settled. It seemed to me then, and does now,
that all delegates with credentials from recognized societies should have had a voice in the organization of the
convention, though subject to exclusion afterward.
However, the women sat in a low curtained seat like a
church choir, and modestly listened to the French, British, and American Solons for twelve of the longest days
in June, as did, also, our grand Garrison and Rogers in
the gallery. They scorned a convention that ignored
the rights of the very women who had fought, side by
side, with them in the anti-slavery conflict. "After bat-
tling so many long years," said Garrison, "for the liberties of African slaves, I can take no part in a convention
that strikes down the most sacred rights of all women."

After coming three thousand miles to speak on the subject nearest his heart, he nobly shared the enforced silence of the rejected delegates. It was a great act of self-sacrifice that should never be forgotten by women.

Thomas Clarkson was chosen president of the convention and made a few remarks in opening, but he soon retired, as his age and many infirmities made all public occasions too burdensome, and Joseph Sturge, a Quaker, was made chairman. Sitting next to Mrs. Mott, I said:

" As there is a Quaker in the chair now, what could he do if the spirit should move you to speak? "

" Ah," she replied, evidently not believing such a contingency possible, " where the spirit of the Lord is, there is liberty."

She had not much faith in the sincerity of abolitionists who, while eloquently defending the natural rights of slaves, denied freedom of speech to one-half the people of their own race. Such was the consistency of an assemblage of philanthropists! They would have been horrified at the idea of burning the flesh of the distinguished women present with red-hot irons, but the crucifixion of their pride and self-respect, the humiliation of the spirit, seemed to them a most trifling matter. The action of this convention was the topic of discussion, in public and private, for a long time, and stung many women into new thought and action and gave rise to the movement for women's political equality both in England and the United States.

As the convention adjourned, the remark was heard on all sides, " It is about time some demand was made for new liberties for women." As Mrs. Mott and I walked home, arm in arm, commenting on the incidents of the day, we resolved to hold a convention as soon as we returned home, and form a society to advocate the rights of women. At the lodging house on Queen Street, where a large number of delegates had apartments, the discussions were heated at every meal, and at times so bitter that, at last, Mr. Birney packed his valise and sought more peaceful quarters. Having strongly opposed the admission of women as delegates to the convention it was rather embarrassing to meet them, during the intervals between the various sessions, at the table and in the drawing room.

These were the first women I had ever met who believed in the equality of the sexes and who did not believe in the popular orthodox religion. The acquaintance of Lucretia Mott, who was a broad, liberal thinker on politics, religion, and all questions of reform, opened to me a new world of thought. As we walked about to see the sights of London, I embraced every opportunity to talk with her. It was intensely gratifying to hear all that, through years of doubt, I had dimly thought, so freely discussed by other women, some of them no older than myself—women, too, of rare intelligence, cultivation, and refinement. After six weeks' sojourn under the same roof with Lucretia Mott, whose conversation was uniformly on a high plane, I felt that I knew her too well to sympathize with the orthodox Friends, who denounced her as a dangerous woman because she doubted certain dogmas they fully believed.

As Mr. Birney and my husband were invited to speak all over England, Scotland, and Ireland, and we were uniformly entertained by orthodox Friends, I had abundant opportunity to know the general feeling among them toward Lucretia Mott. Even Elizabeth

Fry seemed quite unwilling to breathe the same atmosphere with her.   During the six weeks that many of
us remained in London after the convention we were
invited to a succession of public and private breakfasts,
dinners, and teas, and on these occasions it was amusing to watch Mrs. Fry's sedulous efforts to keep Mrs.
Mott at a distance.   If Mrs. Mott was on the lawn,
Mrs. Fry would go into the house; if Mrs. Mott was in
the house, Mrs. Fry would stay out on the lawn.   One
evening, when we were all crowded into two parlors,
and there was no escape, the word went round that
Mrs. Fry felt moved to pray with the American delegates, whereupon a profound silence reigned.   After a
few moments Mrs. Fry's voice was heard deploring the
schism among the American Friends; that so many had
been led astray by false doctrines; urging the Spirit of
All Good to show them the error of their way, and
gather them once more into the fold of the great Shepherd of our faith.   The prayer was directed so point-
edly at the followers of Elias Hicks, and at Lucretia
Mott in particular, that I whispered to Lucretia, at the
close, that she should now pray for Mrs. Fry, that her
eyes might be opened to her bigotry and uncharitable-
ness, and be led by the Spirit into higher light.   " Oh,
no! " she replied, " a prayer of this character, under the
circumstances, is an unfair advantage to take of a
stranger, but I would not resent it in the house of her
friends."

In these gatherings we met the leading Quaker families and many other philanthropists of different denominations interested in the anti-slavery movement.
On all these occasions our noble Garrison spoke
most effectively, and thus our English friends had an

opportunity of enjoying his eloquence, the lack of which had been so grave a loss in the convention.

We devoted a month sedulously to sightseeing in London, and, in the line of the traveler's duty, we explored St. Paul's Cathedral, the British Museum, the Tower, various prisons, hospitals, galleries of art, Windsor Castle, and St. James's Palace, the Zoölogical Gardens, the schools and colleges, the chief theaters and churches, Westminster Abbey, the Houses of Parliament, and the Courts. We heard the most famous preachers, actors, and statesmen. In fact, we went to the top and bottom of everything, from the dome of St. Paul to the tunnel under the Thames, just then in the process of excavation. We drove through the parks, sailed up and down the Thames, and then visited every shire but four in England, in all of which we had large meetings, Mr. Birney and Mr. Stanton being the chief speakers. As we were generally invited to stay with Friends, it gave us a good opportunity to see the leading families, such as the Ashursts, the Alexanders, the Priestmans, the Braithwaites, and Buxtons, the Gurneys, the Peases, the Wighams of Edinburgh, and the Webbs of Dublin. We spent a few days with John Joseph Gurney at his beautiful home in Norwich. He had just returned from America, having made a tour through the South. When asked how he liked America, he said, " I like everything but your pie crust and your slavery."

Before leaving London, the whole American delegation, about forty in number, were invited to dine with Samuel Gurney. He and his brother, John Joseph Gurney, were, at that time, the leading bankers in London. Someone facetiously remarked that the Jews were the leading bankers in London until the Quakers crowded them out.

One of the most striking women I met in England at this time was Miss Elizabeth Pease. I never saw a more strongly marked face. Meeting her, forty years after, on the platform of a great meeting in the Town Hall at Glasgow, I knew her at once. She is now Mrs. Nichol of Edinburgh, and, though on the shady side of eighty, is still active in all the reforms of the day.

It surprised us very much at first, when driving into the grounds of some of these beautiful Quaker homes, to have the great bell rung at the lodge, and to see the number of liveried servants on the porch and in the halls, and then to meet the host in plain garb, and to be welcomed in plain language, " How does thee do, Henry? " " How does thee do Elizabeth? " This sounded peculiarly sweet to me—a stranger in a strange land. The wealthy English Quakers we visited at that time, taking them all in all, were the most charming people I had ever seen. They were refined and intelligent on all subjects, and though rather conservative on some points, were not aggressive in pressing their opinions on others. Their hospitality was charming and generous, their homes the beau ideal of comfort and order, the cuisine faultless, while peace reigned over all. The quiet, gentle manner and the soft tones in speaking, and the mysterious quiet in these well-ordered homes were like the atmosphere one finds in a modern convent, where the ordinary duties of the day seem to be accomplished by some magical influence.

Before leaving London we spent a delightful day in June at the home of Samuel Gurney, surrounded by a fine park with six hundred deer roaming about—

always a beautiful feature in the English landscape. As the Duchess of Sutherland and Lord Morpeth had expressed a wish to Mrs. Fry to meet some of the leading American abolitionists, it was arranged that they should call at her brother's residence on this occasion. Soon after we arrived, the Duchess, with her brother and Mrs. Fry, in her state carriage with six horses and outriders, drove up to the door. Mr. Gurney was evidently embarrassed at the prospect of a lord and a duchess under his roof. Leaning on the arm of Mrs. Fry, the duchess was formally introduced to us individually. Mrs. Mott conversed with the distinguished guests with the same fluency and composure as with her own countrywomen. However anxious the English people were as to what they should say and do, the Americans were all quite at their ease.

As Lord Morpeth had some interesting letters from the island of Jamaica to read to us, we formed a circle on the lawn to listen. England had just paid one hundred millions of dollars to emancipate the slaves, and we were all interested in hearing the result of the experiment. The distinguished guest in turn had many questions to ask in regard to American slavery. We found none of that prejudice against color in England which is so inveterate among the American people; at my first dinner in England I found myself beside a gentleman from Jamaica, as black as the ace of spades. After the departure of the duchess, dinner was announced. It was a sumptuous meal, most tastefully served. There were half a dozen wineglasses at every plate, but abolitionists, in those days, were all converts to temperance, and, as the bottles went around there was a general headshaking, and the right hand ex-

tended over the glasses. Our English friends were
amazed that none of us drank wine. Mr. Gurney said
he had never before seen such a sight as forty ladies and
gentlemen sitting down to dinner and none of them
tasting wine. In talking with him on that point, he
said:

" I suppose your nursing mothers drink beer? "

I laughed, and said, " Oh, no! We should be afraid
of befogging the brains of our children."

" No danger of that," said he; " we are all bright
enough, and yet a cask of beer is rolled into the cellar
for the mother with each newborn child."

Colonel Miller from Vermont, one of our American
delegation, was in the Greek war with Lord Byron. As
Lady Byron had expressed a wish to see him, that her
daughter might know something of her father's last
days, an interview was arranged, and the colonel kindly
invited me to accompany him. His account of their
acquaintance and the many noble traits of character
Lord Byron manifested, his generous impulses and acts
of self-sacrifice, seemed particularly gratifying to the
daughter. It was a sad interview, arranged chiefly for
the daughter's satisfaction, though Lady Byron listened
with a painful interest. As the colonel was a warm
admirer of the great poet, he no doubt represented him
in the best possible light, and his narration of his last
days was deeply interesting. Lady Byron had a quiet,
reserved manner, a sad face, and a low, plaintive voice,
like one who had known deep sorrow. I had seen her
frequently in the convention and at social teas, and had
been personally presented to her before this occasion.
Altogether I thought her a sweet, attractive-looking
woman.

We had a pleasant interview with Lord Brougham also. The Philadelphia Anti-slavery Society sent him an elaborately carved inkstand, made from the wood of Pennsylvania Hall, which was destroyed by a pro-slavery mob. Mr. Birney made a most graceful speech in presenting the memento, and Lord Brougham was equally happy in receiving it.

One of the most notable characters we met at this time was Daniel O'Connell. He made his first appearance in the London convention a few days after the women were rejected. He paid a beautiful tribute to woman and said that, if he had been present when the question was under discussion, he should have spoken and voted for their admission. He was a tall, well-developed, magnificent-looking man, and probably one of the most effective speakers Ireland ever produced. I saw him at a great India meeting in Exeter Hall, where some of the best orators from France, America, and England were present. There were six natives from India on the platform who, not understanding anything that was said, naturally remained listless throughout the proceedings. But the moment O'Connell began to speak they were all attention, bending forward and closely watching every movement. One could almost tell what he said from the play of his expressive features, his wonderful gestures, and the pose of his whole body. When he finished, the natives joined in the general applause. He had all Wendell Phillips' power of sarcasm and denunciation, and added to that the most tender pathos. He could make his audience laugh or cry at pleasure. It was a rare sight to see him dressed in " Repeal cloth " in one of his Repeal meetings. We were in Dublin in the midst of that excitement, when the hopes of new liberties for that oppressed people all centered on O'Connell. The enthusiasm of the people for the Repeal of the Union was then at white-heat. Dining one day with the "Great Liberator," as he was called, I asked him if he hoped to carry that measure.

"No," he said, "but it is always good policy to claim the uttermost and then you will be sure to get something."

Could he have looked forward fifty years and have seen the present condition of his unhappy country, he would have known that English greed and selfishness could defeat any policy, however wise and far-seeing. The successive steps by which Irish commerce was ruined and religious feuds between her people continually fanned into life, and the nation subjugated, form the darkest page in the history of England. But the people are awakening at last to their duty, and, for the first time, organizing English public sentiment in favor of "Home Rule." I attended several large, enthusiastic meetings when last in England, in which the most radical utterances of Irish patriots were received with prolonged cheers. I trust the day is not far off when the beautiful Emerald Isle will unfurl her banner before the nations of the earth, enthroned as the Queen Republic of those northern seas!

We visited Wordsworth's home at Grasmere, among the beautiful lakes, but he was not there. However, we saw his surroundings—the landscape that inspired some of his poetic dreams, and the dense rows of hollyhocks of every shade and color, leading from his porch to the gate. The gardener told us this was his favorite flower. Though it had no special beauty in itself, taken alone, yet the wonderful combination of royal colors was indeed striking and beautiful. We saw Harriet Martineau at her country home as well as at her house in town. As we were obliged to converse with her through an ear trumpet, we left her to do most of the talking. She gave us many amusing experiences of her travels in America, and her comments on the London Convention were rich and racy. She was not an attractive woman in either manner or appearance, though considered great and good by all who knew her.

We spent a few days with Thomas Clarkson, in Ipswich. He lived in a very old house with long rambling corridors, surrounded by a moat, which we crossed by means of a drawbridge. He had just written an article against the colonization scheme, which his wife read aloud to us. He was so absorbed in the subject that he forgot the article was written by himself, and kept up a running applause with " hear! " " hear! " the English mode of expressing approbation. He told us of the severe struggles he and Wilberforce had gone through in rousing the public sentiment of England to the demand for emancipation in Jamaica. But their trials were mild, compared with what Garrison and his coadjutors had suffered in America.

Having read of all these people, it was difficult to realize, as I visited them in their own homes from day to day, that they were the same persons I had so long worshiped from afar!

CHAPTER VI.

HOMEWARD BOUND.

AFTER taking a view of the wonders and surroundings of London we spent a month in Paris. Fifty years ago there was a greater difference in the general appearance of things between France and England than now. That countries only a few hours' journey apart should differ so widely was to us a great surprise. How changed the sights and sounds! Here was the old diligence, lumbering along with its various compartments and its indefinite number of horses, harnessed with rope and leather, sometimes two, sometimes three abreast, and sometimes one in advance, with an outrider belaboring the poor beasts without cessation, and the driver yelling and cracking his whip. The uproar, confusion, and squabbles at every stopping place are overwhelming; the upper classes, men and women alike, rushing into each other's arms, embrace and kiss, while drivers and hostlers on the slightest provocation hurl at each other all the denunciatory adjectives in the language, and with such vehemence that you expect every moment to see a deadly conflict. But to-day, as fifty years ago, they never arrive at that point. Theirs was and is purely an encounter of words, which they keep up, as they drive off in opposite directions, just as far as they can hear and see each other, with threats of vengeance to come.

Such an encounter between two Englishmen would mean the death of one or the other.

All this was in marked contrast with John Bull and his Island. There the people were as silent as if they had been born deaf and dumb. The English stage-coach was compact, clean, and polished from top to bottom, the horses and harness glossy and in order, the well-dressed, dignified coachman, who seldom spoke a loud word or used his whip, kept his seat at the various stages, while hostlers watered or changed the steeds; the postman blew his bugle blast to have the mail in readiness, and the reserved passengers made no remarks on what was passing; for, in those days, Englishmen were afraid to speak to each other for fear of recognizing one not of their class, while to strangers and foreigners they would not speak except in case of dire necessity. The Frenchman was ready enough to talk, but, unfortunately, we were separated by different languages. Thus the Englishman would not talk, the Frenchman could not, and the intelligent, loquacious American driver, who discourses on politics, religion, national institutions, and social gossip was unknown on that side of the Atlantic. What the curious American traveler could find out himself from observation and pertinacious seeking he was welcome to, but the Briton would waste no breath to enlighten Yankees as to the points of interest or customs of his country.

Our party consisted of Miss Pugh, Abby Kimber, Mr. Stanton, and myself. I had many amusing experiences in making my wants known when alone, having forgotten most of my French. For instance, traveling night and day in the diligence to Paris, as the stops were short, one was sometimes in need of something to eat. One night as my companions were all asleep, I went out to get a piece of cake or a cracker, or whatever of that sort I could obtain, but, owing to my clumsy use of the language, I was misunderstood. Just as the diligence was about to start, and the shout for us to get aboard was heard, the waiter came running with a piping hot plate of sweetbreads nicely broiled. I had waited and wondered why it took so long to get a simple piece of cake or biscuit, and lo! a piece of hot meat was offered me. I could not take the frizzling thing in my hand nor eat it without bread, knife, or fork, so I hurried off to the coach, the man pursuing me to the very door. I was vexed and disappointed, while the rest of the party were convulsed with laughter at the parting salute and my attempt to make my way alone. It was some time before I heard the last of the " sweetbreads."

When we reached Paris we secured a courier who could speak English, to show us the sights of that wonderful city. Every morning early he was at the door, rain or shine, to carry out our plans, which, with the aid of our guidebook, we had made the evening before. In this way, going steadily, day after day, we visited all points of interest for miles round and sailed up and down the Seine. The Palace of the Tuileries, with its many associations with a long line of more or less unhappy kings and queens, was then in its glory, and its extensive and beautiful grounds were always gay with crowds of happy people. These gardens were a great resort for nurses and children and were furnished with all manner of novel appliances for their amusement, including beautiful little carriages drawn by four goats with girls or boys driving, boats sailing in the air, seemingly propelled by oars, and hobby horses flying round on whirligigs with boys vainly trying to catch each other. No people have ever taken the trouble to invent so many amusements for children as have the French. The people enjoyed being always in the open air, night and day. The parks are crowded with amusement seekers, some reading and playing games, some sewing, knitting, playing on musical instruments, dancing, sitting around tables in bevies eating, drinking, and gayly chatting. And yet, when they drive in carriages or go to their homes at night, they will shut themselves in as tight as oysters in their shells. They have a theory that night air is very injurious,—in the house,—although they will sit outside until midnight. I found this same superstition prevalent in France fifty years later.

We visited the Hôtel des Invalides just as they were preparing the sarcophagus for the reception of the remains of Napoleon. We witnessed the wild excitement of that enthusiastic people, and listened with deep interest to the old soldiers' praises of their great general. The ladies of our party chatted freely with them. They all had interesting anecdotes to relate of their chief. They said he seldom slept over four hours, was an abstemious eater, and rarely changed a servant, as he hated a strange face about him. He was very fond of a game of chess, and snuffed continuously; talked but little, was a light sleeper,—the stirring of a mouse would awaken him,—and always on the watchtower. They said that, in his great campaigns, he seemed to be omnipresent. A sentinel asleep at his post would sometimes waken to find Napoleon on duty in his place.

The ship that brought back Napoleon's remains was the *Belle Poule* (the beautiful hen!), which landed at Cherbourg, November 30, 1840. The body was conveyed to the Church of the Invalides, which adjoins the tomb. The Prince de Joinville brought the body from Saint Helena, and Louis Philippe received it.

At that time each soldier had a little patch of land to decorate as he pleased, in which many scenes from their great battles were illustrated. One represented Napoleon crossing the Alps. There were the cannon, the soldiers, Napoleon on horseback, all toiling up the steep ascent, perfect in miniature. In another was Napoleon, flag in hand, leading the charge across the bridge of Lodi. In still another was Napoleon in Egypt, before the Pyramids, seated, impassive, on his horse, gazing at the Sphinx, as if about to utter his immortal words to his soldiers: "Here, forty centuries look down upon us." These object lessons of the past are all gone now and the land used for more prosaic purposes.

I little thought, as I witnessed that great event in France in 1840, that fifty-seven years later I should witness a similar pageant in the American Republic, when our nation paid its last tributes to General Grant. There are many points of similarity in these great events. As men they were alike aggressive and self-reliant. In Napoleon's will he expressed the wish that his last resting place might be in the land and among the people he loved so well. His desire is fulfilled. He rests in the chief city of the French republic, whose shores are washed by the waters of the Seine. General Grant expressed the wish that he might be interred in our metropolis and added: " Wherever I am buried,

I desire that there shall be room for my wife by my side." His wishes, too, are fulfilled. He rests in the chief city of the American Republic, whose shores are washed by the waters of the Hudson, and in his magnificent mausoleum there is room for his wife by his side.

Several members of the Society of Friends from Boston and Philadelphia, who had attended the World's Anti-slavery Convention in London, joined our party for a trip on the Continent. Though opposed to war, they all took a deep interest in the national excitement and in the pageants that heralded the expected arrival of the hero from Saint Helena. As they all wore military coats of the time of George Fox, the soldiers, supposing they belonged to the army of some country, gave them the military salute wherever we went, much to their annoyance and our amusement.

In going the rounds, Miss Pugh amused us by reading aloud the description of what we were admiring and the historical events connected with that particular building or locality. We urged her to spend the time taking in all she could see and to read up afterward; but no, a history of France and Galignani's guide she carried everywhere, and, while the rest of us looked until we were fully satisfied, she took a bird's-eye view and read the description. Dear little woman! She was a fine scholar, a good historian, was well informed on all subjects and countries, proved an invaluable traveling companion, and could tell more of what we saw than all the rest of us together.

On several occasions we chanced to meet Louis Philippe dashing by in an open barouche. We felt great satisfaction in remembering that at one time he was an exile in our country, where he earned his living by teaching school. What an honor for Yankee children to have been taught, by a French king, the rudiments of his language.

Having been accustomed to the Puritan Sunday of restraint and solemnity, I found that day in Paris gay and charming. The first time I entered into some of the festivities, I really expected to be struck by lightning. The libraries, art galleries, concert halls, and theaters were all open to the people. Bands of music were playing in the parks, where whole families, with their luncheons, spent the day—husbands, wives, and children, on an excursion together. The boats on the Seine and all public conveyances were crowded. Those who had but this one day for pleasure seemed determined to make the most of it. A wonderful contrast with that gloomy day in London, where all places of amusement were closed and nothing open to the people but the churches and drinking saloons. The streets and houses in which Voltaire, LaFayette, Mme. de Staël, Mme. Roland, Charlotte Corday, and other famous men and women lived and died, were pointed out to us. We little thought, then, of all the terrible scenes to be enacted in Paris, nor that France would emerge from the dangers that beset her on every side into a sister republic. It has been a wonderful achievement, with kings and Popes all plotting against her experiment, that she has succeeded in putting kingcraft under her feet and proclaimed liberty, equality, fraternity for her people.

After a few weeks in France, we returned to London, traveling through England, Ireland, and Scotland for several months. We visited the scenes that Shakespeare,

Burns, and Dickens had made classic. We spent a few days at Huntingdon, the home of Oliver Cromwell, and visited the estate where he passed his early married life. While there, one of his great admirers read aloud to us a splendid article in one of the reviews, written by Carlyle, giving " The Protector," as his friend said, his true place in history. It was long the fashion of England's historians to represent Cromwell as a fanatic and hypocrite, but his character was vindicated by later writers. " Never," says Macaulay, " was a ruler so conspicuously born for sovereignty. The cup which has intoxicated almost all others sobered him."

We saw the picturesque ruins of Kenilworth Castle, the birthplace of Shakespeare, the homes of Byron and Mary Chaworth, wandered through Newstead Abbey, saw the monument to the faithful dog, and the large dining room where Byron and his boon companions used to shoot at a mark. It was a desolate region. We stopped a day or two at Ayr and drove out to the birthplace of Burns. The old house that had sheltered him was still there, but its walls now echoed to other voices, and the fields where he had toiled were plowed by other hands. We saw the stream and banks where he and Mary sat together, the old stone church where the witches held their midnight revels, the two dogs, and the bridge of Ayr. With Burns, as with Sappho, it was love that awoke his heart to song. A bonny lass who worked with him in the harvest field inspired his first attempts at rhyme. Life, with Burns, was one long, hard struggle. With his natural love for the beautiful, the terrible depression of spirits he suffered from his dreary surroundings was inevitable. The interest great men took in him, when they awoke to

his genius, came too late for his safety and encouragement. In a glass of whisky he found, at last, the rest
and cheer he never knew when sober. Poverty and
ignorance are the parents of intemperance, and that
vice will never be suppressed until the burdens of life
are equally shared by all.

We saw Melrose by moonlight, spent several hours at
Abbotsford, and lingered in the little *sanctum sanctorum*
where Scott wrote his immortal works. It was so small
that he could reach the bookshelves on every side.
We went through the prisons, castles, and narrow
streets of Edinburgh, where the houses are seven and
eight stories high, each story projecting a few feet until,
at the uppermost, opposite neighbors could easily shake
hands and chat together. All the intervals from
active sight-seeing we spent in reading the lives of historical personages in poetry and prose, until our sympathies flowed out to the real and ideal characters.
Lady Jane Grey, Anne Boleyn, Mary Queen of Scots,
Ellen Douglas, Jeanie and Effie Deans, Highland Mary,
Rebecca the Jewess, Di Vernon, and Rob Roy all alike
seemed real men and women, whose shades or descendants we hoped to meet on their native heath.

Here among the Scotch lakes and mountains Mr.
Stanton and I were traveling alone for the first time
since our marriage, and as we both enjoyed walking, we
made many excursions on foot to points that could not
be reached in any other way. We spent some time
among the Grampian Hills, so familiar to every school-
boy, walking, and riding about on donkeys. We sailed
up and down Loch Katrine and Loch Lomond. My
husband was writing letters for some New York newspapers on the entire trip, and aimed to get exact knowl-

edge of all we saw; thus I had the advantage of the information he gathered. On these long tramps I wore a short dress, reaching just below the knee, of dark-blue cloth, a military cap of the same material that shaded my eyes, and a pair of long boots, made on the masculine pattern then generally worn—the most easy style for walking, as the pressure is equal on the whole foot and the ankle has free play. Thus equipped, and early trained by my good brother-in-law to long walks, I found no difficulty in keeping pace with my husband.

Being self-reliant and venturesome in our explorations, we occasionally found ourselves involved in grave difficulties by refusing to take a guide. For instance, we decided to go to the top of Ben Nevis alone. It looked to us a straightforward piece of business to walk up a mountain side on a bee line, and so, in the face of repeated warnings by our host, we started. We knew nothing of zigzag paths to avoid the rocks, the springs, and swamps; in fact we supposed all mountains smooth and dry, like our native hills that we were accustomed to climb. The landlord shook his head and smiled when we told him we should return at noon to dinner, and we smiled, too, thinking he placed a low estimate on our capacity for walking. But we had not gone far when we discovered the difficulties ahead. Some places were so steep that I had to hold on to my companion's coat tails, while he held on to rocks and twigs, or braced himself with a heavy cane. By the time we were half-way up we were in a dripping perspiration, our feet were soaking wet, and we were really too tired to proceed. But, after starting with such supreme confidence in ourselves, we were ashamed to confess our fatigue to each other, and much more to return and verify all the prognostications of the host and his guides. So we determined to push on and do what we had proposed. With the prospect of a magnificent view and an hour's delicious rest on the top, we started with renewed courage. A steady climb of six hours brought us to the goal of promise; our ascent was accomplished. But alas! it was impossible to stop there—the cold wind chilled us to the bone in a minute. So we took one glance at the world below and hurried down the south side to get the mountain between us and the cold northeaster.

When your teeth are chattering with the cold, and the wind threatening to make havoc with your raiment, you are not in a favorable condition to appreciate grand scenery. Like the king of France with twice ten thousand men, we marched up the hill and then, marched down again. We found descending still more difficult, as we were in constant fear of slipping, losing our hold, and rolling to the bottom. We were tired, hungry, and disappointed, and the fear of not reaching the valley before nightfall pressed heavily upon us. Neither confessed to the other the fatigue and apprehension each felt, but, with fresh endeavor and words of encouragement, we cautiously went on. We accidentally struck a trail that led us winding down comfortably some distance, but we lost it, and went clambering down as well as we could in our usual way. To add to our misery, a dense Scotch mist soon enveloped us, so that we could see but a short distance ahead, and not knowing the point from which we started, we feared we might be going far out of our way. The coming twilight, too, made the prospect still darker. Fortunately our host, having less faith in us than we had in ourselves, sent a guide to reconnoiter, and, just at the moment when we began to realize our danger of spending the night on the mountain, and to admit it to each other, the welcome guide hailed us in his broad accent. His shepherd dog led the way into the beaten path. As I could hardly stand I took the guide's arm, and when we reached the bottom two donkeys were in readiness to take us to the hotel.

We did not recover from the fatigue of that expedition in several days, and we made no more experiments of exploring strange places without guides. We learned, too, that mountains are not so hospitable as they seem nor so gently undulating as they appear in the distance, and that guides serve other purposes besides extorting money from travelers. If, under their guidance, we had gone up and down easily, we should always have thought we might as well have gone alone. So our experience gave us a good lesson in humility. We had been twelve hours on foot with nothing to eat, when at last we reached the hotel. We were in no mood for boasting of the success of our excursion, and our answers were short to inquiries as to how we had passed the day.

Being tired of traveling and contending about woman's sphere with the Rev. John Scoble, an Englishman, who escorted Mr. Birney and Mr. Stanton on their tour through the country, I decided to spend a month in Dublin; while the gentlemen held meetings in Cork, Belfast, Waterford, Limerick, and other chief towns, finishing the series with a large, enthusiastic gathering in Dublin, at which O'Connell made one of his most withering speeches on American slavery; the inconsistency of such an " institution " with the principles of a republican government giving full play to his powers of sarcasm. On one occasion, when introduced to a slaveholder, he put his hands behind his back, refusing to recognize a man who bought and sold his fellow-beings. The Rev. John Scoble was one of the most conceited men I ever met. His narrow ideas in regard to woman, and the superiority of the royal and noble classes in his own country, were to me so exasperating that I grew more and more bellicose every day we traveled in company. He was terribly seasick crossing the Channel, to my intense satisfaction. As he always boasted of his distinguished countrymen, I suggested, in the midst of one of his most agonizing spasms, that he ought to find consolation in the fact that Lord Nelson was always seasick on the slightest provocation.

The poverty in Ireland was a continual trial to our sensibilities; beggars haunted our footsteps everywhere, in the street and on the highways, crouching on the steps of the front door and on the curbstones, and surrounding our carriage wherever and whenever we stopped to shop or make a visit. The bony hands and sunken eyes and sincere gratitude expressed for every penny proved their suffering real. As my means were limited and I could not pass one by, I got a pound changed into pennies, and put them in a green bag, which I took in the carriage wherever I went. It was but a drop in the ocean, but it was all I could do to relieve that unfathomed misery. The poverty I saw everywhere in the Old World, and especially in Ireland, was a puzzling problem to my mind, but I rejected the idea that it was a necessary link in human experience—that it always had been and always must be.

As we drove, day by day, in that magnificent Phœnix Park, of fifteen hundred acres, one of the largest parks, I believe, in the world, I would often put the question to myself, what right have the few to make a pleasure ground of these acres, while the many have nowhere to lay their heads, crouching under stiles and bridges, clothed in rags, and feeding on sea-weed with no hope, in the slowly passing years, of any change for the better? The despair stamped on every brow told the sad story of their wrongs. Those accustomed to such everyday experiences brush beggars aside as they would so many flies, but those to whom such sights are new cannot so easily quiet their own consciences. Everyone in the full enjoyment of all the blessings of life, in his normal condition, feels some individual responsibility for the poverty of others. When the sympathies are not blunted by any false philosophy, one feels reproached by one's own abundance. I once heard a young girl, about to take her summer outing, when asked by her grandmother if she had all the dresses she needed, reply, " Oh, yes! I was oppressed with a constant sense of guilt, when packing, to see how much I had, while so many girls have nothing decent to wear."

More than half a century has rolled by since I stood on Irish soil, and shed tears of pity for the wretchedness I saw, and no change for the better has as yet come to that unhappy people—yet this was the land of Burke, Grattan, Shiel, and Emmett; the land into which Christianity was introduced in the fifth century, St. Patrick being the chief apostle of the new faith. In the sixth century Ireland sent forth missionaries from her monasteries to convert Great Britain and the nations of

Northern Europe. From the eighth to the twelfth century Irish scholars held an enviable reputation. In fact, Ireland was the center of learning at one time. The arts, too, were cultivated by her people; and the round towers, still pointed out to travelers, are believed to be the remains of the architecture of the tenth century. The ruin of Ireland must be traced to other causes than the character of the people or the Catholic religion. Historians give us facts showing English oppressions sufficient to destroy any nation.

The short, dark days of November intensified, in my eyes, the gloomy prospects of that people, and made the change to the *Sirius* of the Cunard Line, the first regular Atlantic steamship to cross the ocean, most enjoyable. Once on the boundless ocean, one sees no beggars, no signs of human misery, no crumbling ruins of vast cathedral walls, no records of the downfall of mighty nations, no trace, even, of the mortal agony of the innumerable host buried beneath her bosom. Byron truly says:

> " Time writes no wrinkle on thine azure brow—
> Such as creation's dawn beheld, thou rollest now."

When we embarked on the *Sirius*, we had grave doubts as to our safety and the probability of our reaching the other side, as we did not feel that ocean steamers had yet been fairly tried. But, after a passage of eighteen days, eleven hours, and fifteen minutes, we reached Boston, having spent six hours at Halifax. We little thought that the steamer *Sirius* of fifty years ago would ever develop into the magnificent floating palaces of to-day—three times as large and three times as swift. In spite of the steamer, however, we had a cold, rough, dreary voyage, and I have no pleasant memories connected with it. Our fellow-passengers were all in their staterooms most of the time. Our good friend Mr. Birney had sailed two weeks before us, and as Mr. Stanton was confined to his berth, I was thrown on my own resources. I found my chief amusement in reading novels and playing chess with a British officer on his way to Canada. When it was possible I walked on deck with the captain, or sat in some sheltered corner, watching the waves. We arrived in New York, by rail, the day before Christmas. Everything looked bright and gay in our streets. It seemed to me that the sky was clearer, the air more refreshing, and the sunlight more brilliant than in any other land!

CHAPTER VII.

MOTHERHOOD.

WE found my sister Harriet in a new home in Clinton Place (Eighth Street), New York city, then considered so far up town that Mr. Eaton's friends were continually asking him why he went so far away from the social center, though in a few months they followed him. Here we passed a week. I especially enjoyed seeing my little niece and nephew, the only grandchildren in the family. The girl was the most beautiful child I ever saw, and the boy the most intelligent and amusing. He was very fond of hearing me recite the poem by Oliver Wendell Holmes entitled " The Height of the Ridiculous," which I did many times, but he always wanted to see the lines that almost killed the man with laughing. He went around to a number of the bookstores one day and inquired for them. I told him afterward they were never published; that when Mr. Holmes saw the effect on his servant he suppressed them, lest they should produce the same effect on the typesetters, editors, and the readers of the Boston newspapers. My explanation never satisfied him. I told him he might write to Mr. Holmes, and ask the privilege of reading the original manuscript, if it still was or ever had been in existence. As one of my grandnephews was troubled in exactly the same way, I decided to appeal myself to Dr. Holmes for the enlightenment of this second generation. So I wrote him the

following letter, which he kindly answered, telling us
that his " wretched man " was a myth like the heroes
in " Mother Goose's Melodies ":

" DEAR DR. HOLMES:
  " I have a little nephew to whom I often recite ' The
Height of the Ridiculous,' and he invariably asks for
the lines that produced the fatal effect on your servant.
He visited most of the bookstores in New York city to
find them, and nothing but your own word, I am sure,
will ever convince him that the ' wretched man ' is but
a figment of your imagination.   I tried to satisfy him
by saying you did not dare to publish the lines lest they
should produce a similar effect on the typesetters, editors, and the readers of the Boston journals.
  " However, he wishes me to ask you whether you
kept a copy of the original manuscript, or could reproduce the lines with equal power.   If not too much
trouble, please send me a few lines on this point, and
greatly oblige,
          " Yours sincerely,
                  " ELIZABETH CADY STANTON."

" MY DEAR MRS. STANTON:
  " I wish you would explain to your little nephew that
the story of the poor fellow who almost died laughing
was a kind of a dream of mine, and not a real thing that
happened, any more than that an old woman ' lived in
a shoe and had so many children she didn't know what
to do,' or that Jack climbed the bean stalk and found
the giant who lived at the top of it.   You can explain
to him what is meant by imagination, and thus turn my
youthful rhymes into a text for a discourse worthy of

the Concord School of Philosophy. I have not my
poems by me here, but I remember that ' The Height
of the Ridiculous ' ended with this verse:

> " Ten days and nights, with sleepless eye,
>   I watched that wretched man,
>   And since, I never dare to write
>   As funny as I can."

"But tell your nephew he mustn't cry about it any
more than because geese go barefoot and bald eagles
have no nightcaps. The verses are in all the editions
of my poems.

"Believe me, dear Mrs. Stanton,

"Very Truly and Respectfully Yours,

"OLIVER WENDELL HOLMES."

After spending the holidays in New York city, we
started for Johnstown in a " stage sleigh, conveying the
United States mail," drawn by spanking teams of four
horses, up the Hudson River valley. We were three
days going to Albany, stopping over night at various
points; a journey now performed in three hours. The
weather was clear and cold, the sleighing fine, the
scenery grand, and our traveling companions most
entertaining, so the trip was very enjoyable. From Albany to Schenectady we went in the railway cars; then
another sleighride of thirty miles brought us to Johnstown. My native hills, buried under two feet of snow,
tinted with the last rays of the setting sun, were a beautiful and familiar sight. Though I had been absent but
ten months, it seemed like years, and I was surprised to
find how few changes had occurred since I left. My
father and mother, sisters Madge and Kate, the old
house and furniture, the neighbors, all looked precisely

the same as when I left them. I had seen so much and
been so constantly on the wing that I wondered that all
things here should have stood still. I expected to hear
of many births, marriages, deaths, and social upheavals,
but the village news was remarkably meager. This
hunger for home news on returning is common, I suppose, to all travelers.

Our trunks unpacked, wardrobes arranged in closets
and drawers, the excitement of seeing friends over, we
spent some time in making plans for the future.

My husband, after some consultation with my father,
decided to enter his office and commence the study of
the law. As this arrangement kept me under the
parental roof, I had two added years of pleasure, walking, driving, and riding on horseback with my sisters.
Madge and Kate were dearer to me than ever, as I saw
the inevitable separation awaiting us in the near future.
In due time they were married and commenced housekeeping—Madge in her husband's house near by, and
Kate in Buffalo. All my sisters were peculiarly fortunate in their marriages; their husbands being men of
fine presence, liberal education, high moral character,
and marked ability. These were pleasant and profitable
years. I devoted them to reading law, history, and
political economy, with occasional interruptions to take
part in some temperance or anti-slavery excitement.

Eliza Murray and I had classes of colored children in
the Sunday school. On one occasion, when there was
to be a festival, speaking in the church, a procession
through the streets, and other public performances for
the Sunday-school celebration, some narrow-minded
bigots objected to the colored children taking part.
They approached Miss Murray and me with most per-

suasive tones on the wisdom of not allowing them to march in the procession to the church. We said, " Oh, no! It won't do to disappoint the children. They are all dressed, with their badges on, and looking forward with great pleasure to the festivities of the day. Besides, we would not cater to any of these contemptible prejudices against color." We were all assembled in the courthouse preparatory to forming in the line of march. Some were determined to drive the colored children home, but Miss Murray and I, like two defiant hens, kept our little brood close behind us, determined to conquer or perish in the struggle. At last milder counsels prevailed, and it was agreed that they might march in the rear. We made no objection and fell into line, but, when we reached the church door, it was promptly closed as the last white child went in. We tried two other doors, but all were guarded. We shed tears of vexation and pity for the poor children, and, when they asked us the reason why they could not go in, we were embarrassed and mortified with the explanation we were forced to give. However, I invited them to my father's house, where Miss Murray and I gave them refreshments and entertained them for the rest of the day.

The puzzling questions of theology and poverty that had occupied so much of my thoughts, now gave place to the practical one, " what to do with a baby." Though motherhood is the most important of all the professions,—requiring more knowledge than any other department in human affairs,—yet there is not sufficient attention given to the preparation for this office. If we buy a plant of a horticulturist we ask him many questions as to its needs, whether it thrives best in sunshine or in shade, whether it needs much or little water, what degrees of heat or cold; but when we hold in our arms for the first time, a being of infinite possibilities, in whose wisdom may rest the destiny of a nation, we take it for granted that the laws governing its life, health, and happiness are intuitively understood, that there is nothing new to be learned in regard to it. Yet here is a science to which philosophers have, as yet, given but little attention. An important fact has only been discovered and acted upon within the last ten years, that children come into the world tired, and not hungry, exhausted with the perilous journey. Instead of being thoroughly bathed and dressed, and kept on the rack while the nurse makes a prolonged toilet and feeds it some nostrum supposed to have much needed medicinal influence, the child's face, eyes, and mouth should be hastily washed with warm water, and the rest of its body thoroughly oiled, and then it should be slipped into a soft pillow case, wrapped in a blanket, and laid to sleep. Ordinarily, in the proper conditions, with its face uncovered in a cool, pure atmosphere, it will sleep twelve hours. Then it should be bathed, fed, and clothed in a high-necked, long-sleeved silk shirt and a blanket, all of which could be done in five minutes. As babies lie still most of the time the first six weeks, they need no dressing. I think the nurse was a full hour bathing and dressing my firstborn, who protested with a melancholy wail every blessed minute.

Ignorant myself of the initiative steps on the threshold of time, I supposed this proceeding was approved by the best authorities. However, I had been thinking, reading, observing, and had as little faith in the popular theories in regard to babies as on any other subject. I saw them, on all sides, ill half the time, pale and peevish, dying early, having no joy in life. I heard parents complaining of weary days and sleepless nights, while each child, in turn, ran the gauntlet of red gum, jaundice, whooping cough, chicken-pox, mumps, measles, scarlet fever, and fits. They all seemed to think these inflictions were a part of the eternal plan—that Providence had a kind of Pandora's box, from which he scattered these venerable diseases most liberally among those whom he especially loved. Having gone through the ordeal of bearing a child, I was determined, if possible, to keep him, so I read everything I could find on the subject. But the literature on this subject was as confusing and unsatisfactory as the longer and shorter catechisms and the Thirty-nine Articles of our faith. I had recently visited our dear friends, Theodore and Angelina Grimke-Weld, and they warned me against books on this subject. They had been so misled by one author, who assured them that the stomach of a child could only hold one tablespoonful, that they nearly starved their firstborn to death. Though the child dwindled, day by day, and, at the end of a month, looked like a little old man, yet they still stood by the distinguished author. Fortunately, they both went off, one day, and left the child with Sister "Sarah," who thought she would make an experiment and see what a child's stomach could hold, as she had grave doubts about the tablespoonful theory. To her surprise the baby took a pint bottle full of milk, and had the sweetest sleep thereon he had known in his earthly career. After that he was permitted to take what he wanted, and " the author " was informed of his libel on the infantile stomach.

So here, again, I was entirely afloat, launched on the seas of doubt without chart or compass. The life and well-being of the race seemed to hang on the slender thread of such traditions as were handed down by ignorant mothers and nurses. One powerful ray of light illuminated the darkness; it was the work of Andrew Combe on " Infancy." He had, evidently watched some of the manifestations of man in the first stages of his development, and could tell, at least, as much of babies as naturalists could of beetles and bees. He did give young mothers some hints of what to do, the whys and wherefores of certain lines of procedure during antenatal life, as well as the proper care thereafter. I read several chapters to the nurse. Although, out of her ten children, she had buried five, she still had too much confidence in her own wisdom and experience to pay much attention to any new idea that might be suggested to her. Among other things, Combe said that a child's bath should be regulated by the thermometer, in order to be always of the same temperature. She ridiculed the idea, and said her elbow was better than any thermometer, and, when I insisted on its use, she would invariably, with a smile of derision, put her elbow in first, to show how exactly it tallied with the thermometer. When I insisted that the child should not be bandaged, she rebelled outright, and said she would not take the responsibility of nursing a child without a bandage. I said, " Pray, sit down, dear nurse, and let us reason together. Do not think I am setting up my judgment against yours, with all your experience. I am simply trying to act on the opinions of a distinguished physician, who says there should be no pressure on a child anywhere; that the limbs and body should be free; that it is cruel to bandage an infant from hip to armpit, as is usually done in America; or both body and legs, as is done in Europe; or strap them to boards, as is done by savages on both continents. Can you give me one good reason, nurse, why a child should be bandaged?"

"Yes," she said emphatically, "I can give you a dozen."

"I only asked for one," I replied.

"Well," said she, after much hesitation, "the bones of a newborn infant are soft, like cartilage, and, unless you pin them up snugly, there is danger of their falling apart."

"It seems to me," I replied, "you have given the strongest reason why they should be carefully guarded against the slightest pressure. It is very remarkable that kittens and puppies should be so well put together that they need no artificial bracing, and the human family be left wholly to the mercy of a bandage. Suppose a child was born where you could not get a bandage, what then? Now I think this child will remain intact without a bandage, and, if I am willing to take the risk, why should you complain?"

"Because," said she, "if the child should die, it would injure my name as a nurse. I therefore wash my hands of all these new-fangled notions."

So she bandaged the child every morning, and I as regularly took it off. It has been fully proved since to be as useless an appendage as the vermiform. She had several cups with various concoctions of herbs standing on the chimney-corner, ready for insomnia, colic, indigestion, etc., etc., all of which were spirited away when she was at her dinner. In vain I told her we were homeopathists, and afraid of everything in the animal, vegetable, or mineral kingdoms lower than the two-hundredth dilution. I tried to explain the Hahnemann system of therapeutics, the philosophy of the principle *similia similibus curantur*, but she had no capacity for first principles, and did not understand my discourse. I told her that, if she would wash the baby's mouth with pure cold water morning and night and give it a tea-spoonful to drink occasionally during the day, there would be no danger of red gum; that if she would keep the blinds open and let in the air and sunshine, keep the temperature of the room at sixty-five degrees, leave the child's head uncovered so that it could breathe freely, stop rocking and trotting it and singing such melancholy hymns as " Hark, from the tombs a dole-ful sound!" the baby and I would both be able to weather the cape without a bandage. I told her I should nurse the child once in two hours, and that she must not feed it any of her nostrums in the meantime; that a child's stomach, being made on the same general plan as our own, needed intervals of rest as well as ours. She said it would be racked with colic if the stomach was empty any length of time, and that it would surely have rickets if it were kept too still. I told her if the child had no anodynes, nature would regulate its sleep and motions. She said she could not stay in a room with the thermometer at sixty-five degrees, so I told her to sit in the next room and regulate the heat to suit herself; that I would ring a bell when her services were needed.

The reader will wonder, no doubt, that I kept such a

cantankerous servant. I could get no other. Dear "Mother Monroe," as wise as she was good, and as tender as she was strong, who had nursed two generations of mothers in our village, was engaged at that time, and I was compelled to take an exotic. I had often watched "Mother Monroe" with admiration, as she turned and twisted my sister's baby. It lay as peacefully in her hands as if they were lined with eider down. She bathed and dressed it by easy stages, turning the child over and over like a pancake. But she was so full of the magnetism of human love, giving the child, all the time, the most consoling assurance that the operation was to be a short one, that the whole proceeding was quite entertaining to the observer and seemingly agreeable to the child, though it had a rather surprised look as it took a bird's-eye view, in quick succession, of the ceiling and the floor. Still my nurse had her good points. She was very pleasant when she had her own way. She was neat and tidy, and ready to serve me at any time, night or day. She did not wear false teeth that rattled when she talked, nor boots that squeaked when she walked. She did not snuff nor chew cloves, nor speak except when spoken to. Our discussions, on various points, went on at intervals, until I succeeded in planting some ideas in her mind, and when she left me, at the end of six weeks, she confessed that she had learned some valuable lessons. As the baby had slept quietly most of the time, had no crying spells, nor colic, and I looked well, she naturally came to the conclusion that pure air, sunshine, proper dressing, and regular feeding were more necessary for babies than herb teas and soothing syrups.

Besides the obstinacy of the nurse, I had the ignorance of physicians to contend with. When the child was four days old we discovered that the collar bone was bent. The physician, wishing to get a pressure on the shoulder, braced the bandage round the wrist. " Leave that," he said, " ten days, and then it will be all right." Soon after he left I noticed that the child's hand was blue, showing that the circulation was impeded. " That will never do," said I; " nurse, take it off." " No, indeed," she answered, " I shall never interfere with the doctor." So I took it off myself, and sent for another doctor, who was said to know more of surgery. He expressed great surprise that the first physician called should have put on so severe a bandage. " That," said he, " would do for a grown man, but ten days of it on a child would make him a cripple." However, he did nearly the same thing, only fastening it round the hand instead of the wrist. I soon saw that the ends of the fingers were all purple, and that to leave that on ten days would be as dangerous as the first. So I took that off.

" What a woman!" exclaimed the nurse. " What do you propose to do?"

" Think out something better, myself; so brace me up with some pillows and give the baby to me."

She looked at me aghast and said, "You'd better trust the doctors, or your child will be a helpless cripple."

" Yes," I replied, " he would be, if we had left either of those bandages on, but I have an idea of something better."

" Now," said I, talking partly to myself and partly to her, " what we want is a little pressure on that bone; that is what both those men aimed at. How can we get it without involving the arm, is the question?"

"I am sure I don't know," said she, rubbing her hands and taking two or three brisk turns round the room.

"Well, bring me three strips of linen, four double." I then folded one, wet in arnica and water, and laid it on the collar bone, put two other bands, like a pair of suspenders, over the shoulders, crossing them both in front and behind, pinning the ends to the diaper, which gave the needed pressure without impeding the circulation anywhere. As I finished she gave me a look of budding confidence, and seemed satisfied that all was well. Several times, night and day, we wet the compress and readjusted the bands, until all appearances of inflammation had subsided.

At the end of ten days the two sons of Æsculapius appeared and made their examination and said all was right, whereupon I told them how badly their bandages worked and what I had done myself. They smiled at each other, and one said:

"Well, after all, a mother's instinct is better than a man's reason."

"Thank you, gentlemen, there was no instinct about it. I did some hard thinking before I saw how I could get a pressure on the shoulder without impeding the circulation, as you did."

Thus, in the supreme moment of a young mother's life, when I needed tender care and support, I felt the whole responsibility of my child's supervision; but though uncertain at every step of my own knowledge, I learned another lesson in self-reliance. I trusted neither men nor books absolutely after this, either in regard to the heavens above or the earth beneath, but continued to use my "mother's instinct," if "reason " is too dignified a term to apply to woman's thoughts. My advice to every mother is, above all other arts and sciences, study first what relates to babyhood, as there is no department of human action in which there is such lamentable ignorance.

At the end of six weeks my nurse departed, and I had a good woman in her place who obeyed my orders, and now a new difficulty arose from an unexpected quarter. My father and husband took it into their heads that the child slept too much. If not awake when they wished to look at him or to show him to their friends, they would pull him out of his crib on all occasions. When I found neither of them was amenable to reason on this point, I locked the door, and no amount of eloquent pleading ever gained them admittance during the time I considered sacred to the baby's slumbers. At six months having, as yet, had none of the diseases supposed to be inevitable, the boy weighed thirty pounds. Then the stately Peter came again into requisition, and in his strong arms the child spent many of his waking hours. Peter, with a long, elephantine gait, slowly wandered over the town, lingering especially in the busy marts of trade. Peter's curiosity had strengthened with years, and, wherever a crowd gathered round a monkey and hand organ, a vender's wagon, an auction stand, or the post office at mail time, there stood Peter, black as coal, with " the beautiful boy in white," the most conspicuous figure in the crowd. As I told Peter never to let children kiss the baby, for fear of some disease, he kept him well aloft, allowing no affectionate manifestations except toward himself.

My reading, at this time, centered on hygiene. I

came to the conclusion, after much thought and observation, that children never cried unless they were uncomfortable. A professor at Union College, who used to combat many of my theories, said he gave one of his children a sound spanking at six weeks, and it never disturbed him a night afterward. Another Solomon told me that a very weak preparation of opium would keep a child always quiet and take it through the dangerous period of teething without a ripple on the surface of domestic life. As children cannot tell what ails them, and suffer from many things of which parents are ignorant, the crying of the child should arouse them to an intelligent examination. To spank it for crying is to silence the watchman on the tower through fear, to give soothing syrup is to drug the watchman while the evils go on. Parents may thereby insure eight hours' sleep at the time, but at the risk of greater trouble in the future with sick and dying children. Tom Moore tells us " the heart from love to one, grows bountiful to all." I know the care of one child made me thoughtful of all. I never hear a child cry, now, that I do not feel that I am bound to find out the reason.

In my extensive travels on lecturing tours, in after years, I had many varied experiences with babies. One day, in the cars, a child was crying near me, while the parents were alternately shaking and slapping it. First one would take it with an emphatic jerk, and then the other. At last I heard the father say in a spiteful tone, " If you don't stop I'll throw you out of the window." One naturally hesitates about interfering between parents and children, so I generally restrain myself as long as I can endure the torture of witnessing such outrages, but at length I turned and said:

" Let me take your child and see if I can find out what ails it."

" Nothing ails it," said the father, " but bad temper."

The child readily came to me. I felt all around to see if its clothes pinched anywhere, or if there were any pins pricking. I took off its hat and cloak to see if there were any strings cutting its neck or choking it. Then I glanced at the feet, and lo! there was the trouble. The boots were at least one size too small. I took them off, and the stockings, too, and found the feet as cold as ice and the prints of the stockings clearly traced on the tender flesh. We all know the agony of tight boots. I rubbed the feet and held them in my hands until they were warm, when the poor little thing fell asleep. I said to the parents, " You are young people, I see, and this is probably your first child." They said, " Yes." " You don't intend to be cruel, I know, but if you had thrown those boots out of the window, when you threatened to throw the child, it would have been wiser. This poor child has suffered ever since it was dressed this morning." I showed them the marks on the feet, and called their attention to the fact that the child fell asleep as soon as its pain was relieved. The mother said she knew the boots were tight, as it was with difficulty she could get them on, but the old ones were too shabby for the journey and they had no time to change the others.

" Well," said the husband, " if I had known those boots were tight, I would have thrown them out of the window."

" Now," said I, " let me give you one rule: when your child cries, remember it is telling you, as well as it can, that something hurts it, either outside or in, and do not rest until you find what it is.   Neither spanking, shaking, or scolding can relieve pain."

I have seen women enter the cars with their babies' faces completely covered with a blanket shawl.   I have often thought I would like to cover their faces for an hour and see how they would bear it.   In such circumstances, in order to get the blanket open, I have asked to see the baby, and generally found it as red as a beet. Ignorant nurses and mothers have discovered that children sleep longer with their heads covered.   They don't know why, nor the injurious effect of breathing over and over the same air that has been thrown off the lungs polluted with carbonic acid gas.   This stupefies the child and prolongs the unhealthy slumber.

One hot day, in the month of May, I entered a crowded car at Cedar Rapids, Ia., and took the only empty seat beside a gentleman who seemed very nervous about a crying child.   I was scarcely seated when he said:

" Mother, do you know anything about babies? "

" Oh, yes! " I said, smiling, " that is a department of knowledge on which I especially pride myself."

" Well," said he, " there is a child that has cried most of the time for the last twenty-four hours.   What do you think ails it? "

Making a random supposition, I replied, " It probably needs a bath."

He promptly rejoined, " If you will give it one, I will provide the necessary means."

I said, " I will first see if the child will come to me and if the mother is willing."

I found the mother only too glad to have a few minutes' rest, and the child too tired to care who took it. She gave me a suit of clean clothes throughout, the gentleman spread his blanket shawl on the seat, securing the opposite one for me and the bathing appliances. Then he produced a towel, sponge, and an india-rubber bowl full of water, and I gave the child a generous drink and a thorough ablution. It stretched and seemed to enjoy every step of the proceeding, and, while I was brushing its golden curls as gently as I could, it fell asleep; so I covered it with the towel and blanket shawl, not willing to disturb it for dressing. The poor mother, too, was sound asleep, and the gentleman very happy. He had children of his own and, like me, felt great pity for the poor, helpless little victim of ignorance and folly. I engaged one of the ladies to dress it when it awoke, as I was soon to leave the train. It slept the two hours I remained—how much longer I never heard.

A young man, who had witnessed the proceeding, got off at the same station and accosted me, saying:

"I should be very thankful if you would come and see my baby. It is only one month old and cries all the time, and my wife, who is only sixteen years old, is worn out with it and neither of us know what to do, so we all cry together, and the doctor says he does not see what ails it."

So I went on my mission of mercy and found the child bandaged as tight as a drum. When I took out the pins and unrolled it, it fairly popped like the cork out of a champagne bottle. I rubbed its breast and its back and soon soothed it to sleep. I remained a long time, telling them how to take care of the child and the mother, too. I told them everything I could think of in regard to clothes, diet, and pure air. I asked the mother why she bandaged her child as she did. She said her nurse told her that there was danger of hernia unless the abdomen was well bandaged. I told her that the only object of a bandage was to protect the navel, for a few days, until it was healed, and for that purpose all that was necessary was a piece of linen four inches square, well oiled, folded four times double, with a hole in the center, laid over it. I remembered, next day, that I forgot to tell them to give the child water, and so I telegraphed them, "Give the baby water six times a day." I heard of that baby afterward. It lived and flourished, and the parents knew how to administer to the wants of the next one. The father was a telegraph operator and had many friends—knights of the key— throughout Iowa. For many years afterward, in leisure moments, these knights would "call up" this parent and say, over the wire, "Give the baby water six times a day." Thus did they "repeat the story, and spread the truth from pole to pole."

CHAPTER VIII.

In the autumn of 1843 my husband was admitted to the bar and commenced the practice of law in Boston with Mr. Bowles, brother-in-law of the late General John A. Dix. This gave me the opportunity to make many pleasant acquaintances among the lawyers in Boston, and to meet, intimately, many of the noble men and women among reformers, whom I had long worshiped at a distance. Here, for the first time, I met Lydia Maria Child, Abby Kelly, Paulina Wright, Elizabeth Peabody, Maria Chapman and her beautiful sisters, the Misses Weston, Oliver and Marianna Johnson, Joseph and Thankful Southwick and their three bright daughters. The home of the Southwicks was always a harbor of rest for the weary, where the anti-slavery hosts were wont to congregate, and where one was always sure to meet someone worth knowing. Their hospitality was generous to an extreme, and so boundless that they were, at last, fairly eaten out of house and home. Here, too, for the first time, I met Theodore Parker, John Pierpont, John G. Whittier, Emerson, Alcott, Lowell, Hawthorne, Mr. and Mrs. Samuel E. Sewall, Sidney Howard Gay, Pillsbury, Foster, Frederick Douglass, and last though not least, those noble men, Charles Hovey and Francis Jackson, the only men who ever left any money to the cause of woman suffrage. I also met Miss Jackson, afterward

Mrs. Eddy, who left half her fortune, fifty thousand dollars, for the same purpose.

I was a frequent visitor at the home of William Lloyd Garrison. Though he had a prolonged battle to fight in the rough outside world, his home was always a haven of rest. Mrs. Garrison was a sweet-tempered, conscientious woman, who tried, under all circumstances, to do what was right. She had sound judgment and rare common sense, was tall and fine-looking, with luxuriant brown hair, large tender blue eyes, delicate features, and affable manners. They had an exceptionally fine family of five sons and one daughter. Fanny, now the wife of Henry Villard, the financier, was the favorite and pet. All the children, in their maturer years, have fulfilled the promises of their childhood. Though always in straitened circumstances, the Garrisons were very hospitable. It was next to impossible for Mr. Garrison to meet a friend without inviting him to his house, especially at the close of a convention.

I was one of twelve at one of his impromptu tea parties. We all took it for granted that his wife knew we were coming, and that her preparations were already made. Surrounded by half a dozen children, she was performing the last act in the opera of Lullaby, wholly unconscious of the invasion downstairs. But Mr. Garrison was equal to every emergency, and, after placing his guests at their ease in the parlor, he hastened to the nursery, took off his coat, and rocked the baby until his wife had disposed of the remaining children. Then they had a consultation about the tea, and when, basket in hand, the good man sallied forth for the desired viands, Mrs. Garrison, having made a hasty toilet, came

down to welcome her guests. She was as genial and
self-possessed as if all things had been prepared. She
made no apologies for what was lacking in the general
appearance of the house nor in the variety of the *menu*
—it was sufficient for her to know that Mr. Garrison
was happy in feeling free to invite his friends. The impromptu meal was excellent, and we had a most
enjoyable evening. I have no doubt that Mrs. Garrison
had more real pleasure than if she had been busy all
day making preparations and had been tired out when
her guests arrived.

The anti-slavery conventions and fairs, held every
year during the holidays, brought many charming people from other States, and made Boston a social center
for the coadjutors of Garrison and Phillips. These conventions surpassed any meetings I had ever attended;
the speeches were eloquent and the debates earnest and
forcible. Garrison and Phillips were in their prime, and
slavery was a question of national interest. The hall
in which the fairs were held, under the auspices of Mrs.
Chapman and her cohorts, was most artistically decorated. There one could purchase whatever the fancy
could desire, for English friends, stimulated by the
appeals of Harriet Martineau and Elizabeth Pease, used
to send boxes of beautiful things, gathered from all
parts of the Eastern Continent. There, too, one could
get a most *recherché* luncheon in the society of the
literati of Boston; for, however indifferent many were
to slavery *per se*, they enjoyed these fairs, and all
classes flocked there till far into the night. It was a
kind of ladies' exchange for the holiday week, where
each one was sure to meet her friends. The fair and the
annual convention, coming in succession, intensified

the interest in both. I never grew weary of the conventions, though I attended all the sessions, lasting, sometimes, until eleven o'clock at night. The fiery eloquence of the abolitionists, the amusing episodes that occurred when some crank was suppressed and borne out on the shoulders of his brethren, gave sufficient variety to the proceedings to keep the interest up to high-water mark.

There was one old man dressed in white, carrying a scythe, who imagined himself the personification of "Time," though called "Father Lampson." Occasionally he would bubble over with some prophetic vision, and, as he could not be silenced, he was carried out. He usually made himself as limp as possible, which added to the difficulty of his exit and the amusement of the audience. A ripple of merriment would unsettle, for a moment, even the dignity of the platform when Abigail Folsom, another crank, would shout from the gallery, "Stop not, my brother, on the order of your going, but go." The abolitionists were making the experiment, at this time, of a free platform, allowing everyone to speak as moved by the spirit, but they soon found that would not do, as those evidently moved by the spirit of mischief were quite as apt to air their vagaries as those moved by the spirit of truth.

However, the Garrisonian platform always maintained a certain degree of freedom outside its regular programme, and, although this involved extra duty in suppressing cranks, yet the meeting gained enthusiasm by some good spontaneous speaking on the floor as well as on the platform. A number of immense mass meetings were held in Faneuil Hall, a large, dreary place, with its bare walls and innumerable dingy windows. The only attempt at an ornament was the American eagle, with its wings spread and claws firmly set, in the middle of the gallery. The gilt was worn off its beak, giving it the appearance, as Edmund Quincy said, of having a bad cold in the head.

This old hall was sacred to so many memories connected with the early days of the Revolution that it was a kind of Mecca for the lovers of liberty visiting Boston. The anti-slavery meetings held there were often disturbed by mobs that would hold the most gifted orator at bay hour after hour, and would listen only to the songs of the Hutchinson family. Although these songs were a condensed extract of the whole anti-slavery constitution and by-laws, yet the mob was as peaceful under these pæans to liberty as a child under the influence of an anodyne. What a welcome and beautiful vision that was when the four brothers, in blue broadcloth and white collars, turned down *à la* Byron, and little sister Abby in silk, soft lace, and blue ribbon, appeared on the platform to sing their quaint ballads of freedom! Fresh from the hills of New Hampshire, they looked so sturdy, so vigorous, so pure, so true that they seemed fitting representatives of all the cardinal virtues, and even a howling mob could not resist their influence. Perhaps, after one of their ballads, the mob would listen five minutes to Wendell Phillips or Garrison until he gave them some home thrusts, when all was uproar again. The Northern merchants who made their fortunes out of Southern cotton, the politicians who wanted votes, and the ministers who wanted to keep peace in the churches, were all as much opposed to the anti-slavery agitation as were the slaveholders themselves. These were the classes the mob represented, though seemingly composed of gamblers, liquor dealers, and demagogues. For years the anti-slavery struggle at the North was carried on against statecraft, priestcraft, the cupidity of the moneyed classes, and the ignorance of the masses, but, in spite of all these forces of evil, it triumphed at last.

I was in Boston at the time that Lane and Wright, some metaphysical Englishmen, and our own Alcott held their famous philosophical conversations, in which Elizabeth Peabody took part. I went to them regularly. I was ambitious to absorb all the wisdom I could, but, really, I could not give an intelligent report of the points under discussion at any sitting. Oliver Johnson asked me, one day, if I enjoyed them. I thought, from a twinkle in his eye, that he thought I did not, so I told him I was ashamed to confess that I did not know what they were talking about. He said, " Neither do I,—very few of their hearers do,—so you need not be surprised that they are incomprehensible to you, nor think less of your own capacity."

I was indebted to Mr. Johnson for several of the greatest pleasures I enjoyed in Boston. He escorted me to an entire course of Theodore Parker's lectures, given in Marlborough Chapel. This was soon after the great preacher had given his famous sermon on " The Permanent and Transient in Religion," when he was ostracised, even by the Unitarians, for his radical utterances, and not permitted to preach in any of their pulpits. His lectures were deemed still more heterodox than that sermon. He shocked the orthodox churches of that day—more, even, than Ingersoll has in our times.

The lectures, however, were so soul-satisfying to me

that I was surprised at the bitter criticisms I heard expressed. Though they were two hours long, I never grew weary, and, when the course ended, I said to Mr. Johnson:

" I wish I could hear them over again."

" Well, you can," said he, " Mr. Parker is to repeat them in Cambridgeport, beginning next week." Accordingly we went there and heard them again with equal satisfaction.

During the winter in Boston I attended all the lectures, churches, theaters, concerts, and temperance, peace, and prison-reform conventions within my reach. I had never lived in such an enthusiastically literary and reform latitude before, and my mental powers were kept at the highest tension. We went to Chelsea, for the summer, and boarded with the Baptist minister, the Rev. John Wesley Olmstead, afterward editor of *The Watchman and Reflector.* He had married my cousin, Mary Livingston, one of the most lovely, unselfish characters I ever knew. There I had the opportunity of meeting several of the leading Baptist ministers in New England, and, as I was thoroughly imbued with Parker's ideas, we had many heated discussions on theology. There, too, I met Orestes Bronson, a remarkably well-read man, who had gone through every phase of religious experience from blank atheism to the bosom of the Catholic Church, where I believe he found repose at the end of his days. He was so arbitrary and dogmatic that most people did not like him; but I appreciated his acquaintance, as he was a liberal thinker and had a world of information which he readily imparted to those of a teachable spirit. As I was then in a hungering, thirsting condition for truth on every subject, the friendship of such a man was, to me, an inestimable blessing. Reading Theodore Parker's lectures, years afterward, I was surprised to find how little there was in them to shock anybody—the majority of thinking people having grown up to them.

While living in Chelsea two years, I used to walk (there being no public conveyances running on Sunday) from the ferry to Marlborough Chapel to hear Mr. Parker preach. It was a long walk, over two miles, and I was so tired, on reaching the chapel, that I made it a point to sleep through all the preliminary service, so as to be fresh for the sermon, as the friend next whom I sat always wakened me in time. One Sunday, when my friend was absent, it being a very warm day and I unusually fatigued, I slept until the sexton informed me that he was about to close the doors! In an unwary moment I imparted this fact to my Baptist friends. They made all manner of fun ever afterward of the soothing nature of Mr. Parker's theology, and my long walk, every Sunday, to repose in the shadow of a heterodox altar. Still, the loss of the sermon was the only vexatious part of it, and I had the benefit of the walk and the refreshing slumber, to the music of Mr. Parker's melodious voice and the deep-toned organ.

Mrs. Oliver Johnson and I spent two days at the Brook Farm Community when in the height of its prosperity. There I met the Ripleys,—who were, I believe, the backbone of the experiment,—William Henry Channing, Bronson Alcott, Charles A. Dana, Frederick Cabot, William Chase, Mrs. Horace Greeley, who was spending a few days there, and many others, whose names I cannot recall. Here was a charming family of intelligent men and women, doing their own farm and house work, with lectures, readings, music, dancing, and games when desired; realizing, in a measure, Edward Bellamy's beautiful vision of the equal conditions of the human family in the year 2000. The story of the beginning and end of this experiment of community life has been told so often that I will simply say that its failure was a grave disappointment to those most deeply interested in its success. Mr. Channing told me, years after, when he was pastor of the Unitarian church in Rochester, as we were wandering through Mount Hope one day, that, when the Roxbury community was dissolved and he was obliged to return to the old life of competition, he would gladly have been laid under the sod, as the isolated home seemed so solitary, silent, and selfish that the whole atmosphere was oppressive.

In 1843 my father moved to Albany, to establish my brothers-in-law, Mr. Wilkeson and Mr. McMartin, in the legal profession. That made Albany the family rallying point for a few years. This enabled me to spend several winters at the Capital and to take an active part in the discussion of the Married Woman's Property Bill, then pending in the legislature. William H. Seward, Governor of the State from 1839 to 1843, recommended the Bill, and his wife, a woman of rare intelligence, advocated it in society. Together we had the opportunity of talking with many members, both of the Senate and the Assembly, in social circles, as well as in their committee rooms. Bills were pending from 1836 until 1848, when the measure finally passed.

My second son was born in Albany, in March, 1844, under more favorable auspices than the first, as I knew, then, what to do with a baby. Returning to Chelsea we commenced housekeeping, which afforded me another chapter of experience. A new house, newly furnished, with beautiful views of Boston Bay, was all I could desire. Mr. Stanton announced to me, in starting, that his business would occupy all his time, and that I must take entire charge of the housekeeping. So, with two good servants and two babies under my sole supervision, my time was pleasantly occupied.

When first installed as mistress over an establishment, one has that same feeling of pride and satisfaction that a young minister must have in taking charge of his first congregation. It is a proud moment in a woman's life to reign supreme within four walls, to be the one to whom all questions of domestic pleasure and economy are referred, and to hold in her hand that little family book in which the daily expenses, the outgoings and incomings, are duly registered. I studied up everything pertaining to housekeeping, and enjoyed it all. Even washing day—that day so many people dread—had its charms for me. The clean clothes on the lines and on the grass looked so white, and smelled so sweet, that it was to me a pretty sight to contemplate. I inspired my laundress with an ambition to have her clothes look white and to get them out earlier than our neighbors, and to have them ironed and put away sooner.

As Mr. Stanton did not come home to dinner, we made a picnic of our noon meal on Mondays, and all thoughts and energies were turned to speed the washing. No unnecessary sweeping or dusting, no visiting nor entertaining angels unawares on that day— it was held sacred to soap suds, blue-bags, and clotheslines. The children, only, had no deviation in the regularity of their lives. They had their drives and walks, their naps and rations, in quantity and time, as usual. I had all the most approved cook books, and spent half my time preserving, pickling, and experimenting in new dishes. I felt the same ambition to excel in all departments of the culinary art that I did at school in the different branches of learning. My love of order and cleanliness was carried throughout, from parlor to kitchen, from the front door to the back. I gave a man an extra shilling to pile the logs of firewood with their smooth ends outward, though I did not have them scoured white, as did our Dutch grandmothers. I tried, too, to give an artistic touch to everything—the dress of my children and servants included. My dining table was round, always covered with a clean cloth of a pretty pattern and a centerpiece of flowers in their season, pretty dishes, clean silver, and set with neatness and care. I put my soul into everything, and hence enjoyed it. I never could understand how housekeepers could rest with rubbish all round their back doors; eggshells, broken dishes, tin cans, and old shoes scattered round their premises; servants ragged and dirty, with their hair in papers, and with the kitchen and dining room full of flies. I have known even artists to be indifferent to their personal appearance and their surroundings. Surely a mother and child, tastefully dressed, and a pretty home for a framework, is, as a picture, even more attractive than a domestic scene hung on the wall. The love of the beautiful can be illustrated as well in life as on canvas. There is such a struggle among women to become artists that I really wish some of their gifts could be illustrated in clean, orderly, beautiful homes.

Our house was pleasantly situated on the Chelsea Hills, commanding a fine view of Boston, the harbor, and surrounding country. There, on the upper piazza, I spent some of the happiest days of my life, enjoying, in turn, the beautiful outlook, my children, and my books. Here, under the very shadow of Bunker Hill Monument, my third son was born. Shortly after this Gerrit Smith and his wife came to spend a few days with us, so this boy, much against my will, was named after my cousin. I did not believe in old family names unless they were peculiarly euphonious. I had a list of beautiful names for sons and daughters, from which to designate each newcomer; but, as yet, not one on my list had been used. However, I put my foot down, at No. 4, and named him Theodore, and, thus far, he has proved himself a veritable " gift of God," doing his uttermost, in every way possible, to fight the battle of freedom for woman.

During the visit of my cousin I thought I would venture on a small, select dinner party, consisting of the Rev. John Pierpont and his wife, Charles Sumner, John G. Whittier, and Joshua Leavitt. I had a new cook, Rose, whose viands, thus far, had proved delicious, so I had no anxiety on that score. But, unfortunately, on this occasion I had given her a bottle of wine for the pudding sauce and whipped cream, of which she imbibed too freely, and hence there were some glaring blunders in the *menu* that were exceedingly mortifying. As Mr. Smith and my husband were both good talkers, I told them they must cover all defects with their brilliant conversation, which they promised to do.

Rose had all the points of a good servant, phrenologically and physiologically. She had a large head, with great bumps of caution and order, her eyes were large and soft and far apart. In selecting her, scientifically, I had told my husband, in triumph, several times what a treasure I had found. Shortly after dinner, one evening when I was out, she held the baby while the nurse was eating her supper, and carelessly burned his foot against the stove. Then Mr. Stanton suggested that, in selecting the next cook, I would better not trust to science, but inquire of the family where she lived as to her practical virtues. Poor Rose! she wept over her lapses when sober, and made fair promises for the future, but I did not dare to trust her, so we parted. The one drawback to the joys of housekeeping was then, as it is now, the lack of faithful, competent servants. The hope of co-operative housekeeping, in the near future, gives us some promise of a more harmonious domestic life.

One of the books in my library I value most highly is the first volume of Whittier's poems, published in 1838, "Dedicated to Henry B. Stanton, as a token of the author's personal friendship, and of his respect for the unreserved devotion of exalted talents to the cause of humanity and freedom." Soon after our marriage we spent a few days with our gifted Quaker poet, on his farm in Massachusetts.

I shall never forget those happy days in June; the long walks and drives, and talks under the old trees of anti-slavery experiences, and Whittier's mirth and indignation as we described different scenes in the World's Anti-slavery Convention in London. He laughed immoderately at the Tom Campbell episode. Poor fellow! he had taken too much wine that day, and when Whittier's verses, addressed to the convention, were read, he criticised them severely, and wound up by saying that the soul of a poet was not in him. Mr. Stanton sprang to his feet and recited some of Whittier's stirring stanzas on freedom, which electrified the audience, and, turning to Campbell, he said: " What do you say to that? " " Ah! that's real poetry," he replied. " And John Greenleaf Whittier is its author," said Mr. Stanton.

I enjoyed, too, the morning and evening service, when the revered mother read the Scriptures and we all bowed our heads in silent worship. There was, at times, an atmosphere of solemnity pervading everything, that was oppressive in the midst of so much that appealed to my higher nature. There was a shade of sadness in even the smile of the mother and sister, and a rigid plainness in the house and its surroundings, a depressed look in Whittier himself that the songs of the birds, the sunshine, and the bracing New England air seemed powerless to chase away, caused, as I afterward heard, by pecuniary embarrassment, and fears in regard to the delicate health of the sister. She, too, had rare poetical talent, and in her Whittier found not only a helpful companion in the practical affairs of life, but one who sympathized with him in the highest flights of which his muse was capable. Their worst fears were realized in the death of the sister not long after. In his last volume several of her poems were published, which are quite worthy the place the brother's appreciation has given them. Whittier's love and reverence for his mother and sister, so marked in every word and look, were charming features of his home life. All his poems to our sex breathe the same tender, worshipful sentiments.

Soon after this visit at Amesbury, our noble friend spent a few days with us in Chelsea, near Boston. One evening, after we had been talking a long time of the unhappy dissensions among anti-slavery friends, by way of dissipating the shadows I opened the piano, and proposed that we should sing some cheerful songs. "Oh, no!" exclaimed Mr. Stanton, "do not touch a note; you will put every nerve of Whittier's body on edge." It seemed, to me, so natural for a poet to love music that I was surprised to know that it was a torture to him.

From our upper piazza we had a fine view of Boston harbor. Sitting there late one moonlight night, admiring the outlines of Bunker Hill Monument and the weird effect of the sails and masts of the vessels lying in the harbor, we naturally passed from the romance of our surroundings to those of our lives. I have often noticed that the most reserved people are apt to grow confidential at such an hour. It was under such circumstances that the good poet opened to me a deeply interesting page of his life, a sad romance of love and disappointment, that may not yet be told, as some who were interested in the events are still among the living.

Whittier's poems were not only one of the most important factors in the anti-slavery war and victory, but they have been equally potent in emancipating the minds of his generation from the gloomy superstitions of the puritanical religion. Oliver Wendell Holmes, in his eulogy of Whittier, says that his influence on the religious thought of the American people has been far greater than that of the occupant of any pulpit.

As my husband's health was delicate, and the New England winters proved too severe for him, we left Boston, with many regrets, and sought a more genial climate in Central New York.

CHAPTER IX.

IN the spring of 1847 we moved to Seneca Falls. Here we spent sixteen years of our married life, and here our other children—two sons and two daughters— were born.

Just as we were ready to leave Boston, Mr. and Mrs. Eaton and their two children arrived from Europe, and we decided to go together to Johnstown, Mr. Eaton being obliged to hurry to New York on business, and Mr. Stanton to remain still in Boston a few months. At the last moment my nurse decided she could not leave her friends and go so far away. Accordingly my sister and I started, by rail, with five children and seventeen trunks, for Albany, where we rested over night and part of the next day. We had a very fatiguing journey, looking after so many trunks and children, for my sister's children persisted in standing on the platform at every opportunity, and the younger ones would follow their example. This kept us constantly on the watch. We were thankful when safely landed once more in the old homestead in Johnstown, where we arrived at midnight. As our beloved parents had received no warning of our coming, the whole household was aroused to dispose of us. But now in safe harbor, 'mid familiar scenes and pleasant memories, our slumbers were indeed refreshing. How rapidly one throws off all care and anxiety under the parental roof, and how at sea one feels, no matter what the age may be, when the loved ones are gone forever and the home of childhood is but a dream of the past.

After a few days of rest I started, alone, for my new home, quite happy with the responsibility of repairing a house and putting all things in order. I was already acquainted with many of the people and the surroundings in Seneca Falls, as my sister, Mrs. Bayard, had lived there several years, and I had frequently made her long visits. We had quite a magnetic circle of reformers, too, in central New York. At Rochester were William Henry Channing, Frederick Douglass, the Anthonys, Posts, Hallowells, Stebbins,—some grand old Quaker families at Farmington,—the Sedgwicks, Mays, Mills, and Matilda Joslyn Gage at Syracuse; Gerrit Smith at Peterboro, and Beriah Green at Whitesboro.

The house we were to occupy had been closed for some years and needed many repairs, and the grounds, comprising five acres, were overgrown with weeds. My father gave me a check and said, with a smile, " You believe in woman's capacity to do and dare; now go ahead and put your place in order." After a minute survey of the premises and due consultation with one or two sons of Adam, I set the carpenters, painters, paperhangers, and gardeners at work, built a new kitchen and woodhouse, and in one month took possession. Having left my children with my mother, there were no impediments to a full display of my executive ability. In the purchase of brick, timber, paint, etc., and in making bargains with workmen, I was in frequent consultation with Judge Sackett and Mr. Bascom. The latter was a member of the Constitutional

Convention, then in session in Albany, and as he used to walk down whenever he was at home, to see how my work progressed, we had long talks, sitting on boxes in the midst of tools and shavings, on the status of women. I urged him to propose an amendment to Article II, Section 3, of the State Constitution, striking out the word " male," which limits the suffrage to men. But, while he fully agreed with all I had to say on the political equality of women, he had not the courage to make himself the laughing-stock of the convention. Whenever I cornered him on this point, manlike he turned the conversation to the painters and carpenters. However, these conversations had the effect of bringing him into the first woman's convention, where he did us good service.

In Seneca Falls my life was comparatively solitary, and the change from Boston was somewhat depressing. There, all my immediate friends were reformers, I had near neighbors, a new home with all the modern conveniences, and well-trained servants. Here our residence was on the outskirts of the town, roads very often muddy and no sidewalks most of the way, Mr. Stanton was frequently from home, I had poor servants, and an increasing number of children. To keep a house and grounds in good order, purchase every article for daily use, keep the wardrobes of half a dozen human beings in proper trim, take the children to dentists, shoemakers, and different schools, or find teachers at home, altogether made sufficient work to keep one brain busy, as well as all the hands I could impress into the service. Then, too, the novelty of housekeeping had passed away, and much that was once attractive in domestic life was now irksome. I had so many cares that the company I needed for intellectual stimulus was a trial rather than a pleasure.

There was quite an Irish settlement at a short distance, and continual complaints were coming to me that my boys threw stones at their pigs, cows, and the roofs of their houses. This involved constant diplomatic relations in the settlement of various difficulties, in which I was so successful that, at length, they constituted me a kind of umpire in all their own quarrels. If a drunken husband was pounding his wife, the children would run for me. Hastening to the scene of action, I would take Patrick by the collar, and, much to his surprise and shame, make him sit down and promise to behave himself. I never had one of them offer the least resistance, and in time they all came to regard me as one having authority. I strengthened my influence by cultivating good feeling. I lent the men papers to read, and invited their children into our grounds; giving them fruit, of which we had abundance, and my children's old clothes, books, and toys. I was their physician, also—with my box of homeopathic medicines I took charge of the men, women, and children in sickness. Thus the most amicable relations were established, and, in any emergency, these poor neighbors were good friends and always ready to serve me.

But I found police duty rather irksome, especially when called out dark nights to prevent drunken fathers from disturbing their sleeping children, or to minister to poor mothers in the pangs of maternity. Alas! alas! who can measure the mountains of sorrow and suffering endured in unwelcome motherhood in the abodes of ignorance, poverty, and vice, where terror-stricken women and children are the victims of strong men frenzied with passion and intoxicating drink?

Up to this time life had glided by with comparative ease, but now the real struggle was upon me. My duties were too numerous and varied, and none sufficiently exhilarating or intellectual to bring into play my higher faculties. I suffered with mental hunger, which, like an empty stomach, is very depressing. I had books, but no stimulating companionship. To add to my general dissatisfaction at the change from Boston, I found that Seneca Falls was a malarial region, and in due time all the children were attacked with chills and fever which, under homeopathic treatment in those days, lasted three months. The servants were afflicted in the same way. Cleanliness, order, the love of the beautiful and artistic, all faded away in the struggle to accomplish what was absolutely necessary from hour to hour. Now I understood, as I never had before, how women could sit down and rest in the midst of general disorder. Housekeeping, under such conditions, was impossible, so I packed our clothes, locked up the house, and went to that harbor of safety, home, as I did ever after in stress of weather.

I now fully understood the practical difficulties most women had to contend with in the isolated household, and the impossibility of woman's best development if in contact, the chief part of her life, with servants and children. Fourier's phalansterie community life and co-operative households had a new significance for me. Emerson says, " A healthy discontent is the first step to progress." The general discontent I felt with woman's portion as wife, mother, housekeeper, physician, and spiritual guide, the chaotic conditions into which everything fell without her constant supervision, and the wearied, anxious look of the majority of women impressed me with a strong feeling that some active measures should be taken to remedy the wrongs of society in general, and of women in particular. My experience at the World's Anti-slavery Convention, all I had read of the legal status of women, and the oppression I saw everywhere, together swept across my soul, intensified now by many personal experiences. It seemed as if all the elements had conspired to impel me to some onward step. I could not see what to do or where to begin—my only thought was a public meeting for protest and discussion.

In this tempest-tossed condition of mind I received an invitation to spend the day with Lucretia Mott, at Richard Hunt's, in Waterloo. There I met several members of different families of Friends, earnest, thoughtful women. I poured out, that day, the torrent of my long-accumulating discontent, with such vehemence and indignation that I stirred myself, as well as the rest of the party, to do and dare anything. My discontent, according to Emerson, must have been healthy, for it moved us all to prompt action, and we decided, then and there, to call a " Woman's Rights Convention." We wrote the call that evening and published it in the *Seneca County Courier* the next day, the 14th of July, 1848, giving only five days' notice, as the convention was to be held on the 19th and 20th. The call was inserted without signatures,—in fact it was a mere announcement of a meeting,—but the chief movers and managers were Lucretia Mott, Mary Ann McClintock, Jane Hunt, Martha C. Wright, and my-

self. The convention, which was held two days in the
Methodist Church, was in every way a grand success.
The house was crowded at every session, the speaking
good, and a religious earnestness dignified all the proceedings.

These were the hasty initiative steps of "the most
momentous reform that had yet been launched on the
world—the first organized protest against the injustice
which had brooded for ages over the character and
destiny of one-half the race." No words could express
our astonishment on finding, a few days afterward, that
what seemed to us so timely, so rational, and so sacred,
should be a subject for sarcasm and ridicule to the entire
press of the nation. With our Declaration of Rights
and Resolutions for a text, it seemed as if every man
who could wield a pen prepared a homily on "woman's
sphere." All the journals from Maine to Texas
seemed to strive with each other to see which could
make our movement appear the most ridiculous. The
anti-slavery papers stood by us manfully and so did
Frederick Douglass, both in the convention and in his
paper, *The North Star,* but so pronounced was the popular voice against us, in the parlor, press, and pulpit, that
most of the ladies who had attended the convention
and signed the declaration, one by one, withdrew their
names and influence and joined our persecutors. Our
friends gave us the cold shoulder and felt themselves
disgraced by the whole proceeding.

If I had had the slightest premonition of all that
was to follow that convention, I fear I should not have
had the courage to risk it, and I must confess that it
was with fear and trembling that I consented to attend
another, one month afterward, in Rochester. Fortu-

nately, the first one seemed to have drawn all the fire, and of the second but little was said. But we had set the ball in motion, and now, in quick succession, conventions were held in Ohio, Indiana, Massachusetts, Pennsylvania, and in the City of New York, and have been kept up nearly every year since.

The most noteworthy of the early conventions were those held in Massachusetts, in which such men as Garrison, Phillips, Channing, Parker, and Emerson took part. It was one of these that first attracted the attention of Mrs. John Stuart Mill, and drew from her pen that able article on " The Enfranchisement of Woman," in the *Westminster Review* of October, 1852.

The same year of the convention, the Married Woman's Property Bill, which had given rise to some discussion on woman's rights in New York, had passed the legislature. This encouraged action on the part of women, as the reflection naturally arose that, if the men who make the laws were ready for some onward step, surely the women themselves should express some interest in the legislation. Ernestine L. Rose, Paulina Wright (Davis), and I had spoken before committees of the legislature years before, demanding equal property rights for women. We had circulated petitions for the Married Woman's Property Bill for many years, and so also had the leaders of the Dutch aristocracy, who desired to see their life-long accumulations descend to their daughters and grandchildren rather than pass into the hands of dissipated, thriftless sons-in-law. Judge Hertell, Judge Fine, and Mr. Geddes of Syracuse prepared and championed the several bills, at different times, before the legislature. Hence the demands made in the convention were not entirely new to the reading and thinking public of New York—the first State to take any action on the question. As New York was the first State to put the word "male" in her constitution in 1778, it was fitting that she should be first in more liberal legislation. The effect of the convention on my own mind was most salutary. The discussions had cleared my ideas as to the primal steps to be taken for woman's enfranchisement, and the opportunity of expressing myself fully and freely on a subject I felt so deeply about was a great relief. I think all women who attended the convention felt better for the statement of their wrongs, believing that the first step had been taken to right them.

Soon after this I was invited to speak at several points in the neighborhood. One night, in the Quaker Meeting House at Farmington, I invited, as usual, discussion and questions when I had finished. We all waited in silence for a long time; at length a middle-aged man, with a broad-brimmed hat, arose and responded in a sing-song tone: "All I have to say is, if a hen can crow, let her crow," emphasizing "crow" with an upward inflection on several notes of the gamut. The meeting adjourned with mingled feelings of surprise and merriment. I confess that I felt somewhat chagrined in having what I considered my unanswerable arguments so summarily disposed of, and the serious impression I had made on the audience so speedily dissipated. The good man intended no disrespect, as he told me afterward. He simply put the whole argument in a nutshell: "Let a woman do whatever she can."

With these new duties and interests, and a broader outlook on human life, my petty domestic annoyances gradually took a subordinate place.   Now I began to write articles for the press, letters to conventions held in other States, and private letters to friends, to arouse them to thought on this question.

The pastor of the Presbyterian Church, Mr. Bogue, preached several sermons on Woman's Sphere, criticising the action of the conventions in Seneca Falls and Rochester.   Elizabeth McClintock and I took notes and answered him in the county papers.   Gradually we extended our labors and attacked our opponents in the New York *Tribune,* whose columns were open to us in the early days, Mr. Greeley being, at that time, one of our most faithful champions.

In answering all the attacks, we were compelled to study canon and civil law, constitutions, Bibles, science, philosophy, and history, sacred and profane.   Now my mind, as well as my hands, was fully occupied, and instead of mourning, as I had done, over what I had lost in leaving Boston, I tried in every way to make the most of life in Seneca Falls.   Seeing that elaborate refreshments prevented many social gatherings, I often gave an evening entertainment without any.   I told the young people, whenever they wanted a little dance or a merry time, to make our house their rallying point, and I would light up and give them a glass of water and some cake.   In that way we had many pleasant informal gatherings.   Then, in imitation of Margaret Fuller's Conversationals, we started one which lasted several years.   We selected a subject each week on which we all read and thought; each, in turn, preparing an essay ten minutes in length.

These were held, at different homes, Saturday of each week.   On coming together we chose a presiding officer for the evening, who called the meeting to order, and introduced the essayist. That finished, he asked each member, in turn, what he or she had read or thought on the subject, and if any had criticisms to make on the essay. Everyone was expected to contribute something. Much information was thus gained, and many spicy discussions followed. All the ladies, as well as the gentlemen, presided in turn, and so became familiar with parliamentary rules. The evening ended with music, dancing, and a general chat. In this way we read and thought over a wide range of subjects and brought together the best minds in the community. Many young men and women who did not belong to what was considered the first circle,—for in every little country village there is always a small clique that constitutes the aristocracy,—had the advantages of a social life otherwise denied them. I think that all who took part in this Conversation Club would testify to its many good influences.

I had three quite intimate young friends in the village who spent much of their spare time with me, and who added much to my happiness: Frances Hoskins, who was principal of the girls' department in the academy, with whom I discussed politics and religion; Mary Bascom, a good talker on the topics of the day, and Mary Crowninshield, who played well on the piano. As I was very fond of music, Mary's coming was always hailed with delight. Her mother, too, was a dear friend of mine, a woman of rare intelligence, refinement, and conversational talent. She was a Schuyler, and belonged to the Dutch aristocracy in Albany. She died suddenly, after a short illness. I was with her in the last hours and held her hand until the gradually fading spark of life went out. Her son is Captain A. S. Crowninshield of our Navy.

My nearest neighbors were a very agreeable, intelligent family of sons and daughters. But I always felt that the men of that household were given to domineering. As the mother was very amiable and self-sacrificing, the daughters found it difficult to rebel. One summer, after general house-cleaning, when fresh paint and paper had made even the kitchen look too dainty for the summer invasion of flies, the queens of the household decided to move the sombre cook-stove into a spacious woodhouse, where it maintained its dignity one week, in the absence of the head of the home. The mother and daughters were delighted with the change, and wondered why they had not made it before during the summer months. But their pleasure was shortlived. Father and sons rose early the first morning after his return and moved the stove back to its old place. When the wife and daughters came down to get their breakfast (for they did all their own work) they were filled with grief and disappointment. The breakfast was eaten in silence, the women humbled with a sense of their helplessness, and the men gratified with a sense of their power. These men would probably all have said " home is woman's sphere," though they took the liberty of regulating everything in her sphere.

MRS. STANTON AND SON, 1854.

Susan B. Anthony
1820 – Feb. 15 – 1856 –

CHAPTER X.

THE reports of the conventions held in Seneca Falls and Rochester, N. Y., in 1848, attracted the attention of one destined to take a most important part in the new movement—Susan B. Anthony, who, for her courage and executive ability, was facetiously called by William Henry Channing, the Napoleon of our struggle. At this time she was teaching in the academy at Canajoharie, a little village in the beautiful valley of the Mohawk.

" The Woman's Declaration of Independence " issued from those conventions startled and amused her, and she laughed heartily at the novelty and presumption of the demand. But, on returning home to spend her vacation, she was surprised to find that her sober Quaker parents and sister, having attended the Rochester meetings, regarded them as very profitable and interesting, and the demands made as proper and reasonable. She was already interested in the anti-slavery and temperance reforms, was an active member of an organization called " The Daughters of Temperance," and had spoken a few times in their public meetings. But the new gospel of " Woman's Rights," found a ready response in her mind, and, from that time, her best efforts have been given to the enfranchisement of women.

As, from this time, my friend is closely connected

with my narrative and will frequently appear therein, a sketch of her seems appropriate.

Lord Bacon has well said: " He that hath wife and children hath given hostages to fortune; for they are impediments to great enterprises either of virtue or mischief. Certainly the best works, and of greatest merit for the public, have proceeded from the unmarried or childless men; which, both in affection and means, have married and endowed the public."

This bit of Baconian philosophy, as alike applicable to women, was the subject, not long since, of a conversation with a remarkably gifted Englishwoman. She was absorbed in many public interests and had conscientiously resolved never to marry, lest the cares necessarily involved in matrimony should make inroads upon her time and thought, to the detriment of the public good. " Unless," said she, " some women dedicate themselves to the public service, society is robbed of needed guardians for the special wants of the weak and unfortunate. There should be, in the secular world, certain orders corresponding in a measure to the grand sisterhoods of the Catholic Church, to the members of which, as freely as to men, all offices, civic and ecclesiastical, should be open." That this ideal will be realized may be inferred from the fact that exceptional women have, in all ages, been leaders in great projects of charity and reform, and that now many stand waiting only the sanction of their century, ready for wide altruistic labors.

The world has ever had its vestal virgins, its holy women, mothers of ideas rather than of men; its Marys, as well as its Marthas, who, rather than be busy housewives, preferred to sit at the feet of divine wisdom, and ponder the mysteries of the unknown. All hail to Maria Mitchell, Harriet Hosmer, Charlotte Cushman, Alice and Phœbe Cary, Louisa Alcott, Dr. Elizabeth Blackwell, Frances Willard, and Clara Barton! All honor to the noble women who have devoted earnest lives to the intellectual and moral needs of mankind!

Susan B. Anthony was of sturdy New England stock, and it was at the foot of Old Greylock, South Adams, Mass., that she gave forth her first rebellious cry. There the baby steps were taken, and at the village school the first stitches were learned, and the A B C duly mastered. When five winters had passed over Susan's head, there came a time of great domestic commotion, and, in her small way, the child seized the idea that permanence is not the rule of life. The family moved to Battenville, N. Y., where Mr. Anthony became one of the wealthiest men in Washington County. Susan can still recall the stately coldness of the great house—how large the bare rooms, with their yellow-painted floors, seemed, in contrast with her own diminutiveness, and the outlook of the schoolroom where for so many years, with her brothers and sisters, she pursued her studies under private tutors.

Mr. Anthony was a stern Hicksite Quaker. In Susan's early life he objected on principle to all forms of frivolous amusement, such as music, dancing, or novel reading, while games and even pictures were regarded as meaningless luxuries. Such puritanical convictions might have easily degenerated into mere cant; but underlying all was a broad and firm basis of wholesome respect for individual freedom and a brave adherence to truth. He was a man of good business capacity, and a thorough manager of his wide and lucrative interests. He saw that compensation and not chance ruled in the commercial world, and he believed in the same just, though often severe, law in the sphere of morals. Such a man was not apt to walk humbly in the path mapped out by his religious sect. He early offended by choosing a Baptist for a wife. For this first offense he was " disowned," and, according to Quaker usage, could only be received into fellowship again by declaring himself " sorry " for his crime in full meeting. He was full of devout thankfulness for the good woman by his side, and destined to be thankful to the very end for this companion, so calm, so just, so farseeing. He rose in meeting, and said he was " sorry " that the rules of the society were such that, in marrying the woman he loved, he had committed offense! He admitted that he was " sorry " for something, so was taken back into the body of the faithful! But his faith had begun to weaken in many minor points of discipline. His coat soon became a cause of offense and called forth another reproof from those buttoned up in conforming garments. The petty forms of Quakerism began to lose their weight with him altogether, and he was finally disowned for allowing the village youth to be taught dancing in an upper room of his dwelling. He was applied to for this favor on the ground that young men were under great temptation to drink if the lessons were given in the hotel; and, being a rigid temperance man, he readily consented, though his principles, in regard to dancing, would not allow his own sons and daughters to join in the amusement. But the society could accept no such discrimination in what it deemed sin, nor such compromise with worldly frivolity, and so Mr. Anthony was seen no more in meeting. But, in later years, in Rochester he was an attentive listener to Rev. William Henry Channing.

The effect of all this on Susan is the question of interest. No doubt she early weighed the comparative moral effects of coats cut with capes and those cut without, of purely Quaker conjugal love and that deteriorated with Baptist affection. Susan had an earnest soul and a conscience tending to morbidity; but a strong, well-balanced body and simple family life soothed her too active moral nature and gave the world, instead of a religious fanatic, a sincere, concentrated worker. Every household art was taught her by her mother, and so great was her ability that the duty demanding especial care was always given into her hands. But ever, amid school and household tasks, her day-dream was that, in time, she might be a " high-seat " Quaker. Each Sunday, up to the time of the third disobedience, Mr. Anthony went to the Quaker meeting house, some thirteen miles from home, his wife and children usually accompanying him, though, as non-members, they were rigidly excluded from all business discussions. Exclusion was very pleasant in the bright days of summer; but, on one occasion in December, decidedly unpleasant for the seven-year-old Susan. When the blinds were drawn, at the close of the religious meeting, and non-members retired, Susan sat still. Soon she saw a thin old lady with blue goggles come down from the " high seat." Approaching her, the Quakeress said softly, " Thee is not a member—thee must go out." " No; my mother told me not to go out in the cold," was the child's firm response. "Yes, but thee must go out—thee is not a member." " But my father is a member." " Thee is not a member," and Susan felt as if the spirit was moving her and soon found herself in outer coldness. Fingers and toes becoming numb, and a bright fire in a cottage over the way beckoning warmly to her, the exile from the chapel resolved to seek secular shelter. But alas! she was confronted by a huge dog, and just escaped with whole skin though capeless jacket. We may be sure there was much talk, that night, at the home fireside, and the good Baptist wife declared that no child of hers should attend meeting again till made a member. Thereafter, by request of her father, Susan became a member of the Quaker church.

Later, definite convictions took root in Miss Anthony's heart. Hers is, indeed, a sincerely religious nature. To be a simple, earnest Quaker was the aspiration of her girlhood; but she shrank from adopting the formal language and plain dress. Dark hours of conflict were spent over all this, and she interpreted her disinclination as evidence of unworthiness. Poor little Susan! As we look back with the knowledge of our later life, we translate the heart-burnings as unconscious protests against labeling your free soul, against testing your reasoning conviction of to-morrow by any shibboleth of to-day's belief. We hail this child-intuition as a prophecy of the uncompromising truthfulness of the mature woman. Susan Anthony was taught simply that she must enter into the holy of holies of her own self, meet herself, and be true to the revelation. She first found words to express her convictions in listening to Rev. William Henry Channing, whose teaching had a lasting spiritual influence upon her. To-day Miss Anthony is an agnostic. As to the nature of the Godhead and of the life beyond her horizon she does not profess to know anything. Every energy of her soul is centered upon the needs of this world. To her, work is worship. She has not stood aside, shivering in the cold shadows of uncertainty, but has moved on with the whirling world, has done the good given her to do, and thus, in darkest hours, has been sustained by an unfaltering faith in the final perfection of all things. Her belief is not orthodox, but it is religious. In ancient Greece she would have been a Stoic; in the era of the Reformation, a Calvinist; in King Charles' time, a Puritan; but in this nineteenth century, by the very laws of her being, she is a Reformer.

For the arduous work that awaited Miss Anthony her years of young womanhood had given preparation. Her father, though a man of wealth, made it a matter of conscience to train his girls, as well as his boys, to self-support. Accordingly Susan chose the profession of teacher, and made her first essay during a summer vacation in a school her father had established for the children of his employés. Her success was so marked, not only in imparting knowledge, but also as a disciplinarian, that she followed this career steadily for fifteen years, with the exception of some months given in Philadelphia to her own training. Of the many school rebellions which she overcame, one rises before me, prominent in its ludicrous aspect. This was in the district school at Center Falls, in the year 1839. Bad reports were current there of male teachers driven out by a certain strapping lad. Rumor next told of a

Quaker maiden coming to teach—a Quaker maiden of peace principles. The anticipated day and Susan arrived. She looked very meek to the barbarian of fifteen, so he soon began his antics. He was called to the platform, told to lay aside his jacket, and, thereupon, with much astonishment received from the mild Quaker maiden, with a birch rod applied calmly but with precision, an exposition of the *argumentum ad hominem* based on the *a posteriori* method of reasoning. Thus Susan departed from her principles, but not from the school.

But, before long, conflicts in the outside world disturbed our young teacher. The multiplication table and spelling book no longer enchained her thoughts; larger questions began to fill her mind. About the year 1850 Susan B. Anthony hid her ferule away. Temperance, anti-slavery, woman suffrage,—three pregnant questions,—presented themselves, demanding her consideration. Higher, ever higher, rose their appeals, until she resolved to dedicate her energy and thought to the burning needs of the hour. Owing to early experience of the disabilities of her sex, the first demand for equal rights for women found echo in Susan's heart. And, though she was in the beginning startled to hear that women had actually met in convention, and by speeches and resolutions had declared themselves man's peer in political rights, and had urged radical changes in State constitutions and the whole system of American jurisprudence; yet the most casual review convinced her that these claims were but the logical outgrowth of the fundamental theories of our republic.

At this stage of her development I met my future friend and coadjutor for the first time. How well I remember the day! George Thompson and William Lloyd Garrison having announced an anti-slavery meeting in Seneca Falls, Miss Anthony came to attend it. These gentlemen were my guests. Walking home, after the adjournment, we met Mrs. Bloomer and Miss Anthony on the corner of the street, waiting to greet us. There she stood, with her good, earnest face and genial smile, dressed in gray delaine, hat and all the same color, relieved with pale blue ribbons, the perfection of neatness and sobriety. I liked her thoroughly, and why I did not at once invite her home with me to dinner, I do not know. She accuses me of that neglect, and has never forgiven me, as she wished to see and hear all she could of our noble friends. I suppose my mind was full of what I had heard, or my coming dinner, or the probable behavior of three mischievous boys who had been busily exploring the premises while I was at the meeting.

That I had abundant cause for anxiety in regard to the philosophical experiments these young savages might try the reader will admit, when informed of some of their performances. Henry imagined himself possessed of rare powers of invention (an ancestral weakness for generations), and so made a life preserver of corks, and tested its virtues on his brother, who was about eighteen months old. Accompanied by a troop of expectant boys, the baby was drawn in his carriage to the banks of the Seneca, stripped, the string of corks tied under his arms, and set afloat in the river, the philosopher and his satellites, in a rowboat, watching the experiment. The baby, accustomed to a morning bath in a large tub, splashed about joyfully, keeping his head above water. He was as blue as indigo and as cold as a frog when rescued by his anxious mother. The next day the same victimized infant was seen, by a passing friend, seated on the chimney, on the highest peak of the house. Without alarming anyone, the friend hurried up to the housetop and rescued the child. Another time the three elder brothers entered into a conspiracy, and locked up the fourth, Theodore, in the smoke-house. Fortunately, he sounded the alarm loud and clear, and was set free in safety, whereupon the three were imprisoned in a garret with two barred windows. They summarily kicked out the bars, and, sliding down on the lightning rod, betook themselves to the barn for liberty. The youngest boy, Gerrit, then only five years old, skinned his hands in the descent. This is a fair sample of the quiet happiness I enjoyed in the first years of motherhood.

It was 'mid such exhilarating scenes that Miss Anthony and I wrote addresses for temperance, anti-slavery, educational, and woman's rights conventions. Here we forged resolutions, protests, appeals, petitions, agricultural reports, and constitutional arguments; for we made it a matter of conscience to accept every invitation to speak on every question, in order to maintain woman's right to do so. To this end we took turns on the domestic watchtowers, directing amusements, settling disputes, protecting the weak against the strong, and trying to secure equal rights to all in the home as well as the nation. I can recall many a stern encounter between my friend and the young experimenter. It is pleasant to remember that he never seriously injured any of his victims, and only once came near fatally shooting himself with a pistol. The ball went through his hand;

happily a brass button prevented it from penetrating his heart.

It is often said, by those who know Miss Anthony best, that she has been my good angel, always pushing and goading me to work, and that but for her pertinacity I should never have accomplished the little I have. On the other hand it has been said that I forged the thunderbolts and she fired them. Perhaps all this is, in a measure, true. With the cares of a large family I might, in time, like too many women, have become wholly absorbed in a narrow family selfishness, had not my friend been continually exploring new fields for missionary labors. Her description of a body of men on any platform, complacently deciding questions in which woman had an equal interest, without an equal voice, readily roused me to a determination to throw a firebrand into the midst of their assembly.

Thus, whenever I saw that stately Quaker girl coming across my lawn, I knew that some happy convocation of the sons of Adam was to be set by the ears, by one of our appeals or resolutions. The little portmanteau, stuffed with facts, was opened, and there we had what the Rev. John Smith and Hon. Richard Roe had said: false interpretations of Bible texts, the statistics of women robbed of their property, shut out of some college, half paid for their work, the reports of some disgraceful trial; injustice enough to turn any woman's thoughts from stockings and puddings. Then we would get out our pens and write articles for papers, or a petition to the legislature; indite letters to the faithful, here and there; stir up the women in Ohio, Pennsylvania, or Massachusetts; call on *The Lily*, *The Una*, *The Liberator*, *The Standard* to remember our wrongs as well as those of the slave. We never met without issuing a pronunciamento on some question. In thought and sympathy we were one, and in the division of labor we exactly complemented each other. In writing we did better work than either could alone. While she is slow and analytical in composition, I am rapid and synthetic. I am the better writer, she the better critic. She supplied the facts and statistics, I the philosophy and rhetoric, and, together, we have made arguments that have stood unshaken through the storms of long years; arguments that no one has answered. Our speeches may be considered the united product of our two brains.

So entirely one are we that, in all our associations, ever side by side on the same platform, not one feeling of envy or jealousy has ever shadowed our lives. We have indulged freely in criticism of each other when alone, and hotly contended whenever we have differed, but in our friendship of years there has never been the break of one hour. To the world we always seem to agree and uniformly reflect each other. Like husband and wife, each has the feeling that we must have no differences in public. Thus united, at an early day we began to survey the state and nation, the future field of our labors. We read, with critical eyes, the proceedings of Congress and legislatures, of general assemblies and synods, of conferences and conventions, and discovered that, in all alike, the existence of woman was entirely ignored.

Night after night, by an old-fashioned fireplace, we plotted and planned the coming agitation; how, when, and where each entering wedge could be driven, by which women might be recognized and their rights secured. Speedily the State was aflame with disturbances in temperance and teachers' conventions, and the press heralded the news far and near that women delegates had suddenly appeared, demanding admission in men's conventions; that their rights had been hotly contested session after session, by liberal men on the one side, the clergy and learned professors on the other; an overwhelming majority rejecting the women with terrible anathemas and denunciations. Such battles were fought over and over in the chief cities of many of the Northern States, until the bigotry of men in all the reforms and professions was thoroughly exposed. Every right achieved, to enter a college, to study a profession, to labor in some new industry, or to advocate a reform measure was contended for inch by inch.

Many of those enjoying all these blessings now complacently say, " If these pioneers in reform had only pressed their measures more judiciously, in a more lady-like manner, in more choice language, with a more deferential attitude, the gentlemen could not have behaved so rudely." I give, in these pages, enough of the characteristics of these women, of the sentiments they expressed, of their education, ancestry, and position to show that no power could have met the prejudice and bigotry of that period more successfully than they did who so bravely and persistently fought and conquered them.

Miss Anthony first carried her flag of rebellion into the State conventions of teachers, and there fought, almost single-handed, the battle for equality. At the close of the first decade she had compelled conservatism to yield its ground so far as to permit women to participate in all debates, deliver essays, vote, and hold honored positions as officers. She labored as sincerely in the temperance movement, until convinced that woman's moral power amounted to little as a civil agent, until backed by ballot and coined into State law. She still never loses an occasion to defend coeducation and prohibition, and solves every difficulty with the refrain, " woman suffrage," as persistent as the " never more " of Poe's raven.

CHAPTER XI.

SUSAN B. ANTHONY—*Continued.*

IT was in 1852 that anti-slavery, through the eloquent lips of such men as George Thompson, Phillips, and Garrison, first proclaimed to Miss Anthony its pressing financial necessities. To their inspired words she gave answer, four years afterward, by becoming a regularly employed agent in the Anti-slavery Society. For her espoused cause she has always made boldest demands. In the abolition meetings she used to tell each class why it should support the movement financially; invariably calling upon Democrats to give liberally, as the success of the cause would enable them to cease bowing the knee to the slave power.

There is scarce a town, however small, from New York to San Francisco, that has not heard her ringing voice. Who can number the speeches she has made on lyceum platforms, in churches, schoolhouses, halls, barns, and in the open air, with a lumber wagon or a cart for her rostrum? Who can describe the varied audiences and social circles she has cheered and interested? Now we see her on the far-off prairies, entertaining, with sterling common sense, large gatherings of men, women, and children, seated on rough boards in some unfinished building; again, holding public debates in some town with half-fledged editors and clergymen; next, sailing up the Columbia River and, in hot haste to meet some appointment, jolting over the rough mountains of Oregon and Washington; and then, before legislative assemblies, constitutional conventions, and congressional committees, discussing with senators and judges the letter and spirit of constitutional law.

Miss Anthony's style of speaking is rapid and vehement. In debate she is ready and keen, and she is always equal to an emergency. Many times in traveling with her through the West, especially on our first trip to Kansas and California, we were suddenly called upon to speak to the women assembled at the stations. Filled with consternation, I usually appealed to her to go first; and, without a moment's hesitation, she could always fill five minutes with some appropriate words and inspire me with thoughts and courage to follow. The climax of these occasions was reached in an institution for the deaf and dumb in Michigan. I had just said to my friend, " There is one comfort in visiting this place; we shall not be asked to speak," when the superintendent, approaching us, said, " Ladies, the pupils are assembled in the chapel, ready to hear you. I promised to invite you to speak to them as soon as I heard you were in town." The possibility of addressing such an audience was as novel to Miss Anthony as to me; yet she promptly walked down the aisle to the platform, as if to perform an ordinary duty, while I, half distracted with anxiety, wondering by what process I was to be placed in communication with the deaf and dumb, reluctantly followed. But the manner was simple enough, when illustrated. The superintendent, standing by our side, repeated, in the sign language, what was said as fast as uttered; and by laughter, tears, and applause, the pupils showed that they fully appreciated the pathos, humor, and argument.

One night, crossing the Mississippi at McGregor, Iowa, we were icebound in the middle of the river. The boat was crowded with people, hungry, tired, and cross with the delay. Some gentlemen, with whom we had been talking on the cars, started the cry, "Speech on woman suffrage!" Accordingly, in the middle of the Mississippi River, at midnight, we presented our claims to political representation, and debated the question of universal suffrage until we landed. Our voyagers were quite thankful that we had shortened the many hours, and we equally so at having made several converts and held a convention on the very bosom of the great "Mother of Waters." Only once in all these wanderings was Miss Anthony taken by surprise, and that was on being asked to speak to the inmates of an insane asylum. "Bless me!" said she, "it is as much as I can do to talk to the sane! What could I say to an audience of lunatics?" Her companion, Virginia L. Minor of St. Louis, replied: "This is a golden moment for you, the first opportunity you have ever had, according to the constitutions, to talk to your 'peers,' for is not the right of suffrage denied to 'idiots, criminals, lunatics, and women'?"

Much curiosity has been expressed as to the love-life of Miss Anthony; but, if she has enjoyed or suffered any of the usual triumphs or disappointments of her sex, she has not yet vouchsafed this information to her biographers. While few women have had more sincere and lasting friendships, or a more extensive correspondence with a large circle of noble men, yet I doubt if one of them can boast of having received from her any exceptional attention. She has often playfully said, when questioned on this point, that she could not consent that the man she loved, described in the Constitution as a white male, native born, American citizen, possessed of the right of self-government, eligible to the office of President of the great Republic, should unite his destinies in marriage with a political slave and pariah. " No, no; when I am crowned with all the rights, privileges, and immunities of a citizen, I may give some consideration to this social institution; but until then I must concentrate all my energies on the enfranchisement of my own sex." Miss Anthony's love-life, like her religion, has manifested itself in steadfast, earnest labors for men in general. She has been a watchful and affectionate daughter, sister, friend, and those who have felt the pulsations of her great heart know how warmly it beats for all.

As the custom has long been observed, among married women, of celebrating the anniversaries of their wedding-day, quite properly the initiative has been taken, in late years, of doing honor to the great events in the lives of single women. Being united in closest bonds to her profession, Dr. Harriet K. Hunt of Boston celebrated her twenty-fifth year of faithful services as a physician by giving to her friends and patrons a large reception, which she called her silver wedding. From a feeling of the sacredness of her life work, the admirers of Susan B. Anthony have been moved to mark, by reception and convention, her rapid-flowing years and the passing decades of the suffrage movement. To the most brilliant occasion of this kind, the invitation cards were as follows:

The ladies of the Woman's Bureau invite you to a reception on Tuesday evening, February 15th, to celebrate the fiftieth birthday of Susan B. Anthony, when her friends will have an opportunity to show their appreciation of her long services in behalf of woman's emancipation.

No. 49 East 23d St., New York,
February 10, 1870.

ELIZABETH B. PHELPS,
ANNA B. DARLING,
CHARLOTTE BEEBE WILBOUR.

In response to the invitation, the parlors of the bureau were crowded with friends to congratulate Miss Anthony on the happy event, many bringing valuable gifts as an expression of their gratitude. Among other presents were a handsome gold watch and checks to the amount of a thousand dollars. The guests were entertained with music, recitations, the reading of many piquant letters of regret from distinguished people, and witty rhymes written for the occasion by the Cary sisters. Miss Anthony received her guests with her usual straightforward simplicity, and in a few earnest words expressed her thanks for the presents and praises showered upon her. The comments of the leading journals, next day, were highly complimentary, and as genial as amusing. All dwelt on the fact that, at last, a woman had arisen brave enough to assert her right to grow old and openly declare that half a century had rolled over her head.

Of carefully prepared written speeches Miss Anthony has made few; but these, by the high praise they called forth, prove that she can—in spite of her own declaration to the contrary—put her sterling thoughts on paper concisely and effectively. After her exhaustive plea, in 1880, for a Sixteenth Amendment before

the Judiciary Committee of the Senate, Senator Ed-
munds accosted her, as she was leaving the Capitol, and
said he neglected to tell her, in the committee room,
that she had made an argument, no matter what his
personal feelings were as to the conclusions reached,
which was unanswerable—an argument, unlike the
usual platform oratory given at hearings, suited to a
committee of men trained to the law.

It was in 1876 that Miss Anthony gave her much
criticised lecture on " Social Purity " in Boston. As
to the result she felt very anxious; for the intelligence
of New England composed her audience, and it did not
still her heart-beats to see, sitting just in front of the
platform, her revered friend, William Lloyd Garrison.
But surely every fear vanished when she felt the grand
old abolitionist's hand warmly pressing hers, and heard
him say that to listen to no one else would he have had
courage to leave his sick room, and that he felt fully re-
paid by her grand speech, which neither in matter nor
manner would he have changed in the smallest particular.   But into Miss Anthony's private correspondence
one must look for examples of her most effective writing.   Verb or substantive is often wanting, but you
can always catch the thought, and will ever find it clear
and suggestive.   It is a strikingly strange dialect, but
one that touches, at times, the deepest chords of pathos
and humor, and, when stirred by some great event, is
highly eloquent.

From being the most ridiculed and mercilessly persecuted woman, Miss Anthony has become the most
honored and respected in the nation. Witness the
praises of press and people, and the enthusiastic ova-
tions she received on her departure for Europe in

1883. Never were warmer expressions of regret for an absence, nor more sincere prayers for a speedy return, accorded to any American on leaving his native shores. This slow awaking to the character of her services shows the abiding sense of justice in the human soul. Having spent the winter of 1882-83 in Washington, trying to press to a vote the bill for a Sixteenth Amendment before Congress, and the autumn in a vigorous campaign through Nebraska, where a constitutional amendment to enfranchise women had been submitted to the people, she felt the imperative need of an entire change in the current of her thoughts. Accordingly, after one of the most successful conventions ever held at the national capital, and a most flattering ovation in the spacious parlors of the Riggs House, and a large reception in Philadelphia, she sailed for Europe.

Fortunate in being perfectly well during the entire voyage, our traveler received perpetual enjoyment in watching the ever varying sea and sky. To the captain's merry challenge to find anything so grand as the ocean, she replied, " Yes, these mighty forces in nature do indeed fill me with awe; but this vessel, with deep-buried fires, powerful machinery, spacious decks, and tapering masts, walking the waves like a thing of life, and all the work of man, impresses one still more deeply. Lo! in man's divine creative power is fulfilled the prophecy, ' Ye shall be as Gods! ' "

In all her journeyings through Germany, Italy, and France, Miss Anthony was never the mere sight-seer, but always the humanitarian and reformer in traveler's guise. Few of the great masterpieces of art gave her real enjoyment. The keen appreciation of the beauties of sculpture, painting, and architecture, which one would have expected to find in so deep a religious nature, was wanting, warped, no doubt, by her early Quaker training. That her travels gave her more pain than pleasure was, perhaps, not so much that she had no appreciation of æsthetic beauty, but that she quickly grasped the infinitude of human misery; not because her soul did not feel the heights to which art had risen, but that it vibrated in every fiber to the depths to which mankind had fallen. Wandering through a gorgeous palace one day, she exclaimed, " What do you find to admire here? If it were a school of five hundred children being educated into the right of self-government I could admire it, too; but standing for one man's pleasure, I say no!" In the quarters of one of the devotees, at the old monastery of the Certosa, at Florence, there lies, on a small table, an open book, in which visitors register. On the occasion of Miss Anthony's visit the pen and ink proved so unpromising that her entire party declined this opportunity to make themselves famous, but she made the rebellious pen inscribe, " Perfect equality for women, civil, political, religious. Susan B. Anthony, U. S. A." Friends, who visited the monastery next day, reported that lines had been drawn through this heretical sentiment.

During her visit at the home of Mr. and Mrs. Sargent, in Berlin, Miss Anthony quite innocently posted her letters in the official envelopes of our Suffrage Association, which bore the usual mottoes, " No just government can be formed without the consent of the governed," etc. In a few days an official brought back a large package, saying, " Such sentiments are not allowed to pass through the post office."

Probably nothing saved her from arrest as a socialist, under the tyrannical police regulations, but the fact that she was the guest of the Minister Plenipotentiary of the United States.

My son Theodore wrote of Miss Anthony's visit in Paris: " I had never before seen her in the rôle of tourist. She seemed interested only in historical monuments, and in the men and questions of the hour. The galleries of the Louvre had little attraction for her, but she gazed with deep pleasure at Napoleon's tomb, Nôtre Dame, and the ruins of the Tuileries. She was always ready to listen to discussions on the political problems before the French people, the prospects of the Republic, the divorce agitation, and the education of women. 'I had rather see Jules Ferry than all the pictures of the Louvre, Luxembourg, and Salon,' she remarked at table. A day or two later she saw Ferry at Laboulaye's funeral. The three things which made the deepest impression on Miss Anthony, during her stay at Paris, were probably the interment of Laboulaye (the friend of the United States and of the woman movement); the touching anniversary demonstration of the Communists, at the Cemetery of Père La Chaise, on the very spot where the last defenders of the Commune of 1871 were ruthlessly shot and buried in a common grave; and a woman's rights meeting, held in a little hall in the Rue de Rivoli, at which the brave, far-seeing Mlle. Hubertine Auchet was the leading spirit."

While on the Continent Miss Anthony experienced the unfortunate sensation of being deaf and dumb; to speak and not to be understood, to hear and not to comprehend, were to her bitter realities. We can imagine to what desperation she was brought when her Quaker prudishness could hail an emphatic oath in English from a French official with the exclamation, " Well, it sounds good to hear someone even swear in old Anglo-Saxon! " After two months of enforced silence, she was buoyant in reaching the British Islands once more, where she could enjoy public speaking and general conversation. Here she was the recipient of many generous social attentions, and, on May 25, a large public meeting of representative people, presided over by Jacob Bright, was called, in our honor, by the National Association of Great Britain. She spoke on the educational and political status of women in America, I of their religious and social position.

Before closing my friend's biography I shall trace two golden threads in this closely woven life of incident. One of the greatest services rendered by Miss Anthony to the suffrage cause was in casting a vote in the Presidential election of 1872, in order to test the rights of women under the Fourteenth Amendment. For this offense the brave woman was arrested, on Thanksgiving Day, the national holiday handed down to us by Pilgrim Fathers escaped from England's persecutions. She asked for a writ of habeas corpus. The writ being flatly refused, in January, 1873, her counsel gave bonds. The daring defendant finding, when too late, that this not only kept her out of jail, but her case out of the Supreme Court of the United States, regretfully determined to fight on, and gain the uttermost by a decision in the United States Circuit Court. Her trial was set down for the Rochester term in May. Quickly she canvassed the whole county, laying before every probable juror the strength of her case. When the time for the trial arrived, the District Attorney, fearing the result, if the decision were left to a jury drawn from Miss Anthony's enlightened county, transferred the trial to the Ontario County term, in June, 1873.

It was now necessary to instruct the citizens of another county. In this task Miss Anthony received valuable assistance from Matilda Joslyn Gage; and, to meet all this new expense, financial aid was generously given, unsolicited, by Thomas Wentworth Higginson, Gerrit Smith, and other sympathizers. But in vain was every effort; in vain the appeal of Miss Anthony to her jurors; in vain the moral influence of the leading representatives of the bar of Central New York filling the courtroom, for Judge Hunt, without precedent to sustain him, declaring it a case of law and not of fact, refused to give the case to the jury, reserving to himself final decision. Was it not an historic scene which was enacted there in that little courthouse in Canandaigua? All the inconsistencies were embodied in that Judge, punctilious in manner, scrupulous in attire, conscientious in trivialities, and obtuse on great principles, fitly described by Charles O'Conor—" A very ladylike Judge." Behold him sitting there, balancing all the niceties of law and equity in his Old World scales, and at last saying, " The prisoner will stand up." Whereupon the accused arose. " The sentence of the court is that you pay a fine of one hundred dollars and the costs of the prosecution." Then the unruly defendant answers: " May it please your Honor, I shall never pay a dollar of your unjust penalty," and more to the same effect, all of which she has lived up to. The " ladylike " Judge had gained some insight into the determination of the prisoner; so, not wishing to incarcerate her to all eternity, he added gently:

"Madam, the court will not order you committed until the fine is paid."

It was on the 17th of June that the verdict was given. On that very day, a little less than a century before, the brave militia was driven back at Bunker Hill—back, back, almost wiped out; yet truth was in their ranks, and justice, too. But how ended that rebellion of weak colonists? The cause of American womanhood, embodied for the moment in the liberty of a single individual, received a rebuff on June 17, 1873; but, just as surely as our Revolutionary heroes were in the end victorious, so will the inalienable rights of our heroines of the nineteenth century receive final vindication.

In his speech of 1880, before the Phi Beta Kappa Society at Harvard, Wendell Phillips said—what as a rule is true—that " a reformer, to be conscientious, must be free from bread-winning." I will open Miss Anthony's accounts and show that this reformer, being, perhaps, the exception which proves the rule, has been consistently and conscientiously in debt. Turning over her year-books the pages give a fair record up to 1863. Here began the first herculean labor. The Woman's Loyal League, sadly in need of funds, was not an incorporated association, so its secretary assumed the debts. Accounts here became quite lamentable, the deficit reaching five thousand dollars. It must be paid, and, in fact, will be paid. Anxious, weary hours were spent in crowding the Cooper Institute, from week to week, with paying audiences, to listen to such men as Phillips, Curtis, and Douglass, who contributed their services, and lifted the secretary out of debt. At last, after many difficulties, her cash-book of 1863 was honorably pigeon-holed. In

1867 we can read account of herculean labor the second. Twenty thousand tracts are needed to convert the voters of Kansas to woman suffrage. Traveling expenses to Kansas, and the tracts, make the debtor column overreach the creditor some two thousand dollars. There is recognition on these pages of more than one thousand dollars obtained by soliciting advertisements, but no note is made of the weary, burning July days spent in the streets of New York to procure this money, nor of the ready application of the savings made by petty economies from her salary from the Hovey Committee.

It would have been fortunate for my brave friend, if cash-books 1868, 1869, and 1870 had never come down from their shelves; for they sing and sing, in notes of debts, till all unite in one vast chorus of far more than ten thousand dollars. These were the days of the *Revolution*, the newspaper, not the war, though it was warfare for the debt-ridden manager. Several thousand dollars she paid with money earned by lecturing, and with money given her for personal use. One Thanksgiving was, in truth, a time for returning thanks; for she received, canceled, from her cousin, Anson Lapham, her note for four thousand dollars. After the funeral of Paulina Wright Davis, the bereaved widower pressed into Miss Anthony's hand canceled notes for five hundred dollars, bearing on the back the words, "In memory of my beloved wife." One other note was canceled in recognition of her perfect forgetfulness of self-interest and ready sacrifice to the needs of others. When laboring, in 1874, to fill every engagement, in order to meet her debts, her mother's sudden illness called her home. Without one selfish regret, the anxious daughter hastened to Rochester. When recovery was certain, and Miss Anthony was about to return to her fatiguing labors, her mother gave her, at parting, her note for a thousand dollars, on which was written, in trembling lines, " In just consideration of the tender sacrifice made to nurse me in severe illness." At last all the *Revolution* debt was paid, except that due to her generous sister, Mary Anthony, who used often humorously to assure her she was a fit subject for the bankrupt act.

There is something humorously pathetic in the death of the *Revolution*—that firstborn of Miss Anthony. Mrs. Laura Curtis Bullard generously assumed the care of the troublesome child, and, in order to make the adoption legal, gave the usual consideration—one dollar. The very night of the transfer Miss Anthony went to Rochester with the dollar in her pocket, and the little change left after purchasing her ticket. She arrived safely with her debts, but nothing more—her pocket had been picked! Oh, thief, could you but know what value of faithful work you purloined!

From the close of the year 1876 Miss Anthony's accounts showed favorable signs as to the credit column. Indeed, at the end of five years there was a solid balance of several thousand dollars earned on lecturing tours. But alas! the accounts grow dim again—in fact the credit column fades away. " The History of Woman Suffrage " ruthlessly swallowed up every vestige of Miss Anthony's bank account. But, in 1886, by the will of Mrs. Eddy, daughter of Francis Jackson of Boston, Miss Anthony received twenty-four thousand dollars for the Woman's Suffrage Movement, which lifted her out of debt once more.

In vain will you search these telltale books for evidence of personal extravagance; for, although Miss Anthony thinks it true economy to buy the best, her tastes are simple. Is there not something very touching in the fact that she never bought a book or picture for her own enjoyment? The meager personal balance-sheets show four lapses from discipline,—lapses that she even now regards as ruthless extravagance,—viz.: the purchase of two inexpensive brooches, a much needed watch, and a pair of cuffs to match a point-lace collar presented by a friend. Those interested in Miss Anthony's personal appearance long ago ceased to trust her with the purchase-money for any ornament; for, however firm her resolution to comply with their wish, the check invariably found its way to the credit column of those little cash-books as " money received for the cause." Now, reader, you have been admitted to a private view of Miss Anthony's financial records, and you can appreciate her devotion to an idea. Do you not agree with me that a " bread-winner " can be a conscientious reformer?

In finishing this sketch of the most intimate friend I have had for the past forty-five years,—with whom I have spent weeks and months under the same roof,—I can truly say that she is the most upright, courageous, self-sacrificing, magnanimous human being I have ever known. I have seen her beset on every side with the most petty annoyances, ridiculed and misrepresented, slandered and persecuted; I have known women refuse to take her extended hand; women to whom she presented copies of " The History of Woman Suffrage," return it unnoticed; others to keep it without one word of acknowledgment; others to write most insulting letters in answer to hers of affectionate conciliation. And yet, under all the cross-fires incident to a reform, never has her hope flagged, her self-respect wavered, or a feeling of resentment shadowed her mind. Oftentimes, when I have been sorely discouraged, thinking that the prolonged struggle was a waste of force which in other directions might be rich in achievement, with her sublime faith in humanity, she would breathe into my soul renewed inspiration, saying, " Pity rather than blame those who persecute us." So closely interwoven have been our lives, our purposes, and experiences that, separated, we have a feeling of incompleteness—united, such strength of self-assertion that no ordinary obstacles, difficulties, or dangers ever appear to us insurmountable. Reviewing the life of Susan B. Anthony, I ever liken her to the Doric column in Grecian architecture, so simply, so grandly she stands, free from every extraneous ornament, supporting her one vast idea—the enfranchisement of woman.

As our estimate of ourselves and our friendship may differ somewhat from that taken from an objective point of view, I will give an extract from what our common friend Theodore Tilton wrote of us in 1868:

" Miss Susan B. Anthony, a well-known, indefatigable, and lifelong advocate of temperance, anti-slavery, and woman's rights, has been, since 1851, Mrs. Stanton's intimate associate in reformatory labors. These celebrated women are of about equal age, but of the most opposite characteristics, and illustrate the theory of counterparts in affection by entertaining for each other a friendship of extraordinary strength.

" Mrs. Stanton is a fine writer, but a poor executant; Miss Anthony is a thorough manager, but a poor writer. Both have large brains and great hearts; neither has any selfish ambition for celebrity; but each vies with the other in a noble enthusiasm for the cause to which they are devoting their lives.

" Nevertheless, to describe them critically, I ought to say that, opposites though they be, each does not so much supplement the other's deficiencies as augment the other's eccentricities. Thus they often stimulate each other's aggressiveness, and, at the same time, diminish each other's discretion.

" But, whatever may be the imprudent utterances of the one or the impolitic methods of the other, the animating motives of both are evermore as white as the light. The good that they do is by design; the harm by accident. These two women, sitting together in their parlors, have, for the last thirty years, been diligent forgers of all manner of projectiles, from fireworks to thunderbolts, and have hurled them with unexpected explosion into the midst of all manner of educational, reformatory, religious, and political assemblies; sometimes to the pleasant surprise and half welcome of the members, more often to the bewilderment and prostration of numerous victims; and, in a few signal instances, to the gnashing of angry men's teeth. I know of no two more pertinacious incendiaries in the whole country. Nor will they themselves deny the charge. In fact this noise-making twain are the two sticks of a drum, keeping up what Daniel Webster called ' The rub-a-dub of agitation.' "

CHAPTER XII.

WOMEN had been willing so long to hold a subordinate position, both in private and public affairs, that a gradually growing feeling of rebellion among them quite exasperated the men, and their manifestations of hostility in public meetings were often as ridiculous as humiliating.

True, those gentlemen were all quite willing that women should join their societies and churches to do the drudgery; to work up the enthusiasm in fairs and revivals, conventions and flag presentations; to pay a dollar apiece into their treasury for the honor of being members of their various organizations; to beg money for the Church; to circulate petitions from door to door; to visit saloons; to pray with or defy rumsellers; to teach school at half price, and sit round the outskirts of a hall, in teachers' State conventions, like so many wallflowers; but they would not allow them to sit on the platform, address the assembly, or vote for men and measures.

Those who had learned the first lessons of human rights from the lips of Henry B. Stanton, Samuel J. May, and Gerrit Smith would not accept any such position. When women abandoned the temperance reform, all interest in the question gradually died out in the State, and practically nothing was done in New

York for nearly twenty years. Gerrit Smith made one or two attempts toward an " anti-dramshop " party, but, as women could not vote, they felt no interest in the measure, and failure was the result.

I soon convinced Miss Anthony that the ballot was the key to the situation; that when we had a voice in the laws we should be welcome to any platform. In turning the intense earnestness and religious enthusiasm of this great-souled woman into this channel, I soon felt the power of my convert in goading me forever forward to more untiring work. Soon fastened, heart to heart, with hooks of steel in a friendship that years of confidence and affection have steadily strengthened, we have labored faithfully together.

From the year 1850 conventions were held in various States, and their respective legislatures were continually besieged; New York was thoroughly canvassed by Miss Anthony and others. Appeals, calls for meetings, and petitions were circulated without number. In 1854 I prepared my first speech for the New York legislature. That was a great event in my life. I felt so nervous over it, lest it should not be worthy the occasion, that Miss Anthony suggested that I should slip up to Rochester and submit it to the Rev. William Henry Channing, who was preaching there at that time. I did so, and his opinion was so favorable as to the merits of my speech that I felt quite reassured. My father felt equally nervous when he saw, by the Albany *Evening Journal,* that I was to speak at the Capitol, and asked me to read my speech to him also. Accordingly, I stopped at Johnstown on my way to Albany, and, late one evening, when he was alone in his office, I entered and took my seat on the opposite side of his table. On no occasion, before or since, was I ever more embarrassed—an audience of one, and that the one of all others whose approbation I most desired, whose disapproval I most feared. I knew he condemned the whole movement, and was deeply grieved at the active part I had taken. Hence I was fully aware that I was about to address a wholly unsympathetic audience. However, I began, with a dogged determination to give all the power I could to my manuscript, and not to be discouraged or turned from my purpose by any tender appeals or adverse criticisms. I described the widow in the first hours of her grief, subject to the intrusions of the coarse minions of the law, taking inventory of the household goods, of the old armchair in which her loved one had breathed his last, of the old clock in the corner that told the hour he passed away. I threw all the pathos I could into my voice and language at this point, and, to my intense satisfaction, I saw tears filling my father's eyes. I cannot express the exultation I felt, thinking that now he would see, with my eyes, the injustice women suffered under the laws he understood so well.

Feeling that I had touched his heart I went on with renewed confidence, and, when I had finished, I saw he was thoroughly magnetized. With beating heart I waited for him to break the silence. He was evidently deeply pondering over all he had heard, and did not speak for a long time. I believed I had opened to him a new world of thought. He had listened long to the complaints of women, but from the lips of his own daughter they had come with a deeper pathos and power. At last, turning abruptly, he said: " Surely you have had a happy, comfortable life, with all your wants and needs supplied; and yet that speech fills me with self-reproach; for one might naturally ask, how can a young woman, tenderly brought up, who has had no bitter personal experience, feel so keenly the wrongs of her sex? Where did you learn this lesson?" "I learned it here," I replied, "in your office, when a child, listening to the complaints women made to you. They who have sympathy and imagination to make the sorrows of others their own can readily learn all the hard lessons of life from the experience of others." "Well, well!" he said, "you have made your points clear and strong; but I think I can find you even more cruel laws than those you have quoted." He suggested some improvements in my speech, looked up other laws, and it was one o'clock in the morning before we kissed each other good-night. How he felt on the question after that I do not know, as he never said anything in favor of or against it. He gladly gave me any help I needed, from time to time, in looking up the laws, and was very desirous that whatever I gave to the public should be carefully prepared.

Miss Anthony printed twenty thousand copies of this address, laid it on the desk of every member of the legislature, both in the Assembly and Senate, and, in her travels that winter, she circulated it throughout the State. I am happy to say I never felt so anxious about the fate of a speech since.

The first woman's convention in Albany was held at this time, and we had a kind of protracted meeting for two weeks after. There were several hearings before both branches of the legislature, and a succession of meetings in Association Hall, in which Phillips, Channing, Ernestine L. Rose, Antoinette L. Brown, and

Susan B. Anthony took part.   Being at the capital of the State, discussion was aroused at every fireside, while the comments of the press were numerous and varied. Every little country paper had something witty or silly to say about the uprising of the " strong-minded." Those editors whose heads were about the size of an apple were the most opposed to the uprising of women, illustrating what Sidney Smith said long ago: " There always was, and there always will be a class of men so small that, if women were educated, there would be nobody left below them."   Poor human nature loves to have something to look down upon!

Here is a specimen of the way such editors talked at that time.   The *Albany Register,* in an article on " Woman's Rights in the Legislature," dated March 7, 1854, says:

" While the feminine propagandists of women's rights confined themselves to the exhibition of short petti-coats and long-legged boots, and to the holding of conventions and speech-making in concert rooms, the people were disposed to be amused by them, as they are by the wit of the clown in the circus, or the per-formances of Punch and Judy on fair days, or the min-strelsy of gentlemen with blackened faces, on banjos, the tambourine, and bones.   But the joke is becoming stale.   People are getting cloyed with these perform-ances, and are looking for some healthier and more intellectual amusement.   The ludicrous is wearing away, and disgust is taking the place of pleasurable sen-sations, arising from the novelty of this new phase of hypocrisy and infidel fanaticism.

"People are beginning to inquire how far public senti-ment should sanction or tolerate these unsexed women, who would step out from the true sphere of the mother, the wife, and the daughter, and taking upon themselves the duties and the business of men, stalk into the public gaze, and, by engaging in the politics, the rough controversies and trafficking of the world, upheave existing institutions, and overrun all the social relations of life.

"It is a melancholy reflection that, among our American women, who have been educated to better things, there should be found any who are willing to follow the lead of such foreign propagandists as the ringleted, gloved exotic, Ernestine L. Rose. We can understand how such a man as the Rev. Mr. May, or the sleek-headed Dr. Channing, may be deluded by her into becoming one of her disciples. They are not the first instances of infatuation that may overtake weak-minded men, if they are honest in their devotion to her and her doctrines; nor would they be the first examples of a low ambition that seeks notoriety as a substitute for true fame, if they are dishonest. Such men there are always, and, honest or dishonest, their true position is that of being tied to the apron strings of some strong-minded woman, and to be exhibited as rare specimens of human wickedness or human weakness and folly. But that one educated American should become her disciple and follow her insane teachings is a marvel."

When we see the abuse and ridicule to which the best of men were subjected for standing on our platform in the early days, we need not wonder that so few have been brave enough to advocate our cause in later years, either in conventions or in the halls of legislation.

After twelve added years of agitation, following the passage of the Property Bill, New York conceded other civil rights to married women. Pending the discussion

of these various bills, Susan B. Anthony circulated petitions, both for the civil and political rights of women,
throughout the State, traveling in stage coaches, open
wagons, and sleighs in all seasons, and on foot, from
door to door through towns and cities, doing her uttermost to rouse women to some sense of their natural
rights as human beings, and to their civil and political
rights as citizens of a republic.   And while expending
her time, strength, and money to secure these blessings
for the women of the State, they would gruffly tell her
that they had all the rights they wanted, or rudely shut
the door in her face; leaving her to stand outside, petition in hand, treating her with as much contempt as
if she was asking alms for herself.   None but those who
did that work in the early days, for the slaves and the
women, can ever know the hardships and humiliations
that were endured.   But it was done because it was
only through petitions—a power seemingly so ineffi-
cient—that disfranchised classes could be heard in the
State and National councils; hence their importance.

The frivolous objections some women made to our
appeals were as exasperating as they were ridiculous.
To reply to them politely, at all times, required a divine
patience.   On one occasion, after addressing the legislature, some of the ladies, in congratulating me, inquired, in a deprecating tone, " What do you do with
your children? "   " Ladies," I said, " it takes me no
longer to speak, than you to listen; what have you done
with your children the two hours you have been sitting
here?   But, to answer your question, I never leave
my children to go to Saratoga, Washington, Newport,
or Europe, or even to come here.   They are, at this
moment, with a faithful nurse at the Delevan House,

and, having accomplished my mission, we shall all return home together."

When my children reached the magic number of seven, my good angel, Susan B. Anthony, would sometimes take one or two of them to her own quiet home, just out of Rochester, where, on a well-cultivated little farm, one could enjoy uninterrupted rest and the choicest fruits of the season. That was always a safe harbor for my friend, as her family sympathized fully in the reforms to which she gave her life. I have many pleasant memories of my own flying visits to that hospitable Quaker home and the broad catholic spirit of Daniel and Lucy Anthony. Whatever opposition and ridicule their daughter endured elsewhere, she enjoyed the steadfast sympathy and confidence of her own home circle. Her faithful sister Mary, a most successful teacher in the public schools of Rochester for a quarter of a century, and a good financier, who with her patrimony and salary had laid by a competence, took on her shoulders double duty at home in cheering the declining years of her parents, that Susan might do the public work in the reforms in which they were equally interested. Now, with life's earnest work nearly accomplished, the sisters are living happily together; illustrating another of the many charming homes of single women, so rapidly multiplying of late.

Miss Anthony, who was a frequent guest at my home, sometimes stood guard when I was absent. The children of our household say that among their earliest recollections is the tableau of " Mother and Susan," seated by a large table covered with books and papers, always writing and talking about the Constitution, interrupted with occasional visits from others of the faith-

ful. Hither came Elizabeth Oakes Smith, Paulina
Wright Davis, Frances Dana Gage, Dr. Harriet Hunt,
Rev. Antoinette Brown, Lucy Stone, and Abby Kelly,
until all these names were as familiar as household
words to the children.

Martha C. Wright of Auburn was a frequent visitor
at the center of the rebellion, as my sequestered cottage
on Locust Hill was facetiously called. She brought
to these councils of war not only her own wisdom, but that of the wife and sister of William H.
Seward, and sometimes encouraging suggestions from
the great statesman himself, from whose writings we
often gleaned grand and radical sentiments. Lucretia
Mott, too, being an occasional guest of her sister,
Martha C. Wright, added the dignity of her presence at many of these important consultations. She
was uniformly in favor of toning down our fiery
pronunciamentos. For Miss Anthony and myself,
the English language had no words strong enough
to express the indignation we felt at the prolonged injustice to women. We found, however,
that, after expressing ourselves in the most vehement manner and thus in a measure giving our
feelings an outlet, we were reconciled to issue the
documents in milder terms. If the men of the State
could have known the stern rebukes, the denunciations, the wit, the irony, the sarcasm that were
garnered there, and then judiciously pigeonholed and
milder and more persuasive appeals substituted, they
would have been truly thankful that they fared no
worse.

Senator Seward frequently left Washington to visit
in our neighborhood, at the house of Judge G. V.

Sackett, a man of wealth and political influence. One of the Senator's standing anecdotes, at dinner, to illustrate the purifying influence of women at the polls, which he always told with great zest for my especial benefit, was in regard to the manner in which his wife's sister exercised the right of suffrage.

He said: "Mrs. Worden having the supervision of a farm near Auburn, was obliged to hire two or three men for its cultivation. It was her custom, having examined them as to their capacity to perform the required labor, their knowledge of tools, horses, cattle, and horticulture, to inquire as to their politics. She informed them that, being a widow and having no one to represent her, she must have Republicans to do her voting and to represent her political opinions, and it always so happened that the men who offered their services belonged to the Republican party. I remarked to her, one day, 'Are you sure your men vote as they promise?' 'Yes,' she replied, 'I trust nothing to their discretion. I take them in my carriage within sight of the polls and put them in charge of some Republican who can be trusted. I see that they have the right tickets and then I feel sure that I am faithfully represented, and I know I am right in so doing. I have neither husband, father, nor son; I am responsible for my own taxes; am amenable to all the laws of the State; must pay the penalty of my own crimes if I commit any; hence I have the right, according to the principles of our government, to representation, and so long as I am not permitted to vote in person, I have a right to do so by proxy; hence I hire men to vote my principles.'"

These two sisters, Mrs. Worden and Mrs. Seward,

daughters of Judge Miller, an influential man, were women of culture and remarkable natural intelligence, and interested in all progressive ideas. They had rare common sense and independence of character, great simplicity of manner, and were wholly indifferent to the little arts of the toilet.

I was often told by fashionable women that they objected to the woman's rights movement because of the publicity of a convention, the immodesty of speaking from a platform, and the trial of seeing one's name in the papers. Several ladies made such remarks to me one day, as a bevy of us were sitting together in one of the fashionable hotels in Newport. We were holding a convention there at that time, and some of them had been present at one of the sessions. " Really," said I, " ladies, you surprise me; our conventions are not as public as the ballroom where I saw you all dancing last night. As to modesty, it may be a question, in many minds, whether it is less modest to speak words of soberness and truth, plainly dressed on a platform, than gorgeously arrayed, with bare arms and shoulders, to waltz in the arms of strange gentlemen. And as to the press, I noticed you all reading, in this morning's papers, with evident satisfaction, the personal compliments and full descriptions of your dresses at the last ball. I presume that any one of you would have felt slighted if your name had not been mentioned in the general description. When my name is mentioned, it is in connection with some great reform movement. Thus we all suffer or enjoy the same publicity—we are alike ridiculed. Wise men pity and ridicule you, and fools pity and ridicule me—you as the victims of folly and fashion, me as the representative of many of the disagreeable

'isms' of the age, as they choose to style liberal
opinions. It is amusing, in analyzing prejudices, to see
on what slender foundation they rest." And the ladies
around me were so completely cornered that no one
attempted an answer.

I remember being at a party at Secretary Seward's
home, at Auburn, one evening, when Mr. Burlingame,
special ambassador from China to the United States,
with a Chinese delegation, were among the guests. As
soon as the dancing commenced, and young ladies and
gentlemen, locked in each other's arms, began to whirl
in the giddy waltz, these Chinese gentlemen were so
shocked that they covered their faces with their fans,
occasionally peeping out each side and expressing their
surprise to each other. They thought us the most im-
modest women on the face of the earth. Modesty and
taste are questions of latitude and education; the more
people know,—the more their ideas are expanded by
travel, experience, and observation,—the less easily they
are shocked. The narrowness and bigotry of women
are the result of their circumscribed sphere of thought
and action.

A few years after Judge Hurlbert had published his
work on "Human Rights," in which he advocated
woman's right to the suffrage, and I had addressed the
legislature, we met at a dinner party in Albany.
Senator and Mrs. Seward were there. The Senator
was very merry on that occasion and made Judge
Hurlbert and myself the target for all his ridicule
on the woman's rights question, in which the most
of the company joined, so that we stood quite
alone. Sure that we had the right on our side
and the arguments clearly defined in our minds,

and both being cool and self-possessed, and in wit and sarcasm quite equal to any of them, we fought the Senator, inch by inch, until he had a very narrow platform to stand on. Mrs. Seward maintained an unbroken silence, while those ladies who did open their lips were with the opposition, supposing, no doubt, that Senator Seward represented his wife's opinions.

When we ladies withdrew from the table my embarrassment may be easily imagined. Separated from the Judge, I would now be an hour with a bevy of ladies who evidently felt repugnance to all my most cherished opinions. It was the first time I had met Mrs. Seward, and I did not then know the broad, liberal tendencies of her mind. What a tide of disagreeable thoughts rushed through me in that short passage from the dining room to the parlor. How gladly I would have glided out the front door! But that was impossible, so I made up my mind to stroll round as if self-absorbed, and look at the books and paintings until the Judge appeared; as I took it for granted that, after all I had said at the table on the political, religious, and social equality of women, not a lady would have anything to say to me.

Imagine, then, my surprise when, the moment the parlor door was closed upon us, Mrs. Seward, approaching me most affectionately, said:

" Let me thank you for the brave words you uttered at the dinner table, and for your speech before the legislature, that thrilled my soul as I read it over and over."

I was filled with joy and astonishment. Recovering myself, I said, " Is it possible, Mrs. Seward, that you agree with me? Then why, when I was so hard pressed by foes on every side, did you not come to the defense? I supposed that all you ladies were hostile to every one of my ideas on this question."

" No, no! " said she; " I am with you thoroughly, but I am a born coward; there is nothing I dread more than Mr. Seward's ridicule.   I would rather walk up to the cannon's mouth than encounter it."   " I, too, am with you," " And I," said two or three others, who had been silent at the table.

I never had a more serious, heartfelt conversation than with these ladies.   Mrs. Seward's spontaneity and earnestness had moved them all deeply, and when the Senator appeared the first words he said were:

" Before we part I must confess that I was fairly vanquished by you and the Judge, on my own principles " (for we had quoted some of his most radical utterances). " You have the argument, but custom and prejudice are against you, and they are stronger than truth and logic."

CHAPTER XIII.

THERE was one bright woman among the many in our Seneca Falls literary circle to whom I would give more than a passing notice—Mrs. Amelia Bloomer, who represented three novel phases of woman's life. She was assistant postmistress; an editor of a reform paper advocating temperance and woman's rights; and an advocate of the new costume which bore her name!

In 1849 her husband was appointed postmaster, and she became his deputy, was duly sworn in, and, during the administration of Taylor and Fillmore, served in that capacity. When she assumed her duties the improvement in the appearance and conduct of the office was generally acknowledged. A neat little room adjoining the public office became a kind of ladies' exchange, where those coming from different parts of the town could meet to talk over the news of the day and read the papers and magazines that came to Mrs. Bloomer as editor of the *Lily*. Those who enjoyed the brief reign of a woman in the post office can readily testify to the void felt by the ladies of the village when Mrs. Bloomer's term expired and a man once more reigned in her stead. However, she still edited the *Lily*, and her office remained a fashionable center for several years. Although she wore the bloomer dress, its originator was Elizabeth Smith Miller, the only daughter of Gerrit Smith. In the winter of 1852 Mrs. Miller came to visit me in Seneca Falls, dressed somewhat in the Turkish style—short skirt, full trousers of fine black broadcloth; a Spanish cloak, of the same material, reaching to the knee; beaver hat and feathers and dark furs; altogether a most becoming costume and exceedingly convenient for walking in all kinds of weather. To see my cousin, with a lamp in one hand and a baby in the other, walk upstairs with ease and grace, while, with flowing robes, I pulled myself up with difficulty, lamp and baby out of the question, readily convinced me that there was sore need of reform in woman's dress, and I promptly donned a similar attire. What incredible freedom I enjoyed for two years! Like a captive set free from his ball and chain, I was always ready for a brisk walk through sleet and snow and rain, to climb a mountain, jump over a fence, work in the garden, and, in fact, for any necessary locomotion.

Bloomer is now a recognized word in the English language. Mrs. Bloomer, having the *Lily* in which to discuss the merits of the new dress, the press generally took up the question, and much valuable information was elicited on the physiological results of woman's fashionable attire; the crippling effect of tight waists and long skirts, the heavy weight on the hips, and high heels, all combined to throw the spine out of plumb and lay the foundation for all manner of nervous diseases. But, while all agreed that some change was absolutely necessary for the health of women, the press stoutly ridiculed those who were ready to make the experiment.

A few sensible women, in different parts of the country, adopted the costume, and farmers' wives especially proved its convenience. It was also worn by skaters, gymnasts, tourists, and in sanitariums. But, while the few realized its advantages, the many laughed it to scorn, and heaped such ridicule on its wearers that they soon found that the physical freedom enjoyed did not compensate for the persistent persecution and petty annoyances suffered at every turn. To be rudely gazed at in public and private, to be the conscious subjects of criticism, and to be followed by crowds of boys in the streets, were all, to the very last degree, exasperating. A favorite doggerel that our tormentors chanted, when we appeared in public places, ran thus:

> "Heigh! ho! in rain and snow,
> The bloomer now is all the go.
> Twenty tailors take the stitches,
> Twenty women wear the breeches.
> Heigh! ho! in rain or snow,
> The bloomer now is all the go."

The singers were generally invisible behind some fence or attic window. Those who wore the dress can recall countless amusing and annoying experiences. The patience of most of us was exhausted in about two years; but our leader, Mrs. Miller, bravely adhered to the costume for nearly seven years, under the most trying circumstances. While her father was in Congress, she wore it at many fashionable dinners and receptions in Washington. She was bravely sustained, however, by her husband, Colonel Miller, who never flinched in escorting his wife and her coadjutors, however inartistic their costumes might be. To tall, gaunt women with large feet and to those who were short and stout, it was equally trying. Mrs. Miller was also encouraged by the intense feeling of her father on the question of woman's dress. To him the whole revolution in woman's position turned on her dress. The long skirt was the symbol of her degradation.

The names of those who wore the bloomer costume, besides those already mentioned, were Paulina Wright Davis, Lucy Stone, Susan B. Anthony, Sarah and Angelina Grimke, Mrs. William Burleigh, Celia Burleigh, Charlotte Beebe Wilbour, Helen Jarvis, Lydia Jenkins, Amelia Willard, Dr. Harriet N. Austin, and many patients in sanitariums, whose names I cannot recall. Looking back to this experiment, I am not surprised at the hostility of men in general to the dress, as it made it very uncomfortable for them to go anywhere with those who wore it. People would stare, many men and women make rude remarks, boys followed in crowds, with jeers and laughter, so that gentlemen in attendance would feel it their duty to show fight, unless they had sufficient self-control to pursue the even tenor of their way, as the ladies themselves did, without taking the slightest notice of the commotion they created. But Colonel Miller went through the ordeal with coolness and dogged determination, to the vexation of his acquaintances, who thought one of his duties as a husband was to prescribe his wife's costume.

Though we did not realize the success we hoped for by making the dress popular, yet the effort was not lost. We were well aware that the dress was not artistic, and though we made many changes, our own good taste was never satisfied until we threw aside the loose trousers and adopted buttoned leggins. After giving up the experiment, we found that the costume in which Diana the Huntress is represented, and that worn on the

stage by Ellen Tree in the play of " Ion," would have
been more artistic and convenient.   But we, who had
made the experiment, were too happy to move about
unnoticed and unknown, to risk, again, the happiness of
ourselves and our friends by any further experiments.
I have never wondered since that the Chinese women
allow their daughters' feet to be encased in iron shoes,
nor that the Hindoo widows walk calmly to the funeral
pyre; for great are the penalties of those who dare resist
the behests of the tyrant Custom.

Nevertheless the agitation has been kept up, in a
mild form, both in England and America. Lady
Harberton, in 1885, was at the head of an organized
movement in London to introduce the bifurcated skirt;
Mrs. Jenness Miller, in this country, is making an
entire revolution in every garment that belongs to a
woman's toilet; and common-sense shoemakers have
vouchsafed to us, at last, a low, square heel to our boots
and a broad sole in which the five toes can spread themselves at pleasure.   Evidently a new day of physical
freedom is at last dawning for the most cribbed and
crippled of Eve's unhappy daughters.

It was while living in Seneca Falls, and at one
of the most despairing periods of my young life, that
one of the best gifts of the gods came to me in the form
of a good, faithful housekeeper. She was indeed a
treasure, a friend and comforter, a second mother to my
children, and understood all life's duties and gladly bore
its burdens. She could fill any department in domestic life, and for thirty years was the joy of our household. But for this noble, self-sacrificing woman, much
of my public work would have been quite impossible.
If by word or deed I have made the journey of life easier

for any struggling soul, I must in justice share the meed of praise accorded me with my little Quaker friend Amelia Willard.

There are two classes of housekeepers—one that will get what they want, if in the range of human possibilities, and then accept the inevitable inconveniences with cheerfulness and heroism; the other, from a kind of chronic inertia and a fear of taking responsibility, accept everything as they find it, though with gentle, continuous complainings. The latter are called amiable women. Such a woman was our congressman's wife in 1854, and, as I was the reservoir of all her sorrows, great and small, I became very weary of her amiable non-resistance. Among other domestic trials, she had a kitchen stove that smoked and leaked, which could neither bake nor broil,—a worthless thing,—and too small for any purpose. Consequently half their viands were spoiled in the cooking, and the cooks left in disgust, one after another.

In telling me, one day, of these kitchen misadventures, she actually shed tears, which so roused my sympathies that, with surprise, I exclaimed: " Why do you not buy a new stove? " To my unassisted common sense that seemed the most practical thing to do. " Why," she replied, " I have never purchased a darning needle, to put the case strongly, without consulting Mr. S., and he does not think a new stove necessary." " What, pray," said I, " does he know about stoves, sitting in his easy-chair in Washington? If he had a dull old knife with broken blades, he would soon get a new one with which to sharpen his pens and pencils, and, if he attempted to cook a meal—granting he knew how—on your old stove, he would set it out of doors the next hour.   Now my advice to you is to buy a new one this very day! "

" Bless me! " she said, " that would make him furious; he would blow me sky-high."   " Well," I replied, " suppose he did go into a regular tantrum and use all the most startling expletives in the vocabulary for fifteen minutes!   What is that compared with a good stove 365 days in the year?   Just put all he could say on one side, and all the advantages you would enjoy on the other, and you must readily see that his wrath would kick the beam."   As my logic was irresistible, she said, " Well, if you will go with me, and help select a stove, I think I will take the responsibility."

Accordingly we went to the hardware store and selected the most approved, largest-sized stove, with all the best cooking utensils, best Russian pipe, etc. " Now," said she, " I am in equal need of a good stove in my sitting room, and I would like the pipes of both stoves to lead into dumb stoves above, and thus heat two or three rooms upstairs for my children to play in, as they have no place except the sitting room, where they must be always with me; but I suppose it is not best to do too much at one time."   " On the contrary," I replied, " as your husband is wealthy, you had better get all you really need now.   Mr. S. will probably be no more surprised with two stoves than with one, and, as you expect a hot scene over the matter, the more you get out of it the better."

So the stoves and pipes were ordered, holes cut through the ceiling, and all were in working order next day.   The cook was delighted over her splendid stove and shining tins, copper-bottomed tea kettle and boiler, and warm sleeping room upstairs; the children were delighted with their large playrooms, and madam jubilant with her added comforts and that newborn feeling of independence one has in assuming responsibility.

She was expecting Mr. S. home in the holidays, and occasionally weakened at the prospect of what she feared might be a disagreeable encounter. At such times she came to consult with me, as to what she would say and do when the crisis arrived. Having studied the *genus homo* alike on the divine heights of exaltation and in the valleys of humiliation, I was able to make some valuable suggestions.

" Now," said I, " when your husband explodes, as you think he will, neither say nor do anything; sit and gaze out of the window with that far-away, sad look women know so well how to affect. If you can summon tears at pleasure, a few would not be amiss; a gentle shower, not enough to make the nose and eyes red or to detract from your beauty. Men cannot resist beauty and tears. Never mar their effect with anything bordering on sobs and hysteria; such violent manifestations being neither refined nor artistic. A scene in which one person does the talking must be limited in time. No ordinary man can keep at white heat fifteen minutes; if his victim says nothing, he will soon exhaust himself. Remember every time you speak in the way of defense, you give him a new text on which to branch out again. If silence is ever golden, it is when a husband is in a tantrum."

In due time Mr. S. arrived, laden with Christmas presents, and Charlotte came over to tell me that she had passed through the ordeal. I will give the scene in her own words as nearly as possible. " My husband came yesterday, just before dinner, and, as I expected him, I had all things in order. He seemed very happy to see me and the children, and we had a gay time looking at our presents and chatting about Washington and all that had happened since we parted. It made me sad, in the midst of our happiness, to think how soon the current of his feelings would change, and I wished in my soul that I had not bought the stoves. But, at last, dinner was announced, and I knew that the hour had come. He ran upstairs to give a few touches to his toilet, when lo! the shining stoves and pipes caught his eyes. He explored the upper apartments and came down the back stairs, glanced at the kitchen stove, then into the dining room, and stood confounded, for a moment, before the nickel-plated 'Morning Glory.' Then he exclaimed, 'Heavens and earth! Charlotte, what have you been doing?' I remembered what you told me and said nothing, but looked steadily out of the window. I summoned no tears, however, for I felt more like laughing than crying; he looked so ridiculous flying round spasmodically, like popcorn on a hot griddle, and talking as if making a stump speech on the corruptions of the Democrats. The first time he paused to take breath I said, in my softest tones: 'William, dinner is waiting; I fear the soup will be cold.' Fortunately he was hungry, and that great central organ of life and happiness asserted its claims on his attention, and he took his seat at the table. I broke what might have been an awkward silence, chatting with the older children about their school lessons. Fortunately they were late, and did not know what had happened, so they talked to their father and gradually restored his equilibrium. We had a very good dinner, and I have not heard a word about the stoves since. I suppose we shall have another scene when the bill is presented."

A few years later, Horace Greeley came to Seneca Falls to lecture on temperance. As he stayed with us, we invited Mr. S., among others, to dinner. The chief topic at the table was the idiosyncrasies of women. Mr. Greeley told many amusing things about his wife, of her erratic movements and sudden decisions to do and dare what seemed most impracticable. Perhaps, on rising some morning, she would say: " I think I'll go to Europe by the next steamer, Horace. Will you get tickets to-day for me, the nurse, and children?" " Well," said Mr. S., " she must be something like our hostess. Every time her husband goes away she cuts a door or window. They have only ten doors to lock every night, now."

" Yes," I said, " and your own wife, too, Mrs. S., has the credit of some high-handed measures when you are in Washington." Then I told the whole story, amid peals of laughter, just as related above. The dinner table scene fairly convulsed the Congressman. The thought that he had made such a fool of himself in the eyes of Charlotte that she could not even summon a tear in her defense, particularly pleased him. When sufficiently recovered to speak, he said: " Well, I never could understand how it was that Charlotte suddenly emerged from her thraldom and manifested such rare executive ability. Now I see to whom I am indebted for the most comfortable part of my married life. I am a thousand times obliged to you; you did just right and so did she, and she has been a happier woman ever since. She now gets what she needs, and frets no more, to me, about ten thousand little things. How can a man know what implements are necessary for the work he never does? Of all agencies for upsetting the equanimity of family life, none can surpass an old, broken-down kitchen stove!"

In the winter of 1861, just after the election of Lincoln, the abolitionists decided to hold a series of conventions in the chief cities of the North. All their available speakers were pledged for active service. The Republican party, having absorbed the political abolitionists within its ranks by its declared hostility to the extension of slavery, had come into power with overwhelming majorities. Hence the Garrisonian abolitionists, opposed to all compromises, felt that this was the opportune moment to rouse the people to the necessity of holding that party to its declared principles, and pushing it, if possible, a step or two forward.

I was invited to accompany Miss Anthony and Beriah Green to a few points in Central New York. But we soon found, by the concerted action of Republicans all over the country, that anti-slavery conventions would not be tolerated. Thus Republicans and Democrats made common cause against the abolitionists. The John Brown raid, the year before, had intimidated Northern politicians as much as Southern slaveholders, and the general feeling was that the discussion of the question at the North should be altogether suppressed.

From Buffalo to Albany our experience was the same, varied only by the fertile resources of the actors and their surroundings. Thirty years of education had somewhat changed the character of Northern mobs. They no longer dragged men through the streets with ropes around their necks, nor broke up women's prayer meetings; they no longer threw eggs and brickbats at the apostles of reform, nor dipped them in barrels of tar and feathers, they simply crowded the halls, and, with laughing, groaning, clapping, and cheering, effectually interrupted the proceedings. Such was our experience during the two days we attempted to hold a convention in St. James' Hall, Buffalo. As we paid for the hall, the mob enjoyed themselves, at our expense, in more ways than one. Every session, at the appointed time, we took our places on the platform, making, at various intervals of silence, renewed efforts to speak. Not succeeding, we sat and conversed with each other and the many friends who crowded the platform and anterooms. Thus, among ourselves, we had a pleasant reception and a discussion of many phases of the question that brought us together. The mob not only vouchsafed to us the privilege of talking to our friends without interruption, but delegations of their own came behind the scenes, from time to time, to discuss with us the right of free speech and the constitutionality of slavery.

These Buffalo rowdies were headed by ex-Justice Hinson, aided by younger members of the Fillmore and Seymour families, and the chief of police and fifty subordinates, who were admitted to the hall free, for the express purpose of protecting our right of free speech, but who, in defiance of the mayor's orders, made not the slightest effort in our defense. At Lockport there was a feeble attempt in the same direction. At Albion neither hall, church, nor schoolhouse could be obtained, so we held small meetings in the dining room of the hotel. At Rochester, Corinthian Hall was packed long before the hour advertised. This was a delicately appreciative, jocose mob. At this point Aaron Powell joined us.   As he had just risen from a bed of sickness, looking pale and emaciated, he slowly mounted the platform.   The mob at once took in his look of exhaustion, and, as he seated himself, they gave an audible simultaneous sigh, as if to say, what a relief it is to be seated!   So completely did the tender manifestation reflect Mr. Powell's apparent condition that the whole audience burst into a roar of laughter.   Here, too, all attempts to speak were futile.   At Port Byron a generous sprinkling of cayenne pepper on the stove soon cut short all constitutional arguments and pæans to liberty.

And so it was all the way to Albany.   The whole State was aflame with the mob spirit, and from Boston and various points in other States the same news reached us.   As the legislature was in session, and we were advertised in Albany, a radical member sarcastically moved "That as Mrs. Stanton and Miss Anthony were about to move on Albany, the militia be ordered out for the protection of the city."   Happily, Albany could then boast of a Democratic mayor, a man of courage and conscience, who said the right of free speech should never be trodden under foot where he had the right to prevent it.   And grandly did that one determined man maintain order in his jurisdiction.   Through all the sessions of the convention Mayor Thatcher sat on the platform, his police stationed in different parts of the hall and outside the building, to disperse the crowd as fast as it collected.   If a man or boy hissed or made the slightest interruption, he was immediately ejected.   And not only did the mayor preserve order in the meetings, but, with a company of armed police, he escorted us, every time, to and from the Delevan House. The last night Gerrit Smith addressed the mob from the steps of the hotel, after which they gave him three cheers and dispersed in good order.

When proposing for the Mayor a vote of thanks, at the close of the convention, Mr. Smith expressed his fears that it had been a severe ordeal for him to listen to these prolonged anti-slavery discussions. He smiled, and said: " I have really been deeply interested and instructed. I rather congratulate myself that a convention of this character has, at last, come in the line of my business; otherwise I should have probably remained in ignorance of many important facts and opinions I now understand and appreciate."

While all this was going on publicly, an equally trying experience was progressing, day by day, behind the scenes. Miss Anthony had been instrumental in helping a much abused mother, with her child, to escape from a husband who had immured her in an insane asylum. The wife belonged to one of the first families of New York, her brother being a United States senator, and the husband, also, a man of position; a large circle of friends and acquaintances was interested in the result. Though she was incarcerated in an insane asylum for eighteen months, yet members of her own family again and again testified that she was not insane. Miss Anthony, knowing that she was not, and believing fully that the unhappy mother was the victim of a conspiracy, would not reveal her hiding place.

Knowing the confidence Miss Anthony felt in the wisdom of Mr. Garrison and Mr. Phillips, they were implored to use their influence with her to give up the fugitives. Letters and telegrams, persuasions, arguments, and warnings from Mr. Garrison, Mr. Phillips, and the Senator on the one side, and from Lydia Mott, Mrs. Elizabeth F. Ellet, and Abby Hopper Gibbons, on the other, poured in upon her, day after day; but Miss Anthony remained immovable, although she knew that she was defying and violating the law and might be arrested any moment on the platform. We had known so many aggravated cases of this kind that, in daily counsel, we resolved that this woman should not be recaptured if it were possible to prevent it. To us it looked as imperative a duty to shield a sane mother, who had been torn from a family of little children and doomed to the companionship of lunatics, and to aid her in fleeing to a place of safety, as to help a fugitive from slavery to Canada. In both cases an unjust law was violated; in both cases the supposed owners of the victims were defied; hence, in point of law and morals, the act was the same in both cases. The result proved the wisdom of Miss Anthony's decision, as all with whom Mrs. P. came in contact for years afterward, expressed the opinion that she was, and always had been, perfectly sane. Could the dark secrets of insane asylums be brought to light we should be shocked to know the great number of rebellious wives, sisters, and daughters who are thus sacrificed to false customs and barbarous laws made by men for women.

CHAPTER XIV.

THE widespread discussion we are having, just now, on the subject of marriage and divorce, reminds me of an equally exciting one in 1860. A very liberal bill, introduced into the Indiana legislature by Robert Dale Owen, and which passed by a large majority, roused much public thought on the question, and made that State free soil for unhappy wives and husbands. A similar bill was introduced into the legislature of New York by Mr. Ramsey, which was defeated by four votes, owing, mainly, to the intense opposition of Horace Greeley. He and Mr. Owen had a prolonged discussion, in the New York *Tribune*, in which Mr. Owen got decidedly the better of the argument.

There had been several aggravated cases of cruelty to wives among the Dutch aristocracy, so that strong influences in favor of the bill had been brought to bear on the legislature, but the *Tribune* thundered every morning in its editorial column its loudest peals, which reverberated through the State. So bitter was the opposition to divorce, for any cause, that but few dared to take part in the discussion. I was the only woman, for many years, who wrote and spoke on the question. Articles on divorce, by a number of women, recently published in the *North American Review*, are a sign of progress, showing that women dare speak out now more freely on the relations that most deeply concern them.

My feelings had been stirred to their depths very early in life by the sufferings of a dear friend of mine, at whose wedding I was one of the bridesmaids. In listening to the facts in her case, my mind was fully made up as to the wisdom of a liberal divorce law. We read Milton's essays on divorce, together, and were thoroughly convinced as to the right and duty not only of separation, but of absolute divorce. While the New York bill was pending, I was requested, by Lewis Benedict, one of the committee who had the bill in charge, to address the legislature. I gladly accepted, feeling that here was an opportunity not only to support my friend in the step she had taken, but to make the path clear for other unhappy wives who might desire to follow her example. I had no thought of the persecution I was drawing down on myself for thus attacking so venerable an institution. I was always courageous in saying what I saw to be true, for the simple reason that I never dreamed of opposition. What seemed to me to be right I thought must be equally plain to all other rational beings. Hence I had no dread of denunciation. I was only surprised when I encountered it, and no number of experiences have, as yet, taught me to fear public opinion. What I said on divorce thirty-seven years ago seems quite in line with what many say now. The trouble was not in what I said, but that I said it too soon, and before the people were ready to hear it. It may be, however, that I helped them to get ready; who knows?

As we were holding a woman suffrage convention in Albany, at the time appointed for the hearing, Ernestine L. Rose and Lucretia Mott briefly added their views on the question. Although Mrs. Mott had urged Mrs. Rose and myself to be as moderate as possible in our demands, she quite unconsciously made the most radical utterance of all, in saying that marriage was a question beyond the realm of legislation, that must be left to the parties themselves. We rallied Lucretia on her radicalism, and some of the journals criticised us severely; but the following letter shows that she had no thought of receding from her position:

"ROADSIDE, near Philadelphia,
"4th Mo., 30th, '61.

" MY DEAR LYDIA MOTT:

" I have wished, ever since parting with thee and our other dear friends in Albany, to send thee a line, and have only waited in the hope of contributing a little ' substantial aid ' toward your neat and valuable ' depository.' The twenty dollars inclosed is from our Female Anti-slavery Society.

" I see the annual meeting, in New York, is not to be held this spring. Sister Martha is here, and was expecting to attend both anniversaries. But we now think the woman's rights meeting had better not be attempted, and she has written Elizabeth C. Stanton to this effect.

" I was well satisfied with being at the Albany meeting. I have since met with the following, from a speech of Lord Brougham's, which pleased me, as being as radical as mine in your stately Hall of Representatives:

" ' Before women can have any justice by the laws of England, there must be a total reconstruction of the whole marriage system; for any attempt to amend it would prove useless. The great charter, in establishing the supremacy of law over prerogative, provides only for justice between man and man; for woman nothing is left but common law, accumulations and modifications of original Gothic and Roman heathenism, which no amount of filtration through ecclesiastical courts could change into Christian laws. They are declared unworthy a Christian people by great jurists; still they remain unchanged.'

" So Elizabeth Stanton will see that I have authority for going to the root of the evil.

" Thine,

" LUCRETIA MOTT."

Those of us who met in Albany talked the matter over in regard to a free discussion of the divorce question at the coming convention in New York. It was the opinion of those present that, as the laws on marriage and divorce were very unequal for man and woman, this was a legitimate subject for discussion on our platform; accordingly I presented a series of resolutions, at the annual convention, in New York city, to which I spoke for over an hour. I was followed by Antoinette L. Brown, who also presented a series of resolutions in opposition to mine. She was, in turn, answered by Ernestine L. Rose. Wendell Phillips then arose, and, in an impressive manner pronounced the whole discussion irrelevant to our platform, and moved that neither the speeches nor resolutions go on the records of the convention. As I greatly admired Wendell Phillips, and appreciated his good opinion, I was surprised and humiliated to find myself under the ban of his disapprobation. My face was scarlet, and I trembled with mingled feelings of doubt and fear—doubt as to the wisdom of my position and fear lest the convention should repudiate the whole discussion. My emotion was so apparent that Rev. Samuel Longfellow, a brother of the poet, who sat beside me, whispered in my ear, " Nevertheless you are right, and the convention will sustain you."

Mr. Phillips said that as marriage concerned man and woman alike, and the laws bore equally on them, women had no special ground for complaint, although, in my speech, I had quoted many laws to show the reverse. Mr. Garrison and Rev. Antoinette L. Brown were alike opposed to Mr. Phillips' motion, and claimed that marriage and divorce were legitimate subjects for discussion on our platform. Miss Anthony closed the debate. She said: " I hope Mr. Phillips will withdraw his motion that these resolutions shall not appear on the records of the convention. I am very sure that it would be contrary to all parliamentary usage to say that, when the speeches which enforced and advocated the resolutions are reported and published in the proceedings, the resolutions shall not be placed there. And as to the point that this question does not belong to this platform—from that I totally dissent. Marriage has ever been a one-sided matter, resting most unequally upon the sexes. By it man gains all; woman loses all; tyrant law and lust reign supreme with him; meek submission and ready obedience alone befit her. Woman has never been consulted; her wish has never been taken into consideration as regards the terms of the marriage compact. By law, public sentiment, and religion,—from the time of Moses down to the present day,—woman has never been thought of other than as a piece of property, to be disposed of at the will and pleasure of man. And at this very hour, by our statute books, by our (so-called) enlightened Christian civilization, she has no voice whatever in saying what shall be the basis of the relation. She must accept marriage as man proffers it, or not at all.

"And then, again, on Mr. Phillips' own ground, the discussion is perfectly in order, since nearly all the wrongs of which we complain grow out of the inequality of the marriage laws, that rob the wife of the right to herself and her children; that make her the slave of the man she marries. I hope, therefore, the resolutions will be allowed to go out to the public; that there may be a fair report of the ideas which have actually been presented here; that they may not be left to the mercy of the secular press. I trust the convention will not vote to forbid the publication of those resolutions with the proceedings."

Rev. William Hoisington (the blind preacher) followed Miss Anthony, and said: "Publish all that you have done here, and let the public know it."

The question was then put, on the motion of Mr. Phillips, and it was lost.

As Mr. Greeley, in commenting on the convention, took the same ground with Mr. Phillips, that the laws on marriage and divorce were equal for man and woman, I answered them in the following letter to the New York *Tribune.*

"*To the Editor of the New York Tribune:*

"SIR: At our recent National Woman's Rights Convention many were surprised to hear Wendell Phillips object to the question of marriage and divorce as irrelevant to our platform. He said: ' We had no right to discuss here any laws or customs but those where inequality existed for the sexes; that the laws on marriage and divorce rested equally on man and woman; that he suffers, as much as she possibly could, the wrongs and abuses of an ill-assorted marriage.'

" Now it must strike every careful thinker that an immense difference rests in the fact that man has made the laws cunningly and selfishly for his own purpose. From Coke down to Kent, who can cite one clause of the marriage contract where woman has the advantage? When man suffers from false legislation he has his remedy in his own hands. Shall woman be denied the right of protest against laws in which she had no voice; laws which outrage the holiest affections of her nature; laws which transcend the limits of human legislation, in a convention called for the express purpose of considering her wrongs? He might as well object to a protest against the injustice of hanging a woman, because capital punishment bears equally on man and woman.

"The contract of marriage is by no means equal. The law permits the girl to marry at twelve years of age, while it requires several years more of experience on the part of the boy. In entering this compact, the man gives up nothing that he before possessed, he is a man still; while the legal existence of the woman is suspended during marriage, and, henceforth, she is known but in and through the husband. She is nameless, purseless, childless—though a woman, an heiress, and a mother.

" Blackstone says: ' The husband and wife are one, and that one is the husband.' Chancellor Kent, in his

'Commentaries,' says: 'The legal effects of marriage are generally deducible from the principle of the common law, by which the husband and wife are regarded as one person, and her legal existence and authority lost or suspended during the continuance of the matrimonial union.'

" The wife is regarded by all legal authorities as a *feme covert*, placed wholly *sub potestate viri*. Her moral responsibility, even, is merged in her husband. The law takes it for granted that the wife lives in fear of her husband; that his command is her highest law; hence a wife is not punishable for the theft committed in the presence of her husband. An unmarried woman can make contracts, sue and be sued, enjoy the rights of property, to her inheritance—to her wages—to her person—to her children; but, in marriage, she is robbed by law of all and every natural and civil right. Kent further says: 'The disability of the wife to contract, so as to bind herself, arises not from want of discretion, but because she has entered into an indissoluble connection by which she is placed under the power and protection of her husband.' She is possessed of certain rights until she is married; then all are suspended, to revive, again, the moment the breath goes out of the husband's body. (See ' Cowen's Treatise,' vol. 2, p. 709.)

" If the contract be equal, whence come the terms ' marital power,' ' marital rights,' ' obedience and restraint,' ' dominion and control,' ' power and protection,' etc., etc.? Many cases are stated, showing the exercise of a most questionable power over the wife, sustained by the courts. (See ' Bishop on Divorce,' p. 489.)

" The laws on divorce are quite as unequal as those on

marriage; yea, far more so. The advantages seem to be all on one side and the penalties on the other. In case of divorce, if the husband be not the guilty party, the wife goes out of the partnership penniless. (Kent, vol. 2, p. 33; ' Bishop on Divorce,' p. 492.)

" In New York, and some other States, the wife of the guilty husband can now sue for a divorce in her own name, and ,the costs come out of the husband's estate; but, in the majority of the States, she is still compelled to sue in the name of another, as she has no means for paying costs, even though she may have brought her thousands into the partnership. ' The allowance to the innocent wife of *ad interim* alimony and money to sustain the suit, is not regarded as a strict right in her, but of sound discretion in the court.' (' Bishop on Divorce,' p. 581.)

" ' Many jurists,' says Kent, ' are of opinion that the adultery of the husband ought not to be noticed or made subject to the same animadversions as that of the wife, because it is not evidence of such entire depravity nor equally injurious in its effects upon the morals, good order, and happiness of the domestic life. Montesquieu, Pothier, and Dr. Taylor all insist that the cases of husband and wife ought to be distinguished, and that the violation of the marriage vow, on the part of the wife, is the most mischievous, and the prosecution ought to be confined to the offense on her part. (" Esprit des Lois," tom. 3, 186; " Traité du Contrat de Mariage," No. 516; " Elements of Civil Law," p. 254).'

" Say you, ' These are but the opinions of men '? On what else, I ask, are the hundreds of women depending, who, this hour, demand in our courts a release from burdensome contracts? Are not these delicate matters left wholly to the discretion of courts? Are not young women from the first families dragged into our courts, —into assemblies of men exclusively,—the judges all men, the jurors all men? No true woman there to shield them, by her presence, from gross and impertinent questionings, to pity their misfortunes, or to protest against their wrongs?

" The administration of justice depends far more on the opinions of eminent jurists than on law alone, for law is powerless when at variance with public sentiment.

" Do not the above citations clearly prove inequality? Are not the very letter and spirit of the marriage contract based on the idea of the supremacy of man as the keeper of woman's virtue—her sole protector and support? Out of marriage, woman asks nothing, at this hour, but the elective franchise. It is only in marriage that she must demand her right to person, children, property, wages, life, liberty, and the pursuit of happiness. How can we discuss all the laws and conditions of marriage, without perceiving its essential essence, end, and aim? Now, whether the institution of marriage be human or divine, whether regarded as indissoluble by ecclesiastical courts or dissoluble by civil courts, woman, finding herself equally degraded in each and every phase of it, always the victim of the institution, it is her right and her duty to sift the relation and the compact through and through, until she finds out the true cause of her false position. How can we go before the legislatures of our respective States and demand new laws, or no laws, on divorce, until we have some idea of what the true relation is?

" We decide the whole question of slavery by settling the sacred rights of the individual. We assert that man cannot hold property in man, and reject the whole code of laws that conflicts with the self-evident truth of the assertion.

"Again, I ask, is it possible to discuss all the laws of a relation, and not touch the relation itself?

"Yours respectfully,

"ELIZABETH CADY STANTON."

The discussion on the question of marriage and divorce occupied one entire session of the convention, and called down on us severe criticisms from the metropolitan and State press. So alarming were the comments on what had been said that I began to feel that I had inadvertently taken out the underpinning from the social system. Enemies were unsparing in their denunciations, and friends ridiculed the whole proceeding. I was constantly called on for a definition of marriage and asked to describe home life as it would be when men changed their wives every Christmas. Letters and newspapers poured in upon me, asking all manner of absurd questions, until I often wept with vexation. So many things, that I had neither thought nor said, were attributed to me that, at times, I really doubted my own identity.

However, in the progress of events the excitement died away, the earth seemed to turn on its axis as usual, women were given in marriage, children were born, fires burned as brightly as ever at the domestic altars, and family life, to all appearances, was as stable as usual.

Public attention was again roused to this subject by the McFarland-Richardson trial, in which the former shot the latter, being jealous of his attentions to his wife. McFarland was a brutal, improvident husband, who had completely alienated his wife's affections, while Mr. Richardson, who had long been a cherished acquaintance of the family, befriended the wife in the darkest days of her misery. She was a very refined, attractive woman, and a large circle of warm friends stood by her through the fierce ordeal of her husband's trial.

Though McFarland did not deny that he killed Richardson, yet he was acquitted on the plea of insanity, and was, at the same time, made the legal guardian of his child, a boy, then, twelve years of age, and walked out of the court with him, hand in hand. What a travesty on justice and common sense that, while a man is declared too insane to be held responsible for taking the life of another, he might still be capable of directing the life and education of a child! And what an insult to that intelligent mother, who had devoted twelve years of her life to his care, while his worthless father had not provided for them the necessaries of life!

She married Mr. Richardson on his deathbed. The ceremony was performed by Henry Ward Beecher and Rev. O. B. Frothingham, while such men as Horace Greeley and Joshua Leavitt witnessed the solemn service. Though no shadow had ever dimmed Mrs. Richardson's fair fame, yet she was rudely treated in the court and robbed of her child, though by far the most fitting parent to be intrusted with his care.

As the indignation among women was general and at white heat with regard to her treatment, Miss Anthony suggested to me, one day, that it would be a golden opportunity to give women a lesson on their helplessness under the law—wholly in the power of man as to their domestic relations, as well as to their civil and political rights. Accordingly we decided to hold some

meetings, for women alone, to protest against the decision of this trial, the general conduct of the case, the
tone of the press, and the laws that made it possible
to rob a mother of her child.

Many ladies readily enlisted in the movement. I was
invited to make the speech on the occasion, and Miss
Anthony arranged for two great meetings, one in
Apollo Hall, New York city, and one in the Academy of
Music, in Brooklyn. The result was all that we could
desire. Miss Anthony, with wonderful executive
ability, made all the arrangements, taking on her own
shoulders the whole financial responsibility.

My latest thought on this question I gave in *The
Arena* of April, 1894, from which I quote the following:

" There is a demand just now for an amendment to
the United States Constitution that shall make the laws
of marriage and divorce the same in all the States of
the Union. As the suggestion comes uniformly from
those who consider the present divorce laws too liberal,
we may infer that the proposed national law is to place
the whole question on a narrower basis, rendering null
and void the laws that have been passed in a broader
spirit, according to the needs and experiences, in certain
sections, of the sovereign people. And here let us bear
in mind that the widest possible law would not make divorce obligatory on anyone, while a restricted law, on
the contrary, would compel many, marrying, perhaps,
under more liberal laws, to remain in uncongenial
relations.

" As we are still in the experimental stage on this
question, we are not qualified to make a perfect law
that would work satisfactorily over so vast an area
as our boundaries now embrace. I see no evidence in

what has been published on this question, of late, by statesmen, ecclesiastics, lawyers, and judges, that any of them have thought sufficiently on the subject to prepare a well-digested code, or a comprehensive amendment to the national Constitution. Some view it as a civil contract, though not governed by the laws of other contracts; some view it as a religious ordinance—a sacrament; some think it a relation to be regulated by the State, others by the Church, and still others think it should be left wholly to the individual. With this wide divergence of opinion among our leading minds, it is quite evident that we are not prepared for a national law.

" Moreover, as woman is the most important factor in the marriage relation, her enfranchisement is the primal step in deciding the basis of family life. Before public opinion on this question crystallizes into an amendment to the national Constitution, the wife and mother must have a voice in the governing power and must be heard, on this great problem, in the halls of legislation.

" There are many advantages in leaving all these questions, as now, to the States. Local self-government more readily permits of experiments on mooted questions, which are the outcome of the needs and convictions of the community. The smaller the area over which legislation extends, the more pliable are the laws. By leaving the States free to experiment in their local affairs, we can judge of the working of different laws under varying circumstances, and thus learn their comparative merits. The progress education has achieved in America is due to the fact that we have left our system of public instruction in the hands of local authorities.   How different would be the solution of the great educational question of manual labor in the schools, if the matter had to be settled at Washington!

" The whole nation might find itself pledged to a scheme that a few years would prove wholly impracticable.   Not only is the town meeting, as Emerson says, ' the cradle of American liberties,' but it is the nursery of Yankee experiment and wisdom.   England, with its clumsy national code of education, making one inflexible standard of scholarship for the bright children of the manufacturing districts and the dull brains of the agricultural counties, should teach us a lesson as to the wisdom of keeping apart state and national government.

" Before we can decide the just grounds for divorce, we must get a clear idea of what constitutes marriage.   In a true relation the chief object is the loving companionship of man and woman, their capacity for mutual help and happiness and for the development of all that is noblest in each other.   The second object is the building up a home and family, a place of rest, peace, security, in which child-life can bud and blossom like flowers in the sunshine.

" The first step toward making the ideal the real, is to educate our sons and daughters into the most exalted ideas of the sacredness of married life and the responsibilities of parenthood.   I would have them give, at least, as much thought to the creation of an immortal being as the artist gives to his landscape or statue. Watch him in his hours of solitude, communing with great Nature for days and weeks in all her changing moods, and when at last his dream of beauty is realized and takes a clearly defined form, behold how patiently he works through long months and years on sky and lake, on tree and flower; and when complete, it represents to him more love and life, more hope and ambition, than the living child at his side, to whose conception and antenatal development not one soulful thought was ever given. To this impressible period of human life, few parents give any thought; yet here we must begin to cultivate virtues that can alone redeem the world.

" The contradictory views in which woman is represented are as pitiful as varied. While the Magnificat to the Virgin is chanted in all our cathedrals round the globe on each returning Sabbath day, and her motherhood extolled by her worshipers, maternity for the rest of womankind is referred to as a weakness, a disability, a curse, an evidence of woman's divinely ordained subjection. Yet surely the real woman should have some points of resemblance in character and position with the ideal one, whom poets, novelists, and artists portray.

" It is folly to talk of the sacredness of marriage and maternity, while the wife is practically regarded as an inferior, a subject, a slave. Having decided that companionship and conscientious parenthood are the only true grounds for marriage, if the relation brings out the worst characteristics of each party, or if the home atmosphere is unwholesome for children, is not the very *raison d'être* of the union wanting, and the marriage practically annulled? It cannot be called a holy relation,—no, not a desirable one,— when love and mutual respect are wanting. And let us bear in mind one other important fact: the lack of sympathy and content in the parents indicates radical physical unsuitability, which results in badly organized offspring. If, then, the real object of marriage is defeated, it is for the interest of the State, as well as the individual concerned, to see that all such pernicious unions be legally dissolved. Inasmuch, then, as incompatibility of temper defeats the two great objects of marriage, it should be the primal cause for divorce.

" The true standpoint from which to view this question is individual sovereignty, individual happiness. It is often said that the interests of society are paramount, and first to be considered. This was the Roman idea, the Pagan idea, that the individual was made for the State. The central idea of barbarism has ever been the family, the tribe, the nation—never the individual. But the great doctrine of Christianity is the right of individual conscience and judgment. The reason it took such a hold on the hearts of the people was because it taught that the individual was primary; the State, the Church, society, the family, secondary. However, a comprehensive view of any question of human interest, shows that the highest good and happiness of the individual and society lie in the same direction.

" The question of divorce, like marriage, should be settled, as to its most sacred relations, by the parties themselves; neither the State nor the Church having any right to intermeddle therein. As to property and children, it must be viewed and regulated as a civil contract. Then the union should be dissolved with at least as much deliberation and publicity as it was formed. There might be some ceremony and witnesses to add to the dignity and solemnity of the occasion. Like the Quaker marriage, which the parties conduct themselves, so, in this case, without any statement of their disagreements, the parties might simply declare that, after living together for several years, they found themselves unsuited to each other, and incapable of making a happy home.

" If divorce were made respectable, and recognized by society as a duty, as well as a right, reasonable men and women could arrange all the preliminaries, often, even, the division of property and guardianship of children, quite as satisfactorily as it could be done in the courts. Where the mother is capable of training the children, a sensible father would leave them to her care rather than place them in the hands of a stranger.

" But, where divorce is not respectable, men who have no paternal feeling will often hold the child, not so much for its good or his own affection, as to punish the wife for disgracing him. The love of children is not strong in most men, and they feel but little responsibility in regard to them. See how readily they turn off young sons to shift for themselves, and, unless the law compelled them to support their illegitimate children, they would never give them a second thought. But on the mother-soul rest forever the care and responsibility of human life. Her love for the child born out of wedlock is often intensified by the infinite pity she feels through its disgrace. Even among the lower animals we find the female ever brooding over the young and helpless.

" Limiting the causes of divorce to physical defects or delinquencies; making the proceedings public; prying into all the personal affairs of unhappy men and women; regarding the step as quasi criminal; punishing the guilty party in the suit; all this will not strengthen frail human nature, will not insure happy homes, will not banish scandals and purge society of prostitution.

"No, no; the enemy of marriage, of the State, of society is not liberal divorce laws, but the unhealthy atmosphere that exists in the home itself. A legislative act cannot make a unit of a divided family."

CHAPTER XV.

ON April 15, 1861, the President of the United States called out seventy-five thousand militia, and summoned Congress to meet July 4, when four hundred thousand men were called for, and four hundred millions of dollars were voted to suppress the Rebellion.

These startling events roused the entire people, and turned the current of their thoughts in new directions. While the nation's life hung in the balance, and the dread artillery of war drowned, alike, the voices of commerce, politics, religion, and reform, all hearts were filled with anxious forebodings, all hands were busy in solemn preparations for the awful tragedies to come.

At this eventful hour the patriotism of woman shone forth as fervently and spontaneously as did that of man; and her self-sacrifice and devotion were displayed in as many varied fields of action. While he buckled on his knapsack and marched forth to conquer the enemy, she planned the campaigns which brought the nation victory; fought in the ranks, when she could do so without detection; inspired the sanitary commission; gathered needed supplies for the grand army; provided nurses for the hospitals; comforted the sick; smoothed the pillows of the dying; inscribed the last messages of love to those far away; and marked the resting places where the brave men fell. The labor women accomplished, the hardships they endured, the time and strength they sacrificed in the War that summoned three million men to arms, can never be fully appreciated.

Indeed, we may safely say that there is scarcely a loyal woman in the North who did not do something in aid of the cause; who did not contribute time, labor, and money to the comfort of our soldiers and the success of our arms. The story of the War will never be fully written if the achievements of women are left untold. They do not figure in the official reports; they are not gazetted for gallant deeds; the names of thousands are unknown beyond the neighborhood where they lived, or the hospitals where they loved to labor; yet there is no feature in our War more creditable to us as a nation, none from its positive newness so well worthy of record.

While the mass of women never philosophize on the principles that underlie national existence, there were those in our late War who understood the political significance of the struggle; the " irrepressible conflict " between freedom and slavery, between National and State rights. They saw that to provide lint, bandages, and supplies for the army, while the War was not conducted on a wise policy, was to labor in vain; and while many organizations, active, vigilant, and self-sacrificing, were multiplied to look after the material wants of the army, these few formed themselves into a National Loyal League, to teach sound principles of government and to impress on the nation's conscience that freedom for the slaves was the only way to victory. Accustomed, as most women had been to works of charity and to the relief of outward suffering, it was difficult to rouse their enthusiasm for an idea, to persuade them to labor for a principle. They clamored for practical work, something for their hands to do; for fairs and sewing societies to raise money for soldier's families, for tableaux, readings, theatricals—anything but conventions to discuss principles and to circulate petitions for emancipation. They could not see that the best service they could render the army was to suppress the Rebellion, and that the most effective way to accomplish that was to transform the slaves into soldiers. This Woman's Loyal League voiced the solemn lessons of the War: Liberty to all; national protection for every citizen under our flag; universal suffrage, and universal amnesty.

After consultation with Horace Greeley, William Lloyd Garrison, Governor Andrews, and Robert Dale Owen, Miss Anthony and I decided to call a meeting of women in Cooper Institute and form a Woman's Loyal League, to advocate the immediate emancipation and enfranchisement of the Southern slaves, as the most speedy way of ending the War, so we issued, in tract form, and extensively circulated the following call:

" In this crisis of our country's destiny, it is the duty of every citizen to consider the peculiar blessings of a republican form of government, and decide what sacrifices of wealth and life are demanded for its defense and preservation. The policy of the War, our whole future life, depend on a clearly defined idea of the end proposed and the immense advantages to be secured to ourselves and all mankind by its accomplishment. No mere party or sectional cry, no technicalities of constitutional or military law, no mottoes of craft or policy are big enough to touch the great heart of a nation in the midst of revolution. A grand idea—such as freedom or justice—is needful to kindle and sustain the fires of a high enthusiasm.

"At this hour, the best word and work of every man and woman are imperatively demanded. To man, by common consent, are assigned the forum, camp, and field. What is woman's legitimate work and how she may best accomplish it, is worthy our earnest counsel one with another. We have heard many complaints of the lack of enthusiasm among Northern women; but when a mother lays her son on the altar of her country, she asks an object equal to the sacrifice. In nursing the sick and wounded, knitting socks, scraping lint, and making jellies the bravest and best may weary if the thoughts mount not in faith to something beyond and above it all. Work is worship only when a noble purpose fills the soul. Woman is equally interested and responsible with man in the final settlement of this problem of self-government; therefore let none stand idle spectators now. When every hour is big with destiny, and each delay but complicates our difficulties, it is high time for the daughters of the Revolution, in solemn council, to unseal the last will and testaments of the fathers, lay hold of their birthright of freedom, and keep it a sacred trust for all coming generations.

"To this end we ask the Loyal Women of the Nation to meet in the Church of the Puritans (Dr. Cheever's), New York, on Thursday, the 14th of May next.

"Let the women of every State be largely represented in person or by letter.

"On behalf of the Woman's Central Committee,
"Elizabeth Cady Stanton,
"Susan B. Anthony."

Among other resolutions adopted at the meeting were the following:

" *Resolved,* There never can be a true peace in this Republic until the civil and political rights of all citizens of African descent and all women are practically established.

" *Resolved,* That the women of the Revolution were not wanting in heroism and self-sacrifice, and we, their daughters, are ready, in this War, to pledge our time, our means, our talents, and our lives, if need be, to secure the final and complete consecration of America to freedom."

It was agreed that the practical work to be done to secure freedom for the slaves was to circulate petitions through all the Northern States. For months these petitions were circulated diligently everywhere, as the signatures show—some signed on fence posts, plows, the anvil, the shoemaker's bench—by women of fashion and those in the industries, alike in the parlor and the kitchen; by statesmen, professors in colleges, editors, bishops; by sailors, and soldiers, and the hard-handed children of toil, building railroads and bridges, and digging canals, and in mines in the bowels of the earth. Petitions, signed by three hundred thousand persons, can now be seen in the national archives in the Capitol at Washington. Three of my sons spent weeks in our office in Cooper Institute, rolling up the petitions from each State separately, and inscribing on the outside the number of names of men and women contained therein. We sent appeals to the President the House of Representatives, and the Senate, from time to time, urging emancipation and the passage of the proposed Thirteenth, Fourteenth, and Fifteenth Amendments to the National Constitution. During these eventful months we received many letters from Senator Sumner, saying, " Send on the petitions as fast as received; they give me opportunities for speech."

Robert Dale Owen, chairman of the Freedman's Commission, was most enthusiastic in the work of the Loyal League, and came to our rooms frequently to suggest new modes of agitation and to give us an inkling of what was going on behind the scenes in Washington. Those who had been specially engaged in the Woman Suffrage movement suspended their conventions during the war, and gave their time and thought wholly to the vital issues of the hour. Seeing the political significance of the war, they urged the emancipation of the slaves as the sure, quick way of cutting the Gordian knot of the Rebellion. To this end they organized a national league, and rolled up a mammoth petition, urging Congress so to amend the Constitution as to prohibit the existence of slavery in the United States. From their headquarters in Cooper Institute, New York city, they sent out the appeals to the President, Congress, and the people at large; tracts and forms of petition, franked by members of Congress, were scattered like snowflakes from Maine to Texas. Meetings were held every week, in which the policy of the Government was freely discussed, and approved or condemned.

That this League did a timely educational work is manifested by the letters received from generals, statesmen, editors, and from women in most of the Northern States, fully indorsing its action and principles. The clearness to thinking women of the cause of the War;

the true policy in waging it; their steadfastness in maintaining the principles of freedom, are worthy of consideration. With this League abolitionists and Republicans heartily co-operated. A course of lectures was delivered for its benefit in Cooper Institute, by such men as Horace Greeley, George William Curtis, William D. Kelly, Wendell Phillips, E. P. Whipple, Frederick Douglass, Theodore D. Weld, Rev. Dr. Tyng, and Dr. Bellows. Many letters are on its files from Charles Sumner, approving its measures, and expressing great satisfaction at the large number of emancipation petitions being rolled into Congress. The Republican press, too, was highly complimentary. The New York *Tribune* said: " The women of the Loyal League have shown great practical wisdom in restricting their efforts to one subject, the most important which any society can aim at in this hour, and great courage in undertaking to do what never has been done in the world before, to obtain one million of names to a petition."

The leading journals vied with each other in praising the patience and prudence, the executive ability, the loyalty, and the patriotism of the women of the League, and yet these were the same women who, when demanding civil and political rights, privileges, and immunities for themselves, had been uniformly denounced as " unwise," " imprudent," " fanatical," and " impracticable." During the six years they held their own claims in abeyance to those of the slaves of the South, and labored to inspire the people with enthusiasm for the great measures of the Republican party, they were highly honored as "wise, loyal, and clear-sighted." But when the slaves were emancipated, and these women asked that they should be recognized in the reconstruction as citizens of the Republic, equal before the law, all these transcendent virtues vanished like dew before the morning sun. And thus it ever is: so long as woman labors to second man's endeavors and exalt his sex above her own, her virtues pass unquestioned; but when she dares to demand rights and privileges for herself, her motives, manners, dress, personal appearance, and character are subjects for ridicule and detraction.

Liberty, victorious over slavery on the battlefield, had now more powerful enemies to encounter at Washington. The slaves set free, the master conquered, the South desolate; the two races standing face to face, sharing alike the sad results of war, turned with appealing looks to the general government, as if to say, "How stand we now?" "What next?" Questions our statesmen, beset with dangers, with fears for the nation's life, of party divisions, of personal defeat, were wholly unprepared to answer. The reconstruction of the South involved the reconsideration of the fundamental principles of our Government and the natural rights of man. The nation's heart was thrilled with prolonged debates in Congress and State legislatures, in the pulpits and public journals, and at every fireside on these vital questions, which took final shape in the three historic amendments to the Constitution.

The first point, his emancipation, settled, the political status of the negro was next in order; and to this end various propositions were submitted to Congress. But to demand his enfranchisement on the broad principle of natural rights was hedged about with difficulties, as the logical result of such action must be the enfranchisement of all ostracized classes; not only the white

women of the entire country, but the slave women of
the South. Though our senators and representatives
had an honest aversion to any proscriptive legislation
against loyal women, in view of their varied and self-
sacrificing work during the War, yet the only way they
could open the constitutional door just wide enough to
let the black man pass in was to introduce the word
" male " into the national Constitution. After the
generous devotion of such women as Anna Carroll and
Anna Dickinson in sustaining the policy of the Republicans, both in peace and war, they felt it would come
with a bad grace from that party to place new barriers
in woman's path to freedom. But how could the
amendment be written without the word " male," was
the question.

Robert Dale Owen being at Washington, and behind
the scenes at the time, sent copies of the various bills
to the officers of the Loyal League, in New York, and
related to us some of the amusing discussions. One of
the committee proposed " persons " instead of " males."
" That will never do," said another, " it would enfranchise wenches." " Suffrage for black men will be all
the strain the Republican party can stand," said another. Charles Sumner said, years afterward, that he
wrote over nineteen pages of foolscap to get rid of the
word " male " and yet keep " negro suffrage " as a
party measure intact; but it could not be done.

Miss Anthony and I were the first to see the full significance of the word " male " in the Fourteenth
Amendment, and we at once sounded the alarm, and
sent out petitions for a constitutional amendment to
" prohibit the States from disfranchising any of their
citizens on the ground of sex." Miss Anthony, who

had spent the year in Kansas, started for New York the moment she saw the proposition before Congress to put the word " male" into the national Constitution, and made haste to rouse the women in the East to the fact that the time had come to begin vigorous work again for woman's enfranchisement.

Leaving Rochester, October 11, she called on Martha Wright at Auburn; Phebe Jones and Lydia Mott at Albany; Mmes. Rose, Gibbons, Davis, at New York city; Lucy Stone and Antoinette Brown Blackwell in New Jersey; Stephen and Abby Foster at Worcester; Mmes. Severance, Dall, Nowell, Dr. Harriet K. Hunt, Dr. M. E. Zackesewska, and Messrs. Phillips and Garrison in Boston, urging them to join in sending protests to Washington against the pending legislation. Mr. Phillips at once consented to devote five hundred dollars from the " Jackson Fund " to commence the work. Miss Anthony and I spent all our Christmas holidays in writing letters and addressing appeals and petitions to every part of the country, and, before the close of the session of 1865-66, petitions with ten thousand signatures were poured into Congress.

One of my letters was as follows:

" *To the Editor of the Standard:*

"SIR: Mr. Broomall of Pennsylvania, Mr. Schenck of Ohio, Mr. Jenckes of Rhode Island, and Mr. Stevens of Pennsylvania, have each a resolution before Congress to amend the Constitution.

"Article First, Section Second, reads thus: 'Representatives and direct taxes shall be apportioned among the several States which may be included within this Union, according to their respective numbers.'

"Mr. Broomall proposes to amend by saying, 'male electors'; Mr. Schenck, 'male citizens'; Mr. Jenckes, 'male citizens'; Mr. Stevens, 'male voters,' as, in process of time, women may be made 'legal voters' in the several States, and would then meet that requirement of the Constitution. But those urged by the other gentlemen, neither time, effort, nor State Constitutions could enable us to meet, unless, by a liberal interpretation of the amendment, a coat of mail to be worn at the polls might be judged all-sufficient. Mr. Jenckes and Mr. Schenck, in their bills, have the grace not to say a word about taxes, remembering, perhaps, that 'taxation without representation is tyranny.' But Mr. Broomall, though unwilling that we should share in the honors of government, would fain secure us a place in its burdens; for, while he apportions representatives to "male electors" only, he admits "all the inhabitants" into the rights, privileges, and immunities of taxation. Magnanimous M. C.!

"I would call the attention of the women of the nation to the fact that, under the Federal Constitution, as it now exists, there is not one word that limits the right of suffrage to any privileged class. This attempt to turn the wheels of civilization backward, on the part of Republicans claiming to be the liberal party, should rouse every woman in the nation to a prompt exercise of the only right she has in the Government, the right of petition. To this end a committee in New York have sent out thousands of petitions, which should be circulated in every district and sent to its representative at Washington as soon as possible.

"ELIZABETH CADY STANTON.
"NEW YORK, January 2, 1866."

CHAPTER XVI.

IN 1867 the proposition to extend the suffrage to
women and to colored men was submitted to the people
of the State of Kansas, and, among other Eastern
speakers, I was invited to make a campaign through
the State. As the fall elections were pending, there
was great excitement everywhere. Suffrage for colored
men was a Republican measure, which the press and
politicians of that party advocated with enthusiasm.

As woman suffrage was not a party question, we
hoped that all parties would favor the measure; that we
might, at last, have one green spot on earth where
women could enjoy full liberty as citizens of the United
States. Accordingly, in July, Miss Anthony and I
started, with high hopes of a most successful trip, and,
after an uneventful journey of one thousand five hundred miles, we reached the sacred soil where John
Brown and his sons had helped to fight the battles that
made Kansas a free State.

Lucy Stone, Mr. Blackwell, and Olympia Brown had
preceded us and opened the campaign with large meetings in all the chief cities. Miss Anthony and I did the
same. Then it was decided that, as we were to go to
the very borders of the State, where there were no
railroads, we must take carriages, and economize our
forces by taking different routes. I was escorted by

ex-Governor Charles Robinson. We had a low, easy carriage, drawn by two mules, in which we stored about a bushel of tracts, two valises, a pail for watering the mules, a basket of apples, crackers, and other such refreshments as we could purchase on the way. Some things were suspended underneath the carriage, some packed on behind, and some under the seat and at our feet. It required great skill to compress the necessary baggage into the allotted space. As we went to the very verge of civilization, wherever two dozen voters could be assembled, we had a taste of pioneer life. We spoke in log cabins, in depots, unfinished schoolhouses, churches, hotels, barns, and in the open air.

I spoke in a large mill one night. A solitary tallow candle shone over my head like a halo of glory; a few lanterns around the outskirts of the audience made the darkness perceptible; but all I could see of my audience was the whites of their eyes in the dim distance. People came from twenty miles around to these meetings, held either in the morning, afternoon, or evening, as was most convenient.

As the regular State election was to take place in the coming November, the interest increased from week to week, until the excitement of the people knew no bounds. There were speakers for and against every proposition before the people. This involved frequent debates on all the general principles of government, and thus a great educational work was accomplished, which is one of the advantages of our frequent elections.

The friends of woman suffrage were doomed to disappointment. Those in the East, on whom they relied for influence through the liberal newspapers, were silent, and we learned, afterward, that they used what influence they had to keep the abolitionists and Republicans of the State silent, as they feared the discussion of the woman question would jeopardize the enfranchisement of the black man. However, we worked untiringly and hopefully, not seeing through the game of the politicians until nearly the end of the canvass, when we saw that our only chance was in getting the Democratic vote. Accordingly, George Francis Train, then a most effective and popular speaker, was invited into the State to see what could be done to win the Democracy. He soon turned the tide, strengthened the weak-kneed Republicans and abolitionists, and secured a large Democratic vote.

For three months we labored diligently, day after day, enduring all manner of discomforts in traveling, eating, and sleeping. As there were no roads or guide-posts, we often lost our way. In going through cañons and fording streams it was often so dark that the Governor was obliged to walk ahead to find the way, taking off his coat so that I could see his white shirt and slowly drive after him. Though seemingly calm and cool, I had a great dread of these night adventures, as I was in constant fear of being upset on some hill and rolled into the water. The Governor often complimented me on my courage, when I was fully aware of being tempest-tossed with anxiety. I am naturally very timid, but, being silent under strong emotions of either pleasure or pain, I am credited with being courageous in the hour of danger.

For days, sometimes, we could find nothing at a public table that we could eat. Then passing through a little settlement we could buy dried herring, crackers, gum arabic, and slippery elm; the latter, we were told, was very nutritious. We frequently sat down to a table with bacon floating in grease, coffee without milk, sweetened with sorghum, and bread or hot biscuit, green with soda, while vegetables and fruit were seldom seen. Our nights were miserable, owing to the general opinion among pioneers that a certain species of insect must necessarily perambulate the beds in a young civilization. One night, after traveling over prairies all day, eating nothing but what our larder provided, we saw a light in a cottage in the distance which seemed to beckon to us. Arriving, we asked the usual question,—if we could get a night's lodging,—to which the response was inevitably a hearty, hospitable " Yes." One survey of the premises showed me what to look for in the way of midnight companionship, so I said to the Governor, " I will resign in your favor the comforts provided for me to-night, and sleep in the carriage, as you do so often." I persisted against all the earnest persuasions of our host, and in due time I was ensconced for the night, and all about the house was silent.

I had just fallen into a gentle slumber, when a chorus of pronounced grunts and a spasmodic shaking of the carriage revealed to me the fact that I was surrounded by those long-nosed black pigs, so celebrated for their courage and pertinacity. They had discovered that the iron steps of the carriage made most satisfactory scratching posts, and each one was struggling for his turn. This scratching suggested fleas. Alas! thought I, before morning I shall be devoured. I was mortally tired and sleepy, but I reached for the whip and plied it lazily from side to side; but I soon found nothing but a constant and most vigorous application of the whip could hold them at bay one moment. I had heard that this type of pig was very combative when thwarted in its desires, and they seemed in such sore need of relief that I thought there was danger of their jumping into the carriage and attacking me. This thought was more terrifying than that of the fleas, so I decided to go to sleep and let them alone to scratch at their pleasure. I had a sad night of it, and never tried the carriage again, though I had many equally miserable experiences within four walls.

After one of these border meetings we stopped another night with a family of two bachelor brothers and two spinster sisters. The home consisted of one large room, not yet lathed and plastered. The furniture included a cooking stove, two double beds in remote corners, a table, a bureau, a washstand, and six wooden chairs. As it was late, there was no fire in the stove and no suggestion of supper, so the Governor and I ate apples and chewed slippery elm before retiring to dream of comfortable beds and well-spread tables in the near future.

The brothers resigned their bed to me just as it was. I had noticed that there was no ceremonious changing of bed linen under such circumstances, so I had learned to nip all fastidious notions of individual cleanliness in the bud, and to accept the inevitable. When the time arrived for retiring, the Governor and the brothers went out to make astronomical observations or smoke, as the case might be, while the sisters and I made our evening toilet, and disposed ourselves in the allotted corners. That done, the stalwart sons of Adam made their beds with skins and blankets on the floor. When all was still and darkness reigned, I reviewed the situation with a heavy heart, seeing that I was bound to remain a prisoner in the corner all night, come what might. I had just congratulated myself on my power of adaptability to circumstances, when I suddenly started with an emphatic " What is that? " A voice from the corner asked, " Is your bed comfortable? " " Oh, yes," I replied, " but I thought I felt a mouse run over my head." " Well," said the voice from the corner, " I should not wonder. I have heard such squeaking from that corner during the past week that I told sister there must be a mouse nest in that bed." A confession she probably would not have made unless half asleep. This announcement was greeted with suppressed laughter from the floor. But it was no laughing matter to me. Alas! what a prospect—to have mice running over one all night. But there was no escape. The sisters did not offer to make any explorations, and, in my fatigue costume, I could not light a candle and make any on my own account. The house did not afford an armchair in which I could sit up. I could not lie on the floor, and the other bed was occupied. Fortunately, I was very tired and soon fell asleep. What the mice did the remainder of the night I never knew, so deep were my slumbers. But, as my features were intact, and my facial expression as benign as usual next morning, I inferred that their gambols had been most innocently and decorously conducted. These are samples of many similar experiences which we encountered during the three months of those eventful travels.

Heretofore my idea had been that pioneer life was a period of romantic freedom. When the long, white-covered wagons, bound for the far West, passed by, I thought of the novelty of a six-months' journey through the bright spring and summer days in a house on wheels, meals under shady trees and beside babbling brooks, sleeping in the open air, and finding a home, at last, where land was cheap, the soil rich and deep, and where the grains, vegetables, fruit, and flowers grew bountifully with but little toil. But a few months of pioneer life permanently darkened my rosy ideal of the white-covered wagon, the charming picnics by the way, and the paradise at last. I found many of these adventurers in unfinished houses and racked with malaria; in one case I saw a family of eight, all ill with chills and fever. The house was half a mile from the spring water on which they depended and from which those best able, from day to day, carried the needed elixir to others suffering with the usual thirst. Their narrations of all the trials of the long journey were indeed heartrending.

In one case a family of twelve left their comfortable farm in Illinois, much against the earnest protests of the mother; she having ten children, the youngest a baby then in her arms. All their earthly possessions were stored in three wagons, and the farm which the mother owned was sold before they commenced their long and perilous journey. There was no reason for going except that the husband had the Western fever. They were doing well in Illinois, on a large farm within two miles of a village, but he had visions of a bonanza near the setting sun. Accordingly they started. At the end of one month the baby died. A piece of wood from the cradle was all they had to mark its lonely resting place. With sad hearts they went on, and, in a few weeks, with grief for

her child, her old home, her kindred and friends, the
mother also died.   She, too, was left alone on the far-
off prairies, and the sad pageant moved on.   Another
child soon shared the same fate, and then a span of
horses died, and one wagon, with all the things they
could most easily spare, was abandoned.   Arrived at
their destination none of the golden dreams was realized.   The expensive journey, the struggles in starting
under new circumstances, and the loss of the mother's
thrift and management, made the father so discouraged
and reckless that much of his property was wasted, and
his earthly career was soon ended.   Through the heroic
energy and good management of the eldest daughter,
the little patrimony, in time, was doubled, and the children well brought up and educated in the rudiments of
learning, so that all became respectable members of
society.   Her advice to all young people is, if you are
comfortably established in the East, stay there.   There
is no royal road to wealth and ease, even in the Western
States!

In spite of the discomforts we suffered in the Kansas
campaign, I was glad of the experience.   It gave me
added self-respect to know that I could endure such
hardships and fatigue with a great degree of cheerfulness.   The Governor and I often laughed heartily, as we
patiently chewed our gum arabic and slippery elm, to
think on what a gentle stimulus we were accomplishing
such wonderful feats as orators and travelers.   It was
fortunate our intense enthusiasm for the subject gave
us all the necessary inspiration, as the supplies we
gathered by the way were by no means sufficiently in-
vigorating for prolonged propagandism.

I enjoyed these daily drives over the vast prairies, listening to the Governor's descriptions of the early days when the " bushwhackers and jayhawkers " made their raids on the inhabitants of the young free State. The courage and endurance of the women, surrounded by dangers and discomforts, surpassed all description. I count it a great privilege to have made the acquaintance of so many noble women and men who had passed through such scenes and conquered such difficulties. They seemed to live in an atmosphere altogether beyond their surroundings. Many educated families from New England, disappointed in not finding the much talked of bonanzas, were living in log cabins, in solitary places, miles from any neighbors. But I found Emerson, Parker, Holmes, Hawthorne, Whittier, and Lowell on their bookshelves to gladden their leisure hours.

Miss Anthony and I often comforted ourselves mid adverse winds with memories of the short time we spent under Mother Bickerdyke's hospitable roof at Salina. There we had clean, comfortable beds, delicious viands, and everything was exquisitely neat. She entertained us with her reminiscences of the War. With great self-denial she had served her country in camp and hospital, and was with Sherman's army in that wonderful march to the sea, and here we found her on the outpost of civilization, determined to start what Kansas most needed—a good hotel. But alas! it was too good for that latitude and proved a financial failure. It was, to us, an oasis in the desert, where we would gladly have lingered if the opposition would have come to us for conversion. But, as we had to carry the gospel of woman's equality into the highways and hedges, we left dear Mother Bickerdyke with profound regret. The seed sown in Kansas in 1867 is now bearing its

legitimate fruits.   There was not a county in the State
where meetings were not held or tracts scattered with
a generous hand.   If the friends of our cause in the East
had been true and had done for woman what they did
for the colored man, I believe both propositions would
have been carried; but with a narrow policy, playing off
one against the other, both were defeated.   A policy
of injustice always bears its own legitimate fruit in
failure.

However, women learned one important lesson—
namely, that it is impossible for the best of men
to understand women's feelings or the humiliation
of their position.   When they asked us to be silent
on our question during the War, and labor for the
emancipation of the slave, we did so, and gave
five years to his emancipation and enfranchisement.
To this proposition my friend, Susan B. Anthony,
never consented, but was compelled to yield because no one stood with her.   I was convinced, at
the time, that it was the true policy.   I am now equally
sure that it was a blunder, and, ever since, I have
taken my beloved Susan's judgment against the world.
I have always found that, when we see eye to eye, we
are sure to be right, and when we pull together we are
strong.   After we discuss any point together and fully
agree, our faith in our united judgment is immovable
and no amount of ridicule and opposition has the
slightest influence, come from what quarter it may.

Together we withstood the Republicans and abolitionists, when, a second time, they made us the most
solemn promises of earnest labor for our enfranchisement, when the slaves were safe beyond a peradventure.
They never redeemed their promise made during the

War, hence, when they urged us to silence in the Kansas campaign, we would not for a moment entertain the proposition. The women generally awoke to their duty to themselves. They had been deceived once and could not be again. If the leaders in the Republican and abolition camps could deceive us, whom could we trust?

Again we were urged to be silent on our rights, when the proposition to take the word "white" out of the New York Constitution was submitted to a vote of the people of the State, or, rather, to one-half the people, as women had no voice in the matter. Again we said "No, no, gentlemen! if the 'white' comes out of the Constitution, let the 'male' come out also. Women have stood with the negro, thus far, on equal ground as ostracized classes, outside the political paradise; and now, when the door is open, it is but fair that we both should enter and enjoy all the fruits of citizenship. Heretofore ranked with idiots, lunatics, and criminals in the Constitution, the negro has been the only respectable compeer we had; so pray do not separate us now for another twenty years, ere the constitutional door will again be opened."

We were persistently urged to give all our efforts to get the word "white" out, and thus secure the enfranchisement of the colored man, as that, they said, would prepare the way for us to follow. Several editors threatened that, unless we did so, their papers should henceforth do their best to defeat every measure we proposed. But we were deaf alike to persuasions and threats, thinking it wiser to labor for women, constituting, as they did, half the people of the State, rather than for a small number of colored men; who, viewing all things from the same standpoint as white men, would be an added power against us.

The question settled in Kansas, we returned, with George Francis Train, to New York. He offered to pay all the expenses of the journey and meetings in all the chief cities on the way, and see that we were fully and well reported in their respective journals. After prolonged consultation Miss Anthony and I thought best to accept the offer and we did so. Most of our friends thought it a grave blunder, but the result proved otherwise. Mr. Train was then in his prime—a large, fine-looking man, a gentleman in dress and manner, neither smoking, chewing, drinking, nor gormandizing. He was an effective speaker and actor, as one of his speeches, which he illustrated, imitating the poor wife at the washtub and the drunken husband reeling in, fully showed. He gave his audience charcoal sketches of everyday life rather than argument. He always pleased popular audiences, and even the most fastidious were amused with his caricatures. As the newspapers gave several columns to our meetings at every point through all the States, the agitation was widespread and of great value. To be sure our friends, on all sides, fell off, and those especially who wished us to be silent on the question of woman's rights, declared " the cause too sacred to be advocated by such a charlatan as George Francis Train." We thought otherwise, as the accession of Mr. Train increased the agitation twofold. If these fastidious ladies and gentlemen had come out to Kansas and occupied the ground and provided " the sinews of war," there would have been no field for Mr. Train's labors, and we should have accepted their services. But, as the ground was unoccupied, he

had, at least, the right of a reform " squatter " to cultivate the cardinal virtues and reap a moral harvest
wherever he could.

Reaching New York, Mr. Train made it possible for
us to establish a newspaper, which gave another impe-
tus to our movement. The *Revolution,* published by
Susan B. Anthony and edited by Parker Pillsbury and
myself, lived two years and a half and was then con-
solidated with the New York *Christian Enquirer,* edited
by the Rev. Henry Bellows, D. D. I regard the brief
period in which I edited the *Revolution* as one of the
happiest of my life, and I may add the most useful. In
looking over the editorials I find but one that I sincerely
regret, and that was a retort on Mr. Garrison, written
under great provocation, but not by me, which circumstances, at the time, forbade me to disown. Considering the pressure brought to bear on Miss Anthony
and myself, I feel now that our patience and forbear-
ance with our enemies in their malignant attacks on our
good name, which we never answered, were indeed
marvelous.

We said at all times and on all other subjects just
what we thought, and advertised nothing that we did
not believe in. No advertisements of quack remedies
appeared in our columns. One of our clerks once published a bread powder advertisement, which I did not
see until the paper appeared; so, in the next number,
I said, editorially, what I thought of it. I was alone in
the office, one day, when a man blustered in. " Who,"
said he, " runs this concern? " " You will find the
names of the editors and publishers," I replied, " on
the editorial page." " Are you one of them? " " I am,"
I replied. " Well, do you know that I agreed to pay

twenty dollars to have that bread powder advertised for one month, and then you condemn it editorially?" "I have nothing to do with the advertising; Miss Anthony pays me to say what I think." "Have you any more thoughts to publish on that bread powder?" "Oh, yes," I replied, "I have not exhausted the subject yet." "Then," said he, "I will have the advertisement taken out. What is there to pay for the one insertion?" "Oh, nothing," I replied, "as the editorial probably did you more injury than the advertisement did you good." On leaving, with prophetic vision, he said, "I prophesy a short life for this paper; the business world is based on quackery, and you cannot live without it." With melancholy certainty, I replied, "I fear you are right."

CHAPTER XVII.

LYCEUMS AND LECTURERS.

THE Lyceum Bureau was, at one time, a great feature in American life. The three leading bureaus were in Boston, New York, and Chicago. The managers, map in hand, would lay out trips, more or less extensive according to the capacity or will of the speakers, and then, with a dozen or more victims in hand, make arrangements with the committees in various towns and cities to set them all in motion. As the managers of the bureaus had ten per cent. of what the speakers made, it was to their interest to keep the time well filled. Hence the engagements were made without the slightest reference to the comfort of the travelers. With our immense distances, it was often necessary to travel night and day, sometimes changing cars at midnight, and perhaps arriving at the destination half an hour or less before going on the platform, and starting again on the journey immediately upon leaving it. The route was always carefully written out, giving the time the trains started from and arrived at various points; but as cross trains often failed to connect, one traveled, guidebook in hand, in a constant fever of anxiety. As, in the early days, the fees were from one to two hundred dollars a night, the speakers themselves were desirous of accomplishing as much as possible.

In 1869 I gave my name, for the first time, to the New York Bureau, and on November 14 began the long, weary pilgrimages, from Maine to Texas, that lasted twelve years; speaking steadily for eight months—from October to June—every season. That was the heyday of the lecturing period, when a long list of bright men and women were constantly on the wing. Anna Dickinson, Olive Logan, Kate Field,—later, Mrs. Livermore and Mrs. Howe, Alcott, Phillips, Douglass, Tilton, Curtis, Beecher, and, several years later, General Kilpatrick, with Henry Vincent, Bradlaugh, and Matthew Arnold from England; these and many others were stars of the lecture platform.

Some of us occasionally managed to spend Sunday together, at a good hotel in some city, to rest and feast and talk over our joys and sorrows, the long journeys, the hard fare in the country hotels, the rainy nights when committees felt blue and tried to cut down our fees; the being compelled by inconsiderate people to talk on the train; the overheated, badly ventilated cars; the halls, sometimes too warm, sometimes too cold; babies crying in our audiences; the rain pattering on the roof overhead or leaking on the platform—these were common experiences. In the West, women with babies uniformly occupied the front seats so that the little ones, not understanding what you said, might be amused with your gestures and changing facial expression. All these things, so trying, at the time, to concentrated and enthusiastic speaking, afterward served as subjects of amusing conversation. We unanimously complained of the tea and coffee. Mrs. Livermore had the wisdom to carry a spirit lamp with her own tea and coffee, and thus supplied herself with the needed stimu-

ELIZABETH SMITH MILLER.

STANTON

DANIEL CADY   THEODORE   GERRIT SMITH

THEODORE'S CHILDREN

lants for her oratorical efforts. The hardships of these lyceum trips can never be appreciated except by those who have endured them. With accidents to cars and bridges, with floods and snow blockades, the pitfalls in one of these campaigns were without number.

On one occasion, when engaged to speak at Maquoketa, Iowa, I arrived at Lyons about noon, to find the road was blocked with snow, and no chance of the cars running for days. "Well," said I to the landlord, "I must be at Maquoketa at eight o'clock to-night; have you a sleigh, a span of fleet horses, and a skillful driver? If so, I will go across the country." "Oh, yes, madam!" he replied, "I have all you ask; but you could not stand a six-hours' drive in this piercing wind." Having lived in a region of snow, with the thermometer down to twenty degrees below zero, I had no fears of winds and drifts, so I said, "Get the sleigh ready and I will try it." Accordingly I telegraphed the committee that I would be there, and started. I was well bundled up in a fur cloak and hood, a hot oak plank at my feet, and a thick veil over my head and face. As the landlord gave the finishing touch, by throwing a large buffalo robe over all and tying the two tails together at the back of my head and thus effectually preventing me putting my hand to my nose, he said, "There, if you can only sit perfectly still, you will come out all right at Maquoketa; that is, if you get there, which I very much doubt." It was a long, hard drive against the wind and through drifts, but I scarcely moved a finger, and, as the clock struck eight, we drove into the town. The hall was warm, and the church bell having announced my arrival, a large audience was assembled. As I learned that all the roads in Northern Iowa were blocked, I made the entire circuit, from point to point, in a sleigh, traveling forty and fifty miles a day.

At the Sherman House, in Chicago, three weeks later, I met Mr. Bradlaugh and General Kilpatrick, who were advertised on the same route ahead of me. " Well," said I, " where have you gentlemen been? " " Waiting here for the roads to be opened. We have lost three weeks' engagements," they replied. As the General was lecturing on his experiences in Sherman's march to the sea, I chaffed him on not being able, in an emergency, to march across the State of Iowa. They were much astonished and somewhat ashamed, when I told them of my long, solitary drives over the prairies from day to day. It was the testimony of all the bureaus that the women could endure more fatigue and were more conscientious than the men in filling their appointments.

The pleasant feature of these trips was the great educational work accomplished for the people through their listening to lectures on all the vital questions of the hour. Wherever any of us chanced to be on Sunday, we preached in some church; and wherever I had a spare afternoon, I talked to women alone, on marriage, maternity, and the laws of life and health. We made many most charming acquaintances, too, scattered all over our Western World, and saw how comfortable and happy sensible people could be, living in most straitened circumstances, with none of the luxuries of life. If most housekeepers could get rid of one-half their clothes and furniture and put their bric-a-brac in the town museum, life would be simplified and they would begin to know what leisure means. When I see so many of our American women struggling to be artists, who cannot make a good loaf of bread nor a palatable cup of coffee, I think of what Theodore Parker said when art was a craze in Boston. " The fine arts do not interest me so much as the coarse arts which feed, clothe, house, and comfort a people. I would rather be a great man like Franklin than a Michael Angelo— nay, if I had a son, I should rather see him a mechanic, like the late George Stephenson, in England, than a great painter like Rubens, who only copied beauty."

One day I found at the office of the *Revolution* an invitation to meet Mrs. Moulton in the Academy of Music, where she was to try her voice for the coming concert for the benefit of the Woman's Medical College. And what a voice for power, pathos, pliability! I never heard the like. Seated beside her mother, Mrs. W. H. Greenough, I enjoyed alike the mother's anxious pride and the daughter's triumph. I felt, as I listened, the truth of what Vieuxtemps said the first time he heard her, " That is the traditional voice for which the ages have waited and longed." When, on one occasion, Mrs. Moulton sang a song of Mozart's to Auber's accompaniment, someone present asked, " What could be added to make this more complete? Auber looked up to heaven, and, with a sweet smile, said, " Nothing but that Mozart should have been here to listen." Looking and listening, " Here," thought I, " is another jewel in the crown of womanhood, to radiate and glorify the lives of all." I have such an intense pride of sex that the triumphs of woman in art, literature, oratory, science, or song rouse my enthusiasm as nothing else can.

Hungering, that day, for gifted women, I called on Alice and Phebe Cary and Mary Clemmer Ames, and together we gave the proud white male such a serving up as did our souls good and could not hurt him, intrenched, as he is, behind creeds, codes, customs, and constitutions, with vizor and breastplate of self-complacency and conceit. In criticising Jessie Boucherett's essay on " Superfluous Women," in which she advises men in England to emigrate in order to leave room and occupation for women, the *Tribune* said: " The idea of a home without a man in it!" In visiting the Carys one always felt that there was a home—a very charming one, too—without a man in it.

Once when Harriet Beecher Stowe was at Dr. Taylor's, I had the opportunity to make her acquaintance. In her sanctum, surrounded by books and papers, she was just finishing her second paper on the Byron family, and her sister Catherine was preparing papers on her educational work, preparatory to a coming meeting of the ladies of the school board. The women of the Beecher family, though most of them wives and mothers, all had a definite life-work outside the family circle, and other objects of intense interest beside husbands, babies, cook stoves, and social conversations. Catherine said she was opposed to woman suffrage, and if she thought there was the least danger of our getting it, she would write and talk against it vehemently. But, as the nation was safe against such a calamity, she was willing to let the talk go on, because the agitation helped her work. " It is rather paradoxical," I said to her, " that the pressing of a false principle can help a true one; but when you get the women all thoroughly educated, they will step off to the polls and vote in spite of you."

One night on the train from New York to Williamsport, Pennsylvania, I found abundant time to think over the personal peculiarities of the many noble women who adorn this nineteenth century, and, as I recalled them, one by one, in America, England, France, and Germany, and all that they are doing and saying, I wondered that any man could be so blind as not to see that woman has already taken her place as the peer of man. While the lords of creation have been debating her sphere and drawing their chalk marks here and there, woman has quietly stepped outside the barren fields where she was compelled to graze for centuries, and is now in green pastures and beside still waters, a power in the world of thought.

These pleasant cogitations were cut short by my learning that I had taken the wrong train, and must change at Harrisburg at two o'clock in the morning. How soon the reflection that I must leave my comfortable berth at such an unchristian hour changed the whole hue of glorious womanhood and every other earthly blessing! However, I lived through the trial and arrived at Williamsport as the day dawned. I had a good audience at the opera house that evening, and was introduced to many agreeable people, who declared themselves converted to woman suffrage by my ministrations. Among the many new jewels in my crown, I added, that night, Judge Bently.

In November, 1869, I passed one night in Philadelphia, with Miss Anthony, at Anna Dickinson's home— a neat, three-story brick house in Locust Street. This haven of rest, where the world-famous little woman came, ever and anon, to recruit her overtaxed energies, was very tastefully furnished, adorned with engravings, books, and statuary. Her mother, sister, and brother

made up the household—a pleasing, cultivated trio.
The brother was a handsome youth of good judgment,
and given to sage remarks; the sister, witty, intuitive,
and incisive in speech; the mother, dressed in rich
Quaker costume, and though nearly seventy, still possessed of great personal beauty. She was intelligent,
dignified, refined, and, in manner and appearance, reminded one of Angelina Grimké as she looked in her
younger days. Everything about the house and its
appointments indicated that it was the abode of genius
and cultivation, and, although Anna was absent, the
hospitalities were gracefully dispensed by her family.
Napoleon and Shakespeare seemed to be Anna's patron
saints, looking down, on all sides, from the wall. The
mother amused us with the sore trials her little orator
had inflicted on the members of the household by her
vagaries in the world of fame.

On the way to Kennett Square, a young gentleman pointed out to us the home of Benjamin West,
who distinguished himself, to the disgust of broad-
brims generally, as a landscape painter. In com-
mencing his career, it is said he made use of the
tail of a cat in lieu of a brush. Of course Benjamin's first attempts were on the sly, and he could
not ask paterfamilias for money to buy a brush
without encountering the good man's scorn. Whether,
in the hour of his need and fresh enthusiasm,
poor puss was led to the sacrificial altar, or whether
he found her reposing by the roadside, having paid the
debt of Nature, our informant could not say; enough
that, in time, he owned a brush and immortalized himself by his skill in its use. Such erratic ones as Whittier, West, and Anna Dickinson go to prove that even

the prim, proper, perfect Quakers are subject to like infirmities with the rest of the human family.

I had long heard of the " Progressive Friends " in the region round Longwood; had read the many bulls they issued from their " yearly meetings " on every question, on war, capital punishment, temperance, slavery, woman's rights; had learned that they were turning the cold shoulder on the dress, habits, and opinions of their Fathers; listening to the ministrations of such worldlings as William Lloyd Garrison, Theodore Tilton, and Oliver Johnson, in a new meeting house, all painted and varnished, with cushions, easy seats, carpets, stoves, a musical instrument—shade of George Fox, forgive—and three brackets with vases on the " high seat," and, more than all that, men and women were indiscriminately seated throughout the house.

All this Miss Anthony and I beheld with our own eyes, and, in company with Sarah Pugh and Chandler Darlington, did sit together in the high seat and talk in the congregation of the people. There, too, we met Hannah Darlington and Dinah Mendenhall,—names long known in every good work,—and, for the space of one day, did enjoy the blissful serenity of that earthly paradise. The women of Kennett Square were celebrated not only for their model housekeeping but also for their rare cultivation on all subjects of general interest.

In November I again started on one of my Western trips, but, alas! on the very day the trains were changed, and so I could not make connections to meet my engagements at Saginaw and Marshall, and just saved myself at Toledo by going directly from the cars before the audience, with the dust of twenty-four hours' travel on my garments. Not being able to reach Saginaw, I went straight to Ann Arbor, and spent three days most pleasantly in visiting old friends, making new ones, and surveying the town, with its grand University. I was invited to Thanksgiving dinner at the home of Mr. Seaman, a highly cultivated Democratic editor, author of " Progress of Nations." A choice number of guests gathered round his hospitable board on that occasion, over which his wife presided with dignity and grace. Woman suffrage was the target for the combined wit and satire of the company, and, after four hours of uninterrupted sharpshooting, pyrotechnics, and laughter, we dispersed to our several abodes, fairly exhausted with the excess of enjoyment.

One gentleman had the moral hardihood to assert that men had more endurance than women, whereupon a lady remarked that she would like to see the thirteen hundred young men in the University laced up in steel-ribbed corsets, with hoops, heavy skirts, trains, high heels, panniers, chignons, and dozens of hairpins sticking in their scalps, cooped up in the house year after year, with no exhilarating exercise, no hopes, aims, nor ambitions in life, and know if they could stand it as well as the girls. " Nothing," said she, " but the fact that women, like cats, have nine lives, enables them to survive the present *régime* to which custom dooms the sex."

While in Ann Arbor I gave my lecture on " Our Girls " in the new Methodist church—a large building, well lighted, and filled with a brilliant audience. The students, in large numbers, were there, and strengthened the threads of my discourse with frequent and generous applause; especially when I urged on the Regents of the University the duty of opening its doors to the daughters of the State. There were several splendid girls in Michigan, at that time, preparing themselves for admission to the law department. As Judge Cooley, one of the professors, was a very liberal man, as well as a sound lawyer, and strongly in favor of opening the college to girls, I had no doubt the women of Michigan would soon distinguish themselves at the bar. Some said the chief difficulty in the way of the girls of that day being admitted to the University was the want of room. That could have been easily obviated by telling the young men from abroad to betake themselves to the colleges in their respective States, that Michigan might educate her daughters. As the women owned a good share of the property of the State, and had been heavily taxed to build and endow that institution, it was but fair that they should share in its advantages.

The Michigan University, with its extensive grounds, commodious buildings, medical and law schools, professors' residences, and the finest laboratory in the country, was an institution of which the State was justly proud, and, as the tuition was free, it was worth the trouble of a long, hard siege by the girls of Michigan to gain admittance there. I advised them to organize their forces at once, get their minute guns, battering rams, monitors, projectiles, bombshells, cannon, torpedoes, and crackers ready, and keep up a brisk cannonading until the grave and reverend seigniors opened the door, and shouted, " Hold, enough! "

The ladies of Ann Arbor had a fine library of their own, where their clubs met once a week. They had just formed a suffrage association. My visit ended with a pleasant reception, at which I was introduced to the chaplain, several professors, and many ladies and gentlemen ready to accept the situation. Judge Cooley gave me a glowing account of the laws of Michigan— how easy it was for wives to get possession of all the property, and then sunder the marriage tie and leave the poor husband to the charity of the cold world, with their helpless children about him. I heard of a rich lady, there, who made a will, giving her husband a handsome annuity as long as he remained her widower. It was evident that the poor " white male," sooner or later, was doomed to try for himself the virtue of the laws he had made for women. I hope, for the sake of the race, he will not bear oppression with the stupid fortitude we have for six thousand years.

At Flint I was entertained by Mr. and Mrs. Jenny. Mr. Jenny was a Democratic editor who believed in progress, and in making smooth paths for women in this great wilderness of life. His wife was a remarkable woman. She inaugurated the Ladies' Libraries in Michigan. In Flint they had a fine brick building and nearly two thousand volumes of choice books, owned by the association, and money always in the treasury. Here, too, I had a fine audience and gave my lecture entitled " Open the Door."

At Coldwater, in spite of its name, I found a warm, appreciative audience. The president of the lyceum was a sensible young man who, after graduating at Ann Arbor, decided, instead of starving at the law, to work with his hands and brains at the same time. When all men go to their legitimate business of creating wealth, developing the resources of the country, and leave its mere exchange to the weaker sex, we shall not have so many superfluous women in the world with nothing to do. It is evident the time has come to hunt man into his appropriate sphere. Coming from Chicago, I met Governor Fairchild and Senator Williams of Wisconsin. It was delightful to find them thoroughly grounded in the faith of woman suffrage. They had been devout readers of the *Revolution* ever since Miss Anthony induced them to subscribe, the winter before, at Madison. Of course a new glow of intelligence irradiated their fine faces (for they were remarkably handsome men) and there was a new point to all their words. Senator Williams, like myself, was on a lecturing tour. " Man " was his theme, for which I was devoutly thankful; for, if there are any of God's creatures that need lecturing, it is this one that is forever advising us. I thought of all men, from Father Gregory down to Horace Bushnell, who had wearied their brains to describe woman's sphere, and how signally they had failed.

Throughout my lyceum journeys I was of great use to the traveling public, in keeping the ventilators in the cars open, and the dampers in fiery stoves shut up, especially in sleeping cars at night. How many times a day I thought what the sainted Horace Mann tried to impress on his stupid countrymen, that, inasmuch as the air is forty miles deep around the globe, it is a useless piece of economy to breathe any number of cubic feet over more than seven times! The babies, too, need to be thankful that I was in a position to witness their wrongs. Many, through my intercessions, received their first drink of water, and were emancipated from woolen hoods, veils, tight strings under their chins, and endless swaddling bands.   It is a startling assertion, but true, that I have met few women who know how to take care of a baby.   And this fact led me, on one trip, to lecture to my fair countrywomen on " Marriage and Maternity," hoping to aid in the inauguration of a new era of happy, healthy babies.

After twenty-four hours in the express I found myself in a pleasant room in the International Hotel at La Crosse, looking out on the Great Mother of Waters, on whose cold bosom the ice and the steamers were struggling for mastery.   Beyond stretched the snow-clad bluffs, sternly looking down on the Mississippi, as if to say, " ' Thus far shalt thou come and no farther '—though sluggish, you are aggressive, ever pushing where you should not; but all attempts in this direction are alike vain; since creation's dawn, we have defied you, and here we stand, to-day, calm, majestic, immovable.   Coquette as you will in other latitudes, with flowery banks and youthful piers in the busy marts of trade, and undermine them, one and all, with your deceitful wooings, but bow in reverence as you gaze on us.   We have no eyes for your beauty; no ears for your endless song; our heads are in the clouds, our hearts commune with gods; you have no part in the eternal problems of the ages that fill our thoughts, yours the humble duty to wash our feet, and then pass on, remembering to keep in your appropriate sphere, within the barks that wise geographers have seen fit to mark."

As I listened to these complacent hills and watched the poor Mississippi weeping as she swept along, to lose her sorrows in ocean's depths, I thought how like the attitude of man to woman.   Let these proud hills remember that they, too, slumbered for centuries in deep valleys down, down, when, perchance, the sparkling Mississippi rolled above their heads, and but for some generous outburst, some upheaval of old Mother Earth, wishing that her rock-ribbed sons, as well as graceful daughters, might enjoy the light, the sunshine and the shower—but for this soul of love in matter as well as mind—these bluffs and the sons of Adam, too, might not boast the altitude they glory in to-day. Those who have ears to hear discern low, rumbling noises that foretell convulsions in our social world that may, perchance, in the next upheaval, bring woman to the surface; up, up, from gloomy ocean depths, dark caverns, and damper valleys. The struggling daughters of earth are soon to walk in the sunlight of a higher civilization.

Escorted by Mr. Woodward, a member of the bar, I devoted a day to the lions of La Crosse. First we explored the courthouse, a large, new brick building, from whose dome we had a grand view of the surrounding country. The courtroom where justice is administered was large, clean, airy—the bench carpeted and adorned with a large, green, stuffed chair, in which I sat down, and, in imagination, summoned up advocates, jurors, prisoners, and people, and wondered how I should feel pronouncing sentence of death on a fellow-being, or, like Portia, wisely checkmating the Shylocks of our times. Here I met Judge Hugh Cameron, formerly of Johnstown. He invited us into his sanctum, where we had a pleasant chat about our native hills, Scotch affiliations, the bench and bar of New York, and the Wisconsin laws for women. The Judge, having maintained a happy bachelor state, looked placidly on the aggressive movements of the sex, as his domestic felicity would be no way affected, whether woman was voted up or down.

We next surveyed the Pomeroy building, which contained a large, tastefully finished hall and printing establishment, where the La Crosse *Democrat* was formerly published. As I saw the perfection, order, and good taste, in all arrangements throughout, and listened to Mr. Huron's description of the life and leading characteristics of its chief, it seemed impossible to reconcile the tone of the *Democrat* with the moral status of its editor. I never saw a more complete business establishment, and the editorial sanctum looked as if it might be the abiding place of the Muses. Mirrors, pictures, statuary, books, music, rare curiosities, and fine specimens of birds and minerals were everywhere. Over the editor's table was a beautiful painting of his youthful daughter, whose flaxen hair, blue eyes, and angelic face should have inspired a father to nobler, purer, utterances than he was wont, at that time, to give to the world.

But Pomeroy's good deeds will live long after his profane words are forgotten. Throughout the establishment cards, set up in conspicuous places, said, "Smoking here is positively forbidden." Drinking, too, was forbidden to all his employés. The moment a man was discovered using intoxicating drinks, he was dismissed. In the upper story of the building was a large, pleasant room, handsomely carpeted and furnished, where the employés, in their leisure hours, could talk, write, read, or amuse themselves in any rational way.

Mr. Pomeroy was humane and generous with his employés, honorable in his business relations, and boundless in his charities to the poor. His charity, business honor, and public spirit were highly spoken of by those who knew him best. That a journal does not always reflect the editor is as much the fault of society as of the man. So long as the public will pay for gross personalities, obscenity, and slang, decent journals will be outbidden in the market. The fact that the La Crosse *Democrat* found a ready sale in all parts of the country showed that Mr. Pomeroy fairly reflected the popular taste. While multitudes turned up the whites of their eyes and denounced him in public, they bought his paper and read it in private.

I left La Crosse in a steamer, just as the rising sun lighted the hilltops and gilded the Mississippi. It was a lovely morning, and, in company with a young girl of sixteen, who had traveled alone from some remote part of Canada, bound for a northern village in Wisconsin, I promenaded the deck most of the way to Winona, a pleased listener to the incidents of my young companion's experiences. She said that, when crossing Lake Huron, she was the only woman on board, but the men were so kind and civil that she soon forgot she was alone. I found many girls, traveling long distances, who had never been five miles from home before, with a self-reliance that was remarkable. They all spoke in the most flattering manner of the civility of our American men in looking after their baggage and advising them as to the best routes.

As you approach St. Paul, at Fort Snelling, where the Mississippi and Minnesota join forces, the country grows bold and beautiful. The town itself, then boasting about thirty thousand inhabitants, is finely situated, with substantial stone residences. It was in one of these charming homes I found a harbor of rest during my stay in the city.   Mrs. Stuart, whose hospitalities I enjoyed, was a woman of rare common sense and sound health.   Her husband, Dr. Jacob H. Stuart, was one of the very first surgeons to volunteer in the late war. In the panic at Bull Run, instead of running, as everybody else did, he stayed with the wounded, and was taken prisoner while taking a bullet from the head of a rebel.   When exchanged, Beauregard gave him his sword for his devotion to the dying and wounded.

I had the pleasure of seeing several of the leading gentlemen and ladies of St. Paul at the Orphans' Fair, where we all adjourned, after my lecture, to discuss woman's rights, over a bounteous supper.   Here I met William L. Banning, the originator of the Lake Superior and Mississippi Railroad.   He besieged Congress and capitalists for a dozen years to build this road, but was laughed at and put off with sneers and contempt, until, at last, Jay Cooke became so weary of his continual coming that he said: " I will build the road to get rid of you."

Whittier seems to have had a prophetic vision of the peopling of this region.   When speaking of the Yankee, he says:

> " He's whittling by St. Mary's Falls,
>   Upon his loaded wain ;
> He's measuring o'er the Pictured Rocks,
>   With eager eyes of gain.

> " I hear the mattock in the mine,
>   The ax-stroke in the dell,
> The clamor from the Indian lodge,
>   The Jesuits' chapel bell !

" I hear the tread of pioneers
    Of nations yet to be ;
    The first low wash of waves, where soon
    Shall roll a human sea."

The opening of these new outlets and mines of
wealth was wholly due to the forecast and perseverance of Mr. Banning. The first engine that went
over a part of the road had been christened at St.
Paul, with becoming ceremonies; the officiating priest-
ess being a beautiful maiden. A cask of water from the
Pacific was sent by Mr. Banning's brother from California, and a small keg was brought from Lake Superior for the occasion. A glass was placed in the
hands of Miss Ella B. Banning, daughter of the president, who then christened the engine, saying: " With
the waters of the Pacific Ocean in my right hand, and
the waters of Lake Superior in my left, invoking the
Genius of Progress to bring together, with iron band,
two great commercial systems of the globe, I dedicate
this engine to the use of the Lake Superior and Mississippi Railroad, and name it William L. Banning."

From St. Paul to Dubuque, as the boats had ceased
running, a circuitous route and a night of discomfort
were inevitable. Leaving the main road to Chicago at
Clinton Junction, I had the pleasure of waiting at a small
country inn until midnight for a freight train. This
was indeed dreary, but, having Mrs. Child's sketches
of Mmes. De Staël and Roland at hand, I read of
Napoleon's persecutions of the one and Robespierre's
of the other, until, by comparison, my condition was
tolerable, and the little meagerly furnished room, with
its dull fire and dim lamp, seemed a paradise compared
with years of exile from one's native land or the prison

cell and guillotine. How small our ordinary, petty trials seem in contrast with the mountains of sorrow that have been piled up on the great souls of the past! Absorbed in communion with them twelve o'clock soon came, and with it the train.

A burly son of Adam escorted me to the passenger car filled with German immigrants, with tin cups, babies, bags, and bundles innumerable. The ventilators were all closed, the stoves hot, and the air was like that of the Black Hole of Calcutta. So, after depositing my cloak and bag in an empty seat, I quietly propped both doors open with a stick of wood, shut up the stoves, and opened all the ventilators with the poker. But the celestial breeze, so grateful to me, had the most unhappy effect on the slumbering exiles. Paterfamilias swore outright; the companion of his earthly pilgrimage said, " We must be going north," and, as the heavy veil of carbonic acid gas was lifted from infant faces, and the pure oxygen filled their lungs and roused them to new life, they set up one simultaneous shout of joy and gratitude, which their parents mistook for agony. Altogether there was a general stir. As I had quietly slipped into my seat and laid my head down to sleep, I remained unobserved—the innocent cause of the general purification and vexation.

We reached Freeport at three o'clock in the morning. As the dépot for Dubuque was nearly half a mile on the other side of the town, I said to a solitary old man who stood shivering there to receive us, " How can I get to the other station? " " Walk, madam." " But I do not know the way." " There is no one to go with you." " How is my trunk going? " said I. " I have a donkey and cart to take that." " Then," said I, " you, the donkey, the trunk, and I will go together." So I stepped into the cart, sat down on the trunk, and the old man laughed heartily as we jogged along through the mud of that solitary town in the pale morning starlight. Just as the day was dawning, Dubuque, with its rough hills and bold scenery, loomed up. Soon, under the roof of Myron Beach, one of the distinguished lawyers of the West, with a good breakfast and sound nap, my night's sorrows were forgotten.

I was sorry to find that Mrs. Beach, though a native of New York, and born on the very spot where the first woman's rights convention was held in this country, was not sound on the question of woman suffrage. She seemed to have an idea that voting and housekeeping could not be compounded; but I suggested that, if the nation could only enjoy a little of the admirable system with which she and other women administered their domestic affairs, Uncle Sam's interests would be better secured. This is just what the nation needs to-day, and women must wake up to the consideration that they, too, have duties as well as rights in the State. A splendid audience greeted me in the Opera House, and I gave " Our Girls," bringing many male sinners to repentance, and stirring up some lethargic *femmes coverts* to a state of rebellion against the existing order of things.

From Dubuque I went to Dixon, a large town, where I met a number of pleasant people, but I have one cause of complaint against the telegraph operator, whose negligence to send a dispatch to Mt. Vernon, written and paid for, came near causing me a solitary night on the prairie, unsheltered and unknown. Hearing that the express train went out Sunday afternoon,

I decided to go, so as to have all day at Mt. Vernon before speaking; but on getting my trunk checked, the baggageman said the train did not stop there. "Well," said I, "check the trunk to the nearest point at which it does stop," resolving that I would persuade the conductor to stop one minute, anyway. Accordingly, when the conductor came round, I presented my case as persuasively and eloquently as possible, telling him that I had telegraphed friends to meet me, etc., etc. He kindly consented to do so and had my trunk rechecked. On arriving, as there was no light, no sound, and the depot was half a mile from the town, the conductor urged me to go to Cedar Rapids and come back the next morning, as it was Sunday night and the dépôt might not be opened, and I might be compelled to stay there on the platform all night in the cold.

But, as I had telegraphed, I told him I thought someone would be there, and I would take the risk. So off went the train, leaving me solitary and alone. I could see the lights in the distant town and the dark outlines of two great mills near by, which suggested dams and races. I heard, too, the distant barking of dogs, and I thought there might be wolves, too; but no human sound. The platform was high and I could see no way down, and I should not have dared to go down if I had. So I walked all round the house, knocked at every door and window, called "John!" "James!" "Patrick!" but no response. Dressed in all their best, they had, no doubt, gone to visit Sally, and I knew they would stay late. The night wind was cold. What could I do? The prospect of spending the night there filled me with dismay. At last I thought I would try my vocal powers; so I hallooed as loud as I could, in every note of the gamut, until I was hoarse. At last I heard a distant sound, a loud halloo, which I returned, and so we kept it up until the voice grew near, and, when I heard a man's heavy footsteps close at hand, I was relieved. He proved to be the telegraph operator, who had been a brave soldier in the late war. He said that no message had come from Dixon. He escorted me to the hotel, where some members of the Lyceum Committee came in and had a hearty laugh at my adventure, especially that, in my distress, I should have called on James and John and Patrick, instead of Jane, Ann, and Bridget. They seemed to argue that that was an admission, on my part, of man's superiority, but I suggested that, as my sex had not yet been exalted to the dignity of presiding in dépots and baggage rooms, there would have been no propriety in calling Jane and Ann.

Mt. Vernon was distinguished for a very flourishing Methodist college, open to boys and girls alike. The president and his wife were liberal and progressive people. I dined with them in their home near the college, and met some young ladies from Massachusetts, who were teachers in the institution. All who gathered round the social board on that occasion were of one mind on the woman question. Even the venerable mother of the president seemed to light up with the discussion of the theme. I gave " Our Girls " in the Methodist church, and took the opportunity to compliment them for taking the word " obey " out of their marriage ceremony. I heard the most encouraging reports of the experiment of educating the sexes together. It was the rule in all the Methodist institutions in Iowa,

and I found that the young gentlemen fully approved
of it.

At Mt. Vernon I also met Mr. Wright, former
Secretary of State, who gave me several interesting facts in regard to the women of Iowa. The
State could boast one woman who was an able
lawyer, Mrs. Mansfield. Mrs. Berry and Mrs. Stebbins were notaries public. Miss Addington was
superintendent of schools in Mitchell County. She
was nominated by a convention in opposition to a
Mr. Brown. When the vote was taken, lo! there was
a tie. Mr. Brown offered to yield through courtesy,
but she declined; so they drew lots and Miss Addington
was the victor. She once made an abstract of
titles of all the lands in the county where she
lived, and had received an appointment to office
from the Governor of the State, who requested the
paper to be made out " L." instead of Laura Addington. He said it was enough for Iowa to appoint women
to such offices, without having it known the world over.
I was sorry to tell the Governor's secrets,—which I
did everywhere,—but the cause of womanhood made it
necessary.

CHAPTER XVIII.

WESTWARD HO!

IN the month of June, 1871, Miss Anthony and I went to California, holding suffrage meetings in many of the chief cities from New York to San Francisco, where we arrived about the middle of July, in time to experience the dry, dusty season.

We tarried, on the way, one week in Salt Lake City. It was at the time of the Godby secession, when several hundred Mormons abjured that portion of the faith of their fathers which authorized polygamy. A decision had just been rendered by the United States Supreme Court declaring the first wife and her children the only legal heirs. Whether this decision hastened the secession I do not know; however, it gave us the advantage of hearing all the arguments for and against the system. Those who were opposed to it said it made slaves of men. To support four wives and twenty children was a severe strain on any husband. The women who believed in polygamy had much to say in its favor, especially in regard to the sacredness of motherhood during the period of pregnancy and lactation; a lesson of respect for that period being religiously taught all Mormons.

We were very thankful for the privilege granted us of speaking to the women alone in the smaller Tabernacle. Our meeting opened at two o'clock and lasted until seven, giving us five hours of uninterrupted conversation. Judge McKeon had informed me of the recent decisions and the legal aspects of the questions, which he urged me to present to them fully and frankly, as no one had had such an opportunity before to speak to Mormon women alone. So I made the most of my privilege. I gave a brief history of the marriage institution in all times and countries, of the matriarchate, when the mother was the head of the family and owned the property and children; of the patriarchate, when man reigned supreme and woman was enslaved; of polyandry, polygamy, monogamy, and prostitution. We had a full and free discussion of every phase of the question, and we all agreed that we were still far from having reached the ideal position for woman in marriage, however satisfied man might be with his various experiments. Though the Mormon women, like all others, stoutly defend their own religion, yet they are no more satisfied than any other sect. All women are dissatisfied with their position as inferiors, and their dissatisfaction increases in exact ratio with their intelligence and development.

After this convocation the doors of the Tabernacle were closed to our ministrations, as we thought they would be, but we had crowded an immense amount of science, philosophy, history, and general reflections into the five hours of such free talk as those women had never heard before. As the seceders had just built a new hall, we held meetings there every day, discussing all the vital issues of the hour; the Mormon men and women taking an active part.

We attended the Fourth of July celebration, and saw the immense Tabernacle filled to its utmost capacity.

The various States of the Union were represented by young girls, gayly dressed, carrying beautiful flags and banners. When that immense multitude joined in our national songs, and the deep-toned organ filled the vast dome the music was very impressive, and the spirit of patriotism manifested throughout was deep and sincere.

As I stood among these simple people, so earnest in making their experiment in religion and social life, and remembered all the persecutions they had suffered and all they had accomplished in that desolate, far-off region, where they had, indeed, made " the wilderness blossom like the rose," I appreciated, as never before, the danger of intermeddling with the religious ideas of any people. Their faith finds abundant authority in the Bible, in the example of God's chosen people. When learned ecclesiastics teach the people that they can safely take that book as the guide of their lives, they must expect them to follow the letter and the specific teachings that lie on the surface. The ordinary mind does not generalize nor see that the same principles of conduct will not do for all periods and latitudes. When women understand that governments and religions are human inventions; that Bibles, prayerbooks, catechisms, and encyclical letters are all emanations from the brain of man, they will no longer be oppressed by the injunctions that come to them with the divine authority of " Thus saith the Lord."

That thoroughly democratic gathering in the Tabernacle impressed me more than any other Fourth of July celebration I ever attended. As most of the Mormon families keep no servants, mothers must take their children wherever they go—to churches, theatres, concerts, and military reviews—everywhere and anywhere,

Hence the low, pensive wail of the individual baby, combining in large numbers, becomes a deep monotone, like the waves of the sea, a sort of violoncello accompaniment to all their holiday performances. It was rather trying to me at first to have my glowing periods punctuated with a rhythmic wail from all sides of the hall; but as soon as I saw that it did not distract my hearers, I simply raised my voice, and, with a little added vehemence, fairly rivaled the babies. Commenting on this trial, to one of the theatrical performers, he replied: " It is bad enough for you, but alas! imagine me in a tender death scene, when the most profound stillness is indispensable, having my last gasp, my farewell message to loved ones, accentuated with the joyful crowings or impatient complainings of fifty babies." I noticed in the Tabernacle that the miseries of the infantile host were in a measure mitigated by constant draughts of cold water, borne around in buckets by four old men.

The question of the most profound interest to us at that time, in the Mormon experiment, was the exercise of the suffrage by women. Emeline B. Wells, wife of the Mayor of the city, writing to a Washington convention, in 1894, said of the many complications growing out of various bills before Congress to rob women of this right:

" Women have voted in Utah fourteen years, but, because of the little word ' male ' that still stands upon the statutes, no woman is eligible to any office of emolument or trust. In three successive legislatures, bills have been passed, providing that the word ' male ' be erased; but, each time, the Governor of the Territory, who has absolute veto power, has refused his signature. Yet women attend primary meetings in the various precincts and are chosen as delegates. They are also members of county and territorial central committees, and are thus gaining practical political experience, and preparing themselves for positions of trust.

" In 1882 a convention was held to frame a constitution to be submitted to the people and presented to the Congress of the United States. Women were delegates to this convention, and took part in all its deliberations, and were appointed to act on committees with equal privileges. It is the first instance on record, I think, where women have been members and taken an active part in a constitutional convention.

" Much has been said and written, and justly, too, of suffrage for women in Wyoming; but, in my humble opinion, had Utah stood on the same ground as Wyoming, and women been eligible to office, as they are in that Territory, they would, ere this, have been elected to the legislative Assembly of Utah.

" It is currently reported that Mormon women vote as they are told by their husbands. I most emphatically deny the assertion. All Mormon women vote who are privileged to register. Every girl born here, as soon as she is twenty-one years old, registers, and considers it as much a duty as to say her prayers. Our women vote with the same freedom that characterizes any class of people in the most conscientious acts of their lives."

These various questions were happily solved in 1895, when Utah became a State. Its Constitution gives women the right to vote on all questions, and makes them eligible to any office.

The journey over the Rocky Mountains was more interesting and wonderful than I had imagined. A heavy shower the morning we reached the alkali plains made the trip through that region, where travelers suffer so much, quite endurable. Although we reached California in its hot, dry season, we found the atmosphere in San Francisco delightful, fanned with the gentle breezes of the Pacific, cooled with the waters of its magnificent harbor. The Golden Gate does indeed open to the eye of the traveler one of the most beautiful harbors in the world.

Friends had engaged for us a suite of apartments at the Grand Hotel, then just opened. Our rooms were constantly decked with fresh flowers, which our "suffrage children," as they called themselves, brought us from day to day. So many brought tokens of their good will—in fact, all our visitors came with offerings of fruits and flowers—that not only our apartments, but the public tables were crowded with rare and beautiful specimens of all varieties. We spoke every night, to crowded houses, on all phases of the woman question, and had a succession of visitors during the day. In fact, for one week, we had a perfect ovation. As Senator Stanford and his wife were at the same hotel, we had many pleasant interviews with them.

While in San Francisco we had many delightful sails in the harbor and drives to the seashore and for miles along the beach. We spent several hours at the little Ocean House, watching the gambols of the celebrated seals. These, like the big trees, were named after distinguished statesmen. One very black fellow was named Charles Sumner, in honor of his love of the black race; another, with a little squint in his eye, was called Ben Butler; a stout, rotund specimen that seemed to take life philosophically, was named Senator Davis of Illinois; a very belligerent one, who appeared determined to crowd his confrères into the sea, was called Secretary Stanton. Grant and Lincoln, on a higher ledge of the rocks, were complacently observing the gambols of the rest.

California was on the eve of an important election, and John A. Bingham of Ohio and Senator Cole were stumping the State for the Republican party. At several points we had the use of their great tents for our audiences, and of such of their able arguments as applied to woman. As Mr. Bingham's great speech was on the Thirteenth, Fourteenth, and Fifteenth Amendments, every principle he laid down literally enfranchised the women of the nation. I met the Ohio statesman one morning at breakfast, after hearing him the night before. I told him his logic must compel him to advocate woman suffrage. With a most cynical smile he said " he was not the puppet of logic, but the slave of practical politics."

We met most of our suffrage coadjutors in different parts of California. I spent a few days with Mrs. Elizabeth B. Schenck, one of the earliest pioneers in the suffrage movement. She was a cultivated, noble woman, and her little cottage was a gem of beauty and comfort, surrounded with beautiful gardens and a hedge of fish-geraniums over ten feet high, covered with scarlet flowers. It seemed altogether more like a fairy bower than a human habitation. The windmills all over California, for pumping water, make a very pretty feature in the landscape, as well as an important one, as people are obliged to irrigate their gardens during the dry season. In August the hills are as brown as ours in December.

Here, too, I first met Senator Sargent's family, and visited them in Sacramento City, where we had a suffrage meeting in the evening and one for women alone next day. At a similar meeting in San Francisco six hundred women were present in Platt's Hall. We discussed marriage, maternity, and social life in general. Supposing none but women were present, as all were dressed in feminine costume, the audience were quite free in their questions, and I equally so in my answers. To our astonishment, the next morning, a verbatim report of all that was said appeared in one of the leading papers, with most respectful comments. As I always wrote and read carefully what I had to say on such delicate subjects, the language was well chosen and the presentation of facts and philosophy quite unobjectionable; hence, the information being as important for men as for women, I did not regret the publication. During the day a committee of three gentlemen called to know if I would give a lecture to men alone. As I had no lecture prepared, I declined, with the promise to do so the next time I visited California. The idea was novel, but I think women could do much good in that way.

My readers may be sure that such enterprising travelers as Miss Anthony and myself visited all the wonders, saw the geysers, big trees, the Yosemite Valley, and the immense mountain ranges, piled one above another, until they seemed to make a giant pathway from earth to heaven. We drove down the mountain sides with Fox, the celebrated whip; sixteen people in an open carriage drawn by six horses, down, down, down, as fast as we could go. I expected to be dashed to pieces, but we safely descended in one hour, heights we had taken three to climb. Fox held a steady rein, and seemed as calm as if we were trotting on a level, though any accident, such as a hot axle, a stumbling horse, or a break in the harness would have sent us down the mountain side, two thousand feet, to inevitable destruction. He had many amusing anecdotes to tell of Horace Greeley's trip to the Geysers. The distinguished journalist was wholly unprepared for the race down the mountains and begged Fox to hold up. Sitting in front he made several efforts to seize the lines. But Fox assured him that was the only possible way they could descend in safety, as the horses could guide the stage, but they could not hold it.

At Stockton we met a party of friends just returning from the Yosemite, who gave us much valuable information for the journey. Among other things, I was advised to write to Mr. Hutchins, the chief authority there, to have a good, strong horse in readiness to take me down the steep and narrow path into the valley. We took the same driver and carriage which our friends had found trustworthy, and started early in the morning. The dust and heat made the day's journey very wearisome, but the prospect of seeing the wonderful valley made all hardships of little consequence. Quite a large party were waiting to mount their donkeys and mules when we arrived. One of the attendants, a man about as thin as a stair rod, asked me if I was the lady who had ordered a strong horse; I being the stoutest of the party, he readily arrived at that conclusion, so my steed was promptly produced. But I

knew enough of horses and riding to see at a glance
that he was a failure, with his low withers and high
haunches, for descending steep mountains. In addition to his forward pitch, his back was immensely broad.
Miss Anthony and I decided to ride astride and had suits
made for that purpose; but alas! my steed was so broad
that I could not reach the stirrups, and the moment we
began to descend, I felt as if I were going over his head.
So I fell behind, and, when the party had all gone forward, I dismounted, though my slender guide assured
me there was no danger, he " had been up and down a
thousand times." But, as I had never been at all, his
repeated experiences did not inspire me with courage.
I decided to walk. That, the guide said, was impossible.
" Well," said I, by way of compromise, " I will walk as
far as I can, and when I reach the impossible, I will try
that ill-constructed beast. I cannot see what you men
were thinking of when you selected such an animal for
this journey." And so we went slowly down, arguing
the point whether it were better to ride or walk; to trust
one's own legs, or, by chance, be precipitated thousands
of feet down the mountain side.

It was a hot August day; the sun, in the zenith, shining with full power. My blood was at boiling heat with
exercise and vexation. Alternately sliding and walking, catching hold of rocks and twigs, drinking at every
rivulet, covered with dust, dripping with perspiration,
skirts, gloves, and shoes in tatters, for four long
hours I struggled down to the end, when I laid myself
out on the grass, and fell asleep, perfectly exhausted,
having sent the guide to tell Mr. Hutchins that I had
reached the valley, and, as I could neither ride nor walk,
to send a wheelbarrow, or four men with a blanket to

transport me to the hotel.   That very day the Mariposa
Company had brought the first carriage into the valley,
which, in due time, was sent to my relief.   Miss Anthony, who, with a nice little Mexican pony and narrow
saddle, had made her descent with grace and dignity,
welcomed me on the steps of the hotel, and laughed immoderately at my helpless plight.

As hour after hour had passed, she said, there had
been a general wonderment as to what had become of
me; " but did you ever see such magnificent scenery? "
" Alas! " I replied, " I have been in no mood for scenery.
I have been constantly watching my hands and feet
lest I should come to grief."   The next day I was too
stiff and sore to move a finger.   However, in due time
I awoke to the glory and grandeur of that wonderful
valley, of which no descriptions nor paintings can give
the least idea.   With Sunset Cox, the leading Democratic statesman, and his wife, we had many pleasant
excursions through the valley, and chats, during the
evening, on the piazza.   There was a constant succession of people going and coming, even in that far-off
region, and all had their adventures to relate.   But none
quite equaled my experiences.

We spent a day in the Calaveras Grove, rested beneath the " big trees," and rode on horseback through
the fallen trunk of one of them.   Some vandals sawed
off one of the most magnificent specimens twenty feet
above the ground, and, on this the owners of the hotel
built a little octagonal chapel.   The polished wood,
with bark for a border, made a very pretty floor.   Here
they often had Sunday services, as it held about one
hundred people.   Here, too, we discussed the suffrage
question, amid these majestic trees that had battled

with the winds two thousand years, and had probably never before listened to such rebellion as we preached to the daughters of earth that day.

Here, again, we found our distinguished statesmen immortalized, each with his namesake among these stately trees. We asked our guide if there were any not yet appropriated, might we name them after women. As he readily consented, we wrote on cards the names of a dozen leading women, and tacked them on their respective trees. Whether Lucretia Mott, Lucy Stone, Phœbe Couzins, and Anna Dickinson still retain their identity, and answer when called by the goddess Sylvia in that majestic grove, I know not. Twenty-five years have rolled by since then, and a new generation of visitors and guides may have left no trace of our work behind them. But we whispered our hopes and aspirations to the trees, to be wafted to the powers above, and we left them indelibly pictured on the walls of the little chapel, and for more mortal eyes we scattered leaflets wherever we went, and made all our pleasure trips so many propaganda for woman's enfranchisement.

Returning from California I made the journey straight through from San Francisco to New York. Though a long trip to make without a break, yet I enjoyed every moment, as I found most charming companions in Bishop Janes and his daughter. The Bishop being very liberal in his ideas, we discussed the various theologies, and all phases of the woman question. I shall never forget those pleasant conversations as we sat outside on the platform, day after day, and in the soft moonlight late at night. We took up the thread of our debate each morning where we had dropped it the

night before. The Bishop told me about the resolution
to take the word " obey " from the marriage ceremony
which he introduced, two years before, into the Methodist General Conference and carried with but little opposition. All praise to the Methodist Church! When
our girls are educated into a proper self-respect and
laudable pride of sex, they will scout all these old bar-
barisms of the past that point in any way to the subject
condition of women in either the State, the Church, or
the home. Until the other sects follow her example,
I hope our girls will insist on having their conjugal
knots all tied by Methodist bishops.

The Episcopal marriage service not only still clings
to the word " obey," but it has a most humiliating
ceremony in giving the bride away. I was never
more struck with its odious and ludicrous features
than on once seeing a tall, queenly-looking woman,
magnificently arrayed, married by one of the tiniest
priests that ever donned a surplice and gown,
given away by the smallest guardian that ever
watched a woman's fortunes, to the feeblest, bluest-
looking little groom that ever placed a wedding ring
on bridal finger. Seeing these Lilliputians around
her, I thought, when the little priest said, " Who gives
this woman to this man," that she would take the responsibility and say, " I do," but no! there she stood,
calm, serene, as if it were no affair of hers, while the
little guardian, placing her hand in that of the little
groom, said, " I do." Thus was this stately woman
bandied about by these three puny men, all of whom she
might have gathered up in her arms and borne off to
their respective places of abode.

But women are gradually waking up to the degradation of these ceremonies. Not long since, at a wedding in high life, a beautiful girl of eighteen was struck dumb at the word " obey." Three times the priest pronounced it with emphasis and holy unction, each time slower, louder, than before. Though the magnificent parlors were crowded, a breathless silence reigned. Father, mother, and groom were in agony. The bride, with downcast eyes, stood speechless. At length the priest slowly closed his book and said, " The ceremony is at an end." One imploring word from the groom, and a faint " obey " was heard in the solemn stillness. The priest unclasped his book and the knot was tied. The congratulations, feast, and all, went on as though there had been no break in the proceedings, but the lesson was remembered, and many a rebel made by that short pause.

I think all these reverend gentlemen who insist on the word " obey " in the marriage service should be removed for a clear violation of the Thirteenth Amendment to the Federal Constitution, which says there shall be neither slavery nor involuntary servitude within the United States. As I gave these experiences to Bishop Janes he laughed heartily, and asked me to repeat them to each newcomer. Our little debating society was the center of attraction. One gentleman asked me if our woman suffrage conventions were as entertaining. I told him yes; that there were no meetings in Washington so interesting and so well attended as ours.

As I had some woman-suffrage literature in my valise, I distributed leaflets to all earnest souls who plied me with questions. Like all other things, it requires great discretion in sowing leaflets, lest you expose yourself to a rebuff. I never offer one to a man with a small head and high heels on his boots, with his chin in the air, because I know, in the nature of things, that he will be jealous of superior women; nor to a woman whose mouth has the " prunes and prisms " expression, for I know she will say, " I have all the rights I want." Going up to London one day, a few years later, I noticed a saintly sister, belonging to the Salvation Army, timidly offering some leaflets to several persons on board; all coolly declined to receive them. Having had much experience in the joys and sorrows of propagandism, I put out my hand and asked her to give them to me. I thanked her and read them before reaching London. It did me no harm and her much good in thinking that she might have planted a new idea in my mind. Whatever is given to us freely, I think, in common politeness, we should accept graciously .

While I was enjoying once more the comforts of home, on the blue hills of Jersey, Miss Anthony was lighting the fires of liberty on the mountain tops of Oregon and Washington Territory. All through the months of October, November, and December, 1871, she was jolting about in stages, over rough roads, speaking in every hamlet where a schoolhouse was to be found, and scattering our breezy leaflets to the four winds of heaven.

From 1869 to 1873 Miss Anthony and I made several trips through Iowa, Missouri, Illinois, and Nebraska, holding meetings at most of the chief towns; I speaking in the afternoons to women alone on " Marriage and Maternity." As Miss Anthony had other pressing engagements in Kansas and Nebraska, I went alone to Texas, speaking in Dallas, Sherman, and Houston, where I was delayed two weeks by floods and thus prevented from going to Austin, Galveston, and some points in Louisiana, where I was advertised to lecture. In fact I lost all my appointments for a month. However, there was a fine hotel in Houston and many pleasant people, among whom I made some valuable acquaintances. Beside several public meetings, I had parlor talks and scattered leaflets, so that my time was not lost.

As the floods had upset my plans for the winter, I went straight from Houston to New York over the Iron Mountain Railroad. I anticipated a rather solitary trip; but, fortunately, I met General Baird, whom I knew, and some other army officers, who had been down on the Mexican border to settle some troubles in the " free zone." We amused ourselves on the long journey with whist and woman suffrage discussions. We noticed a dyspeptic-looking clergyman, evidently of a bilious temperament, eying us very steadily and disapprovingly the first day, and in a quiet way we warned each other that, in due time, he would give us a sermon on the sin of card playing.

Sitting alone, early next morning, he seated himself by my side, and asked me if I would allow him to express his opinion on card playing. I said " Oh, yes! I fully believe in free speech." " Well," said he, " I never touch cards. I think they are an invention of the devil to lead unwary souls from all serious thought of the stern duties of life and the realities of eternity! I was sorry to see you, with your white hair, probably near the end of your earthly career, playing cards and talking with those reckless army officers, who delight in killing their fellow-beings. No! I do not believe in war or card playing; such things do not prepare the soul for heaven." " Well," said I, " you are quite right, with your views, to abjure the society of army officers and all games of cards. You, no doubt, enjoy your own thoughts and the book you are reading, more than you would the conversation of those gentlemen and a game of whist. We must regulate our conduct by our own highest ideal. While I deplore the necessity of war, yet I know in our Army many of the noblest types of manhood, whose acquaintance I prize most highly. I enjoy all games, too, from chess down to dominoes. There is so much that is sad and stern in life that we need sometimes to lay down its burdens and indulge in innocent amusements. Thus, you see, what is wise from my standpoint is unwise from yours. I am sorry that you repudiate all amusements, as they contribute to the health of body and soul. You are sorry that I do not think as you do and regulate my life accordingly. You are sure that you are right. I am equally sure that I am. Hence there is nothing to be done in either case but to let each other alone, and wait for the slow process of evolution to give to each of us a higher standard." Just then one of the officers asked me if I was ready for a game of whist, and I excused myself from further discussion. I met many of those dolorous saints in my travels, who spent so much thought on eternity and saving their souls that they lost all the joys of time, as well as those sweet virtues of courtesy and charity that might best fit them for good works on earth and happiness in heaven.

In the spring I went to Nebraska, and Miss Anthony and I again made a Western tour, sometimes together and sometimes by different routes. A constitutional

convention was in session in Lincoln, and it was proposed to submit an amendment to strike the word
" male " from the Constitution.   Nebraska became a
State in March, 1867, and took " Equality before the
law " as her motto.   Her Territorial legislature had
discussed, many times, proposed liberal legislation for
women, and her State legislature had twice considered
propositions for woman's enfranchisement.   I had a
valise with me containing Hon. Benjamin F. Butler's
minority reports as a member of the Judiciary Committee of the United States House of Representatives, in
favor of woman's right to vote under the Fourteenth
Amendment.   As we were crossing the Platte River,
in transferring the baggage to the boat, my valise fell
into the river.   My heart stood still at the thought of
such a fate for all those able arguments.   After the
great General had been in hot water all his life, it was
grievous to think of any of his lucubrations perishing in
cold water at last.   Fortunately they were rescued.
On reaching Lincoln I was escorted to the home of the
Governor, where I spread the documents in the sunshine, and they were soon ready to be distributed among
the members of the constitutional convention.

After I had addressed the convention, some of the
members called on me to discuss the points of my
speech.   All the gentlemen were serious and respectful
with one exception.   A man with an unusually small
head, diminutive form, and crooked legs tried, at my
expense, to be witty and facetious.   During a brief
pause in the conversation he brought his chair directly
before me and said, in a mocking tone, " Don't you
think that the best thing a woman can do is to perform
well her part in the role of wife and mother?   My wife

has presented me with eight beautiful children; is not this a better life-work than that of exercising the right of suffrage? "

I had had my eye on this man during the whole interview, and saw that the other members were annoyed at his behavior. I decided, when the opportune moment arrived, to give him an answer not soon to be forgotten; so I promptly replied to his question, as I slowly viewed him from head to foot, " I have met few men, in my life, worth repeating eight times." The members burst into a roar of laughter, and one of them, clapping him on the shoulder, said: " There, sonny, you have read and spelled; you better go." This scene was heralded in all the Nebraska papers, and, wherever the little man went, he was asked why Mrs. Stanton thought he was not worth repeating eight times.

During my stay in Lincoln there was a celebration of the opening of some railroad. An immense crowd from miles about assembled on this occasion. The collation was spread and speeches were made in the open air. The men congratulated each other on the wonderful progress the State had made since it became an organized Territory in 1854. There was not the slightest reference, at first, to the women. One speaker said: " This State was settled by three brothers, John, James, and Joseph, and from them have sprung the great concourse of people that greet us here to-day." I turned, and asked the Governor if all these people had sprung, Minerva-like, from the brains of John, James, and Joseph. He urged me to put that question to the speaker; so, in one of his eloquent pauses, I propounded the query, which was greeted with loud and prolonged cheers, to the evident satisfaction of the women pres-

ent. The next speaker took good care to give the due
meed of praise to Ann, Jane, and Mary, and to every
mention of the mothers of Nebraska the crowd heartily
responded.

In toasting "the women of Nebraska," at the
collation, I said: "Here's to the mothers, who came
hither by long, tedious journeys, closely packed
with restless children in emigrant wagons, cooking
the meals by day, and nursing the babies by night, while
the men slept. Leaving comfortable homes in the
East, they endured all the hardships of pioneer life, suffered, with the men, the attacks of the Dakota Indians
and the constant apprehension of savage raids, of prairie fires, and the devastating locusts. Man's trials, his
fears, his losses, all fell on woman with double force; yet
history is silent concerning the part woman performed
in the frontier life of the early settlers. Men make no
mention of her heroism and divine patience; they take
no thought of the mental or physical agonies women
endure in the perils of maternity, ofttimes without nurse
or physician in the supreme hour of their need, going,
as every mother does, to the very gates of death in giving life to an immortal being!"

Traveling all over these Western States in the early
days, seeing the privations women suffered, and listening to the tales of sorrow at the fireside, I wondered
that men could ever forget the debt of gratitude they
owed to their mothers, or fail to commemorate their
part in the growth of a great people. Yet the men of
Nebraska have twice defeated the woman suffrage
amendment.

In 1874 Michigan was the point of interest to all
those who had taken part in the woman-suffrage move-

ment. The legislature, by a very large majority, submitted to a vote of the electors an amendment of the Constitution, in favor of striking out the word "male" and thus securing civil and political rights to the women of the State. It was a very active campaign. Crowded meetings were held in all the chief towns and cities. Professor Moses Coit Tyler, and a large number of ministers preached, every Sunday, on the subject of woman's position. The Methodist conference passed a resolution in favor of the amendment by a unanimous vote. I was in the State during the intense heat of May and June, speaking every evening to large audiences; in the afternoon to women alone, and preaching every Sunday in some pulpit. The Methodists, Universalists, Unitarians, and Quakers all threw open their churches to the apostles of the new gospel of equality for women. We spoke in jails, prisons, asylums, dépots, and the open air. Wherever there were ears to hear, we lifted up our voices, and, on the wings of the wind, the glad tidings were carried to the remote corners of the State, and the votes of forty thousand men, on election day, in favor of the amendment were so many testimonials to the value of the educational work accomplished.

I made many valuable acquaintances, on that trip, with whom I have maintained lifelong friendships. One pleasant day I passed in the home of Governor Bagley and his wife, with a group of pretty children. I found the Governor deeply interested in prison reform. He had been instrumental in passing a law giving prisoners lights in their cells and pleasant reading matter until nine o'clock. His ideas of what prisons should be, as unfolded that day, have since been

fully realized in the grand experiment now being successfully tried at Elmira, New York.

I visited the State prison at Jackson, and addressed
seven hundred men and boys, ranging from seventy
down to seventeen years of age. Seated on the dais
with the chaplain, I saw them file in to dinner, and,
while they were eating, I had an opportunity to study
the sad, despairing faces before me. I shall never forget the hopeless expression of one young man, who had
just been sentenced for twenty years, nor how ashamed
I felt that one of my own sex, trifling with two lovers,
had fanned the jealousy of one against the other, until
the tragedy ended in the death of one and the almost
lifelong imprisonment of the other. If girls should be
truthful and transparent in any relations in life, surely
it is in those of love, involving the strongest passions
of which human nature is capable. As the chaplain
told me the sad story, and I noticed the prisoner's refined face and well-shaped head, I felt that the young
man was not under the right influences to learn the
lesson he needed. Fear, coercion, punishment, are the
masculine remedies for moral weakness, but statistics
show their failure for centuries. Why not change the
system and try the education of the moral and intellectual faculties, cheerful surroundings, inspiring influences? Everything in our present system tends to
lower the physical vitality, the self-respect, the moral
tone, and to harden instead of reforming the criminal.

My heart was so heavy I did not know what to say to
such an assembly of the miserable. I asked the chaplain
what I should say. "Just what you please," he replied. Thinking they had probably heard enough of
their sins, their souls, and the plan of salvation, I

thought I would give them the news of the day. So I told them about the woman suffrage amendment, what I was doing in the State, my amusing encounters with opponents, their arguments, my answers. I told them of the great changes that would be effected in prison life when the mothers of the nation had a voice in the buildings and discipline. I told them what Governor Bagley said, and of the good time coming when prisons would no longer be places of punishment but schools of reformation. To show them what women would do to realize this beautiful dream, I told them of Elizabeth Fry and Dorothea L. Dix, of Mrs. Farnham's experiment at Sing Sing, and Louise Michel's in New Caledonia, and, in closing, I said: " Now I want all of you who are in favor of the amendment to hold up your right hands." They gave a unanimous vote, and laughed heartily when I said, " I do wish you could all go to the polls in November and that we could lock our opponents up here until after the election." I felt satisfied that they had had one happy hour, and that I had said nothing to hurt the feelings of the most unfortunate. As they filed off to their respective workshops my faith and hope for brighter days went with them.

Then I went all through the prison. Everything looked clean and comfortable on the surface, but I met a few days after a man, just set free, who had been there five years for forgery. He told me the true inwardness of the system; of the wretched, dreary life they suffered, and the brutality of the keepers. He said the prison was infested with mice and vermin, and that, during the five years he was there, he had never lain down one night to undisturbed slumber. The sufferings endured in summer for want of air, he said, were indescribable. In this prison the cells were in the center or the building, the corridors running all around by the windows, so the prisoners had no outlook and no direct contact with the air. Hence, if a careless keeper forgot to open the windows after a storm, the poor prisoners panted for air in their cells, like fish out of water. My informant worked in the mattress department, over the room where prisoners were punished. He said he could hear the lash and the screams of the victims from morning till night. "Hard as the work is all day," said he, "it is a blessed relief to get out of our cells to march across the yard and get one glimpse of the heavens above, and one breath of pure air, and to be in contact with other human souls in the workshops, for, although we could never speak to each other, yet there was a hidden current of sympathy conveyed by look that made us one in our misery."

Though the press of the State was largely in our favor, yet there were some editors who, having no arguments, exercised the little wit they did possess in low ridicule. It was in this campaign that an editor in a Kalamazoo journal said: "That ancient daughter of Methuselah, Susan B. Anthony, passed through our city yesterday, on her way to the Plainwell meeting, with a bonnet on her head looking as if it had recently descended from Noah's ark." Miss Anthony often referred to this description of herself, and said, "Had I represented twenty thousand voters in Michigan, that political editor would not have known nor cared whether I was the oldest or the youngest daughter of Methuselah, or whether my bonnet came from the ark or from Worth's."

CHAPTER XIX.

THE year 1876 was one of intense excitement and la-
borious activity throughout the country. The anticipation of the centennial birthday of the Republic, to be
celebrated in Philadelphia, stirred the patriotism of the
people to the highest point of enthusiasm. As each
State was to be represented in the great exhibition,
local pride added another element to the public interest.
Then, too, everyone who could possibly afford the journey was making busy preparations to spend the Fourth
of July, the natal day of the Republic, mid the scenes
where the Declaration of Independence was issued in
1776, the Government inaugurated, and the first national councils were held. Those interested in women's
political rights decided to make the Fourth a woman's
day, and to celebrate the occasion, in their various
localities, by delivering orations and reading their own
declaration of rights, with dinners and picnics in the
town halls or groves, as most convenient. But many
from every State in the Union made their arrangements
to spend the historic period in Philadelphia. Owing,
also, to the large number of foreigners who came over
to join in the festivities, that city was crammed to its
utmost capacity. With the crowd and excessive heat,
comfort was everywhere sacrificed to curiosity.

The enthusiasm throughout the country had given a

fresh impulse to the lyceum bureaus. Like the ferry-boats in New York harbor, running hither and thither, crossing each other's tracks, the whole list of lecturers were on the wing, flying to every town and city from San Francisco to New York. As soon as a new railroad ran through a village of five hundred inhabitants that could boast a schoolhouse, a church, or a hotel, and one enterprising man or woman, a course of lectures was at once inaugurated as a part of the winter's entertainments.

On one occasion I was invited, by mistake, to a little town to lecture the same evening when the Christy Minstrels were to perform. It was arranged, as the town had only one hall, that I should speak from seven to eight o'clock and the minstrels should have the remainder of the time. One may readily see that, with the minstrels in anticipation, a lecture on any serious question would occupy but a small place in the hearts of the people in a town where they seldom had entertainments of any kind. All the time I was speaking there was a running to and fro behind the scenes, where the minstrels were transforming themselves with paints and curly wigs into Africans, and laughing at each other's jests. As it was a warm evening, and the windows were open, the hilarity of the boys in the street added to the general din. Under such circumstances it was difficult to preserve my equilibrium. I felt like laughing at my own comical predicament, and I decided to make my address a medley of anecdotes and stories, like a string of beads, held together by a fine thread of argument and illustration. The moment the hand of the clock pointed at eight o'clock the band struck up, thus announcing that the happy hour for the min-

strels had come.   Those of my audience who wished to
stay were offered seats at half price; those who did not,
slipped out, and the crowd rushed in, soon packing the
house to its utmost capacity.   I stayed, and enjoyed the
performance of the minstrels more than I had my own.

As the lyceum season lasted from October to June,
I was late in reaching Philadelphia.   Miss Anthony and
Mrs. Gage had already been through the agony of finding appropriate headquarters for the National Suffrage
Association.   I found them pleasantly situated on the
lower floor of No. 1431 Chestnut Street, with the work
for the coming month clearly mapped out.   As it was
the year for nominating candidates for the presidency of the United States, the Republicans and
Democrats were about to hold their great conventions.   Hence letters were to be written to them
recommending a woman suffrage plank in their platforms, and asking seats for women in the conventions,
with the privilege of being heard in their own behalf.
On these letters our united wisdom was concentrated,
and twenty thousand copies of each were published.

Then it was thought pre-eminently proper that a
Woman's Declaration of Rights should be issued.
Days and nights were spent over that document.   After
many twists from our analytical tweezers, with a critical consideration of every word and sentence, it was at
last, by a consensus of the competent, pronounced very
good.   Thousands were ordered to be printed, and were
folded, put in envelopes, stamped, directed, and scattered.   Miss Anthony, Mrs. Gage, and I worked
sixteen hours, day and night, pressing everyone who
came in, into the service, and late at night carrying immense bundles to be mailed.   With meetings, recep-

tions, and a succession of visitors, all of whom we plied with woman suffrage literature, we felt we had accomplished a great educational work.

Among the most enjoyable experiences at our headquarters were the frequent visits of our beloved Lucretia Mott, who used to come from her country home bringing us eggs, cold chickens, and fine Oolong tea. As she had presented us with a little black teapot that, like Mercury's mysterious pitcher of milk, filled itself for every coming guest, we often improvised luncheons with a few friends. At parting, Lucretia always made a contribution to our depleted treasury. Here we had many prolonged discussions as to the part we should take, on the Fourth of July, in the public celebration. We thought it would be fitting for us to read our Declaration of Rights immediately after that of the Fathers was read, as an impeachment of them and their male descendants for their injustice and oppression. Ours contained as many counts, and quite as important, as those against King George in 1776. Accordingly, we applied to the authorities to allow us seats on the platform and a place in the programme of the public celebration, which was to be held in the historic old Independence Hall. As General Hawley was in charge of the arrangements for the day, I wrote him as follows:

"1431 Chestnut Street, July 1, 1876.
"General Hawley.

"*Honored Sir:* As President of the National Woman's Suffrage Association, I am authorized to ask you for tickets to the platform, at Independence Hall, for the celebration on the Fourth of July. We should like to have seats for at least one representative woman from each State. We also ask your permission to read our Declaration of Rights immediately after the reading of the Declaration of Independence of the Fathers is finished. Although these are small favors to ask as representatives of one-half of the nation, yet we shall be under great obligations to you if granted.

" Respectfully Yours,
" Elizabeth Cady Stanton."

To this I received the following reply:

"U. S. C. C. Headquarters, July 2.

" Mrs. Elizabeth Cady Stanton.

" *Dear Madam:* I send you, with pleasure, half a dozen cards of invitation. As the platform is already crowded, it is impossible to reserve the number of seats you desire. I regret to say it is also impossible for us to make any change in the programme at this late hour. We are crowded for time to carry out what is already proposed.

" Yours Very Respectfully,
" Joseph R. Hawley,
" President, U. S. C. C."

With this rebuff, Mrs. Mott and I decided that we would not accept the offered seats, but would be ready to open our own convention called for that day, at the First Unitarian church, where the Rev. William H. Furness had preached for fifty years. But some of our younger coadjutors decided that they would occupy the seats and present our Declaration of Rights. They said truly, women will be taxed to pay the expenses of this celebration, and we have as good a right to that platform and to the ears of the people as the men have, and we will be heard.

That historic Fourth of July dawned at last, one of the most oppressive days of that heated season. Susan B. Anthony, Matilda Joslyn Gage, Sara Andrews Spencer, Lillie Devereux Blake, and Phœbe W. Couzins made their way through the crowds under the broiling sun of Independence Square, carrying the Woman's Declaration of Rights. This Declaration had been handsomely engrossed by one of their number, and signed by the oldest and most prominent advocates of woman's enfranchisement. Their tickets of admission proved an " open sesame " through the military barriers, and, a few moments before the opening of the ceremonies, these women found themselves within the precincts from which most of their sex were excluded.

The Declaration of 1776 was read by Richard Henry Lee of Virginia, about whose family clusters so much historic fame. The moment he finished reading was determined upon as the appropriate time for the presentation of the Woman's Declaration. Not quite sure how their approach might be met, not quite certain if, at this final moment, they would be permitted to reach the presiding officer, those ladies arose and made their way down the aisle. The bustle of preparation for the Brazilian hymn covered their advance. The foreign guests and the military and civil officers who filled the space directly in front of the speaker's stand, courteously made way, while Miss Anthony, in fitting words, presented the Declaration to the presiding officer. Senator Ferry's face paled as, bowing low, with no word he received the Declaration, which thus became part of the day's proceedings. The ladies turned, scattering printed copies as they deliberately walked down the platform. On every side eager hands were outstretched, men stood on seats and asked for them, while General Hawley, thus defied and beaten in his audacious denial to women of the right to present their Declaration, shouted, " Order, order! "

Passing out, these ladies made their way to a platform, erected for the musicians, in front of Independence Hall. Here, under the shadow of Washington's statue, back of them the old bell that proclaimed " liberty to all the land and all the inhabitants thereof," they took their places, and, to a listening, applauding crowd, Miss Anthony read the Woman's Declaration. During the reading of the Declaration, Mrs. Gage stood beside Miss Anthony and held an umbrella over her head, to shelter her friend from the intense heat of the noonday sun. And thus in the same hour, on opposite sides of old Independence Hall, did the men and women express their opinions on the great principles proclaimed on the natal day of the Republic. The Declaration was handsomely framed, and now hangs in the Vice President's room in the Capitol at Washington.

These heroic ladies then hurried from Independence Hall to the church, already crowded with an expectant audience, to whom they gave a full report of the morning's proceedings. The Hutchinsons of worldwide fame were present in their happiest vein, interspersing the speeches with appropriate songs and felicitous remarks. For five long hours on that hot midsummer day a crowded audience, many standing, listened with profound interest and reluctantly dispersed at last, all agreeing that it was one of the most impressive and enthusiastic meetings they had ever attended.

All through our Civil War the slaves on the Southern plantations had an abiding faith that the terrible conflict would result in freedom for their race. Just so through all the busy preparations of the Centennial, the women of the nation felt sure that the great national celebration could not pass without the concession of some new liberties to them. Hence they pressed their claims at every point, at the Fourth of July celebration in the exposition buildings, and in the Republican and Democratic nominating conventions; hoping to get a plank in the platforms of both the great political parties

The Woman's Pavilion upon the centennial grounds was an afterthought, as theologians claim woman herself to have been. The women of the country, after having contributed nearly one hundred thousand dollars to the centennial stock, found there had been no provision made for the separate exhibition of their work. The centennial board, of which Mrs. Gillespie was president, then decided to raise funds for the erection of a separate building, to be known as the Woman's Pavilion. It covered an acre of ground, and was erected at an expense of thirty thousand dollars—a small sum in comparison with the money which had been raised by women and expended on the other buildings, not to speak of the State and national appropriations, which the taxes levied on them had largely helped to swell.

The Pavilion was no true exhibit of woman's art. Few women are, as yet, owners of the business which their industry largely makes remunerative. Cotton factories, in which thousands of women work, are owned by men. The shoe business, in some branches of which

women are doing more than half the work, is under the
ownership of men.   Rich embroideries from India, rugs
of downy softness from Turkey, the muslin of Decca,
anciently known as " The Woven Wind," the pottery
and majolica ware of P. Pipsen's widow, the cartridges
and envelopes of Uncle Sam, Waltham watches, whose
finest mechanical work is done by women, and ten thousand other industries found no place in the pavilion.
Said United States Commissioner Meeker of Colorado,
" Woman's work comprises three-fourths of the exposition; it is scattered through every building; take it
away, and there would be no exposition."

But this pavilion rendered one good service to
woman in showing her capabilities as an engineer.   The
boiler, which furnished the force for running its work,
was under the charge of a young Canadian girl, Miss
Allison, who, from childhood, had loved machinery,
spending much time in the large saw and grist mills of
her father, run by engines of two and three hundred
horse-power, which she sometimes managed for amusement.   When her name was proposed for running the
pavilion machinery, it caused much opposition.   It was
said that the committee would, some day, find the pavilion blown to atoms; that the woman engineer would
spend her time reading novels instead of watching the
steam gauge; that the idea was impracticable and
should not be thought of.   But Miss Allison soon
proved her capabilities and the falseness of these
prophecies by taking her place in the engine room and
managing its workings with perfect ease.   Six power
looms, on which women wove carpets, webbing, silks,
etc., were run by this engine.   At a later period the
printing of *The New Century for Woman,* a paper pub-

lished by the centennial commission in the woman's building, was done by its means. Miss Allison declared the work to be more cleanly, more pleasant, and infinitely less fatiguing than cooking over a kitchen stove. " Since I have been compelled to earn my own living," she said, " I have never been engaged in work I like so well. Teaching school is much harder, and one is not paid so well." She expressed her confidence in her ability to manage the engines of an ocean steamer, and said that there were thousands of small engines in use in various parts of the country, and no reason existed why women should not be employed to manage them,—following the profession of engineer as a regular business,—an engine requiring far less attention than is given by a nursemaid or a mother to a child.

But to have made the Woman's Pavilion grandly historic, upon. its walls should have been hung the yearly protest of Harriet K. Hunt against taxation without representation; the legal papers served upon the Smith sisters when, for their refusal to pay taxes while unrepresented, their Alderney cows were seized and sold; the papers issued by the city of Worcester for the forced sale of the house and lands of Abby Kelly Foster, the veteran abolitionist, because she refused to pay taxes, giving the same reason our ancestors gave when they resisted taxation; a model of Bunker Hill monument, its foundation laid by Lafayette in 1825, but which remained unfinished nearly twenty years, until the famous German danseuse, Fanny Elssler, gave the proceeds of a public performance for that purpose. With these should have been exhibited framed copies of all the laws bearing unjustly upon women—those which rob her of her name, her earnings, her property, her children, her person; also the legal papers in the case of Susan B. Anthony, who was tried and fined for claiming her right to vote under the Fourteenth Amendment, and the decision of Mr. Justice Miller in the case of Myra Bradwell, denying national protection for woman's civil rights; and the later decision of Chief Justice Waite of the United States Supreme Court against Virginia L. Minor, denying women national protection for their political rights; decisions in favor of State rights which imperil the liberties not only of all women, but of every white man in the nation.

Woman's most fitting contributions to the Centennial Exposition would have been these protests, laws, and decisions, which show her political slavery. But all this was left for rooms outside of the centennial grounds, upon Chestnut Street, where the National Woman's Suffrage Association hoisted its flag, made its protests, and wrote the Declaration of Rights of the women of the United States.

To many thoughtful people it seemed captious and unreasonable for women to complain of injustice in this free land, amidst such universal rejoicings. When the majority of women are seemingly happy, it is natural to suppose that the discontent of the minority is the result of their unfortunate individual idiosyncrasies, and not of adverse influences in established conditions. But the history of the world shows that the vast majority, in every generation, passively accept the conditions into which they are born, while those who demanded larger liberties are ever a small, ostracized minority, whose claims are ridiculed and ignored. From our standpoint we would honor any Chinese woman who claimed the right to her feet and powers of locomotion; the Hindoo widows who refused to ascend the funeral pyre of their husbands; the Turkish women who threw off their masks and veils and left the harem; the Mormon women who abjured their faith and demanded monogamic relations. Why not equally honor the intelligent minority of American women who protest against the artificial disabilities by which their freedom is limited and their development arrested? That only a few, under any circumstances, protest against the injustice of long-established laws and customs, does not disprove the fact of the oppressions, while the satisfaction of the many, if real, only proves their apathy and deeper degradation. That a majority of the women of the United States accept, without protest, the disabilities which grow out of their disfranchisement is simply an evidence of their ignorance and cowardice, while the minority who demand a higher political status clearly prove their superior intelligence and wisdom.

At the close of the Forty-seventh Congress we made two new demands: First, for a special committee to consider all questions in regard to the civil and political rights of women. We naturally asked the question, As Congress has a special committee on the rights of Indians, why not on those of women? Are not women, as a factor in civilization, of more importance than Indians? Secondly, we asked for a room, in the Capitol, where our committee could meet, undisturbed, whenever they saw fit. Though these points were debated a long time, our demands were acceded to at last. We now have our special committee, and our room, with " Woman Suffrage " in gilt letters, over the door. In our struggle to achieve this, while our champion, the senior Senator from Massachusetts, stood up bravely in the discussion, the opposition not only ridiculed the special demand, but all attempts to secure the civil and political rights of women. As an example of the arguments of the opposition, I give what the Senator from Missouri said. It is a fair specimen of all that was produced on that side of the debate. Mr. Vest's poetical flights are most inspiring:

" The Senate now has forty-one committees, with a small army of messengers and clerks, one-half of whom, without exaggeration, are literally without employment. I shall not pretend to specify the committees of this body which have not one single bill, resolution, or proposition of any sort pending before them, and have not had for months. But, Mr. President, out of all committees without business, and habitually without business, in this body, there is one that, beyond any question, could take jurisdiction of this matter and do it ample justice. I refer to that most respectable and antique institution, the Committee on Revolutionary Claims. For thirty years it has been without business. For thirty long years the placid surface of that parliamentary sea has been without one single ripple. If the Senator from Massachusetts desires a tribunal for a calm, judicial equilibrium and examination—a tribunal far from the 'madding crowd's ignoble strife'—a tribunal eminently respectable, dignified and unique; why not send this question to the Committee on Revolutionary Claims? It is eminently proper that this subject should go to that committee because, if there is any revolutionary claim in this country, it is that of woman suffrage. (Laughter.) It revolutionizes society; it

revolutionizes religion; it revolutionizes the Constitution and laws; and it revolutionizes the opinions
of those so old-fashioned among us as to believe that
the legitimate and proper sphere of woman is the family
circle, as wife and mother, and not as politician and
voter—those of us who are proud to believe that

> " Woman's noblest station is retreat :
> Her fairest virtues fly from public sight ;
> Domestic worth—that shuns too strong a light.

" Before that Committee on Revolutionary Claims
why could not this most revolutionary of all claims receive immediate and ample attention? More than
that, as I said before, if there is any tribunal that could
give undivided time and dignified attention, is it not
this committee? If there is one peaceful haven of rest,
never disturbed by any profane bill or resolution of any
sort, it is the Committee on Revolutionary Claims. It
is, in parliamentary life, described by that ecstatic verse
in Watts' hymn—

> " There shall I bathe my wearied soul
> In seas of endless rest,
> And not one wave of trouble roll
> Across my peaceful breast.

" By all natural laws, stagnation breeds disease and
death, and what could stir up this most venerable and
respectable institution more than an application of the
strong-minded, with short hair and shorter skirts, in-
vading its dignified realm and elucidating all the excel-
lences of female suffrage. Moreover, if these ladies
could ever succeed in the providence of God in obtain-
ing a report from that committee, it would end this

question forever; for the public at large and myself included, in view of that miracle of female blandishment and female influence, would surrender at once, and female suffrage would become constitutional and lawful. Sir, I insist upon it that, in deference to this committee, in deference to the fact that it needs this sort of regimen and medicine, this whole subject should be so referred."

This gives a very fair idea of the character of the arguments produced by our opponents, from the inauguration of the movement. But, as there are no arguments in a republican government in favor of an aristocracy of sex, ridicule was really the only available weapon. After declaring " that no just government can be formed without the consent of the governed," " that taxation without representation is tyranny," it is difficult to see on what basis one-half the people are disfranchised.

CHAPTER XX.

THE four years following the Centennial were busy, happy ones, of varied interests and employments, public and private. Sons and daughters graduating from college, bringing troops of young friends to visit us; the usual matrimonial entanglements, with all their promises of celestial bliss intertwined with earthly doubts and fears; weddings, voyages to Europe, business ventures —in this whirl of plans and projects our heads, hearts, and hands were fully occupied. Seven boys and girls dancing round the fireside, buoyant with all life's joys opening before them, are enough to keep the most apathetic parents on the watch-towers by day and anxious even in dreamland by night. My spare time, if it can be said that I ever had any, was given during these days to social festivities. The inevitable dinners, teas, picnics, and dances with country neighbors, all came round in quick succession. We lived, at this time, at Tenafly, New Jersey, not far from the publisher of the *Sun*, Isaac W. England, who also had seven boys and girls as full of frolic as our own. Mrs. England and I entered into all their games with equal zest. The youngest thought half the fun was to see our enthusiasm in " blindman's buff," " fox and geese," and " bean bags." It thrills me with delight, even now, to see these games!

Mr. England was the soul of hospitality. He was

never more happy than when his house was crowded with guests, and his larder with all the delicacies of the season. Though he and Mr. Stanton were both connected with that dignified journal, the New York *Sun*, yet they often joined in the general hilarity. I laugh, as I write, at the memory of all the frolics we had on the blue hills of Jersey.

In addition to the domestic cares which a large family involved, Mrs. Gage, Miss Anthony, and I were already busy collecting material for " The History of Woman Suffrage." This required no end of correspondence. Then my lecturing trips were still a part of the annual programme. Washington conventions, too, with calls, appeals, resolutions, speeches and hearings before the Committees of Congress and State legislatures, all these came round in the year's proceedings as regularly as pumpkin pies for Thanksgiving, plum pudding for Christmas, and patriotism for Washington's birthday. Those who speak for glory or philanthropy are always in demand for college commencements and Fourth of July orations, hence much of Miss Anthony's eloquence, as well as my own, was utilized in this way.

On October 18, 1880, I had an impromptu dinner party. Elizabeth Boynton Harbert, May Wright Thompson (now Sewall), Phœbe W. Couzins, and Arethusa Forbes, returning from a Boston convention, all by chance met under my roof. We had a very merry time talking over the incidents of the convention, Boston proprieties, and the general situation. As I gave them many early reminiscences, they asked if I had kept a diary. " No," I said, " not a pen scratch of the past have I except what might be gathered from many family letters." They urged me to begin a diary at once; so I promised I would on my coming birthday.

My great grief that day was that we were putting in a new range, and had made no preparations for dinner. This completely upset the presiding genius of my culinary department, as she could not give us the bounteous feast she knew was expected on such occasions. I, as usual, when there was any lack in the viands, tried to be as brilliant as possible in conversation; discussing Nirvana, Karma, reincarnation, and thus turning attention from the evanescent things of earth to the joys of a life to come,—not an easy feat to perform with strong-minded women,—but, in parting, they seemed happy and refreshed, and all promised to come again.

But we shall never meet there again, as the old, familiar oaks and the majestic chestnut trees have passed into other hands. Strange lovers now whisper their vows of faith and trust under the tree where a most charming wedding ceremony—that of my daughter Margaret—was solemnized one bright October day. All Nature seemed to do her utmost to heighten the beauty of the occasion. The verdure was brilliant with autumnal tints, the hazy noonday sun lent a peculiar softness to every shadow—even the birds and insects were hushed to silence. As the wedding march rose soft and clear, two stately ushers led the way; then a group of Vassar classmates, gayly decked in silks of different colors, followed by the bride and groom. An immense Saint Bernard dog, on his own account brought up the rear, keeping time with measured tread. He took his seat in full view, watching, alternately, the officiating clergyman, the bride and groom, and guests, as

if to say: "What does all this mean?" No one behaved with more propriety and no one looked more
radiant than he, with a ray of sunlight on his beautiful
coat of long hair, his bright brass collar, and his wonderful head. Bruno did not live to see the old home
broken up, but sleeps peacefully there, under the chestnut trees, and fills a large place in many of our pleasant
memories.

On November 12, 1880, I was sixty-five years old,
and, pursuant to my promise, I then began my diary.
It was a bright, sunny day, but the frost king was at
work; all my grand old trees, that stood like sentinels,
to mark the boundary of my domain, were stripped of
their foliage, and their brilliant colors had faded into
a uniform brown; but the evergreens and the tall, prim
cedars held their own, and, when covered with snow,
their exquisite beauty brought tears to my eyes. One
need never be lonely mid beautiful trees.

My thoughts were with my absent children—Harriot
in France, Theodore in Germany, Margaret with her
husband and brother Gerrit, halfway across the continent, and Bob still in college. I spent the day writing
letters and walking up and down the piazza, and enjoyed,
from my windows, a glorious sunset. Alone, on birth-
days or holidays, one is very apt to indulge in sad retro-
spections. The thought of how much more I might
have done for the perfect development of my children
than I had accomplished, depressed me. I thought of
all the blunders in my own life and in their education.
Little has been said of the responsibilities of parental
life; accordingly little or nothing has been done. I had
such visions of parental duties that day that I came to
the conclusion that parents never could pay the debt

they owe their children for bringing them into this world of suffering, unless they can insure them sound minds in sound bodies, and enough of the good things of this life to enable them to live without a continual struggle for the necessaries of existence. I have no sympathy with the old idea that children owe parents a debt of gratitude for the simple fact of existence, generally conferred without thought and merely for their own pleasure. How seldom we hear of any high or holy preparation for the office of parenthood! Here, in the most momentous act of life, all is left to chance. Men and women, intelligent and prudent in all other directions, seem to exercise no forethought here, but hand down their individual and family idiosyncrasies in the most reckless manner.

On November 13 the New York *Tribune* announced the death of Lucretia Mott, eighty-eight years old. Having known her in the flush of life, when all her faculties were at their zenith, and in the repose of age, when her powers began to wane, her withdrawal from among us seemed as beautiful and natural as the changing foliage, from summer to autumn, of some grand old oak I have watched and loved.

The arrival of Miss Anthony and Mrs. Gage, on November 20, banished all family matters from my mind. What planning, now, for volumes, chapters, footnotes, margins, appendices, paper, and type; of engravings, title, preface, and introduction! I had never thought that the publication of a book required the consideration of such endless details. We stood appalled before the mass of material, growing higher and higher with every mail, and the thought of all the reading involved made us feel as if our life-work lay before us. Six weeks of steady labor all day, and often until midnight, made no visible decrease in the pile of documents. However, before the end of the month we had our arrangements all made with publishers and engravers, and six chapters in print. When we began to correct proof we felt as if something was accomplished. Thus we worked through the winter and far into the spring, with no change except the Washington Convention and an occasional evening meeting in New York city. We had frequent visits from friends whom we were glad to see. Hither came Edward M. Davis, Sarah Pugh, Adeline Thompson, Frederick Cabot of Boston, Dr. William F. Channing, and sweet little Clara Spence, who recited for us some of the most beautiful selections in her repertoire.

In addition we had numberless letters from friends and foes, some praising and some condemning our proposed undertaking, and, though much alone, we were kept in touch with the outside world. But so conflicting was the tone of the letters that, if we had not taken a very fair gauge of ourselves and our advisers, we should have abandoned our project and buried all the valuable material collected, to sleep in pine boxes forever.

At this time I received a very amusing letter from the Rev. Robert Collyer, on " literary righteousness," quizzing me for using one of his anecdotes in my sketch of Lucretia Mott, without giving him credit. I laughed him to scorn, that he should have thought it was my duty to have done so. I told him plainly that he belonged to a class of " white male citizens," who had robbed me of all civil and political rights; of property, children, and personal freedom; and now it

ill became him to call me to account for using one of
his little anecdotes that, ten to one, he had cribbed
from some woman. I told him that I considered his
whole class as fair game for literary pilfering. That
women had been taxed to build colleges to educate
men, and if we could pick up a literary crumb that had
fallen from their feasts, we surely had a right to it.
Moreover, I told him that man's duty in the world was
to work, to dig and delve for jewels, real and ideal, and
lay them at woman's feet, for her to use as she might
see fit; that he should feel highly complimented, instead of complaining, that he had written something I
thought worth using. He answered like the nobleman
he is; susceptible of taking in a new idea. He admitted
that, in view of the shortcomings of his entire sex, he
had not one word to say in the way of accusation, but
lay prostrate at my feet in sackcloth and ashes, wondering that he had not taken my view of the case in
starting.

Only twice in my life have I been accused of quot-
ing without giving due credit. The other case was
that of Matilda Joslyn Gage. I had, on two or three
occasions, used a motto of hers in autograph books,
just as I had sentiments from Longfellow, Lowell,
Shakespeare, Moses, or Paul. In long lyceum trips innumerable autograph books met one at every turn, in
the cars, depots, on the platform, at the hotel and in
the omnibus. "A sentiment, please," cry half a dozen
voices. One writes hastily different sentiments for
each. In this way I unfortunately used a pet sentiment
of Matilda's. So, here and now, I say to my autograph
admirers, from New York to San Francisco, whenever
you see " There is a word sweeter than Mother, Home,

or Heaven—that word is Liberty," remember it belongs
to Matilda Joslyn Gage. I hope, now, that Robert and
Matilda will say, in their posthumous works, that I made
the *amende honorable,* as I always strive to do when
friends feel they have not been fairly treated.

In May, 1881, the first volume of our History appeared; it was an octavo, containing 871 pages, with
good paper, good print, handsome engravings, and
nicely bound. I welcomed it with the same feeling of
love and tenderness as I did my firstborn. I took the
same pleasure in hearing it praised and felt the same
mortification in hearing it criticised. The most hearty
welcome it received was from Rev. William Henry
Channing. He wrote us that it was as interesting and
fascinating as a novel. He gave it a most flattering
notice in one of the London papers. John W. Forney,
too, wrote a good review and sent a friendly letter.
Mayo W. Hazeltine, one of the ablest critics in this country, in the New York *Sun,* also gave it a very careful
and complimentary review. In fact, we received far
more praise and less blame than we anticipated. We
began the second volume in June. In reading over
the material concerning woman's work in the War, I
felt how little our labors are appreciated. Who can
sum up all the ills the women of a nation suffer from
war? They have all of the misery and none of the
glory; nothing to mitigate their weary waiting and
watching for the loved ones who will return no more.

In the spring of 1881, to vary the monotony of
the work on the history, we decided to hold a series
of conventions through the New England States.
We began during the Anniversary week in Boston,
and had several crowded, enthusiastic meetings in

Tremont Temple. In addition to our suffrage meetings, I spoke before the Free Religious, Moral
Education, and Heredity associations. All our speakers
stayed at the Parker House, and we had a very
pleasant time visiting together in our leisure hours.
We were received by Governor Long, at the State
House. He made a short speech, in favor of woman
suffrage, in reply to Mrs. Hooker. We also called on
the Mayor, at the City Hall, and went through Jordan
& Marsh's great mercantile establishment, where the
clerks are chiefly young girls, who are well fed and
housed, and have pleasant rooms, with a good library,
where they sit and read in the evening. We went
through the Sherborn Reformatory Prison for Women,
managed entirely by women. We found it clean and
comfortable, more like a pleasant home than a place of
punishment.

Mrs. Robinson, Miss Anthony, and I were invited to dine with the Bird Club. No woman, other
than I, had ever had that honor before. I dined
with them in 1870, escorted by "Warrington" of
the Springfield *Republican* and Edwin Morton. There
I met Frank Sanborn for the first time. Frank Bird held
about the same place in political life in Massachusetts,
that Thurlow Weed did in the State of New York for
forty years. In the evening we had a crowded reception at the home of Mrs. Fenno Tudor, who occupied
a fine old residence facing the Common, where we met
a large gathering of Boston reformers. On Decora-
tion Day, May 30, we went to Providence, where I was
the guest of Dr. William F. Channing. We had a very
successful convention there. Senator Anthony and ex-
Governor Sprague were in the audience and expressed

great pleasure, afterward, in all they had heard. I preached in Rev. Frederick Hinckley's church the previous Sunday afternoon.

From Providence I hurried home, to meet my son Theodore and his bride, who had just landed from France. We decorated our house and grounds with Chinese lanterns and national flags for their reception. As we had not time to send to New York for bunting, our flags—French and American—were all made of bright red and blue cambric. The effect was fine when they arrived; but, unfortunately, there came up a heavy thunderstorm in the night and so drenched our beautiful flags that they became colorless rags. My little maid announced to me early in the morning that " the French and Americans had had a great battle during the night and that the piazza was covered with blood." This was startling news to one just awakening from a sound sleep. " Why, Emma! " I said, " what do you mean? " " Why," she replied, " the rain has washed all the color out of our flags, and the piazza is covered with red and blue streams of water." As the morning sun appeared in all its glory, chasing the dark clouds away, our decorations did indeed look pale and limp, and were promptly removed.

I was happily surprised with my tall, stately daughter, Marguerite Berry. A fine-looking girl of twenty, straight, strong, and sound, modest and pleasing. She can walk miles, sketches from nature with great skill and rapidity, and speaks three languages. I had always said to my sons: " When you marry, choose a woman with a spine and sound teeth; remember the teeth show the condition of the bones in the rest of the body." So, when Theodore introduced his wife to me,

he said, " You see I have followed your advice; her spine
is as straight as it should be, and every tooth in her head
as sound as ivory." This reminds me of a young man
who used to put my stoves up for the winter. He told
me one day that he thought of getting married.
" Well," I said, " above all things get a wife with a
spine and sound teeth." Stove pipe in hand he turned
to me with a look of surprise, and said: " Do they ever
come without spines? "

In July, 1881, sitting under the trees, Miss Anthony and I read and discussed Wendell Phillips'
magnificent speech before the Phi Beta Kappa
Society at Harvard College. This society had often
talked of inviting him, but was afraid of his
radical utterances. At last, hoping that years might
have modified his opinions and somewhat softened
his speech, an invitation was given. The élite of
Boston, the presidents and college professors from far
and near, were there. A great audience of the wise, the
learned, the distinguished in State and Church assembled. Such a conservative audience, it was supposed,
would surely hold this radical in check. Alas! they
were all doomed, for once, to hear the naked truth, on
every vital question of the day. Thinking this might
be his only opportunity to rouse some liberal thought
in conservative minds, he struck the keynote of every
reform; defended labor strikes, the Nihilists of Russia,
prohibition, woman suffrage, and demanded reformation in our prisons, courts of justice, and halls of legislation. On the woman question, he said:

" Social science affirms that woman's place in society
marks the level of civilization. From its twilight in
Greece, through the Italian worship of the Virgin, the

dreams of chivalry, the justice of the civil law, and the equality of French society, we trace her gradual recognition, while our common law, as Lord Brougham confessed, was, with relation to women, the opprobrium of the age of Christianity. For forty years earnest men and women, working noiselessly, have washed away the opprobrium, the statute books of thirty States have been remodeled, and woman stands, to-day, almost face to face with her last claim—the ballot. It has been a weary and thankless, though successful struggle. But if there be any refuge from that ghastly curse, the vice of great cities, before which social science stands palsied and dumb, it is in this more equal recognition of women.

" If, in this critical battle for universal suffrage, our fathers' noblest legacy to us and the greatest trust God leaves in our hands, there be any weapon, which, once taken from the armory, will make victory certain, it will be as it has been in art, literature, and society, summoning woman into the political arena. The literary class, until within half a dozen years, has taken no note of this great uprising; only to fling every obstacle in its way.

" The first glimpse we get of Saxon blood in history is that line of Tacitus in his ' Germany,' which reads, ' In all grave matters they consult their women.' Years hence, when robust Saxon sense has flung away Jewish superstition and Eastern prejudice, and put under its foot fastidious scholarship and squeamish fashion, some second Tacitus from the valley of the Mississippi will answer to him of the Seven Hills: ' In all grave questions, we consult our women.'

" If the Alps, piled in cold and silence, be the emblem of despotism, we joyfully take the ever restless ocean for ours, only pure because never still. To be as good as

our fathers, we must be better. They silenced their
fears and subdued their prejudices, inaugurating free
speech and equality with no precedent on the file.   Let
us rise to their level, crush appetite, and prohibit temptation if it rots great cities; intrench labor in sufficient
bulwarks against that wealth which, without the ten-
fold strength of modern incorporations, wrecked the
Grecian and Roman states; and, with a sterner effort
still, summon woman into civil life, as re-enforcement to
our laboring ranks, in the effort to make our civilization a success.   Sit not like the figure on our silver
coin, looking ever backward.

> " ' New occasions teach new duties,
>   Time makes ancient good uncouth,
>   They must upward still and onward,
>   Who would keep abreast of truth.
>   Lo ! before us gleam her watch fires—
>   We ourselves must pilgrims be,
>   Launch our *Mayflower*, and steer boldly
>   Through the desperate winter sea,
>   Nor attempt the future's portal
>   With the past's blood-rusted key.' "

That Harvard speech in the face of fashion, bigotry,
and conservatism—so liberal, so eloquent, so brave—is a
model for every young man, who, like the orator, would
devote his talents to the best interests of the race,
rather than to his personal ambition for mere worldly
success.

Toward the end of October, Miss Anthony returned,
after a rest of two months, and we commenced work
again on the second volume of the History. November
2 being election day, the Republican carriage, decorated with flags and evergreens, came to the door for

voters. As I owned the house and paid the taxes, and as none of the white males was home, I suggested that I might go down and do the voting, whereupon the gentlemen who represented the Republican committee urged me, most cordially, to do so. Accompanied by my faithful friend, Miss Anthony, we stepped into the carriage and went to the poll, held in the hotel where I usually went to pay taxes. When we entered the room it was crowded with men. I was introduced to the inspectors by Charles Everett, one of our leading citizens, who said: " Mrs. Stanton is here, gentlemen, for the purpose of voting. As she is a taxpayer, of sound mind, and of legal age, I see no reason why she should not exercise this right of citizenship."

The inspectors were thunderstruck. I think they were afraid that I was about to capture the ballot box. One placed his arms round it, with one hand close over the aperture where the ballots were slipped in, and said, with mingled surprise and pity, "Oh, no, madam! Men only are allowed to vote." I then explained to him that, in accordance with the Constitution of New Jersey, women had voted in New Jersey down to 1801, when they were forbidden the further exercise of the right by an arbitrary act of the legislature, and, by a recent amendment to the national Constitution, Congress had declared that " all persons born or naturalized in the United States, and subject to the jurisdiction thereof, are citizens of the United States and of the State wherein they reside " and are entitled to vote. I told them that I wished to cast my vote, as a citizen of the United States, for the candidates for United States offices. Two of the inspectors sat down and pulled their hats over their eyes, whether from shame or igno-

rance I do not know.   The other held on to the box,
and said " I know nothing about the Constitutions,
State or national.   I never read either; but I do
know that in New Jersey, women have not voted in my
day, and I cannot accept your ballot."   So I laid my
ballot in his hand, saying that I had the same right to
vote that any man present had, and on him must rest
the responsibility of denying me my rights of citizenship.

All through the winter Miss Anthony and I worked
diligently on the History.   My daughter Harriot came
from Europe in February, determined that I should return with her, as she had not finished her studies.   To
expedite my task on the History she seized the laboring
oar, prepared the last chapter and corrected the proof
as opportunity offered.   As the children were scattered
to the four points of the compass and my husband spent
the winter in the city, we decided to lease our house and
all take a holiday.   We spent a month in New York
city, busy on the History to the last hour, with occasional intervals of receiving and visiting friends.   As I
dreaded the voyage, the days flew by too fast for my
pleasure.

CHAPTER XXI.

HAVING worked diligently through nearly two years on the second volume of " The History of Woman Suffrage," I looked forward with pleasure to a rest, in the Old World, beyond the reach and sound of my beloved Susan and the woman suffrage movement. On May 27, 1892, I sailed with my daughter Harriot on the *Château Léoville* for Bordeaux. The many friends who came to see us off brought fruits and flowers, boxes of candied ginger to ward off seasickness, letters of introduction, and light literature for the voyage. We had all the daily and weekly papers, secular and religious, the new monthly magazines, and several novels. We thought we would do an immense amount of reading, but we did very little. Eating, sleeping, walking on deck, and watching the ever-changing ocean are about all that most people care to do. The sail down the harbor that bright, warm evening was beautiful, and, we lingered on deck in the moonlight until a late hour.

I slept but little, that night, as two cats kept running in and out of my stateroom, and my berth was so narrow that I could only lie in one position—as straight as if already in my coffin. Under such circumstances I spent the night, thinking over everything that was painful in my whole life, and imagining all the different calamities that might befall my family in my absence.

It was a night of severe introspection and intense dissatisfaction. I was glad when the morning dawned and I could go on deck. During the day my couch was widened one foot, and, at night, the cats relegated to other quarters.

We had a smooth, pleasant, uneventful voyage, until the last night, when, on nearing the French coast, the weather became dark and stormy. The next morning our good steamer pushed slowly and carefully up the broad, muddy Gironde and landed us on the bustling quays of Bordeaux, where my son Theodore stood waiting to receive us. As we turned to say farewell to our sturdy ship—gazing up at its black iron sides besprinkled with salty foam—a feeling of deep thankfulness took possession of us, for she had been faithful to her trust, and had borne us safely from the New World to the Old, over thousands of miles of treacherous sea.

We spent a day in driving about Bordeaux, enjoying the mere fact of restoration to *terra firma* after twelve days' imprisonment on the ocean. Maritime cities are much the same all the world over. The forests of masts, the heavily laden drays, the lounging sailors, the rough 'longshoremen, and the dirty quays, are no more characteristic of Bordeaux than New York, London, and Liverpool. But Bordeaux was interesting as the birthplace of Montesquieu and as the capital of ancient Guienne and Gascony.

But I must not forget to mention an accident that happened on landing at Bordeaux. We had innumerable pieces of baggage, a baby carriage, rocking chair, a box of " The History of Woman Suffrage " for foreign libraries, besides the usual number of trunks and satchels, and one hamper, in which were many things we were undecided whether to take or leave. Into this, a loaded pistol had been carelessly thrown. The hamper being handled with an emphatic jerk by some jovial French sailor, the pistol exploded, shooting the bearer through the shoulder. He fell bleeding on the quay. The dynamite scare being just at its height, the general consternation was indescribable. Every Frenchman, with vehement gestures, was chattering to his utmost capacity, but keeping at a respectful distance from the hamper. No one knew what had caused the trouble; but Theodore was bound to make an investigation. He proceeded to untie the ropes and examine the contents, and there he found the pistol, from which, pointing upward, he fired two other bullets. " Alas! " said Hattie, " I put that pistol there, never dreaming it was loaded." The wounded man was taken to the hospital. His injuries were very slight, but the incident cost us two thousand francs and no end of annoyance. I was thankful that by some chance the pistol had not gone off in the hold of the vessel and set the ship on fire, and possibly sacrificed three hundred lives through one girl's carelessness. Verily we cannot be too careful in the use of firearms.

Bordeaux is a queer old town, with its innumerable soldiers and priests perambulating in all directions. The priests, in long black gowns and large black hats, have a solemn aspect; but the soldiers, walking lazily along, or guarding buildings that seem in no danger from any living thing, are useless and ridiculous. The heavy carts and harness move the unaccustomed observer to constant pity for the horses. Besides everything that is necessary for locomotion, they have an endless number of ornaments, rising two or three feet above the horses' heads—horns, bells, feathers, and tassels.   One of their carts would weigh as much as three of ours, and all their carriages are equally heavy.

It was a bright, cool day on which we took the train for Toulouse, and we enjoyed the delightful run through the very heart of old Gascony and Languedoc.   It was evident that we were in the South, where the sun is strong, for, although summer had scarcely begun, the country already wore a brown hue.   But the narrow strips of growing grain, the acres of grape vines, looking like young currant bushes, and the fig trees scattered here and there, looked odd to the eye of a native of New York.

We passed many historical spots during that afternoon journey up the valley of the Garonne.   At Portets are the ruins of the Château of Langoiran, built before America was discovered, and, a few miles farther on, we came to the region of the famous wines of Sauterne and Château-Yquem.   Saint Macaire is a very ancient Gallo-Roman town, where they show one churches, walls, and houses built fifteen centuries ago.   One of the largest towns has a history typical of this part of France, where wars of religion and conquest were once the order of the day.   It was taken and re-taken by the Goths, Huns, Burgundians, and Saracens, nobody knows how many times, and belonged, successively, to the kings of France, to the dukes of Aquitaine, to the kings of England, and to the counts of Toulouse. I sometimes wonder whether the inhabitants of our American towns, whose growth and development have been free and untrammeled as that of a favorite child, appreciate the blessings that have been theirs.   How true the lines of Goethe: " America, thou art much hap-

pier than our old continent; thou hast no castles in
ruins, no fortresses; no useless remembrances, no
vain enemies will interrupt the inward workings of
thy life!"

We passed through Moissac, with its celebrated
organ, a gift of Mazarin; through Castle Sarrazin,
founded by the Saracens in the eighth century; through
Montauban, that stronghold of the early Protestants,
which suffered martyrdom for its religious faith;
through Grisolles, built on a Roman highway, and, at
last, in the dusk of the evening, we reached "the Capital of the South," that city of learning—curious, interesting old Toulouse.

Laura Curtis Bullard, in her sketch of me in "Our
Famous Women," says: "In 1882, Mrs. Stanton went
to France, on a visit to her son Theodore, and spent
three months at the convent of La Sagesse, in the city
of Toulouse." This is quite true; but I have sometimes
tried to guess what her readers thought I was doing
for three months in a convent. Weary of the trials
and tribulations of this world, had I gone there to prepare in solitude for the next? Had I taken the veil in
my old age? Or, like high-church Anglicans and
Roman Catholics, had I made this my retreat? Not
at all. My daughter wished to study French advanta-
geously, my son lived in the mountains hard by, and
the garden of La Sagesse, with its big trees, clean
gravel paths, and cool shade, was the most delightful
spot.

In this religious retreat I met, from time to time,
some of the most radical and liberal-minded residents
of the South. Toulouse is one of the most important
university centers of France, and bears with credit

the proud title of " the learned city." With two distinguished members of the faculty, the late Dr. Nicholas Joly and Professor Moliner of the law school, I
often had most interesting discussions on all the great
questions of the hour. That three heretics—I should
say, six, for my daughter, son, and his wife often joined
the circle—could thus sit in perfect security, and debate, in the most unorthodox fashion, in these holy
precincts, all the reforms, social, political, and religious,
which the United States and France need in order to be
in harmony with the spirit of the age, was a striking
proof of the progress the world has made in freedom
of speech. The time was when such acts would have
cost us our lives, even if we had been caught expressing
our heresies in the seclusion of our own homes. But
here, under the oaks of a Catholic convent, with the
gray-robed sisters all around us, we could point out the
fallacies of Romanism itself, without fear or trembling.
Glorious Nineteenth Century, what conquests are
thine!

I shall say nothing of the picturesque streets of
antique Toulouse; nothing of the priests, who swarm
like children in an English town; nothing of the beautifully carved stone façades of the ancient mansions,
once inhabited by the nobility of Languedoc, but now
given up to trade and commerce; nothing of the lofty
brick cathedrals, whose exteriors remind one of London
and whose interiors transfer you to " the gorgeous
East "; nothing of the Capitol, with its gallery rich in
busts of the celebrated sons of the South; nothing of
the museum, the public garden, and the broad river
winding through all. I must leave all these interesting features of Toulouse and hasten up into the Black

Mountains, a few miles away, where I saw the country life of modern Languedoc.

At Jacournassy, the country seat of Mme. Berry, whose daughter my son Theodore married, I spent a month full of surprises. How everything differed from America, and even from the plain below! The peasants, many of them at least, can neither speak French nor understand it. Their language is a patois, resembling both Spanish and Italian, and they cling to it with astonishing pertinacity. Their agricultural implements are not less quaint than their speech. The plow is a long beam with a most primitive share in the middle, a cow at one end, and a boy at the other. The grain is cut with a sickle and threshed with a flail on the barn floor, as in Scripture times. Manure is scattered over the fields with the hands. There was a certain pleasure in studying these old-time ways. I caught glimpses of the anti-revolutionary epoch, when the king ruled the state and the nobles held the lands. Here again I saw, as never before, what vast strides the world has made within one century.

But, indoors, one returns to modern times. The table, beds, rooms of the château were much the same as those of Toulouse and New York city. The cooking is not like ours, however, unless Delmonico's skill be supposed to have extended to all the homes in Manhattan Island, which is, unfortunately, not the case. What an admirable product of French genius is the art of cooking! Of incalculable value have been the culinary teachings of Vatel and his followers.

One of the sources of amusement, during my sojourn at Jacournassy, was of a literary nature. My son Theodore was then busy collecting the materials for his book entitled "The Woman Question in Europe," and every post brought in manuscripts and letters from all parts of the continent, written in almost every tongue known to Babel. So just what I came abroad to avoid, I found on the very threshold where I came to rest. We had good linguists at the château, and every document finally came forth in English dress, which, however, often needed much altering and polishing. This was my part of the work. So, away off in the heart of France, high up in the Black Mountains, surrounded with French-speaking relatives and patois-speaking peasants, I found myself once more putting bad English into the best I could command, just as I had so often done in America, when editor of *The Revolution*, or when arranging manuscript for " The History of Woman Suffrage." But it was labor in the cause of my sex; it was aiding in the creation of " The Woman Question in Europe," and so my pen did not grow slack nor my hand weary.

The scenery in the Black Mountains is very grand, and reminds one of the lofty ranges of mountains around the Yosemite Valley in California. In the distance are the snow-capped Pyrenees, producing a solemn beauty, a profound solitude. We used to go every evening where we could see the sun set and watch the changing shadows in the broad valley below. Another great pleasure here was watching the gradual development of my first grandchild, Elizabeth Cady Stanton, born at Paris, on the 3d of May, 1882. She was a fine child; though only three months old her head was covered with dark hair, and her large blue eyes looked out with intense earnestness from beneath her well-shaped brow.

One night I had a terrible fright. I was the only person sleeping on the ground floor of the château, and my room was at the extreme end of the building, with the staircase on the other side. I had frequently been cautioned not to leave my windows open, as someone might get in. But, as I always slept with an open window, winter and summer, I thought I would take the risk rather than endure a feeling of suffocation night after night. The blinds were solid, and to close them was to exclude all the air, so I left them open about a foot, braced by an iron hook. A favorite resort for a pet donkey was under my window, where he had uniformly slept in profound silence. But one glorious moonlight night, probably to arouse me to enjoy with him the exquisite beauty of our surroundings, he put his nose through this aperture and gave one of the most prolonged, resounding brays I ever heard. Startled from a deep sleep, I was so frightened that at first I could not move. My next impulse was to rush out and arouse the family, but, seeing a dark head in the window, I thought I would slam down the heavy sash and check the intruder before starting. But just as I approached the window, another agonizing bray announced the innocent character of my midnight visitor. Stretching out of the window to frighten him away, a gentleman in the room above me, for the same purpose, dashed down a pail of water, which the donkey and I shared equally. He ran off at a double-quick pace, while I made a hasty retreat.

On August 20, I returned to Toulouse and our quiet convent. The sisters gave me a most affectionate welcome and I had many pleasant chats, sitting in the gardens, with the priests and professors.

Several times my daughter and I attended High Mass in the cathedral, built in the eleventh century. Being entirely new to us it was a most entertaining spectacular performance. With our American ideas of religious devotion, it seemed to us that the people, as well as the building, belonged to the Dark Ages. About fifty priests, in mantles, gowns, and capes, some black, some yellow,—with tinseled fringes and ornamentation,—with all manner of gestures, genuflections, salutations, kneelings, and burning of incense; with prayers, admonitions, and sacraments, filled the altar with constant motion.

A tall man, dressed in red, wheeled in a large basket filled with bread, which the priests, with cups of wine, passed up and down among those kneeling at the altar. At least half a dozen times the places at the altar were filled—chiefly with women. We counted the men,— only seven,—and those were old and tremulous, with one foot in the grave. The whole performance was hollow and mechanical. People walked in, crossed themselves at the door with holy water, and, while kneeling and saying their prayers, looked about examining the dress of each newcomer, their lips moving throughout, satisfied in reeling off the allotted number of prayers in a given time. The one redeeming feature in the whole performance was the grand music. The deep-toned organ, whose sounds reverberated through the lofty arches, was very impressive.

The convent consisted of three large buildings, each three stories high, and a residence for the priests; also a chapel, where women, at their devotions, might be seen at various hours from four o'clock in the morning until evening. Inclosed within a high stone wall were beautiful gardens with fountains and shrines, where images of departed saints, in alcoves lighted with tapers were worshiped on certain days of the year.

Such were our environments, and our minds naturally often dwelt on the nature and power of the religion that had built up and maintained for centuries these peaceful resorts, where cultivated, scholarly men, and women of fine sensibilities, could find rest from the struggles of the outside world. The sisters, who managed this large establishment, seemed happy in the midst of their severe and multifarious duties. Of the undercurrent of their lives I could not judge, but on the surface all seemed smooth and satisfactory. They evidently took great pleasure in the society of each other. Every evening, from six to eight, they all sat in the gardens in a circle together, sewing, knitting, and chatting, with occasional merry bursts of laughter. Their existence is not, by many degrees, as monotonous as that of most women in isolated households—especially of the farmer's wife in her solitary home, miles away from a village and a post office. They taught a school of fifty orphan girls, who lived in the convent, and for whom they frequently had entertainments. They also had a few boarders of the old aristocracy of France, who hate the Republic and still cling to their belief in Popes and Kings. For the purpose of perfecting herself in the language, my daughter embraced every opportunity to talk with all she met, and thus learned the secrets of their inner life. As Sister Rose spoke English, I gleaned from her what knowledge I could as to their views of time and eternity. I found their faith had not made much progress through the terrible upheavals of the French Revolution. Although the Jesuits have been driven out of France, and the pictures of Saints, the Virgin Mary, and Christ, have been banished from the walls of their schools and colleges, the sincere Catholics are more devoted to their religion because of these very persecutions.

Theodore, his wife, and baby, and Mr. Blatch, a young Englishman, came to visit us. The sisters and school children manifested great delight in the baby, and the former equal pleasure in Mr. Blatch's marked attention to my daughter, as babies and courtships were unusual tableaux in a convent. As my daughter was studying for a university degree in mathematics, I went with her to the Lycee, a dreary apartment in a gloomy old building with bare walls, bare floors, dilapidated desks and benches, and an old rusty stove. Yet mid such surroundings, the professor always appeared in full dress, making a stately bow to his class. I had heard so much of the universities of France that I had pictured to myself grand buildings, like those of our universities; but, instead, I found that the lectures were given in isolated rooms, here, there, and anywhere— uniformly dreary inside and outside.

The first day we called on Professor Depesyrons. After making all our arrangements for books and lectures, he suddenly turned to my daughter, and, pointing to the flounces on her dress, her jaunty hat, and some flowers in a buttonhole, he smiled, and said: " All this, and yet you love mathematics? " As we entered the court, on our way to the Lycée and inquired for the professor's lecture room, the students in little groups watched us closely. The one who escorted us asked several questions, and discovered, by our accent, that we were foreigners, a sufficient excuse for the novelty of our proceeding. The professor received us most graciously, and ordered the janitor to bring us chairs, table, paper, and pencils.

Then we chatted pleasantly until the hour arrived for his lecture. As I had but little interest in the subject, and as the problems were pronounced in a foreign tongue, I took my afternoon nap. There was no danger of affronting the professor by such indifference to his eloquence, as he faced the blackboard, filling it with signs and figures as rapidly as possible; then expunging them to refill again and again, without a break in his explanations; talking as fast as his hand moved. Harriot struggled several days to follow him, but found it impossible, so we gave up the chase after cubes and squares, and she devoted herself wholly to the study of the language. These were days, for me, of perfect rest and peace. Everything moved as if by magic, no hurry and bustle, never a cross or impatient word spoken. As only one or two of the sisters spoke English, I could read under the trees uninterruptedly for hours. Emerson, Ruskin, and Carlyle were my chosen companions.

We made several pleasant acquaintances among some Irish families who were trying to live on their reduced incomes in Toulouse. One of these gave us a farewell ball. As several companies of the French army were stationed there, we met a large number of officers at the ball. I had always supposed the French were graceful dancers. I was a quiet "looker on in Vienna," so I had an opportunity of comparing the skill of the different nationalities. All admitted that none glided about so easily and gracefully as the Americans. They seemed to move without the least effort, while the English, the French, and the Germans labored in their dancing, bobbing up and down, jumping and jerking, out of breath and red in the face in five minutes. One great pleasure we had in Toulouse was the music of the military band in the public gardens, where, for half a cent, we could have a chair and enjoy pure air and sweet music for two hours.

We gave a farewell dinner at the Tivollier Hôtel to some of our friends. With speeches and toasts we had a merry time. Professor Joly was the life of the occasion. He had been a teacher in France for forty years and had just retired on a pension. I presented to him " The History of Woman Suffrage," and he wrote a most complimentary review of it in one of the leading French journals. Every holiday must have its end. Other duties called me to England. So, after a hasty good-by to Jacournassy and La Sagesse, to the Black Mountains and Toulouse, to Languedoc and the South, we took train one day in October, just as the first leaves began to fall, and, in fourteen hours, were at Paris. I had not seen the beautiful French capital since 1840. My sojourn within its enchanting walls was short,—too short,—and I woke one morning to find myself, after an absence of forty-two years, again on the shores of England, and before my eyes were fairly open, grim old London welcomed me back. But the many happy hours spent in " merry England " during the winter of 1882-83 have not effaced from my memory the four months in Languedoc.

CHAPTER XXII.

REACHING London in the fogs and mists of November, 1882, the first person I met, after a separation of many years, was our revered and beloved friend William Henry Channing. The tall, graceful form was somewhat bent; the sweet, thoughtful face somewhat sadder; the crimes and miseries of the world seemed heavy on his heart. With his refined, nervous organization, the gloomy moral and physical atmosphere of London was the last place on earth where that beautiful life should have ended. I found him in earnest conversation with my daughter and the young Englishman she was soon to marry, advising them not only as to the importance of the step they were about to take, but as to the minor points to be observed in the ceremony. At the appointed time a few friends gathered in Portland Street Chapel, and as we approached the altar our friend appeared in surplice and gown, his pale, spiritual face more tender and beautiful than ever. This was the last marriage service he ever performed, and it was as pathetic as original. His whole appearance was so in harmony with the exquisite sentiments he uttered, that we who listened felt as if, for the time being, we had entered with him into the Holy of Holies.

Some time after, Miss Anthony and I called on him to return our thanks for the very complimentary review he had written of " The History of Woman Suffrage." He thanked us in turn for the many pleasant memories we had revived in those pages, " but," said he, " they have filled me with indignation, too, at the repeated insults offered to women so earnestly engaged in honest endeavors for the uplifting of mankind. I blushed for my sex more than once in reading these volumes." We lingered long, talking over the events connected with our great struggle for freedom. He dwelt with tenderness on our disappointments, and entered more fully into the humiliations suffered by women, than any man we ever met. His views were as appreciative of the humiliation of woman, through the degradation of sex, as those expressed by John Stuart Mill in his wonderful work on " The Subjection of Women." He was intensely interested in Frances Power Cobbe's efforts to suppress vivisection, and the last time I saw him he was presiding at a parlor meeting where Dr. Elizabeth Blackwell gave an admirable address on the cause and cure of the social evil. Mr. Channing spoke beautifully in closing, paying a warm and merited compliment to Dr. Blackwell's clear and concise review of all the difficulties involved in the question.

Reading so much of English reformers in our journals, of the Brights, McLarens, the Taylors; of Lydia Becker, Josephine Butler, and Octavia Hill, and of their great demonstrations with lords and members of Parliament in the chair,—we had longed to compare the actors in those scenes with our speakers on this side of the water. At last we met them one and all in great public meetings and parlor reunions, at dinners and receptions. We listened to their public men in Parliament, the courts, and the pulpit; to the women in their various assemblies; and came to the conclusion that Americans surpass them in oratory and the conduct of their meetings. A hesitating, apologetic manner seems to be the national custom for an exordium on all questions. Even their ablest men who have visited this country, such as Kingsley, Stanley, Arnold, Tyndall, and Coleridge, have all been criticised by the American public for their elocutionary defects. They have no speakers to compare with Wendell Phillips, George William Curtis, or Anna Dickinson, although John Bright is without peer among his countrymen, as is Mrs. Besant among the women. The women, as a general rule, are more fluent than the men.

I reached England in time to attend the great demonstration in Glasgow, to celebrate the extension of the municipal franchise to the women of Scotland. It was a remarkable occasion. St. Andrew's immense hall was packed with women; a few men were admitted to the gallery at half a crown apiece. Over five thousand people were present. When a Scotch audience is thoroughly roused, nothing can equal the enthusiasm. The arrival of the speakers on the platform was announced with the wildest applause; the entire audience rising, waving their handkerchiefs, and clapping their hands, and every compliment paid the people of Scotland was received with similar outbursts. Mrs. McLaren, a sister of John Bright, presided, and made the opening speech. I had the honor, on this occasion, of addressing an audience for the first time in the Old World. Many others spoke briefly. There were too many speakers; no one had time to warm up to the point of eloquence.

Our system of conventions, of two or three days'

duration, with long speeches discussing pointed and radical resolutions, is quite unknown in England. Their meetings consist of one session of a few hours, into which they crowd all the speakers they can summon. They have a few tame, printed resolutions, on which there can be no possible difference of opinion, with the names of those who are to speak appended. Each of these is read and a few short speeches are made, that may or may not have the slightest reference to the resolutions, which are then passed. The last is usually one of thanks to some lord or member of the House of Commons, who may have condescended to preside at the meeting or do something for the measure in Parliament. The Queen is referred to tenderly in most of the speeches, although she has never done anything to merit the approbation of the advocates of suffrage for women.

From Glasgow quite a large party of the Brights and McLarens went to Edinburgh, where the Hon. Duncan McLaren gave us a warm welcome to Newington House, under the very shadow of the Salisbury crags. These and the Pentland Hills are remarkable features in the landscape as you approach this beautiful city with its mountains and castles. We passed a few charming days driving about, visiting old friends, and discussing the status of woman on both sides of the Atlantic. Here we met Elizabeth Pease Nichol and Jane and Eliza Wigham, whom I had not seen since we sat together in the World's Anti-slavery Convention, in London, in 1840. Yet I knew Mrs. Nichol at once; her strongly marked face was not readily forgotten.

I went with the family on Sunday to the Friends' meeting, where a most unusual manifestation for that decorous sect occurred. I had been told that, if I felt inclined, it would be considered quite proper for me to make some remarks, and just as I was revolving an opening sentence to a few thoughts I desired to present, a man arose in a remote part of the house and began, in a low voice, to give his testimony as to the truth that was in him. All eyes were turned toward him, when suddenly a Friend leaned over the back of the seat, seized his coat tails and jerked him down in a most emphatic manner. The poor man buried his face in his hands, and maintained a profound silence. I learned afterward that he was a bore, and the Friend in the rear thought it wise to nip him in the bud. This scene put to flight all intentions of speaking on my part lest I, too, might get outside the prescribed limits and be suppressed by force. I dined, that day, with Mrs. Nichol, at Huntly Lodge, where she has entertained in turn many of our American reformers. Her walls have echoed to the voices of Garrison, Rogers, Samuel J. May, Parker Pillsbury, Henry C. Wright, Douglass, Remond, and hosts of English philanthropists. Though over eighty years of age, she was still awake to all questions of the hour, and generous in her hospitalities as of yore.

Mrs. Margaret Lucas, whose whole soul was in the temperance movement, escorted me from Edinburgh to Manchester, to be present at another great demonstration in the Town Hall, the finest building in that district. It had just been completed, and, with its ante-room, dining hall, and various apartments for social entertainments, was by far the most perfect hall I had seen in England. There I was entertained by Mrs. Matilda Roby, who, with her husband, gave me a most hospitable reception. She invited several friends to luncheon one day, among others Miss Lydia Becker, editor of the *Suffrage Journal* in that city, and the Rev. Mr. Steinthal, who had visited this country and spoken on our platform. The chief topic at the table was John Stuart Mill, his life, character, writings, and his position with reference to the political rights of women. In the evening we went to see Ristori in " Queen Elizabeth." Having seen her, many years before, in America, I was surprised to find her still so vigorous. And thus, week after week, suffrage meetings, receptions, dinners, luncheons, and theaters pleasantly alternated.

The following Sunday we heard in London a grand sermon from Moncure D. Conway, and had a pleasant interview with him and Mrs. Conway at the close of the session. Later we spent a few days at their artistic home, filled with books, pictures, and mementos from loving friends. A billiard room, with well-worn cues, balls, and table—quite a novel adjunct to a parsonage—may, in a measure, account for his vigorous sermons. A garden reception to Mr. and Mrs. Howells gave us an opportunity to see the American novelist surrounded by his English friends.

Soon after this Mr. Conway asked me to fill his pulpit. I retired Saturday night, very nervous over my sermon for the next day, and the feeling steadily increased until I reached the platform; but once there my fears were all dissipated, and I never enjoyed speaking more than on that occasion, for I had been so long oppressed with the degradation of woman under canon law and church discipline, that I had a sense of relief in pouring out my indignation. My theme was, " What has Christianity done for Woman? " and by the

facts of history I showed clearly that to no form of religion was woman indebted for one impulse of freedom,
as all alike have taught her inferiority and subjection. No lofty virtues can emanate from such a
condition. Whatever heights of dignity and purity
women have individually attained can in no way be attributed to the dogmas of their religion.

With my son Theodore, always deeply interested in
my friends and public work, I called, during my stay in
London, on Mrs. Grey, Miss Jessie Boucherett, and
Dr. Hoggan, who had written essays for " The Woman
Question in Europe "; on our American minister (Mr.
Lowell), Mr. and Mrs. George W. Smalley, and many
other notable men and women. By appointment we
had an hour with the Hon. John Bright, at his residence
on Piccadilly. As his photograph, with his fame, had
reached America, his fine face and head, as well as his
political opinions, were quite familiar to us. He received us with great cordiality, and manifested a clear
knowledge and deep interest in regard to all American
affairs. Free trade and woman suffrage formed the
basis of our conversation; the literature of our respective countries and our great men and women were the
lighter topics of the occasion. He was not sound in
regard to the political rights of women, but it is not
given to any one man to be equally clear on all questions. He voted for John Stuart Mill's amendment to
the Household Suffrage Bill in 1867, but he said,
" that was a personal favor to a friend, without any
strong convictions as to the merits of what I considered
a purely sentimental measure."

We attended the meeting called to rejoice over the
passage of the Married Women's Property Bill, which

gave to the women of England, in 1882, what we had enjoyed in many States in this country since 1848. Mrs. Jacob Bright, Mrs. Scatcherd, Mrs. Elmy, and several members of Parliament made short speeches of congratulation to those who had been instrumental in carrying the measure. It was generally conceded that to the tact and persistence of Mrs. Jacob Bright, more than to any other person, belonged the credit of that achievement. Jacob Bright was at the time a member of Parliament, and fully in sympathy with the bill; and, while Mrs. Bright exerted all her social influence to make it popular with the members, her husband, thoroughly versed in Parliamentary tactics, availed himself of every technicality to push the bill through the House of Commons. Mrs. Bright's chief object in securing this bill, aside from establishing the right that every human being has to his own property, was to place married women on an even plane with widows and spinsters, thereby making them qualified voters.

The next day we went out to Barn Elms to visit Mr. and Mrs. Charles McLaren. He was a member of Parliament, a Quaker by birth and education, and had sustained, to his uttermost ability, the suffrage movement. His charming wife, the daughter of Mrs. Pochin, is worthy of the noble mother who was among the earliest leaders on that question—speaking and writing with ability, on all phases of the subject. Barn Elms is a grand old estate, a few miles out of London. It was the dairy farm of Queen Elizabeth, and was presented by her to Sir Francis Walsingham. Since then it has been inhabited by many persons of note. It has existed as an estate since the time of the early Saxon kings, and the record of the sale of Barn Elms in the time of King Athelstane is still extant. What with its well-kept lawns, fine old trees, glimpses here and there of the Thames winding round its borders, and its wealth of old associations, it is, indeed, a charming spot. Our memory of those days will not go back to Saxon kings, but remain with the liberal host and hostess, the beautiful children, and the many charming acquaintances we met at that fireside. I doubt whether any of the ancient lords and ladies who dispensed their hospitalities under that roof did in any way surpass the present occupants. Mrs. McLaren, interested in all the reforms of the day, is radical in her ideas, a brilliant talker, and, for one so young, remarkably well informed on all political questions.

It was at Barn Elms I met, for the first time, Mrs. Fannie Hertz, to whom I was indebted for many pleasant acquaintances afterward. She is said to know more distinguished literary people than any other woman in London. I saw her, too, several times in her home; meeting, at her Sunday-afternoon receptions, many persons I was desirous to know. On one occasion I found George Jacob Holyoake there, surrounded by several young ladies, all stoutly defending the Nihilists in Russia, and their right to plot their way to freedom. They counted a dynasty of Czars as nothing in the balance with the liberties of a whole people. As I joined the circle, Mr. Holyoake called my attention to the fact that he was the only one in favor of peaceful measures. "Now," said he, "I have often heard it said on your platform that the feminine element in politics would bring about perpetual peace in government, and here all these ladies are advocating the worst forms of vio-

lence in the name of liberty." " Ah! " said I, " lay on
their shoulders the responsibility of governing, and they
would soon become as mild and conservative as you
seem to be." He then gave us his views on co-operation, the only remedy for many existing evils, which he
thought would be the next step toward a higher
civilization.

There, too, I met some Positivists, who, though
liberal on religious questions, were very narrow as
to the sphere of woman. The difference in sex,
which is the very reason why men and women should
be associated in all forms of activity, is to them
the strongest reason why they should be separated.
Mrs. Hertz belongs to the Harrison school of Positivists. I went with her to one of Mrs. Orr's receptions, where we met Robert Browning, a fine-looking
man of seventy years, with white hair and mus-
tache. He was frank, easy, playful, and brilliant in
conversation. Mrs. Orr seemed to be taking a very
pessimistic view of our present sphere of action, which
Mr. Browning, with poetic coloring, was trying to paint
more hopefully.

The next day I dined with Margaret Bright Lucas,
in company with John P. Thomasson, member of
Parliament, and his wife, and, afterward, we went
to the House of Commons and had the good fortune
to hear Gladstone, Parnell, and Sir Charles Dilke.
Seeing Bradlaugh seated outside of the charmed circle,
I sent my card to him, and, in the corridor, we had a
few moments' conversation. I asked him if he thought
he would eventually get his seat. He replied, " Most
assuredly I will. I shall open the next campaign with
such an agitation as will rouse our politicians to some

consideration of the changes gradually coming over the face of things in this country."

The place assigned ladies in the House of Commons is really a disgrace to a country ruled by a queen. This dark perch is the highest gallery, immediately over the speaker's desk and government seats, behind a fine wire netting, so that it is quite impossible to see or hear anything. The sixteen persons who can crowd into the front row, by standing with their noses partly through the open network, can have the satisfaction of seeing the cranial arch of their rulers and hearing an occasional pæan to liberty, or an Irish growl at the lack of it. I was told that this network was to prevent the members on the floor from being disturbed by the beauty of the women. On hearing this I remarked that I was devoutly thankful that our American men were not so easily disturbed, and that the beauty of our women v not of so dangerous a type. I could but contra . our spacious galleries in that magnificent Capitol at Washington, as well as in our grand State Capitols, where hundreds of women can sit at their ease and see and hear their rulers, with these dark, dingy buildings. My son, who had a seat on the floor just opposite the ladies' gallery, said he could compare our appearance to nothing but birds in a cage. He could not distinguish an outline of anybody. All he could see was the moving of feathers and furs or some bright ribbon or flower.

In the libraries, the courts, and the House of Lords, I found many suggestive subjects of thought. It was interesting to find, on the frescoed walls, many historical scenes in which women had taken a prominent part. Among others there was Jane Lane assisting Charles

II. to escape, and Alice Lisle concealing the fugitives after the battle of Sedgemoor. Six wives of Henry VIII. stood forth, a solemn pageant when one recalled their sad fate. Alas! whether for good or ill, women must ever fill a large space in the tragedies of the world.

I passed a few pleasant hours in the house where Macaulay spent his last years. The once spacious library and the large bow-window, looking out on a beautiful lawn, where he sat, from day to day, writing his glowing periods, possessed a peculiar charm for me, as the surroundings of genius always do. I thought, as I stood there, how often he had unconsciously gazed on each object in searching for words rich enough to gild his ideas. The house was owned and occupied by Mr. and Mrs. Stephen Winckworth. It was at one of their sociable Sunday teas that many pleasant memories of the great historian were revived.

One of the most remarkable and genial women I met was Miss Frances Power Cobbe. She called one afternoon, and sipped with me the five o'clock tea, a uniform practice in England. She was of medium height, stout, rosy, and vigorous-looking, with a large, well-shaped head, a strong, happy face, and gifted with rare powers of conversation. I felt very strongly attracted to her. She was frank and cordial, and pronounced in all her views. She gave us an account of her efforts to rescue unhappy cats and dogs from the hands of the vivisectionists. We saw her, too, in her home, and in her office in Victoria Street. The perfect order in which her books and papers were arranged, and the exquisite neatness of the apartments, were refreshing to behold.

My daughter, having decided opinions of her own,

was soon at loggerheads with Miss Cobbe on the question of vivisection. After we had examined several German and French books, with illustrations showing the horrible cruelty inflicted on cats and dogs, she enlarged on the hypocrisy and wickedness of these scientists, and, turning to my daughter, said: " Would you shake hands with one of these vivisectionists? " Yes," said Harriot, " I should be proud to shake hands with Virchow, the great German scientist, for his kindness to a young American girl. She applied to several professors to be admitted to their classes, but all refused except Virchow; he readily assented, and requested his students to treat her with becoming courtesy. ' If any of you behave otherwise,' said he, ' I shall feel myself personally insulted.' She entered his classes and pursued her studies, unmolested and with great success. Now, would you, Miss Cobbe, refuse to shake hands with any of your statesmen, scientists, clergymen, lawyers, or physicians who treat women with constant indignities and insult?" " Oh, no! " said Miss Cobbe. " Then," said Harriot, " you estimate the physical suffering of cats and dogs as of more consequence than the humiliation of human beings. The man who tortures a cat for a scientific purpose is not as low in the scale of beings, in my judgment, as one who sacrifices his own daughter to some cruel custom "

As we were, just then, reading Froude's " Life of Carlyle," we drove by the house where Carlyle had lived, and paused a moment at the door where poor Jennie went in and out so often with a heavy heart. The book gives a painful record of a great soul struggling with poverty and disappointment; the hope of success, as an author, so long deferred and never realized. His

foolish pride of independence and headship, and his utter
indifference to his domestic duties and the comfort of
his wife made the picture still darker.   Poor Jennie!
fitted to shine in any circle, yet doomed, all her married life, to domestic drudgery, instead of associations
with the great man for whose literary companionship
she had sacrificed everything.

At one of Miss Biggs' receptions Miss Anthony and
I met Mr. Stansfeld, M. P., who had labored faithfully
for the repeal of the Contagious Diseases Act, and had
in a measure been successful.   We had the honor of an
interview with Lord Shaftesbury, at one of his crowded
" at homes," and found him a little uncertain as to the
wisdom of allowing married women to vote, for fear of
disturbing the peace of the family.   I have often wondered if men see, in this objection, what a fatal admission
they make as to their love of domination.

Miss Anthony was present at the great Liberal Conference, at Leeds, on October 17, 1882, to which Mrs.
Helen Bright Clark, Miss Jane Cobden, Mrs. Tanner,
Mrs. Scatcherd, and several other ladies were duly
elected delegates from their respective Liberal Leagues.
Mrs. Clark and Miss Cobden, daughters of the
great corn-law reformers, spoke eloquently in favor
of the resolution to extend Parliamentary suffrage
to women, which was presented by Walter McLaren
of Bradford.   As Mrs. Clark made her impassioned
appeal for the recognition of woman's political
equality in the next bill for extension of suffrage,
that immense gathering of sixteen hundred delegates was hushed into profound silence.   For a
daughter to speak thus in that great representative convention, in opposition to her loved and honored father,

the acknowledged leader of that party, was an act of heroism and fidelity to her own highest convictions almost without a parallel in English history, and the effect on the audience was as thrilling as it was surprising. The resolution was passed by a large majority. At the reception given to John Bright that evening, as Mrs. Clark approached the dais on which her noble father stood shaking the hands of passing friends, she remarked to her husband, " I wonder if father has heard of my speech this morning, and if he will forgive me for thus publicly differing with him? " The query was soon answered. As he caught the first glimpse of his daughter he stepped down, and, pressing her hand affectionately, kissed her on either cheek.

The next evening the great Quaker statesman was heard by the admiring thousands who could crowd into Victoria Hall, while thousands, equally desirous to hear, failed to get tickets of admission. It was a magnificent sight, and altogether a most impressive gathering of the people. Miss Anthony, with her friends, sat in the gallery opposite the great platform, where they had a fine view of the whole audience. When John Bright, escorted by Sir Wilfrid Lawson, took his seat, the immense crowd rose, waving hats and handkerchiefs, and, with the wildest enthusiasm, gave cheer after cheer in honor of the great leader. Sir Wilfrid Lawson, in his introductory remarks, facetiously alluded to the resolution adopted by the Conference as somewhat in advance of the ideas of the speaker of the evening. The house broke into roars of laughter, while the Father of Liberalism, perfectly convulsed, joined in the general merriment.

But when at length his time to speak had come, and

Mr. Bright went over the many steps of progress that had been taken by the Liberal party, he cunningly dodged the question of the emancipation of the women of England. He skipped round the agitation of 1867, and John Stuart Mill's amendment presented at that time in the House of Commons; the extension of the municipal suffrage in 1869; the participation of women in the establishment of national schools under the law of 1870, both as voters and members of school boards; the Married Women's Property Bill of 1882; the large and increasing vote for the extension of Parliamentary suffrage in the House of Commons, and the adoption of the resolution by that great Conference the day before. All these successive steps toward woman's emancipation he carefully remembered to forget.

While in London Miss Anthony and I attended several enthusiastic reform meetings. We heard Bradlaugh address his constituency on that memorable day at Trafalgar Square, at the opening of Parliament, when violence was anticipated and the Parliament Houses were surrounded by immense crowds, with the military and police in large numbers, to maintain order. We heard Michael Davitt and Miss Helen Taylor at a great meeting in Exeter Hall; the former on home rule for Ireland, and the latter on the nationalization of land. The facts and figures given in these two lectures, as to the abject poverty of the people and the cruel system by which every inch of land had been grabbed by their oppressors, were indeed appalling. A few days before sailing we made our last visit to Ernestine L. Rose, and found our noble coadjutor, though in delicate health, pleasantly situated in the heart of London, as deeply interested as ever in the struggles of the hour.

A great discomfort, in all English homes, is the inadequate system of heating. A moderate fire in the grate is the only mode of heating, and they seem quite oblivious to the danger of throwing a door open into a cold hall at one's back, while the servants pass in and out with the various courses at dinner. As we Americans were sorely tried, under such circumstances, it was decided, in the home of my son-in-law, Mr. Blatch, to have a hall-stove, which, after a prolonged search, was found in London and duly installed as a presiding deity to defy the dampness that pervades all those ivy-covered habitations, as well as the neuralgia that wrings their possessors. What a blessing it proved, more than any one thing making the old English house seem like an American home! The delightful summer heat we, in America, enjoy in the coldest seasons, is quite unknown to our Saxon cousins. Although many came to see our stove in full working order, yet we could not persuade them to adopt the American system of heating the whole house at an even temperature. They cling to the customs of their fathers with an obstinacy that is incomprehensible to us, who are always ready to try experiments. Americans complain bitterly of the same freezing experiences in France and Germany, and, in turn, foreigners all criticise our overheated houses and places of amusement.

While attending a meeting in Birmingham I stayed with a relative of Joseph Sturge, whose home I had visited forty years before. The meeting was called to discuss the degradation of women under the Contagious Diseases Act. Led by Josephine Butler, the women of England were deeply stirred on the question of its repeal and have since secured it. I heard Mrs.

Butler speak in many of her society meetings as well as on other occasions. Her style was not unlike that one hears in Methodist camp meetings from the best cultivated of that sect; her power lies in her deeply religious enthusiasm. In London we met Emily Faithful, who had just returned from a lecturing tour in the United States, and were much amused with her experiences. Having taken prolonged trips over the whole country, from Maine to Texas, for many successive years, Miss Anthony and I could easily add the superlative to all her narrations.

It was a pleasant surprise to meet the large number of Americans usually at the receptions of Mrs. Peter Taylor. Graceful and beautiful, in full dress, standing beside her husband, who evidently idolized her, Mrs. Taylor appeared quite as refined in her drawing room as if she had never been exposed to the public gaze while presiding over a suffrage convention. Mrs. Taylor is called the mother of the suffrage movement. The reform has not been carried on in all respects to her taste, nor on what she considers the basis of high principle. Neither she nor Mrs. Jacob Bright has ever been satisfied with the bill asking the rights of suffrage for " widows and spinsters " only. To have asked this right " for all women duly qualified," as but few married women are qualified through possessing property in their own right, would have been substantially the same, without making any invidious distinctions. Mrs. Taylor and Mrs. Bright felt that, as married women were the greatest sufferers under the law, they should be the first rather than the last to be enfranchised. The others, led by Miss Becker, claimed that it was good policy to make the demand for " spinsters and widows," and thus exclude the " family unit " and " man's head-ship " from the discussion; and yet these were the very points on which the objections were invariably based. They claimed that, if " spinsters and widows " were enfranchised, they would be an added power to secure to married women their rights. But the history of the past gives us no such assurance. It is not certain that women would be more just than men, and a small privileged class of aristocrats have long governed their fellow-countrymen. The fact that the spinsters in the movement advocated such a bill, shows that they were not to be trusted in extending it. John Stuart Mill, too, was always opposed to the exclusion of married women in the demand for suffrage.

My sense of justice was severely tried by all I heard of the persecutions of Mrs. Besant and Mr. Bradlaugh for their publications on the right and duty of parents to limit population. Who can contemplate the sad condition of multitudes of young children in the Old World whose fate is to be brought up in ignorance and vice—a swarming, seething mass which nobody owns—without seeing the need of free discussion of the philosophical principles that underlie these tangled social problems? The trials of Foote and Ramsey, too, for blasphemy, seemed unworthy a great nation in the nineteenth century. Think of well-educated men of good moral standing thrown into prison in solitary confinement, for speaking lightly of the Hebrew idea of Jehovah and the New Testament account of the birth of Jesus! Our Protestant clergy never hesitate to make the dogmas and superstitions of the Catholic Church seem as absurd as possible, and why should not those who imagine they have outgrown Protestant

superstitions make them equally ridiculous? Whatever is true can stand investigation and ridicule.

In the last of April, when the wildflowers were in their
glory, Mrs. Mellen and her lovely daughter, Daisy, came
down to our home at Basingstoke to enjoy its beauty.
As Mrs. Mellen had known Charles Kingsley and entertained him at her residence in Colorado, she felt a
desire to see his former home.   Accordingly, one bright
morning, Mr. Blatch drove us to Eversley, through
Strathfieldsaye, the park of the Duke of Wellington.
This magnificent place was given to him by the English
government after the battle of Waterloo.   A lofty
statue of the duke, that can be seen for miles around,
stands at one entrance.   A drive of a few miles further
brought us to the parish church of Canon Kingsley,
where he preached many years, and where all that is
mortal of him now lies buried.   We wandered through
the old church, among the moss-covered tombstones,
and into the once happy home, now silent and deserted
—his loved ones being scattered in different quarters of
the globe.   Standing near the last resting place of the
author of " Hypatia," his warning words for women, in
a letter to John Stuart Mill, seemed like a voice from
heaven saying, with new inspiration and power, " This
will never be a good world for women until the last rem-
nant of the canon law is civilized off the face of the
earth."

We heard Mr. Fawcett speak to his Hackney constituents at one of his campaign meetings.   In the
course of his remarks he mentioned with evident favor,
as one of the coming measures, the disestablishment of
the Church, and was greeted with loud applause.   Soon
after he spoke of woman suffrage as another question

demanding consideration, but this was received with laughter and jeers, although the platform was crowded with advocates of the measure, among whom were the wife of the speaker and her sister, Dr. Garrett Anderson. The audience were evidently in favor of releasing themselves from being taxed to support the Church, forgetting that women were taxed not only to support a Church but also a State in the management of neither of which they had a voice. Mr. Fawcett was not an orator, but a simple, straightforward speaker. He made one gesture, striking his right clenched fist into the palm of his left hand at the close of all his strongest assertions, and, although more liberal than his party, he was a great favorite with his constituents.

One pleasant trip I made in England was to Bristol, to visit the Misses Priestman and Mrs. Tanner, sisters-in-law of John Bright. I had stayed at their father's house forty years before, so we felt like old friends. I found them all liberal women, and we enjoyed a few days together, talking over our mutual struggles, and admiring the beautiful scenery for which that part of the country is celebrated. The women of England were just then organizing political clubs, and I was invited to speak before many of them. There is an earnestness of purpose among English women that is very encouraging under the prolonged disappointments reformers inevitably suffer. And the order of English homes, too, among the wealthy classes, is very enjoyable. All go on from year to year with the same servants, the same surroundings, no changes, no moving, no building even; in delightful contrast with our periodical upheavals, always uncertain where we shall go next, or how long our main dependents will stand by us.

From Bristol I went to Greenbank to visit Mrs. Helen Bright Clark. One evening her parlors were crowded and I was asked to give an account of the suffrage movement in America. Some clergymen questioned me in regard to the Bible position of woman, whereupon I gave quite an exposition of its general principles in favor of liberty and equality. As two distinct lines of argument can be woven out of those pages on any subject, on this occasion I selected all the most favorable texts for justice to woman, and closed by stating the limits of its authority. Mrs. Clark, though thoroughly in sympathy with the views I had expressed, feared lest my very liberal utterances might have shocked some of the strictest of the lay-men and clergy. "Well," said I, "if we who do see the absurdities of the old superstitions never unveil them to others, how is the world to make any progress in the theologies? I am in the sunset of life, and I feel it to be my special mission to tell people what they are not prepared to hear, instead of echoing worn-out opin-ions." The result showed the wisdom of my speaking out of my own soul. To the surprise of Mrs. Clark, the Primitive Methodist clergyman called on Sunday morn-ing to invite me to occupy his pulpit in the afternoon and present the same line of thought I had the previous evening. I accepted his invitation. He led the ser-vices, and I took my text from Genesis i. 27, 28, showing that man and woman were a simultaneous creation, en-dowed, in the beginning, with equal power.

Returning to London, I accepted an invitation to take tea one afternoon with Mrs. Jacob Bright, who, in earnest conversation, had helped us each to a cup of tea, and .was turning to help us to something more, when over went table and all—tea, bread and butter, cake, strawberries and cream, silver, china, in one conglomerate mass. Silence reigned. No one started; no one said " Oh! " Mrs. Bright went on with what she was saying as if nothing unusual had occurred, rang the bell, and, when the servant appeared, pointing to the débris, she said, " Charles, remove this." I was filled with admiration at her coolness, and devoutly thankful that we Americans maintained an equally dignified silence.

At a grand reception, given in our honor by the National Central Committee, in Princess' Hall, Jacob Bright, M. P., presided and made an admirable opening speech, followed by his sister, Mrs. McLaren, with a highly complimentary address of welcome. By particular request Miss Anthony explained the industrial, legal, and political status of American women, while I set forth their educational, social, and religious condition. John P. Thomasson, M. P., made the closing address, expressing his satisfaction with our addresses and the progress made in both countries.

Mrs. Thomasson, daughter of Mrs. Lucas, gave several parties, receptions, and dinners,—some for ladies only,—where an abundant opportunity was offered for a critical analysis of the idiosyncrasies of the superior sex, especially in their dealings with women. The patience of even such heroic souls as Lydia Becker and Caroline Biggs was almost exhausted with the tergiversations of Members of the House of Commons. Alas for the many fair promises broken, the hopes deferred, the votes fully relied on and counted, all missing in the hour of action! One crack of Mr. Gladstone's whip put a hundred Liberal members to flight—members whom these noble women had spent years in educating. I never visited the House of Commons that I did not see Miss Becker and Miss Biggs trying to elucidate the fundamental principles of just government to some of the legislators. Verily their divine faith and patience merited more worthy action on the part of their alleged representatives!

Miss Henrietta Müller gave a farewell reception to Miss Anthony and me on the eve of our departure for America, when we had the opportunity of meeting once more most of the pleasant acquaintances we had made in London. Although it was announced for the afternoon, we did, in fact, receive all day, as many could not come at the hour appointed. Dr. Elizabeth Blackwell took breakfast with us; Mrs. Fawcett, Mrs. Saville, and Miss Lord were with us at luncheon; Harriet Hosmer and Olive Logan soon after; Mrs. Peter Taylor later, and from three to six o'clock the parlors were crowded.

Returning from London I passed my birthday, November 12, 1883, in Basingstoke. It was a sad day for us all, knowing that it was the last day with my loved ones before my departure for America. When I imprinted the farewell kiss on the soft cheek of my little granddaughter Nora in the cradle, she in the dawn and I in the sunset of life, I realized how widely the broad ocean would separate us. Miss Anthony met me at Alderly Edge, where we spent a few days with Mr. and Mrs. Jacob Bright. There we found their noble sisters, Mrs. McLaren and Mrs. Lucas, young Walter McLaren and his lovely bride, Eva Müller, whom we had heard several times on the suffrage platform. We rallied her on the step she had lately taken, notwithstanding her sister's able paper on the blessedness of a single life. While there, we visited Dean Stanley's birthplace, but on his death the light and joy went out. The old church whose walls had once echoed to his voice, and the house where he had spent so many useful years, seemed sad and deserted. But the day was bright and warm, the scenery beautiful, cows and sheep were still grazing in the meadows, and the grass was as green as in June. This is England's chief charm,—it is forever green,—perhaps in compensation for the many cloudy days.

As our good friends Mrs. McLaren and Mrs. Lucas had determined to see us safely on board the *Servia*, they escorted us to Liverpool, where we met Mrs. Margaret Parker and Mrs. Scatcherd. Another reception was given us at the residence of Dr. Ewing Whittle. Several short speeches were made, and all present cheered the parting guests with words of hope and encouragement for the good cause. Here the wisdom of forming an international association was first considered. The proposition met with such favor from those present that a committee was appointed to correspond with the friends in different nations. Miss Anthony and I were placed on the committee, and while this project has not yet been fully carried out, the idea of the intellectual co-operation of women to secure equal rights and opportunities for their sex was the basis of the International Council of Women, which was held under the auspices of the National Woman Suffrage Association in Washington, D. C., in March, 1888.

On the Atlantic for ten days we had many opportunities to review all we had seen and heard. Sitting on deck, hour after hour, how often I queried with myself as to the significance of the boon for which we were so earnestly struggling. In asking for a voice in the government under which we live, have we been pursuing a shadow for fifty years? In seeking political power, are we abdicating that social throne where they tell us our influence is unbounded? No, no! the right of suffrage is no shadow, but a substantial entity that the citizen can seize and hold for his own protection and his country's welfare. A direct power over one's own person and property, an individual opinion to be counted, on all questions of public interest, are better than indirect influence, be that ever so far reaching.

Though influence, like the pure white light, is all-pervading, yet it is ofttimes obscured with passing clouds and nights of darkness. Like the sun's rays, it may be healthy, genial, inspiring, though sometimes too direct for comfort, too oblique for warmth, too scattered for any purpose. But as the prism divides the rays, revealing the brilliant colors of the light, so does individual sovereignty reveal the beauty of representative government, and as the burning-glass shows the power of concentrating the rays, so does the combined power of the multitude reveal the beauty of united effort to carry a grand measure.

CHAPTER XXIII.

WOMAN AND THEOLOGY.

RETURNING from Europe in the autumn of 1883, after visiting a large circle of relatives and friends, I spent six weeks with my cousin, Elizabeth Smith Miller, at her home at Geneva, on Seneca Lake.

Through Miss Frances Lord, a woman of rare culture and research, my daughter and I had become interested in the school of theosophy, and read " Isis Unveiled," by Madame Blavatsky, Sinnett's works on the " Occult World," and " The Perfect Way," by Anna Kingsford. Full of these ideas, I soon interested my cousins in the subject, and we resolved to explore, as far as possible, some of these Eastern mysteries, of which we had heard so much. We looked in all directions to find some pilot to start us on the right course. We heard that Gerald Massey was in New York city, lecturing on " The Devil," " Ghosts," and " Evil Spirits " generally, so we invited him to visit us and give a course of lectures in Geneva. But, unfortunately, he was ill, and could not open new fields of thought to us at that time, though we were very desirous to get a glimpse into the unknown world, and hold converse with the immortals. As I soon left Geneva with my daughter, Mrs. Stanton Lawrence, our occult studies were, for a time, abandoned.

My daughter and I often talked of writing a story,

she describing the characters and their environments and I attending to the philosophy and soliloquies. As I had no special duties in prospect, we decided that this was the time to make our experiment. Accordingly we hastened to the family homestead at Johnstown, New York, where we could be entirely alone. Friends on all sides wondered what had brought us there in the depth of the winter. But we kept our secret, and set ourselves to work with diligence, and after three months our story was finished to our entire satisfaction. We felt sure that everyone who read it would be deeply interested and that we should readily find a publisher. We thought of " Our Romance " the first thing in the morning and talked of it the last thing at night. But alas! friendly critics who read our story pointed out its defects, and in due time we reached their conclusions, and the unpublished manuscript now rests in a pigeonhole of my desk. We had not many days to mourn our disappointment, as Madge was summoned to her Western home, and Miss Anthony arrived armed and equipped with bushels of documents for vol. iii. of " The History of Woman Suffrage." The summer and autumn of 1884 Miss Anthony and I passed at Johnstown, working diligently on the History, indulging only in an occasional drive, a stroll round the town in the evening, or a ride in the open street cars.

Mrs. Devereux Blake was holding a series of conventions, at this time, through the State of New York, and we urged her to expend some of her missionary efforts in my native town, which she did with good results. As the school election was near at hand Miss Anthony and I had several preliminary meetings to arouse the women to their duty as voters, and to the necessity of nominating some woman for trustee. When the day for the election arrived the large upper room of the Academy was filled with ladies and gentlemen. Some timid souls who should have been there stayed at home, fearing there would be a row, but everything was conducted with decency and in order. The chairman, Mr. Rosa, welcomed the ladies to their new duties in a very complimentary manner. Donald McMartin stated the law as to what persons were eligible to vote in school elections. Mrs. Horace Smith filled the office of teller on the occasion with promptness and dignity, and Mrs. Elizabeth Wallace Yost was elected trustee by a majority of seven. It is strange that intelligent women, who are supposed to feel some interest in the question of education, should be so indifferent to the power they possess to make our schools all that they should be.

This was the year of the presidential campaign. The Republicans and Democrats had each held their nominating conventions, and all classes participated in the general excitement. There being great dissatisfaction in the Republican ranks, we issued a manifesto: " Stand by the Republican Party," not that we loved Blaine more, but Cleveland less. The latter was elected, therefore it was evident that our efforts did not have much influence in turning the tide of national politics, though the Republican papers gave a broad circulation to our appeal. Dowden's description of the poet Shelley's efforts in scattering one of his suppressed pamphlets, reminded me of ours. He purchased bushels of empty bottles, in which he placed his pamphlets; having corked them up tight, he threw the bottles into the sea at various fashionable watering places, hoping they would wash ashore. Walking the streets of London in the evening he would slip his pamphlets into the hoods of old ladies' cloaks, throw them in shop doors, and leave them in cabs and omnibuses. We scattered ours in the cars, inclosed them in every letter we wrote or newspaper we sent through the country.

The night before election Mr. Stanton and Professor Horace Smith spoke in the Johnstown courthouse, and took rather pessimistic views of the future of the Republic should James G. Blaine be defeated. Cleveland was elected, and we still live as a nation, and are able to digest the thousands of foreign immigrants daily landing at our shores. The night of the election a large party of us sat up until two o'clock to hear the news. Mr. Stanton had long been one of the editorial writers on the New York *Sun,* and they sent him telegrams from that office until a late hour. However, the election was so close that we were kept in suspense several days, before it was definitely decided.

Miss Anthony left in December, 1884, for Washington, and I went to work on an article for the *North American Review,* entitled, "What has Christianity done for Women?" I took the ground that woman was not indebted to any form of religion for the liberty she now enjoys, but that, on the contrary, the religious element in her nature had always been perverted for her complete subjection. Bishop Spaulding, in the same issue of the *Review,* took the opposite ground, but I did not feel that he answered my points.

In January, 1885, my niece Mrs. Baldwin and I went to Washington to attend the Annual Convention of the National Woman Suffrage Association. It was held in the Unitarian church on the 20th, 21st, and 22d days of that month, and went off with great success, as did the usual reception given by Mrs. Spofford at the Riggs House. This dear friend, one of our most ardent coadjutors, always made the annual convention a time for many social enjoyments. The main feature in this convention was the attempt to pass the following resolutions:

"WHEREAS, The dogmas incorporated in religious creeds derived from Judaism, teaching that woman was an after-thought in the creation, her sex a misfortune, marriage a condition of subordination, and maternity a curse, are contrary to the law of God (as revealed in nature), and to the precepts of Christ, and,

"WHEREAS, These dogmas are an insidious poison, sapping the vitality of our civilization, blighting woman, and, through her, paralyzing humanity; therefore be it

"*Resolved*, That we call on the Christian ministry, as leaders of thought, to teach and enforce the fundamental idea of creation, that man was made in the image of God, male and female, and given equal rights over the earth, but none over each other. And, furthermore, we ask their recognition of the scriptural declaration that, in the Christian religion, there is neither male nor female, bond nor free, but all are one in Christ Jesus."

As chairman of the committee I presented a series of resolutions, impeaching the Christian theology—as well as all other forms of religion, for their degrading teachings in regard to woman—which the majority of the committee thought too strong and pointed, and, after much deliberation, they substituted the above, handing over to the Jews what I had laid at the door of the Christians. They thought they had so sugar-coated my ideas that the resolutions would pass without discussion. But some Jews in the convention promptly repudiated this impression of their faith and precipitated the very dis-cussion I desired, but which our more politic friends would fain have avoided.

From the time of the decade meeting in Rochester, in 1878, Matilda Joslyn Gage, Edward M. Davis, and I had sedulously labored to rouse women to a realization of their degraded position in the Church, and presented resolutions at every annual convention for that purpose. But they were either suppressed or so amended as to be meaningless. The resolutions of the annual con-vention of 1885, tame as they are, got into print and roused the ire of the clergy, and upon the following Sunday, Dr. Patton of Howard University preached a sermon on " Woman and Skepticism," in which he un-equivocally took the ground that freedom for woman led to skepticism and immorality. He illustrated his position by pointing to Hypatia, Mary Wollstonecraft, Frances Wright, George Eliot, Harriet Martineau, Mme. Roland, Frances Power Cobbe, and Victoria Woodhull. He made a grave mistake in the last names mentioned, as Mrs. Woodhull was a devout believer in the Christian religion, and surely anyone conversant with Miss Cobbe's writings would never accuse her of skepticism. His sermon was received with intense in-dignation, even by the women of his own congregation. When he found what a whirlwind he had started, he tried to shift his position and explain away much that he had said. We asked him to let us have the sermon for publication, that we might not do him injustice. But as he contradicted himself flatly in trying to restate his discourse, and refused to let us see his sermon, those who heard him were disgusted with his sophistry and tergiversation.

However, our labors in this direction are having an effect. Women are now making their attacks on the Church all along the line. They are demanding their right to be ordained as ministers, elders, deacons, and to be received as delegates in all the ecclesiastical convocations. At last they ask of the Church just what they have asked of the State for the last half century—perfect equality—and the clergy, as a body, are quite as hostile to their demands as the statesmen.

On my way back to Johnstown I spent ten days at Troy, where I preached in the Unitarian church on Sunday evening. During this visit we had two hearings in the Capitol at Albany—one in the Senate Chamber and one in the Assembly, before the Committee on Grievances. On both occasions Mrs. Mary Seymour Howell, Mrs. Devereux Blake, Mrs. Caroline Gilkey Rogers, and I addressed the Committee. Being open to the public, the chamber was crowded. It was nearly forty years since I had made my first appeal in the old Capitol at Albany. My reflections were sad and discouraging, as I sat there and listened to the speakers and remembered how long we had made our appeals at that bar, from year to year, in vain. The members of the committee presented the same calm aspect as their predecessors, as if to say, " Be patient, dear sisters, eternity is before us; this is simply a question of time. What may not come in your day, future generations will surely possess." It is always pleasant to know that our descendants are to enjoy life, liberty, and happiness; but, when one is gasping for one breath of freedom, this reflection is not satisfying.

Returning to my native hills, I found the Lenten season had fairly set in, which I always dreaded on account of the solemn, tolling bell, the Episcopal church being just opposite our residence. On Sunday we had the bells of six churches all going at the same time. It is strange how long customs continue after the original object has ceased to exist. At an early day, when the country was sparsely settled and the people lived at great distances, bells were useful to call them together when there was to be a church service. But now, when the churches are always open on Sunday, and every congregation knows the hour of services and all have clocks, bells are not only useless, but they are a terrible nuisance to invalids and nervous people. If I am ever so fortunate as to be elected a member of a town council, my first efforts will be toward the suppression of bells.

To encourage one of my sex in the trying profession of book agent, I purchased, about this time, Dr. Lord's " Beacon Lights of History," and read the last volume devoted to women, Pagan and Christian, saints and sinners. It is very amusing to see the author's intellectual wriggling and twisting to show that no one can be good or happy without believing in the Christian religion. In describing great women who are not Christians, he attributes all their follies and miseries to that fact. In describing Pagan women, possessed of great virtues, he attributes all their virtues to Nature's gifts, which enable them to rise superior to superstitions. After dwelling on the dreary existence of those not of Christian faith, he forthwith pictures his St. Teresa going through twenty years of doubts and fears about the salvation of her soul. The happiest people I have known have been those who gave themselves no concern about their own souls, but did their uttermost to mitigate the miseries of others.

In May, 1885, we left Johnstown and took possession of our house at Tenafly, New Jersey. It seemed very pleasant, after wandering in the Old World and the New, to be in my own home once more, surrounded by the grand trees I so dearly loved; to see the gorgeous sunsets, the twinkling fireflies; to hear the whippoorwills call their familiar note, while the June bugs and the mosquitoes buzz outside the nets through which they cannot enter. Many people complain of the mosquito in New Jersey, when he can so easily be shut out of the family circle by nets over all the doors and windows. I had a long piazza, encased in netting, where paterfamilias, with his pipe, could muse and gaze at the stars unmolested.

June brought Miss Anthony and a box of fresh documents for another season of work on vol. iii. of our History. We had a flying visit from Miss Eddy of Providence, daughter of Mrs. Eddy who gave fifty thousand dollars to the woman suffrage movement, and a granddaughter of Francis Jackson of Boston, who also left a generous bequest to our reform. We found Miss Eddy a charming young woman with artistic tastes. She showed us several pen sketches she had made of some of our reformers, that were admirable likenesses.

Mr. Stanton's "Random Recollections" were published at this time and were well received. A dinner was given him, on his eightieth birthday (June 27,

1885), by the Press Club of New York city, with speeches and toasts by his lifelong friends. As no ladies were invited I can only judge from the reports in the daily papers, and what I could glean from the honored guest himself, that it was a very interesting occasion.

Sitting in the summerhouse, one day, I witnessed a most amusing scene. Two of the boys, in search of employment, broke up a hornets' nest. Bruno, our large Saint Bernard dog, seeing them jumping about, thought he would join in the fun. The boys tried to drive him away, knowing that the hornets would get in his long hair, but Bruno's curiosity outran his caution and he plunged into the midst of the swarm and was soon completely covered. The buzzing and stinging soon sent the poor dog howling on the run. He rushed as usual, in his distress, to Amelia in the kitchen, where she and the girls were making preserves and ironing. When they saw the hornets, they dropped irons, spoons, jars, everything, and rushed out of doors screaming. I appreciated the danger in time to get safely into the house before Bruno came to me for aid and comfort. At last they played the hose on him until he found some relief; the maidens, armed with towels, thrashed right and left, and the boys, with evergreen branches, fought bravely. I had often heard of " stirring up a hornets' nest," but I had never before seen a practical demonstration of its danger. For days after, if Bruno heard anything buzz, he would rush for the house at the top of his speed. But in spite of these occasional lively episodes, vol. iii. went steadily on.

My suffrage sons and daughters through all the Northern and Western States decided to celebrate, on the 12th of November, 1885, my seventieth birthday,

by holding meetings or sending me gifts and congratulations. This honor was suggested by Mrs. Elizabeth
Boynton Harbert in *The New Era,* a paper she was edit-
ing at that time. The suggestion met with a ready
response. I was invited to deliver an essay on " The
Pleasures of Age," before the suffrage association in
New York city. It took me a week to think them up,
but with the inspiration of Longfellow's " Morituri
Salutamus," I was almost converted to the idea that
" we old folks " had the best of it.

The day was ushered in with telegrams, letters, and
express packages, which continued to arrive during the
week. From England, France, and Germany came
cablegrams, presents, and letters of congratulation, and
from all quarters came books, pictures, silver, bronzes,
California blankets, and baskets of fruits and flowers.
The eulogies in prose and verse were so hearty and
numerous that the ridicule and criticism of forty years
were buried so deep that I shall remember them no
more. There is no class who enjoy the praise of their
fellow-men like those who have had only blame most of
their lives. The evening of the 12th we had a delightful
reunion at the home of Dr. Clemence Lozier, where I
gave my essay, after which Mrs. Lozier, Mrs. Blake, Miss
Anthony, " Jenny June," and some of the younger converts to our platform, all made short speeches of praise
and congratulation, which were followed by music, recitations, and refreshments.

All during the autumn Miss Anthony and I looked
forward to the spring, when we hoped to have completed the third and last volume of our History, and thus
end the labors of ten years. We had neither time nor
eyesight to read aught but the imperative documents

for the History.   I was hungering for some other mental pabulum.

In January, 1886, I was invited to dine with Laura Curtis Bullard, to meet Mme. Durand (Henri Gréville), the novelist. She seemed a politic rather than an earnest woman of principle. As it was often very inconvenient for me to entertain distinguished visitors, who desired to meet me in my country home during the winter, Mrs. Bullard generously offered always to invite them to her home. She and her good mother have done their part in the reform movements in New York by their generous hospitalities.

Reading the debates in Congress, at that time, on a proposed appropriation for a monument to General Grant, I was glad to see that Senator Plumb of Kansas was brave enough to express his opinion against it.   I fully agree with him.   So long as multitudes of our people who are doing the work of the world live in garrets and cellars, in ignorance, poverty, and vice, it is the duty of Congress to apply the surplus in the national treasury to objects which will feed, clothe, shelter, and educate these wards of the State.   If we must keep on continually building monuments to great men, they should be handsome blocks of comfortable homes for the poor, such as Peabody built in London.   Senator Hoar of Massachusetts favored the Grant monument, partly to cultivate the artistic tastes of our people.   We might as well cultivate our tastes on useful dwellings as on useless monuments.   Surely sanitary homes and schoolhouses for the living would be more appropriate monuments to wise statesmen than the purest Parian shafts among the sepulchers of the dead.

The strikes and mobs and settled discontent of the

masses warn us that, although we forget and neglect their interests and our duties, we do it at the peril of all. English statesmen are at their wits' end to-day with their tangled social and industrial problems, threatening the throne of a long line of kings. The impending danger cannot be averted by any surface measures; there must be a radical change in the relations of capital and labor.

In April rumors of a domestic invasion, wafted on every Atlantic breeze, warned us that our children were coming from England and France—a party of six. Fortunately, the last line of the History was written, so Miss Anthony, with vol. iii. and bushels of manuscripts, fled to the peaceful home of her sister Mary at Rochester. The expected party sailed from Liverpool the 26th of May, on the *America*. After being out three days the piston rod broke and they were obliged to return. My son-in-law, W. H. Blatch, was so seasick and disgusted that he remained in England, and took a fresh start two months later, and had a swift passage without any accidents. The rest were transferred to the *Germanic*, and reached New York the 12th of June. Different divisions of the party were arriving until midnight. Five people and twenty pieces of baggage! The confusion of such an invasion quite upset the even tenor of our days, and it took some time for people and trunks to find their respective niches. However crowded elsewhere, there was plenty of room in our hearts, and we were unspeakably happy to have our flock all around us once more.

I had long heard so many conflicting opinions about the Bible—some saying it taught woman's emancipation and some her subjection—that, during this visit of my

children, the thought came to me that it would be well
to collect every biblical reference to women in one small
compact volume, and see on which side the balance of
influence really was.   To this end I proposed to organize a committee of competent women, with some Latin,
Greek, and Hebrew scholars in England and the United
States, for a thorough revision of the Old and New
Testaments, and to ascertain what the status of woman
really was under the Jewish and Christian religion.   As
the Church has thus far interpreted the Bible as teaching woman's subjection, and none of the revisions by
learned ecclesiastics have thrown any new light on the
question, it seemed to me pre-eminently proper and
timely for women themselves to review the book.   As
they are now studying theology in many institutions of
learning, asking to be ordained as preachers, elders, deacons, and to be admitted, as delegates, to Synods and
General Assemblies, and are refused on Bible grounds,
it seemed to me high time for women to consider those
scriptural arguments and authorities.

A happy coincidence enabled me at last to begin this
work.   While my daughter, Mrs. Stanton Blatch, was
with me, our friend Miss Frances Lord, on our earnest
invitation, came to America to visit us.   She landed
in New York the 4th of August, 1886.   As it was
Sunday she could not telegraph, hence there was no
one to meet her, and, as we all sat chatting on the
front piazza, suddenly, to our surprise and delight, she
drove up.   After a few days' rest and general talk of
passing events, I laid the subject so near my heart before
her and my daughter.   They responded promptly and
heartily, and we immediately set to work.   I wrote to
every woman who I thought might join such a commit-

tee, and Miss Lord ran through the Bible in a few days, marking each chapter that in any way referred to women. We found that the work would not be so great as we imagined, as all the facts and teachings in regard to women occupied less than one-tenth of the whole Scriptures. We purchased some cheap Bibles, cut out the texts, pasted them at the head of the page, and, underneath, wrote our commentaries as clearly and concisely as possible. We did not intend to have sermons or essays, but brief comments, to keep " The Woman's Bible " as small as possible.

Miss Lord and I worked several weeks together, and Mrs. Blatch and I, during the winter of 1887, wrote all our commentaries on the Pentateuch. But we could not succeed in forming the committee, nor, after writing innumerable letters, make the women understand what we wanted to do. I still have the commentaries of the few who responded, and the letters of those who declined—a most varied and amusing bundle of manuscripts in themselves. Some said the Bible had no special authority with them; that, like the American Constitution, it could be interpreted to mean anything —slavery, when we protected that " Institution," and freedom, when it existed no longer. Others said that woman's sphere was clearly marked out in the Scriptures, and all attempt at emancipation was flying in the face of Providence. Others said they considered all the revisions made by men thus far, had been so many acts of sacrilege, and they did hope women would not add their influence, to weaken the faith of the people in the divine origin of the Holy Book, for, if men and women could change it in one particular, they could in all. On the whole the correspondence was discouraging.

Later Miss Lord became deeply interested in psychical researches, and I could get no more work out of her. And as soon as we had finished the Pentateuch, Mrs. Blatch declared she would go no farther; that it was the driest history she had ever read, and most derogatory to women. My beloved coadjutor, Susan B. Anthony, said that she thought it a work of supererogation; that when our political equality was recognized and we became full-fledged American citizens, the Church would make haste to bring her Bibles and prayer books, creeds and discipline up to the same high-water mark of liberty.

Helen Gardener said: "I consider this a most important proposal, and if you and I can ever stay on the same side of the Atlantic long enough, we will join hands and do the work. In fact, I have begun already with Paul's Epistles, and am fascinated with the work. The untenable and unscientific positions he takes in regard to women are very amusing. Although the first chapter of Genesis teaches the simultaneous creation of man and woman, Paul bases woman's subjection on the priority of man, and because woman was of the man. As the historical fact is that, as far back as history dates, the man has been of the woman, should he therefore be forever in bondage to her? Logically, according to Paul, he should."

I consulted several friends, such as Dr. William F. Channing, Mr. and Mrs. Moncure D. Conway, Gertrude Garrison, Frederick Cabot, and Edward M. Davis, as to the advisability of the work, and they all agreed that such a volume, showing woman's position under the Jewish and Christian religions, would be valuable, but none of them had time to assist in the project.

Though, owing to all these discouragements, I discontinued my work, I never gave up the hope of renewing it some time, when other of my coadjutors should awake to its importance and offer their services.

On October 27, 1886, with my daughter, nurse, and grandchild, I again sailed for England. Going out of the harbor in the clear early morning, we had a fine view of Bartholdi's statue of Liberty Enlightening the World. We had a warm, gentle rain and a smooth sea most of the way, and, as we had a stateroom on deck, we could have the portholes open, and thus get all the air we desired. With novels and letters, chess and whist the time passed pleasantly, and, on the ninth day, we landed in Liverpool.

CHAPTER XXIV.

ENGLAND AND FRANCE REVISITED.

ON arriving at Basingstoke we found awaiting us cordial letters of welcome from Miss Biggs, Miss Priestman, Mrs. Peter Taylor, Mrs. Priscilla McLaren, Miss Müller, Mrs. Jacob Bright, and Mme. de Barrau. During the winter Mrs. Margaret Bright Lucas, Drs. Kate and Julia Mitchell, Mrs. Charles McLaren, Mrs. Saville, and Miss Balgarnie each spent a day or two with us. The full-dress costume of the ladies was a great surprise to my little granddaughter Nora. She had never seen bare shoulders in a drawing room, and at the first glance she could not believe her eyes. She slowly made the circuit of the room, coming nearer and nearer until she touched the lady's neck to see whether or not it was covered with some peculiar shade of dress, but finding the bare skin she said: " Why, you are not dressed, are you? I see your skin!" The scene suggested to me the amusing description in Holmes' " Elsie Venner," of the efforts of a young lady, seated between two old gentlemen, to show off her white shoulders. The vicar would not look, but steadily prayed that he might not be led into temptation; but the physician, with greater moral hardihood, deliberately surveyed the offered charms, with spectacles on his nose.

In December Hattie and I finished Dowden's " Life of Shelley," which we had been reading together. Here

THREE GENERATIONS.

MY EIGHTIETH BIRTHDAY.

we find a sensitive, refined nature, full of noble purposes, thrown out when too young to meet all life's emergencies, with no loving Mentor to guard him from blunders or to help to retrieve the consequences of his false positions. Had he been surrounded with a few true friends, who could appreciate what was great in him and pity what was weak, his life would have been different. His father was hard, exacting, and unreasonable; hence he had no influence. His mother had neither the wisdom to influence him, nor the courage to rebuke her husband; and alas! poor woman, she was in such thraldom herself to conventionalisms, that she could not understand a youth who set them all at defiance.

We also read Cotton Morrison's " Service of Man," which I hope will be a new inspiration to fresh labors by all for the elevation of humanity, and Carnegie's " Triumphant Democracy," showing the power our country is destined to wield and the vastness of our domain. This book must give every American citizen a feeling of deeper responsibility than ever before to act well his part. We read, too, Harriet Martineau's translation of the works of Auguste Comte, and found the part on woman most unsatisfactory. He criticises Aristotle's belief that slavery is a necessary element of social life, yet seems to think the subjection of woman in modern civilization a matter of no importance.

All through that winter Hattie and I occupied our time studying the Bible and reading the commentaries of Clark, Scott, and Wordsworth (Bishop of Lincoln). We found nothing grand in the history of the Jews nor in the morals inculcated in the Pentateuch. Surely the writers had a very low idea of the nature of their God. They make Him not only anthropomorphic, but of the very lowest type, jealous and revengeful, loving violence rather than mercy. I know no other books that so fully teach the subjection and degradation of woman. Miriam, the eldest sister of Moses and Aaron, a genius, a prophetess, with the family aptitude for diplomacy and government, is continually set aside because of her sex—permitted to lead the women in singing and dancing, nothing more. No woman could offer sacrifices nor eat the holy meats because, according to the Jews, she was too unclean and unholy.

But what is the use, say some, of attaching any importance to the customs and teachings of a barbarous people? None whatever. But when our bishops, archbishops, and ordained clergymen stand up in their pulpits and read selections from the Pentateuch with reverential voice, they make the women of their congregation believe that there really is some divine authority for their subjection. In the Thirty-First Chapter of Numbers, in speaking of the spoils taken from the Midianites, the live stock is thus summarized: " Five thousand sheep, threescore and twelve thousand beeves, threescore and one thousand asses, and thirty-two thousand women and women-children," which Moses said the warriors might keep for themselves. What a pity a Stead had not been there, to protect the child-women of the Midianites and rebuke the Lord's chosen people as they deserved! In placing the women after the sheep, the beeves, and the asses, we have a fair idea of their comparative importance in the scale of being, among the Jewish warriors. No wonder the right reverend bishops and clergy of the Methodist Church, who believe in the divine origin and authority of the Pentateuch, exclude women from their great convocations in the American Republic in the nineteenth century. In view of the fact that our children are taught to reverence the book as of divine origin, I think we have a right to ask that, in the next revision, all such passages be expurgated, and to that end learned, competent women must have an equal place on the revising committee.

Mrs. Margaret Bright Lucas came, in February, to spend a few days with us. She was greatly shocked with many texts in the Old Testament, to which we called her attention, and said: "Here is an insidious influence against the elevation of women, which but few of us have ever taken into consideration." She had just returned from a flying visit to America; having made two voyages across the Atlantic and traveled three thousand miles across the continent in two months, and this at the age of sixty-eight years. She was enthusiastic in her praises of the women she met in the United States. As her name was already on the committee to prepare "The Woman's Bible," we had her hearty approval of the undertaking.

In October Hattie went to London, to attend a meeting to form a Woman's Liberal Federation. Mrs. Gladstone presided. The speeches made were simply absurd, asking women to organize themselves to help the Liberal party, which had steadily denied to them the political rights they had demanded for twenty years. Professor Stuart capped the climax of insult when he urged as "one great advantage in getting women to canvass for the Liberal party was that they would give their services free." The Liberals saw what enthusiasm the Primrose Dames had roused for the Tory party, really carrying the election, and they determined to utilize a similar force in their ranks. But the whole movement was an insult to women.

The one absorbing interest, then, was the Queen's Jubilee. Ladies formed societies to collect funds to place at the disposal of the Queen. Every little village was divided into districts, and different ladies took the rounds, begging pennies at every door of servants and the laboring masses, and pounds of the wealthy people. One of them paid us a visit. She asked the maid who opened the door to see the rest of the servants, and she begged a penny of each of them. She then asked to see the mistress. My daughter descended; but, instead of a pound, she gave her a lecture on the Queen's avarice. When the fund was started the people supposed the Queen was to return it all to the people in liberal endowments of charitable institutions, but her Majesty proposed to build a monument to Prince Albert, although he already had one in London. " The Queen," said my daughter, " should celebrate her Jubilee by giving good gifts to her subjects, and not by filching from the poor their pennies. To give half her worldly possessions to her impoverished people, to give Home Rule to Ireland, or to make her public schools free, would be deeds worthy her Jubilee; but to take another cent from those who are hopelessly poor is a sin against suffering humanity." The young woman realized the situation and said: " I shall go no farther. I wish I could return every penny I have taken from the needy."

The most fitting monuments this nation can build are schoolhouses and homes for those who do the work of the world. It is no answer to say that they are accustomed to rags and hunger. In this world of plenty

every human being has a right to food, clothes, decent
shelter, and the rudiments of education. " Something
is rotten in the state of Denmark " when one-tenth of
the human family, booted and spurred, ride the masses
to destruction. I detest the words " royalty " and
" nobility," and all the ideas and institutions based on
their recognition. In April the great meeting in Hyde
Park occurred—a meeting of protest against the Irish
Coercion Bill. It was encouraging to see that there
is a democratic as well as an aristocratic England. The
London journals gave very different accounts of the
meeting. The Tories said it was a mob of inconsequen-
tial cranks. Reason teaches us, however, that you cannot get up a large, enthusiastic meeting unless there is
some question pending that touches the heart of the
people. Those who say that Ireland has no grievances
are ignorant alike of human nature and the facts of
history.

On April 14 I went to Paris, my daughter escorting
me to Dover, and my son meeting me at Calais. It was
a bright, pleasant day, and I sat on deck and enjoyed
the trip, though many of my fellow passengers were pale
and limp. Whirling to Paris in an easy car, through
the beautiful wheatfields and vineyards, I thought of
the old lumbering diligence, in which we went up to
Paris at a snail's pace forty years before. I remained
in Paris until October, and never enjoyed six months
more thoroughly. One of my chief pleasures was making the acquaintance of my fourth son, Theodore. I
had seen but little of him since he was sixteen years old,
as he then spent five years at Cornell University, and
as many more in Germany and France. He had already
published two works, " The Life of Thiers," and " The

Woman Question in Europe." To have a son interested in the question to which I have devoted my life, is a source of intense satisfaction. To say that I have realized in him all I could desire, is the highest praise a fond mother can give.

My first experience in an apartment, living on an even plane, no running up and down stairs, was as pleasant as it was surprising. I had no idea of the comfort and convenience of this method of keeping house. Our apartment in Paris consisted of drawing room, dining room, library, a good-sized hall, in which stood a large American stove, five bedrooms, bathroom, and kitchen, and a balcony fifty-two feet long and four feet wide. The first few days it made me dizzy to look down from this balcony to the street below. I was afraid the whole structure would give way, it appeared so light and airy, hanging midway between earth and heaven. But my confidence in its steadfastness and integrity grew day by day, and it became my favorite resort, commanding, as it did, a magnificent view of the whole city and distant surroundings.

There were so many Americans in town, and French reformers to be seen, that I gave Wednesday afternoon receptions during my whole visit. To one of our " at homes " came Mlle. Maria Deraismes, the only female Free Mason in France, and the best woman orator in the country; her sister, Mme. Féresse-Deraismes, who takes part in all woman movements; M. Léon Richer, then actively advocating the civil and political rights of women through the columns of his vigorous journal; Mme. Griess Traut, who makes a specialty of Peace work; Mme. Isabelle Bogelot, who afterward attended the Washington Council of 1888, and who is a leader in charity work; the late Mme. Emilie de Morsier, who afterward was the soul of the International Congress of 1889, at Paris; Mme. Pauline Kergomard, the first woman to be made a member of the Superior Council of public Instruction in France, and Mme. Henri Gréville, the novelist.

Among the American guests at our various Wednesday receptions were Mr. and Mrs. John Bigelow, Mr. and Mrs. James G. Blaine, Mr. Daniel C. French, the Concord sculptor; Mrs. J. C. Ayer, Mr. L. White Busbey, one of the editors of the Chicago *Inter-Ocean;* Rev. Dr. Henry M. Field, Charles Gifford Dyer, the painter and father of the gifted young violinist, Miss Hella Dyer; the late Rev. Mr. Moffett, then United States Consul at Athens, Mrs. Governor Bagley and daughter of Michigan; Grace Greenwood and her talented daughter, who charmed everyone with her melodious voice, and Miss Bryant, daughter of the poet. One visitor who interested us most was the Norwegian novelist and republican, Bjornstjorne Bjornson.

We had several pleasant interviews with Frederick Douglass and his wife, some exciting games of chess with Theodore Tilton, in the pleasant apartments of the late W. J. A. Fuller, Esq., and his daughter, Miss Kate Fuller. At this time I also met our brilliant countrywoman, Louise Chandler Moulton. Seeing so many familiar faces, I could easily imagine myself in New York rather than in Paris. I attended several receptions and dined with Mrs. Charlotte Beebe Wilbour, greatly enjoying her clever descriptions of a winter on the Nile in her own dahabeeyeh. I heard Père Hyacinthe preach, and met his American wife on several occasions. I took long drives every day

through the parks and pleasant parts of the city.　With
garden concerts, operas, theaters, and the Hippodrome
I found abundant amusement.　I never grew weary of
the latter performance—the wonderful intelligence displayed there by animals, being a fresh surprise to me
every time I went.

I attended a reception at the Elysée Palace, escorted
by M. Joseph Fabre, then a deputy and now a senator.
M. Fabre is the author of a play and several volumes
devoted to Joan of Arc.　He presented me to the President and to Mme. Jules Grévy.　I was also introduced
to M. Jules Ferry, then Prime Minister, who said, among
other things: " I am sorry to confess it, but it is only too
true, our French women are far behind their sisters in
America."　The beautiful, large garden was thrown
open that evening,—it was in July,—and the fine band
of the Republican Guard gave a delightful concert under
the big trees.　I also met M. Grévy's son-in-law, M.
Daniel Wilson.　He was then a deputy and one of the
most powerful politicians in France.　A few months
later he caused his father's political downfall.　I have
a vivid recollection of him because he could speak English, his father having been a British subject.

I visited the picture galleries once more, after a lapse
of nearly fifty years, and was struck by the fact that, in
that interval, several women had been admitted to
places of honor.　This was especially noticeable in the
Luxembourg Sculpture Gallery, where two women,
Mme. Bertaux and the late Claude Vignon, wife of M.
Rouvier, were both represented by good work—the first
and only women sculptors admitted to that gallery.

At a breakfast party which we gave, I made the acquaintance of General Cluseret, who figured in our

Civil War, afterward became War Minister of the Paris Commune, and is now member of the Chamber of Deputies. He learned English when in America, and had not entirely forgotten it. He told anecdotes of Lincoln, Stanton, Sumner, Frémont, Garibaldi, the Count of Paris, and many other famous men whom he once knew, and proved to be a very interesting conversationalist.

Old bookstands were always attractive centers of interest to Theodore, and, among other treasure-troves, he brought home one day a boy of fourteen years, whose office it had been to watch the books. He was a bright, cheery little fellow of mixed French and German descent, who could speak English, French, and German. He was just what we had desired, to run errands and tend the door. As he was delighted with the idea of coming to us, we went to see his parents. We were pleased with their appearance and surroundings. We learned that they were members of the Lutheran Church, that the boy was one of the shining lights in Sunday school, and the only point in our agreement on which they were strenuous was that he should go regularly to Sunday school and have time to learn his lessons.

So " Immanuel " commenced a new life with us, and as we had unbounded confidence in the boy's integrity, we excused his shortcomings, and, for a time, believed all he said. But before long we found out that the moment we left the house he was in the drawing room, investigating every drawer, playing on the piano, or sleeping on the sofa. Though he was told never to touch the hall stove, he would go and open all the draughts and make it red-hot. Then we adopted the plan of locking up every part of the apartment but the kitchen.   He amused himself burning holes through the pantry shelves, when the cook was out, and boring holes, with a gimlet, through a handsomely carved bread board.   One day, in making up a spare bed for a friend, under the mattress were found innumerable letters he was supposed to have mailed at different times.   When we reprimanded him for his pranks he would look at us steadily, but sorrowfully, and, immediately afterward, we would hear him dancing down the corridor singing, " Safe in the Arms of Jesus."   If he had given heed to one-half we said to him, he would have been safer in our hands than in those of his imaginary protector.   He turned out a thief, an unmitigated liar, a dancing dervish, and, through all our experiences of six weeks with him, his chief reading was his Bible and Sunday-school books.   The experience, however, was not lost on Theodore—he has never suggested a boy since, and a faithful daughter of Eve reigns in his stead.

During the summer I was in the hands of two artists, Miss Anna Klumpke, who painted my portrait, and Paul Bartlett, who molded my head in clay.   To shorten the operation, sometimes I sat for both at the same time.   Although neither was fully satisfied with the results of their labors, we had many pleasant hours together, discussing their art, their early trials, and artists in general.   Each had good places in the *Salon*, and honorable mention that year.   It is sad to see so many American girls and boys, who have no genius for painting or sculpture, spending their days in garrets, in solitude and poverty, with the vain hope of earning distinction.   Women of all classes are awaking to the necessity of self-support, but few are willing to do the ordinary useful work for which they are fitted.

In the *Salon* that year six thousand pictures were offered, and only two thousand accepted, and many of these were " skyed."

It was lovely on our balcony at night to watch the little boats, with their lights, sailing up and down the Seine, especially the day of the great annual fête,— the 14th of July,—when the whole city was magnificently illuminated. We drove about the city on several occasions at midnight, to see the life—men, women, and children enjoying the cool breezes, and the restaurants all crowded with people.

Sunday in Paris is charming—it is the day for the masses of the people. All the galleries of art, the libraries, concert halls, and gardens are open to them. All are dressed in their best, out driving, walking, and having picnics in the various parks and gardens; husbands, wives, and children laughing and talking happily together. The seats in the streets and parks are all filled with the laboring masses. The benches all over Paris— along the curbstones in every street and highway— show the care given to the comfort of the people. You will see mothers and nurses with their babies and children resting on these benches, laboring men eating their lunches and sleeping there at noon, the organ grinders and monkeys, too, taking their comfort. In France you see men and women everywhere together; in England the men generally stagger about alone, caring more for their pipes and beer than their mothers, wives, and sisters. Social life, among the poor especially, is far more natural and harmonious in France than in England, because women mix more freely in business and amusements.

Coming directly from Paris to London, one is forcibly struck with the gloom of the latter city, especially at night.   Paris with its electric lights is brilliant everywhere, while London, with its meager gas jets here and there struggling with the darkness, is as gloomy and desolate as Dore's pictures of Dante's Inferno.   On Sunday, when the shops are closed, the silence and solitude of the streets, the general smoky blackness of the buildings and the atmosphere give one a melancholy impression of the great center of civilization.   Now that it has been discovered that smoke can be utilized and the atmosphere cleared, it is astonishing that the authorities do not avail themselves of the discovery, and thus bring light and joy and sunshine into that city, and then clean the soot of centuries from their blackened buildings.

On my return to England I spent a day with Miss Emily Lord, at her kindergarten establishment.   She had just returned from Sweden, where she spent six weeks in the carpenter's shop, studying the Swedish Slöjd system, in which children of twelve years old learn to use tools, making spoons, forks, and other implements.   Miss Lord showed us some of her work, quite creditable for her first attempts.   She said the children in the higher grades of her school enjoyed the carpenter work immensely and became very deft in the use of tools.

On November 1, 1887, we reached Basingstoke once more, and found all things in order.   My diary tells of several books I read during the winter and what the authors say of women; one the " Religio Medici," by Sir Thomas Browne, M. D., in which the author discourses on many high themes, God, Creation, Heaven, Hell, and vouchsafes one sentence on woman.   Of her he says: " I was never married but once and commend their resolution who never marry twice, not that I disallow of second, nor in all cases of polygamy, which, considering the unequal number of the sexes, may also be necessary. The whole world was made for man, but the twelfth part of man for woman. Man is the whole world—the breath of God; woman the rib and crooked piece of man. I speak not in prejudice nor am averse from that sweet sex, but naturally amorous of all that is beautiful. I can look all day at a handsome picture, though it be but a horse."

Turning to John Paul Friedrich Richter, I found in his chapter on woman many equally ridiculous statements mixed up with much fulsome admiration. After reading some volumes of Richter, I took up Heinrich Heine, the German poet and writer. He said: " Oh, the women! we must forgive them much, for they love much and many. Their hate is, properly, only love turned inside out. Sometimes they attribute some delinquency to us, because they think they can, in this way, gratify another man. When they write they have always one eye on the paper and the other eye on some man. This is true of all authoresses except the Countess Hahn Hahn, who has only one eye." In John Ruskin's biography he gives us a glimpse of his timidity in regard to the sex, when a young man. He was very fond of the society of girls, but never knew how to approach them. He said he " was perfectly happy in serving them, would gladly make a bridge of himself for them to walk over, a beam to fasten a swing to for them—anything but to talk to them." Such are some of the choice specimens of masculine wit I collected during my winter's reading!

At a reception given to me by Drs. Julia and Kate Mitchell, sisters practicing medicine in London, I met Stepniak, the Russian Nihilist, a man of grand presence and fine conversational powers. He was about to go to America, apprehensive lest our Government should make an extradition treaty with Russia to return political offenders, as he knew that proposal had been made. A few weeks later he did visit the United States, and had a hearing before a committee of the Senate. He pointed out the character of the Nihilist movement, declaring Nihilists to be the real reformers, the true lovers of liberty, sacrificing themselves for the best interests of the people, and yet, as political prisoners, they are treated worse than the lowest class of criminals in the prisons and mines of Siberia.

I had a very unpleasant interview, during this visit to London, with Miss Lydia Becker, Miss Caroline Biggs, and Miss Blackburn, at the Metropole, about choosing delegates to the International Council of Women soon to be held in Washington. As there had been some irreconcilable dissensions in the suffrage association, and they could not agree as to whom their delegate should be, they decided to send none at all. I wrote at once to Mrs. Priscilla Bright McLaren, pointing out what a shame it would be if England, above all countries, should not be represented in the first International Council ever called by a suffrage association. She replied promptly that must not be, and immediately moved in the matter, and through her efforts three delegates were soon authorized to go, representing different constituencies—Mrs. Alice Cliff Scatcherd, Mrs. Ormiston Chant, and Mrs. Ashton Dilke.

Toward the last of February, 1888, we went again to

London to make a few farewell visits to dear friends. We spent a few days with Mrs. Mona Caird, who was then reading Karl Pearson's lectures on " Woman," and expounding her views on marriage, which she afterward gave to the *Westminster Review,* and stirred the press to white heat both in England and America. " Is Marriage a Failure? " furnished the heading for our quack advertisements for a long time after. Mrs. Caird was a very graceful, pleasing woman, and so gentle in manner and appearance that no one would deem her capable of hurling such thunderbolts at the longsuffering Saxon people.

We devoted one day to Prince Krapotkine, who lives at Harrow, in the suburbs of London. A friend of his, Mr. Lieneff, escorted us there. We found the prince, his wife, and child in very humble quarters; uncarpeted floors, books and papers on pine shelves, wooden chairs, and the bare necessaries of life—nothing more. They indulge in no luxuries, but devote all they can spare to the publication of liberal opinions to be scattered in Russia, and to help Nihilists in escaping from the dominions of the Czar. The prince and princess took turns in holding and amusing the baby—then only one year old; fortunately it slept most of the time, so that the conversation flowed on for some hours. Krapotkine told us of his sad prison experiences, both in France and Russia. He said the series of articles by George Kennan in the *Century* were not too highly colored, that the sufferings of men and women in Siberia and the Russian prisons could not be overdrawn. One of the refinements of cruelty they practice on prisoners is never to allow them to hear the human voice. A soldier always accompanies the warder who distributes the food, to see that no word is spoken. In vain the poor prisoner asks questions, no answer is ever made, no tidings from the outside world ever given. One may well ask what devil in human form has prescribed such prison life and discipline! I wonder if we could find a man in all Russia who would defend the system, yet someone is responsible for its terrible cruelties!

We returned to Basingstoke, passed the few remaining days in looking over papers and packing for the voyage, and, on March 4, 1888, Mrs. Blatch went with me to Southampton. On the train I met my companions for the voyage, Mrs. Gustafsen, Mrs. Ashton Dilke, and Baroness Gripenberg, from Finland, a very charming woman, to whom I felt a strong attraction. The other delegates sailed from Liverpool. We had a rough voyage and most of the passengers were very sick. Mrs. Dilke and I were well, however, and on deck every day, always ready to play whist and chess with a few gentlemen who were equally fortunate. I was much impressed with Mrs. Dilke's kindness and generosity in serving others. There was a lady on board with two children, whose nurse at the last minute refused to go with her. The mother was sick most of the way, and Mrs. Dilke did all in her power to relieve her, by amusing the little boy, telling him stories, walking with him on deck, and watching him throughout the day, no easy task to perform for an entire stranger. The poor little mother with a baby in her arms must have appreciated such kindly attention.

When the pilot met us off Sandy Hook, he brought news of the terrible blizzard New York had just experienced, by which all communication with the world at large was practically suspended. The captain brought him down into the saloon to tell us all about it. The news was so startling that at first we thought the pilot was joking, but when he produced the metropolitan journals to verify his statements, we listened to the reading and what he had to say with profound astonishment. The second week in March, 1888, will be mem-. orable in the history of storms in the vicinity of New York. The snow was ten feet deep in some places, and the side streets impassable either for carriages or sleighs. I hoped the city would be looking its best, for the first impression on my foreign friends, but it never looked worse, with huge piles of snow everywhere covered with black dust.

I started for Washington at three o'clock, the day after our arrival, reached there at ten o'clock, and found my beloved friends, Miss Anthony and Mrs. Spofford, with open arms and warm hearts to receive me. As the vessel was delayed two days, our friends naturally thought we, too, had encountered a blizzard, but we had felt nothing of it; on the contrary the last days were the most pleasant of the voyage.

CHAPTER XXV.

THE INTERNATIONAL COUNCIL OF WOMEN.

PURSUANT to the idea of the feasibility and need of an International Council of Women, mentioned in a preceding chapter, it was decided to celebrate the fourth decade of the woman suffrage movement in the United States by calling together such a council. At its nineteenth annual convention, held in January, 1887, the National Woman Suffrage Association resolved to assume the entire responsibility of holding a council, and to extend an invitation, for that purpose, to all associations of women in the trades, professions, and reforms, as well as those advocating political rights. Early in June, 1887, a call was issued for such a council to convene under the auspices of the National Woman Suffrage Association at Washington, D. C., on March 25, 1888. The grand assemblage of women, coming from all the countries of the civilized globe, proved that the call for such a council was opportune, while the order and dignity of the proceedings proved the women worthy the occasion. No one doubts now the wisdom of that initiative step nor the added power women have gained over popular thought through the International Council.

As the proceedings of the convention were fully and graphically reported in the *Woman's Tribune* at that time, and as its reports were afterward published in book form, revised and corrected by Miss Anthony,

Miss Foster, and myself, I will merely say that our most sanguine expectations as to its success were more than realized. The large theater was crowded for an entire week, and hosts of able women spoke, as if specially inspired, on all the vital questions of the hour. Although the council was called and conducted by the suffrage association, yet various other societies were represented. Miss Anthony was the financier of the occasion and raised twelve thousand dollars for the purpose, which enabled her to pay all the expenses of the delegates in Washington, and for printing the report in book form. As soon as I reached Washington, Miss Anthony ordered me to remain conscientiously in my own apartment and to prepare a speech for delivery before the committees of the Senate and House, and another, as President, for the opening of the council. However, as Mrs. Spofford placed her carriage at our service, I was permitted to drive an hour or two every day about that magnificent city.

One of the best speeches at the council was made by Helen H. Gardener. It was a criticism of Dr. Hammond's position in regard to the inferior size and quality of woman's brain. As the doctor had never had the opportunity of examining the brains of the most distinguished women, and, probably, those only of paupers and criminals, she felt he had no data on which to base his conclusions. Moreover, she had the written opinion of several leading physicians, that it was quite impossible to distinguish the male from the female brain.

The hearing at the Capitol, after the meeting of the council, was very interesting, as all the foreign delegates were invited to speak each in the language of her own country; to address their alleged representatives in the halls of legislation was a privilege they had never enjoyed at home. It is very remarkable that English women have never made the demand for a hearing in the House of Commons, nor even for a decent place to sit, where they can hear the debates and see the fine proportions of the representatives. The delegates had several brilliant receptions at the Riggs House, and at the houses of Senator Stanford of California and Senator Palmer of Michigan. Miss Anthony and I spent two months in Washington, that winter. One of the great pleasures of our annual conventions was the reunion of our friends at the Riggs House, where we enjoyed the boundless hospitality of Mr. and Mrs. Spofford.

The month of June I spent in New York city, where I attended several of Colonel Robert G. Ingersoll's receptions and saw the great orator and iconoclast at his own fireside, surrounded by his admirers, and heard his beautiful daughters sing, which gave all who listened great pleasure, as they have remarkably fine voices. One has since married, and is now pouring out her richest melodies in the opera of lullaby in her own nursery.

In the fall of 1888, as Ohio was about to hold a Constitutional convention, at the request of the suffrage association I wrote an appeal to the women of the State to demand their right to vote for delegates to such convention. Mrs. Southworth had five thousand copies of my appeal published and distributed at the exposition in Columbus. If ten righteous men could save Sodom, all the brilliant women I met in Cleveland should have saved Ohio from masculine domination.

The winter of 1888-89 I was to spend with my daughter in Omaha. I reached there in time to witness the celebration of the completion of the first bridge between that city and Council Bluffs. There was a grand procession in which all the industries of both towns were represented, and which occupied six hours in passing. We had a desirable position for reviewing the pageant, and very pleasant company to interpret the mottoes, symbols, and banners. The bridge practically brings the towns together, as electric street cars now run from one to the other in ten minutes. Here, for the first time, I saw the cable cars running up hill and down without any visible means of locomotion.

As the company ran an open car all winter, I took my daily ride of nine miles in it for fifteen cents. My son Daniel, who escorted me, always sat inside the car, while I remained on an outside seat. He was greatly amused with the remarks he heard about that " queer old lady that always rode outside in all kinds of wintry weather." One day someone remarked loud enough for all to hear: " It is evident that woman does not know enough to come in when it rains." " Bless me! " said the conductor, who knew me, " that woman knows as much as the Queen of England; too much to come in here by a hot stove." How little we understand the comparative position of those whom we often criticise. There I sat enjoying the bracing air, the pure fresh breezes, indifferent to the fate of an old cloak and hood that had crossed the Atlantic and been saturated with salt water many times, pitying the women inside breathing air laden with microbes that dozens of people had been throwing off from time to time, sacrificing themselves to their stylish bonnets, cloaks, and dresses, suffering with the heat of the red-hot stove; and yet they, in turn, pitying me.

My seventy-third birthday I spent with my son Gerrit Smith Stanton, on his farm near Portsmouth, Iowa. As we had not met in several years, it took us a long time, in the network of life, to pick up all the stitches that had dropped since we parted. I amused myself darning stockings and drawing plans for an addition to his house. But in the spring my son and his wife came to the conclusion that they had had enough of the solitude of farm life and turned their faces eastward.

Soon after my return to Omaha, the editor of the *Woman's Tribune,* Mrs. Clara B. Colby, called and lunched with us one day. She announced the coming State convention, at which I was expected " to make the best speech of my life." She had all the arrangements to make, and invited me to drive round with her, in order that she might talk by the way. She engaged the Opera House, made arrangements at the Paxton House for a reception, called on all her faithful coadjutors to arouse enthusiasm in the work, and climbed up to the sanctums of the editors,—Democratic and Republican alike,—asking them to advertise the convention and to say a kind word for our oppressed class in our struggle for emancipation. They all promised favorable notices and comments, and they kept their promises. Mrs. Colby, being president of the Nebraska Suffrage Association, opened the meeting with an able speech, and presided throughout with tact and dignity.

I came very near meeting with an unfortunate experience at this convention. The lady who escorted me in her carriage to the Opera House carried the manuscript of my speech, which I did not miss until it was nearly time to speak, when I told a lady who sat by my side that our friend had forgotten to give me my manuscript. She went at once to her and asked for it. She remembered taking it, but what she had done with it she did not know. It was suggested that she might have dropped it in alighting from the carriage. And lo! they found it lying in the gutter. As the ground was frozen hard it was not even soiled. When I learned of my narrow escape, I trembled, for I had not prepared any train of thought for extemporaneous use. I should have been obliged to talk when my turn came, and if inspired by the audience or the good angels, might have done well, or might have failed utterly. The moral of this episode is, hold on to your manuscript.

Owing to the illness of my son-in-law, Frank E. Lawrence, he and my daughter went to California to see if the balmy air of San Diego would restore his health, and so we gave up housekeeping in Omaha, and, on April 20, 1889, in company with my eldest son I returned East and spent the summer at Hempstead, Long Island, with my son Gerrit and his wife.

We found Hempstead a quiet, old Dutch town, undisturbed by progressive ideas. Here I made the acquaintance of Chauncey C. Parsons and wife, formerly of Boston, who were liberal in their ideas on most questions. Mrs. Parsons and I attended one of the Seidl club meetings at Coney Island, where Seidl was then giving some popular concerts. The club was composed of two hundred women, to whom I spoke for an hour in the dining room of the hotel. With the magnificent ocean views, the grand concerts, and the beautiful women, I passed two very charming days by the seaside.

My son Henry had given me a phaeton, low and easy as a cradle, and I enjoyed many drives about Long

Island.   We went to Bryant's home on the north side,
several times, and in imagination I saw the old poet in
the various shady nooks, inditing his lines of love and
praise of nature in all her varying moods.   Walking
among the many colored, rustling leaves in the dark
days of November, I could easily enter into his thought
as he penned these lines:

" The melancholy days are come, the saddest of the year,
     Of wailing winds, and naked woods, and meadows brown and sear.
 Heaped in the hollows of the grove, the autumn leaves lie dead ;
     They rustle to the eddying gust, and to the rabbit's tread."

In September, 1889, my daughter, Mrs. Stanton Lawrence, came East to attend a school of physical culture, and my other daughter, Mrs. Stanton Blatch,
came from England to enjoy one of our bracing winters.
Unfortunately we had rain instead of snow, and fogs
instead of frost.   However, we had a pleasant reunion
at Hempstead.   After a few days in and about New
York visiting friends, we went to Geneva and spent
several weeks in the home of my cousin, the daughter of
Gerrit Smith.

She and I have been most faithful, devoted friends all
our lives, and regular correspondents for more than
fifty years.   In the family circle we are ofttimes referred to as " Julius " and " Johnson."   These euphonious names originated in this way: When the Christy
Minstrels first appeared, we went one evening to hear
them.   On returning home we amused our seniors with,
as they said, a capital rehearsal.   The wit and philosopher of the occasion were called, respectively, Julius
and Johnson; so we took their parts and reproduced all
the bright, humorous remarks they made.   The next
morning as we appeared at the breakfast table, Cousin

Gerrit Smith, in his deep, rich voice said: " Good-morning, Julius and Johnson," and he kept it up the few days we were in Albany together. One after another our relatives adopted the pseudonyms, and Mrs. Miller has been " Julius " and I " Johnson " ever since.

From Geneva we went to Buffalo, but, as I had a bad cold and a general feeling of depression, I decided to go to the Dansville Sanatorium and see what Doctors James and Kate Jackson could do for me. I was there six weeks and tried all the rubbings, pinchings, steamings; the Swedish movements of the arms, hands, legs, feet; dieting, massage, electricity, and, though I succeeded in throwing off only five pounds of flesh, yet I felt like a new being. It is a charming place to be in —the home is pleasantly situated and the scenery very fine. The physicians are all genial, and a cheerful atmosphere pervades the whole establishment.

As Christmas was at hand, the women were all half crazy about presents, and while good Doctors James and Kate were doing all in their power to cure the nervous affections of their patients, they would thwart the treatment by sitting in the parlor with the thermometer at seventy-two degrees, embroidering all kinds of fancy patterns,—some on muslin, some on satin, and some with colored worsteds on canvas,—inhaling the poisonous dyes, straining the optic nerves, counting threads and stitches, hour after hour, until utterly exhausted. I spoke to one poor victim of the fallacy of Christmas presents, and of her injuring her health in such useless employment. " What can I do? " she replied, " I must make presents and cannot afford to buy them." " Do you think," said I, " any of your friends would enjoy a present you made at the risk of your

health? I do not think there is any 'must' in the
matter. I never feel that I must give presents, and
never want any, especially from those who make some
sacrifice to give them." This whole custom of presents
at Christmas, New Year's, and at weddings has come to
be a bore, a piece of hypocrisy leading to no end of
unhappiness. I do not know a more pitiful sight than
to see a woman tatting, knitting, embroidering—working cats on the toe of some slipper, or tulips on an
apron. The amount of nervous force that is expended
in this way is enough to make angels weep. The necessary stitches to be taken in every household are quite
enough without adding fancy work.

From Dansville my daughters and I went on to
Washington to celebrate the seventieth birthday of
Miss Anthony, who has always been to them as a second mother. Mrs. Blatch made a speech at the celebration, and Mrs. Lawrence gave a recitation. First
came a grand supper at the Riggs House. The
dining room was beautifully decorated; in fact, Mr.
and Mrs. Spofford spared no pains to make the occasion one long to be remembered. May Wright Sewall
was the mistress of ceremonies. She read the toasts
and called on the different speakers. Phœbe Couzins,
Rev. Anna Shaw, Isabella Beecher Hooker, Matilda
Joslyn Gage, Clara B. Colby, Senator Blair of
New Hampshire, and many others responded. I am
ashamed to say that we kept up the festivities till after
two o'clock. Miss Anthony, dressed in dark velvet and
point lace, spoke at the close with great pathos. Those
of us who were there will not soon forget February 15,
1890.

After speaking before committees of the Senate and

House, I gave the opening address at the annual convention. Mrs. Stanton Blatch spoke a few minutes on the suffrage movement in England, after which we hurried off to New York, and went on board the *Aller*, one of the North German Lloyd steamers, bound for Southampton. At the ship we found Captain Milinowski and his wife and two of my sons waiting our arrival. As we had eighteen pieces of baggage it took Mrs. Blatch some time to review them. My phaeton, which we decided to take, filled six boxes. An easy carriage for two persons is not common in England. The dogcarts prevail, the most uncomfortable vehicles one can possibly use. Why some of our Americans drive in those uncomfortable carts is a question. I think it is because they are " so English." The only reason the English use them is because they are cheap. The tax on two wheels is one-half what it is on four, and in England all carriages are taxed. Before we Americans adopt fashions because they are English, we had better find out the *raison d'être* for their existence.

We had a very pleasant, smooth voyage, unusually so for blustering February and March. As I dislike close staterooms, I remained in the ladies' saloon night and day, sleeping on a sofa. After a passage of eleven days we landed at Southampton, March 2, 1890. It was a beautiful moonlight night and we had a pleasant ride on the little tug to the wharf. We reached Basingstoke at eleven o'clock, found the family well and all things in order.

CHAPTER XXVI.

As soon as we got our carriage put together Hattie and I drove out every day, as the roads in England are in fine condition all the year round. We had lovely weather during the spring, but the summer was wet and cold. With reading, writing, going up to London, and receiving visitors, the months flew by without our accomplishing half the work we proposed.

As my daughter was a member of the Albemarle Club, we invited several friends to dine with us there at different times. There we had a long talk with Mr. Stead, the editor of the *Pall Mall Gazette*, on his position in regard to Russian affairs, " The Deceased Wife's Sister Bill," and the divorce laws of England. Mr. Stead is a fluent talker as well as a good writer. He is the leader of the social purity movement in England. The wisdom of his course toward Sir Charles Dilke and Mr. Parnell was questioned by many; but there is a touch of the religious fanatic in Mr. Stead, as in many of his followers.

There were several problems in social ethics that deeply stirred the English people in the year of our Lord 1890. One was Charles Stewart Parnell's platonic friendship with Mrs. O'Shea, and the other was the Lord Chancellor's decision in the case of Mrs. Jackson. The pulpit, the press, and the people vied with each other in trying to dethrone Mr. Parnell as the great Irish leader, but the united forces did not succeed in destroying his self-respect, nor in hounding him out of the British Parliament, though, after a brave and protracted resistance on his part, they did succeed in hounding him into the grave.

It was pitiful to see the Irish themselves, misled by a hypocritical popular sentiment in England, turn against their great leader, the only one they had had for half a century who was able to keep the Irish question uppermost in the House of Commons year after year. The course of events since his death has proved the truth of what he told them, to wit: that there was no sincerity in the interest English politicians manifested in the question of Home Rule, and that the debates on that point would cease as soon as it was no longer forced on their consideration. And now when they have succeeded in killing their leader, they begin to realize their loss. The question evolved through the ferment of social opinions was concisely stated, thus: " Can a man be a great leader, a statesman, a general, an admiral, a learned chief justice, a trusted lawyer, or skillful physician, if he has ever broken the Seventh Commandment? "

I expressed my opinion in the *Westminster Review*, at the time, in the affirmative. Mrs. Jacob Bright, Mrs. Ellen Battelle Dietrick of Boston, Kate Field, in her *Washington*, agreed with me. Many other women spoke out promptly in the negative, and with a bitterness against those who took the opposite view that was lamentable.

The Jackson case was a profitable study, as it brought out other questions of social ethics, as well as points of

law which were ably settled by the Lord Chancellor.
It seems that immediately after Mr. and Mrs. Jackson
were married, the groom was compelled to go to Aus-
tralia. After two years he returned and claimed his
bride, but in the interval she felt a growing aversion
and determined not to live with him. As she would not
even see him, with the assistance of friends he kid-
naped her one day as she was coming out of church,
and carried her to his home, where he kept her under
surveillance until her friends, with a writ of *habeas
corpus*, compelled him to bring her into court. The
popular idea " based on the common law of England," was, that the husband had this absolute right.
The lower court, in harmony with this idea, maintained
the husband's right, and remanded her to his keeping,
but the friends appealed to the higher court and the
Lord Chancellor reversed the decision.

With regard to the right so frequently claimed, giving husbands the power to seize, imprison, and chastise
their wives, he said: "I am of the opinion that no such
right exists in law. I am of the opinion that no such
right ever did exist in law. I say that no English subject has the right to imprison another English subject,
whether his wife or not." Through this decision the
wife walked out of the court a free woman. The passage of the Married Women's Property Bill in England in 1882 was the first blow at the old idea of
coverture, giving to wives their rights of property,
the full benefit of which they are yet to realize when
clearer-minded men administer the laws. The decision of the Lord Chancellor, rendered March 18, 1891,
declaratory of the personal rights of married women, is
a still more important blow by just so much as the

rights of person are more sacred than the rights of property.

One hundred years ago, Lord Chief Justice Mansfield gave his famous decision in the Somerset case, " That no slave could breathe on British soil," and the slave walked out of court a free man. The decision of the Lord Chancellor, in the Jackson case, is far more important, more momentous in its consequences, as it affects not only one race but one-half of the entire human family. From every point of view this is the greatest legal decision of the century. Like the great Chief Justice of the last century, the Lord Chancellor, with a clearer vision than those about him, rises into a purer atmosphere of thought, and vindicates the eternal principles of justice and the dignity of British law, by declaring all statutes that make wives the bond slaves of their husbands, obsolete.

How long will it be in our Republic before some man will arise, great enough to so interpret our National Constitution as to declare that women, as citizens of the United States, cannot be governed by laws in the making of which they have no part? It is not Constitutional amendments nor statute laws we need, but judges on the bench of our Supreme Court, who, in deciding great questions of human rights, shall be governed by the broad principles of justice rather than precedent. One interesting feature in the trial of the Jackson case, was that both Lady Coleridge and the wife of the Lord Chancellor were seated on the bench, and evidently much pleased with the decision.

It is difficult to account for the fact that, while women of the highest classes in England take the deepest interest in politics and court decisions, American women of wealth and position are wholly indifferent to all public matters.   While English women take an active part in elections, holding meetings and canvassing their districts, here, even the wives of judges, governors, and senators speak with bated breath of political movements, and seem to feel that a knowledge of laws and constitutions would hopelessly unsex them.

Toward the last of April, with my little granddaughter and her nurse, I went down to Bournemouth, one of the most charming watering places in England. We had rooms in the Cliff House with windows opening on the balcony, where we had a grand view of the bay and could hear the waves dashing on the shore. While Nora, with her spade and pail, played all day in the sands, digging trenches and filling them with water, I sat on the balcony reading " Diana of the Crossways," and Bjornson's last novel, " In God's Way," both deeply interesting.   As all the characters in the latter come to a sad end, I could not see the significance of the title.   If they walked in God's way their career should have been successful.

I took my first airing along the beach in an invalid chair.   These bath chairs are a great feature in all the watering places of England.   They are drawn by a man or a donkey.   The first day I took a man, an old sailor, who talked incessantly of his adventures, stopping to rest every five minutes, dissipating all my pleasant reveries, and making an unendurable bore of himself. The next day I told the proprietor to get me a man who would not talk all the time.   The man he supplied jogged along in absolute silence; he would not even answer my questions.   Supposing he had his orders to keep profound silence, after one or two attempts I said nothing. When I returned home, the proprietor asked me how I liked this man. " Ah! " I said, " he was indeed silent and would not even answer a question nor go anywhere I told him; still I liked him better than the talkative man." He laughed heartily and said: " This man is deaf and dumb. I thought I would make sure that you should not be bored." I joined in the laugh and said: " Well, to-morrow get me a man who can hear but cannot speak, if you can find one constructed on that plan."

Bournemouth is noteworthy now as the burial place of Mary Wolstonecraft and the Shelleys. I went to see the monument that had been recently reared to their memory. On one side is the following inscription: " William Godwin, author of ' Political Justice,' born March 3rd, 1756, died April 7th, 1836. Mary Wolstonecraft Godwin, author of the ' Vindication of the Rights of Women,' born April 27th, 1759, died September 10th, 1797." These remains were brought here, in 1851, from the churchyard of St. Pancras, London. On the other side are the following inscriptions: " Mary Wolstonecraft Godwin, daughter of William Godwin and widow of the late Percy Bysshe Shelley, born August 30th, 1797, died February 1st, 1851. Percy Florence Shelley, son of Percy Shelley and Mary Wolstonecraft, third baronet, born November 12th, 1819, died December 5th, 1889." In Christ's Church, six miles from Bournemouth, is a bas-relief in memory of the great poet. He is represented, dripping with seaweed, in the arms of the Angel of Death.

As I sat on my balcony hour after hour, reading and thinking of the Shelleys, watching the changing hues of the clouds and the beautiful bay, and listening to the sad monotone of the waves, these sweet lines of Whittier's came to my mind:

> " Its waves are kneeling on the strand,
>   As kneels the human knee,—
> Their white locks bowing to the sand,
>   The priesthood of the sea !
>
> " The blue sky is the temple's arch,
>   Its transept earth and air,
> The music of its starry march
>   The chorus of a prayer."

American letters, during this sojourn abroad, told of many losses, one after another, from our family circle; nine passed away within two years. The last was my sister Mrs. Bayard, who died in May, 1891. She was the oldest of our family, and had always been a second mother to her younger sisters, and her house our second home.

The last of June my son Theodore's wife and daughter came over from France to spend a month with us. Lisette and Nora, about the same size, played and quarreled most amusingly together. They spent their mornings in the kindergarten school, and the afternoons with their pony, but rainy days I was impressed into their service to dress dolls and tell stories. I had the satisfaction to hear them say that their dolls were never so prettily dressed before, and that my stories were better than any in the books. As I composed the wonderful yarns as I went along, I used to get very tired, and sometimes, when I heard the little feet coming, I would hide, but they would hunt until they found me. When my youngest son was ten years old and could read for himself, I graduated in story telling, having practiced in that line twenty-one years. I vowed that I would expend no more breath in that direction, but the eager face of a child asking for stories is too much for me, and my vow has been often broken. All the time I was in England Nora claimed the twilight hour, and, in France, Lisette was equally pertinacious. When Victor Hugo grew tired telling his grandchildren stories, he would wind up with the story of an old gentleman who, after a few interesting experiences, took up his evening paper and began to read aloud. The children would listen a few moments and then, one by one, slip out of the room. Longfellow's old gentleman, after many exciting scenes in his career, usually stretched himself on the lounge and feigned sleep. But grandmothers are not allowed to shelter themselves with such devices; they are required to spin on until the bedtime really arrives.

On July 16, one of the hottest days of the season, Mrs. Jacob Bright and daughter, Herbert Burroughs, and Mrs. Parkhurst came down from London, and we sat out of doors, taking our luncheon under the trees and discussing theosophy. Later in the month Hattie and I went to Yorkshire to visit Mr. and Mrs. Scatcherd at Morley Hall, and there spent several days. We had a prolonged discussion on personal rights. One side was against all governmental interference, such as compulsory education and the protection of children against cruel parents; the other side in favor of state interference that protected the individual in the enjoyment of life, liberty, and happiness. I took the latter position. Many parents are not fit to have the control of children, hence the State should see that they are sheltered, fed, clothed, and educated. It is far better for the State to make good citizens of

its children in the beginning, than, in the end, to be compelled to care for them as criminals.

While in the north of England we spent a few days at
Howard Castle, the summer residence of Lord and
Lady Carlisle and their ten children. So large a family
in high life is unusual. As I had known Lord and Lady
Amberley in America, when they visited this country in
1867, I enjoyed meeting other members of their family.
Lady Carlisle is in favor of woman suffrage and frequently speaks in public. She is a woman of great force
of character, and of very generous impulses. She is
trying to do her duty in sharing the good things of life
with the needy. The poor for miles round often have
picnics in her park, and large numbers of children from
manufacturing towns spend weeks with her cottage
tenants at her expense. Lord Carlisle is an artist and
a student. As he has a poetical temperament and is
æsthetic in all his tastes, Lady Carlisle is the business manager of the estate. She is a practical
woman with immense executive ability. The castle
with its spacious dining hall and drawing rooms, with
its chapel, library, galleries of paintings and statuary,
its fine outlook, extensive gardens and lawns was
well worth seeing. We enjoyed our visit very much
and discussed every imaginable subject.

When we returned to Basingstoke we had a visit
from Mrs. Cobb, the wife of a member of Parliament,
and sister-in-law of Karl Pearson, whose lectures on
woman I had enjoyed so much. It was through reading
his work, " The Ethic of Free Thought," that the Matriarchate made such a deep impression on my mind and
moved me to write a tract on the subject. People who
have neither read nor thought on this point, question

the facts as stated by Bachofen, Morgan, and Wilkeson; but their truth, I think, cannot be questioned.
They seem so natural in the chain of reasoning
and the progress of human development. Mrs. Cobb
did a very good thing a few days before visiting
us. At a great meeting called to promote Mr. Cobb's
election, John Morley spoke. He did not even say
" Ladies and gentlemen " in starting, nor make the
slightest reference to the existence of such beings as women. When he had finished, Mrs. Cobb
arose mid great cheering and criticised his speech,
making some quotations from his former speeches
of a very liberal nature. The audience laughed and
cheered, fully enjoying the rebuke. The next day in
his speech he remembered his countrywomen, and on
rising said, " Ladies and gentlemen."

During August, 1891, I was busy getting ready for
my voyage, as I was to sail on the *Ems* on August 23.
Although I had crossed the ocean six times in the prior
ten years I dreaded the voyage more than words can
describe. The last days were filled with sadness, in
parting with those so dear to me in foreign countries—
especially those curly-headed little girls, so bright, so
pretty, so winning in all their ways. Hattie and Theodore went with me from Southampton in the little tug
to the great ship *Ems*. It was very hard for us to say
the last farewell, but we all tried to be as brave as
possible.

We had a rough voyage, but I was not seasick one
moment. I was up and dressed early in the morning,
and on deck whenever the weather permitted. I made
many pleasant acquaintances with whom I played chess
and whist; wrote letters to all my foreign friends, ready

to mail on landing; read the "Egotist," by George Meredith, and Ibsen's plays as translated by my friend Frances Lord. I had my own private stewardess, a nice German woman who could speak English. She gave me most of my meals on deck or in the ladies' saloon, and at night she would open the porthole two or three times and air our stateroom; that made the nights endurable. The last evening before landing we got up an entertainment with songs, recitations, readings, and speeches. I was invited to preside and introduce the various performers. We reached Sandy Hook the evening of the 29th day of August and lay there all night, and the next morning we sailed up our beautiful harbor, brilliant with the rays of the rising sun.

Being fortunate in having children in both hemispheres, here, too, I found a son and daughter waiting to welcome me to my native land. Our chief business for many weeks was searching for an inviting apartment where my daughter, Mrs. Stanton Lawrence, my youngest son, Bob, and I could set up our family altar and sing our new psalm of life together. After much weary searching we found an apartment. Having always lived in a large house in the country, the quarters seemed rather contracted at first, but I soon realized the immense saving in labor and expense in having no more room than is absolutely necessary, and all on one floor. To be transported from the street to your apartment in an elevator in half a minute, to have all your food and fuel sent to your kitchen by an elevator in the rear, to have your rooms all warmed with no effort of your own, seemed like a realization of some fairy dream. With an extensive outlook of the heavens above, of the Park and the Boulevard beneath, I had a feeling of freedom, and with a short flight of stairs to the roof (an easy escape in case of fire), of safety, too.

No sooner was I fully established in my eyrie, than I was summoned to Rochester, by my friend Miss Anthony, to fill an appointment she had made for me with Miss Adelaide Johnson, the artist from Washington, who was to idealize Miss Anthony and myself in marble for the World's Fair. I found my friend demurely seated in her mother's rocking-chair hemming table linen and towels for her new home, anon bargaining with butchers, bakers, and grocers, making cakes and puddings, talking with enthusiasm of palatable dishes and the beauties of various articles of furniture that different friends had presented her. All there was to remind one of the " Napoleon of the Suffrage Movement " was a large escritoire covered with documents in the usual state of confusion—Miss Anthony never could keep her papers in order. In search of any particular document she roots out every drawer and pigeon hole, although her mother's little spinning wheel stands right beside her desk, a constant reminder of all the domestic virtues of the good housewife, with whom " order " is of the utmost importance and " heaven's first law." The house was exquisitely clean and orderly, the food appetizing, the conversation pleasant and profitable, and the atmosphere genial.

A room in an adjoining house was assigned to Miss Johnson and myself, where a strong pedestal and huge mass of clay greeted us. And there, for nearly a month, I watched the transformation of that clay into human proportions and expressions, until it gradually emerged with the familiar facial outlines ever so dear to one's self. Sitting there four or five hours every day I used to get very sleepy, so my artist arranged for a series of little naps. When she saw the crisis coming she would say: " I will work now for a time on the ear, the nose, or the hair, as you must be wide awake when I am trying to catch the expression." I rewarded her for her patience and indulgence by summoning up, when awake, the most intelligent and radiant expression that I could command. As Miss Johnson is a charming, cultured woman, with liberal ideas and brilliant in conversation, she readily drew out all that was best in me.

Before I left Rochester, Miss Anthony and her sister Mary gave a reception to me at their house. As some of the professors and trustees of the Rochester University were there, the question of co-education was freely discussed, and the authorities urged to open the doors of the University to the daughters of the people. It was rather aggravating to contemplate those fine buildings and grounds, while every girl in that city must go abroad for higher education. The wife of President Hill of the University had just presented him with twins, a girl and a boy, and he facetiously remarked, " that if the Creator could risk placing sexes in such near relations, he thought they might with safety walk on the same campus and pursue the same curriculum together."

Miss Anthony and I went to Geneva the next day to visit Mrs. Miller and to meet, by appointment, Mrs. Eliza Osborne, the niece of Lucretia Mott, and eldest daughter of Martha C. Wright. We anticipated a merry meeting, but Miss Anthony and I were so tired that we no doubt appeared stupid. In a letter to Mrs. Miller afterward, Mrs. Osborne inquired why I was " so solemn." As I pride myself on being impervious to fatigue or disease, I could not own up to any disability, so I turned the tables on her in the following letter:

"NEW YORK, 26 WEST 61ST STREET,
"November 12, 1891.

"DEAR ELIZA:

"In a recent letter to Mrs. Miller, speaking of the time when we last met, you say, 'Why was Mrs. Stanton so solemn?' to which I reply: Ever since an old German emperor issued an edict, ordering all the women under that flag to knit when walking on the highway, when selling apples in the market place, when sitting in the parks, because 'to keep women out of mischief their hands must be busy,' ever since I read that, I have felt 'solemn' whenever I have seen any daughters of our grand Republic knitting, tatting, embroidering, or occupied with any of the ten thousand digital absurdities that fill so large a place in the lives of Eve's daughters.

"Looking forward to the scintillations of wit, the philosophical researches, the historical traditions, the scientific discoveries, the astronomical explorations, the mysteries of theosophy, palmistry, mental science, the revelations of the unknown world where angels and devils do congregate, looking forward to discussions of all these grand themes, in meeting the eldest daughter of David and Martha Wright, the niece of Lucretia Mott, the sister-in-law of William Lloyd Garrison, a queenly-looking woman five feet eight in height, and well proportioned, with glorious black eyes, rivaling even De Staël's in power and pathos, one can readily imagine the disappointment I experienced when such a woman pulled a cotton wash rag from her pocket and forthwith began to knit with bowed head. Fixing her eyes and concentrating her thoughts on a rag one foot square; it was impossible for conversation to rise above the wash-rag level! It was enough to make the most aged optimist 'solemn' to see such a wreck of glorious womanhood.

"And, still worse, she not only knit steadily, hour after hour, but she bestowed the sweetest words of encouragement on a young girl from the Pacific Coast, who was embroidering rosebuds on another rag, the very girl I had endeavored to rescue from the maelstrom of embroidery, by showing her the unspeakable folly of giving her optic nerves to such base uses, when they were designed by the Creator to explore the planetary world, with chart and compass to guide mighty ships across the sea, to lead the sons of Adam with divinest love from earth to heaven. Think of the great beseeching optic nerves and muscles by which we express our admiration of all that is good and glorious in earth and heaven, being concentrated on a cotton wash rag! Who can wonder that I was 'solemn' that day! I made my agonized protest on the spot, but it fell unheeded, and with satisfied sneer Eliza knit on, and the young Californian continued making the rosebuds. I gazed into space, and, when alone, wept for my degenerate countrywoman. I not only was 'solemn' that day, but I am profoundly 'solemn' whenever I think of that queenly woman and that cotton wash rag. (One can buy a whole dozen of these useful appliances, with red borders and fringed, for twenty-five cents.) Oh, Eliza, I beseech you, knit no more!

"Affectionately yours,

"ELIZABETH CADY STANTON."

To this Mrs. Osborne sent the following reply:

" Dear Mrs. Stanton:

> " In your skit
> Against your sisterhood who knit,
>   Or useful make their fingers,
> I wonder if—deny it not—
> The habit of Lucretia Mott
>   Within your memory lingers !

> " In retrospective vision bright,
>   Can you recall dear Martha Wright
>   Without her work or knitting ?
> The needles flying in her hands,
> On washing rags or baby's bands,
>   Or other work as fitting ?

> " I cannot think they thought the less,
>   Or ceased the company to bless
>   With conversation's riches,
> Because they thus improved their time,
> And never deemed it was a crime
>   To fill the hours with stitches.

> " They even used to preach and plan
>   To spread the fashion, so that man
>   Might have this satisfaction ;
> Instead of idling as men do,
> With nervous meddling fingers too,
>   Why not mate talk with action ?

> " But as a daughter and a niece,
>   I pride myself on every piece
>   Of handiwork created ;
> While reveling in social chat,
> Or listening to gossip flat,
>   My gain is unabated.

> " That German emperor you scorn,
>   Seems to my mind a monarch born,
>   Worthy to lead a column ;

I'll warrant he could talk and work,
And, neither being used to shirk,
    Was rarely very solemn.

" I could say more upon this head,
But must, before I go to bed,
    Your idle precepts mocking,
Get out my needle and my yarn
And, caring not a single darn,
    Just finish up this stocking."

CHAPTER XXVII.

I RETURNED from Geneva to New York city in time to
celebrate my seventy-sixth birthday with my children.
I had traveled about constantly for the last twenty years
in France, England, and my own country, and had so
many friends and correspondents, and pressing invita-
tions to speak in clubs and conventions, that now I decided to turn over a new leaf and rest in an easy-chair.
But so complete a change in one's life could not be
easily accomplished. In spite of my resolution to
abide in seclusion, my daughter and I were induced to
join the Botta Club, which was to meet once a month,
alternately, at the residences of Mrs. Moncure D. Conway and Mrs. Abby Sage Richardson. Though composed of ladies and gentlemen it proved dull and
unprofitable. As the subject for discussion was not announced until each meeting, no one was prepared with
any well-digested train of thought. It was also decided to avoid all questions about which there might
be grave differences of opinion. This negative position reminded me of a book on etiquette which I read
in my young days, in which gentlemen were warned,
" In the presence of ladies discuss neither politics, religion, nor social duties, but confine yourself to art,
poetry, and abstract questions which women cannot
understand. The less they know of a subject the more

439

respectfully they will listen." This club was named in honor of Mrs. Botta, formerly Miss Anne Lynch, whose drawing room for many years was the social center of the literati of New York.

On January 16, 1892, we held the Annual Suffrage Convention in Washington, and, as usual, had a hearing before the Congressional Committee. My speech on the " Solitude of Self " was well received and was published in the Congressional Record. The *Woman's Tribune* struck off many hundreds of copies and it was extensively circulated.

Notwithstanding my determination to rest, I spoke to many clubs, wrote articles for papers and magazines, and two important leaflets, one on " Street Cleaning," another on " Opening the Chicago Exposition on Sunday." As Sunday was the only day the masses could visit that magnificent scene, with its great lake, extensive park, artificial canals, and beautiful buildings, I strongly advocated its being open on that day. One hundred thousand religious bigots petitioned Congress to make no appropriation for this magnificent Exposition, unless the managers pledged themselves to close the gates on Sunday, and hide this vision of beauty from the common people. Fortunately, this time a sense of justice outweighed religious bigotry. I sent my leaflets to every member of Congress and of the State legislatures, and to the managers of the Exposition, and made it a topic of conversation at every opportunity. The park and parts of the Exposition were kept open on Sunday, but some of the machinery was stopped as a concession to narrow Christian sects.

In June, 1892, at the earnest solicitation of Mrs. Russell Sage, I attended the dedication of the Gurley

Memorial Building, presented to the Emma Willard Seminary, at Troy, New York, and made the following address:

" MRS. PRESIDENT, MEMBERS OF THE ALUMNÆ:

" It is just sixty years since the class of '32, to which I belonged, celebrated a commencement in this same room. This was the great event of the season to many families throughout this State. Parents came from all quarters; the *élite* of Troy and Albany assembled here. Principals from other schools, distinguished legislators, and clergymen all came to hear girls scan Latin verse, solve problems in Euclid, and read their own compositions in a promiscuous assemblage. A long line of teachers anxiously waited the calling of their classes, and over all, our queenly Madame Willard presided with royal grace and dignity. Two hundred girls in gala attire, white dresses, bright sashes, and coral ornaments, with their curly hair, rosy cheeks, and sparkling eyes, flitted to and fro, some rejoicing that they had passed through their ordeal, some still on the tiptoe of expectation, some laughing, some in tears—altogether a most beautiful and interesting picture.

" Conservatives then, as now, thought the result of the higher education of girls would be to destroy their delicacy and refinement. But as the graduates of the Troy Seminary were never distinguished in after life for the lack of these feminine virtues, the most timid, even, gradually accepted the situation and trusted their daughters with Mrs. Willard. But that noble woman endured for a long period the same ridicule and persecution that women now do who take an onward step in the march of progress.

" I see around me none of the familiar faces that

greeted my coming or said farewell in parting. I do not know that one of my classmates still lives. Friendship with those I knew and loved best lasted but a few years, then our ways in life parted. I should not know where to find one now, and if I did, probably our ideas would differ on every subject, as I have wandered in latitudes beyond the prescribed sphere of women. I suppose it is much the same with many of you—the familiar faces are all gone, gone to the land of shadows, and I hope of sunshine too, where we in turn will soon follow.

" And yet, though we who are left are strangers to one another, we have the same memories of the past, of the same type of mischievous girls and staid teachers, though with different names. The same long, bare halls and stairs, the recitation rooms with the same old blackboards and lumps of chalk taken for generation after generation, I suppose, from the same pit; the dining room, with its pillars inconveniently near some of the tables, with its thick, white crockery and black-handled knives, and viands that never suited us, because, forsooth, we had boxes of delicacies from home, or we had been out to the baker's or confectioner's and bought pies and cocoanut cakes, candy and chewing gum, all forbidden, but that added to the relish. There, too, were the music rooms, with their old, second-hand pianos, some with rattling keys and tinny sound, on which we were supposed to play our scales and exercises for an hour, though we often slyly indulged in the ' Russian March,' ' Napoleon Crossing the Rhine,' or our national airs, when, as slyly, Mr. Powell, our music teacher, a bumptious Englishman, would softly open the door and say in a stern voice, ' Please practice the lesson I just gave you!'

" Our chief delight was to break the rules, but we did not like to be caught at it. As we were forbidden to talk with our neighbors in study hours, I frequently climbed on top of my bureau to talk through a pipe hole with a daughter of Judge Howell of Canandaigua. We often met afterward, laughed and talked over the old days, and kept our friendship bright until the day of her death. Once while rooming with Harriet Hudson, a sister of Mrs. John Willard, I was moved to a very erratic performance. Miss Theresa Lee had rung the bell for retiring, and had taken her rounds, as usual, to see that the lights were out and all was still, when I peeped out of my door, and seeing the bell at the head of the stairs nearby, I gave it one kick and away it went rolling and ringing to the bottom. The halls were instantly filled with teachers and scholars, all in white robes, asking what was the matter. Harriet and I ran around questioning the rest, and what a frolic we had, helter-skelter, up and down stairs, in each other's rooms, pulling the beds to pieces, changing girls' clothes from one room to another, etc., etc. The hall lamps, dimly burning, gave us just light enough for all manner of depredations without our being recognized, hence the unbounded latitude we all felt for mischief. In our whole seminary course—and I was there nearly three years—we never had such a frolic as that night. It took all the teachers to restore order and quiet us down again for the night. No suspicion of any irregularities were ever attached to Harriet and myself. Our standing for scholarship was good, hence we were supposed to reflect all the moralities.

" Though strangers, we have a bond of union in all these memories, of our bright companions, our good teachers, who took us through the pitfalls of logic, rhetoric, philosophy, and the sciences, and of the noble woman who founded the institution, and whose unselfish devotion in the cause of education we are here to celebrate. The name of Emma Willard is dear to all of us; to know her was to love and venerate her. She was not only good and gifted, but she was a beautiful woman. She had a finely developed figure, well-shaped head, classic features, most genial manners, and a profound self-respect (a rare quality in woman), that gave her a dignity truly royal in every position. Traveling in the Old World she was noticed everywhere as a distinguished personage. And all these gifts she dedicated to the earnest purpose of her life, the higher education of women.

" In opening this seminary she could not find young women capable of teaching the higher branches, hence her first necessity was to train herself. Amos B. Eaton, who was the principal of the Rensselaer Polytechnic School for boys here in Troy, told me Mrs. Willard studied with him every branch he was capable of teaching, and trained a corps of teachers and regular scholars at the same time. She took lessons of the Professor every evening when he had leisure, and studied half the night the branches she was to teach the next day, thus keeping ahead of her classes. Her intense earnestness and mental grasp, the readiness with which she turned from one subject to another, and her retentive memory of every rule and fact he gave her, was a constant surprise to the Professor.

" All her vacation she devoted to training teachers. She was the first to suggest the normal-school system. Remembering her deep interest in the education of women, we can honor her in no more worthy manner than to carry on her special lifework. As we look around at all the educated women assembled here to-day and try to estimate what each has done in her own sphere of action, the schools founded, the teachers sent forth, the inspiration given to girls in general, through the long chain of influences started by our alma mater, we can form some light estimate of the momentous and far-reaching consequences of Emma Willard's life. We have not her difficulties to overcome, her trials to endure, but the imperative duty is laid on each of us to finish the work she so successfully began. Schools and colleges of a high order are now everywhere open to women, public sentiment welcomes them to whatever career they may desire, and our work is to help worthy girls struggling for a higher education, by founding scholarships in desirable institutions in every State in the Union. The most fitting tribute we can pay to Emma Willard is to aid in the production of a generation of thoroughly educated women.

"There are two kinds of scholarships, equally desirable; a permanent one, where the interest of a fund from year to year will support a succession of students, and a temporary one, to help some worthy individual as she may require. Someone has suggested that this association should help young girls in their primary education. But as our public schools possess all the advantages for a thorough education in the rudiments of learning and are free to all, our scholarships should be bestowed on those whose ability and earnestness in the primary department have been proved, and whose capacity for a higher education is fully shown.

"This is the best work women of wealth can do, and

I hope in the future they will endow scholarships for their own sex instead of giving millions of dollars to institutions for boys, as they have done in the past. After all the bequests women have made to Harvard see how niggardly that institution, in its ' annex,' treats their daughters. I once asked a wealthy lady to give a few thousands of dollars to start a medical college and hospital for women in New York. She said before making bequests she always consulted her minister and her Bible. He told her there was nothing said in the Bible about colleges for women. I said, ' Tell him he is mistaken. If he will turn to 2 Chron. xxxiv. 22, he will find that when Josiah, the king, sent the wise men to consult Huldah, the prophetess, about the book of laws discovered in the temple, they found Huldah in the college in Jerusalem, thoroughly well informed on questions of state, while Shallum, her husband, was keeper of the robes. I suppose his business was to sew on the royal buttons.' But in spite of this Scriptural authority, the rich lady gave thirty thousand dollars to Princeton and never one cent for the education of her own sex.

" Of all the voices to which these walls have echoed for over half a century, how few remain to tell the story of the early days, and when we part, how few of us will ever meet again; but I know we shall carry with us some new inspiration for the work that still remains for us to do. Though many of us are old in years, we may still be young in heart. Women trained to concentrate all their thoughts on family life are apt to think—when their children are grown up, their loved ones gone, their servants trained to keep the domestic machinery in motion—that their work in life is done, that no one needs now their thought and care, quite forgetting that the hey-day of woman's life is on the shady side of fifty, when the vital forces heretofore expended in other ways are garnered in the brain, when their thoughts and sentiments flow out in broader channels, when philanthropy takes the place of family selfishness, and when from the depths of poverty and suffering the wail of humanity grows as pathetic to their ears as once was the cry of their own children.

" Or, perhaps, the pressing cares of family life ended, the woman may awake to some slumbering genius in herself for art, science, or literature, with which to gild the sunset of her life. Longfellow's beautiful poem, ' Morituri Salutamus,' written for a similar occasion to this, is full of hope and promise for all of us. He says:

> "'Something remains for us to do or dare ;
> Even the oldest tree some fruit may bear.
> Cato learned Greek at eighty ; Sophocles
> Wrote his grand Œdipus, and Simonides
> Bore off the prize of verse from his compeers,
> When each had numbered more than four-score years,
> And Theophrastus, at three-score and ten,
> Had but begun his Characters of Men ;
> Chaucer, at Woodstock with the nightingales,
> At sixty wrote the Canterbury Tales ;
> Goethe at Weimar, toiling to the last,
> Completed Faust when eighty years were past.
> These are indeed exceptions ; but they show
> How far the gulf-stream of our youth may flow
> Into the Arctic regions of our lives,
> Where little else than life itself survives.
> For age is opportunity no less
> Than youth itself, though in another dress,
> And as the evening twilight fades away
> The sky is filled with stars, invisible by day.'"

On December 21, 1892, we celebrated, for the first time, "Foremothers' Day." Men had celebrated "Forefathers' Day" for many years, but as women were never invited to join in their festivities, Mrs. Devereux Blake introduced the custom of women having a dinner in celebration of that day. Mrs. Isabella Beecher Hooker spent two days with me, and together we attended the feast and made speeches. This custom is now annually observed, and gentlemen sit in the gallery just as ladies had done on similar occasions.

My son Theodore arrived from France in April, 1893, to attend the Chicago Exposition, and spent most of the summer with me at Glen Cove, Long Island, where my son Gerrit and his wife were domiciled. Here we read Captain Charles King's stories of life at military posts, Sanborn's " Biography of Bronson Alcott," and Lecky's " History of Rationalism."

Here I visited Charles A. Dana, the Nestor of journalism, and his charming family. He lived on a beautiful island near Glen Cove. His refined, artistic taste, shown in his city residence in paintings, statuary, and rare bric-a-brac, collected in his frequent travels in the Old World, displayed itself in his island home in the arrangement of an endless variety of trees, shrubs, and flowers, through which you caught glimpses of the Sound and distant shores. One seldom meets so gifted a man as the late editor of the *Sun*. He was a scholar, speaking several languages; an able writer and orator, and a most genial companion in the social circle. His wife and daughter are cultivated women. The name of this daughter, Zoe Dana Underhill, often appears in our popular magazines as the author of short stories, remarkable for their vivid descriptions.

I met Mr. Dana for the first time at the Brook Farm Community in 1843, in that brilliant circle of Boston transcendentalists, who hoped in a few years to transform our selfish, competitive civilization into a Paradise where all the altruistic virtues might make co-operation possible. But alas! the material at hand was not sufficiently plastic for that higher ideal. In due time the community dissolved and the members returned to their ancestral spheres. Margaret Fuller, who was a frequent visitor there, betook herself to matrimony in sunny Italy, William Henry Channing to the Church, Bronson Alcott to the education of the young, Frank Cabot to the world of work, Mr. and Mrs. Ripley to literature, and Charles A. Dana to the press. Mr. Dana was very fortunate in his family relations. His wife, Miss Eunice MacDaniel, and her relatives sympathized with him in all his most liberal opinions. During the summer at Glen Cove I had the pleasure of several long conversations with Miss Frances L. MacDaniel and her brother Osborne, whose wife is the sister of Mr. Dana, and who is now assisting Miss Prestona Mann in trying an experiment, similar to the one at Brook Farm, in the Adirondacks.

Miss Anthony spent a week with us in Glen Cove. She came to stir me up to write papers for every Congress at the Exposition, which I did, and she read them in the different Congresses, adding her own strong words at the close. Mrs. Russell Sage also came and spent a day with us to urge me to write a paper to be read at Chicago at the Emma Willard Reunion, which I did. A few days afterward Theodore and I returned her visit. We enjoyed a few hours' conversation with Mr Sage, who had made a very generous gift of a building to the Emma Willard Seminary at Troy. This school was one of the first established (1820) for girls in our State, and received an appropriation from the New York legislature on the recommendation of the Governor, De Witt Clinton. Mr. Sage gave us a description that night of the time his office was blown up with dynamite thrown by a crank, and of his narrow escape. We found the great financier and his wife in an unpretending cottage with a fine outlook on the sea. Though possessed of great wealth they set a good example of simplicity and economy, which many extravagant people would do well to follow.

Having visited the World's Exposition at Chicago and attended a course of lectures at Chautauqua, my daughter, Mrs. Stanton Lawrence, returned to the city, and as soon as our apartment was in order I joined her. She had recently been appointed Director of Physical Training at the Teachers' College in New York city. I attended several of her exhibitions and lectures, which were very interesting. She is doing her best to develop, with proper exercises and sanitary dress, a new type of womanhood.

My time passed pleasantly these days with a drive in the Park and an hour in the land of Nod, also in reading Henry George's "Progress and Poverty," William Morris on industrial questions, Stevenson's novels, the "Heavenly Twins," and "Marcella," and at twilight, when I could not see to read and write, in playing and singing the old tunes and songs I loved in my youth. In the evening we played draughts and chess. I am fond of all games, also of music and novels, hence the days fly swiftly by; I am never lonely, life is ever very sweet to me and full of interest.

The winter of 1893-94 was full of excitement, as the citizens of New York were to hold a Constitutional Convention. Dr. Mary Putnam Jacobi endeavored to rouse a new class of men and women to action in favor of an amendment granting to women the right to vote. Appeals were sent throughout the State, gatherings were held in parlors, and enthusiastic meetings in Cooper Institute and at the Savoy Hotel. My daughter, Mrs. Stanton Blatch, who was visiting this country, took an active part in the canvass, and made an eloquent speech in Cooper Institute. Strange to say, some of the leading ladies formed a strong party against the proposed amendment and their own enfranchisement. They were called the "Antis." This opposing organization adopted the same plan for the campaign as those in favor of the amendment. They issued appeals, circulated petitions, and had hearings before the Convention.

Mrs. Russell Sage, Mrs. Henry M. Sanders, Mrs. Edward Lauterbach, Mrs. Runkle, and some liberal clergymen did their uttermost to secure the insertion of the amendment in the proposed new constitution, but the Committee on Suffrage of the Constitutional Convention refused even to submit the proposed amendment to a vote of the people, though half a million of our most intelligent and respectable citizens had signed the petition requesting them to do so. Joseph H. Choate and Elihu Root did their uttermost to defeat the amendment, and succeeded.

I spent the summer of 1894 with my son Gerrit, in his home at Thomaston, Long Island. Balzac's novels, and the "Life of Thomas Paine" by Moncure D. Conway, with the monthly magazines and daily papers, were my mental pabulum. My daughter, Mrs. Stanton Lawrence, returned from England in September, 1894, having had a pleasant visit with her sister in Basingstoke. In December Miss Anthony came, and we wrote the woman suffrage article for the new edition of Johnson's Cyclopedia.

On March 3, 1895, Lady Somerset and Miss Frances Willard, on the eve of their departure for England, called to see me. We discussed my project of a " Woman's Bible." They consented to join a revising committee, but before the committee was organized they withdrew their names, fearing the work would be too radical. I especially desired to have the opinions of women from all sects, but those belonging to the orthodox churches declined to join the committee or express their views. Perhaps they feared their faith might be disturbed by the strong light of investigation. Some half dozen members of the Revising Committee began with me to write " Comments on the Pentateuch."

The chief thought revolving in my mind during the years of 1894 and 1895 had been " The Woman's Bible." In talking with friends I began to feel that I might realize my long-cherished plan. Accordingly, I began to read the commentators on the Bible and was surprised to see how little they had to say about the greatest factor in civilization, the mother of the race, and that little by no means complimentary. The more I read, the more keenly I felt the importance of convincing women that the Hebrew mythology had no special claim to a higher origin than that of the Greeks, being far less attractive in style and less refined in sentiment. Its objectionable features would long ago have been apparent had they not been glossed over with a faith in their divine inspiration. For several months I devoted all my time to Biblical criticism and ecclesiastical history, and found no explanation for the degraded status of women under all religions, and in all the so-called " Holy Books."

When Part I. of " The Woman's Bible " was finally published in November, 1895, it created a great sensation. Some of the New York city papers gave a page to its review, with pictures of the commentators, of its critics, and even of the book itself. The clergy denounced it as the work of *Satan*, though it really was the work of Ellen Battelle Dietrick, Lillie Devereux Blake, Rev. Phebe A. Hanaford, Clara Bewick Colby, Ursula N. Gestefeld, Louisa Southworth, Frances Ellen Burr, and myself. Extracts from it, and criticisms of the commentators, were printed in the newspapers throughout America, Great Britain, and Europe. A third edition was found necessary, and finally an edition was published in England. The Revising Committee was enlarged, and it now consists of over thirty of the leading women of America and Europe.*

The month of August, 1895, we spent in Peterboro, on the grand hills of Madison County, nine hundred feet above the valley. Gerrit Smith's fine old mansion still stands, surrounded with magnificent trees, where I had played in childhood, chasing squirrels over lawn and gardens and wading in a modest stream that still creeps slowly round the grounds. I recalled as I sat on the piazza how one time, when Frederick Douglass came to spend a few days at Peterboro, some Southern visitors wrote a note to Mr. Smith asking if Mr. Douglass was to sit in the parlor and at the

---

* Part II. of "The Woman's Bible," which completes the work, will be issued in January, 1898.

dining table; if so, during his visit they would remain in their own apartments.   Mr. Smith replied that
his visitors were always treated by his family as equals,
and such would be the case with Mr. Douglass, who
was considered one of the ablest men reared under
" The Southern Institution."   So these ladies had their
meals in their own apartments, where they stayed most
of the time, and, as Mr. Douglass prolonged his visit,
they no doubt wished in their hearts that they had
never taken that silly position.   The rest of us walked
about with him, arm in arm, played games, and sang
songs together, he playing the accompaniment on the
guitar.   I suppose if our prejudiced countrywomen had
been introduced to Dumas in a French salon, they
would at once have donned their bonnets and ran away.

Sitting alone under the trees I recalled the different
generations that had passed away, all known to me.
Here I had met the grandfather, Peter Sken Smith,
partner of John Jacob Astor.   In their bargains with the
Indians they acquired immense tracts of land in the
Northern part of the State of New York, which were
the nucleus of their large fortunes.   I have often heard
Cousin Gerrit complain of the time he lost managing the
estate.   His son Greene was an enthusiast in the natural
sciences and took but little interest in property matters.
Later, his grandson, Gerrit Smith Miller, assumed the
burden of managing the estate and, in addition, devoted
himself to agriculture.   He imported a fine breed of
Holstein cattle, which have taken the first prize at several fairs.   His son, bearing the same name, is devoted to the natural sciences, like his uncle Greene;
whose fine collection of birds was presented by his
widow to Harvard College.

The only daughter of Gerrit Smith, Elizabeth Smith Miller, is a remarkable woman, possessing many of the traits of her noble father. She has rare executive ability, as shown in the dispatch of her extensive correspondence and in the perfect order of her house and grounds. She has done much in the way of education, especially for the colored race, in helping to establish schools and in distributing literature. She subscribes for many of the best books, periodicals, and papers for friends not able to purchase for themselves. We cannot estimate the good she has done in this way. Every mail brings her letters from all classes, from charitable institutions, prisons, Southern plantations, army posts, and the far-off prairies. To all these pleas for help she gives a listening ear. Her charities are varied and boundless, and her hospitalities to the poor as well as the rich, courteous and generous. The refinement and artistic taste of the Southern mother and the heroic virtues of the father are happily blended in their daughter. In her beautiful home on Seneca Lake, one is always sure to meet some of the most charming representatives of the progressive thought of our times. Representatives of all these generations now rest in the cemetery at Peterboro, and as in review they passed before me they seemed to say, " Why linger you here alone so long? "

My son Theodore arrived from Paris in September, 1895, and rendered most important service during the preparations for my birthday celebration, in answering letters, talking with reporters, and making valuable suggestions to the managers as to many details in the arrangements, and encouraging me to go through the ordeal with my usual heroism. I never felt so nervous in my life, and so unfitted for the part I was in duty bound to perform. From much speaking through many years my voice was hoarse, from a severe fall I was quite lame, and as standing, and distinct speaking are important to graceful oratory, I felt like the king's daughter in Shakespeare's play of " Titus Andronicus," when rude men who had cut her hands off and her tongue out, told her to call for water and wash her hands. However, I lived through the ordeal, as the reader will see in the next chapter.

After my birthday celebration, the next occasion of deep interest to me was the Chicago Convention of 1896, the platform there adopted, and the nomination and brilliant campaign of William J. Bryan. I had long been revolving in my mind questions relating to the tariff and finance, and in the demands of liberal democrats, populists, socialists, and the laboring men and women, I heard the clarion notes of the coming revolution.

During the winter of 1895-96 I was busy writing alternately on this autobiography and " The Woman's Bible," and articles for magazines and journals on every possible subject from Venezuela and Cuba to the bicycle. On the latter subject many timid souls were greatly distressed. Should women ride? What should they wear? What are " God's intentions " concerning them? Should they ride on Sunday? These questions were asked with all seriousness. We had a symposium on these points in one of the daily papers. To me the answer to all these questions was simple—if woman could ride, it was evidently " God's intention " that she be permitted to do so. As to what she should wear, she must decide what is best adapted to her comfort and convenience. Those who prefer a spin of a few hours on a good road in the open air to a close church and a dull sermon, surely have the right to choose, whether with trees and flowers and singing birds to worship in " That temple not made with hands, eternal in the heavens," or within four walls to sleep during the intonation of that melancholy service that relegates us all, without distinction of sex or color, to the ranks of " miserable sinners." Let each one do what seemeth right in her own eyes, provided she does not encroach on the rights of others.

In May, 1896, I again went to Geneva and found the bicycle craze had reached there, with all its most pronounced symptoms; old and young, professors, clergymen, and ladies of fashion were all spinning merrily around on business errands, social calls, and excursions to distant towns. Driving down the avenue one day, we counted eighty bicycles before reaching the post-office. The ancient bandbox, so detested by our sires and sons, has given place to this new machine which our daughters take with them wheresoever they go, boxing and unboxing and readjusting for each journey. It has been a great blessing to our girls in compelling them to cultivate their self-reliance and their mechanical ingenuity, as they are often compelled to mend the wheel in case of accident. Among the visitors at Geneva were Mr. Douglass and his daughter from the island of Cuba. They gave us very sad accounts of the desolate state of the island and the impoverished condition of the people. I had long felt that the United States should interfere in some way to end that cruel warfare, for Spain has proved that she is incompetent to restore order and peace.

CHAPTER XXVIII.

WITHOUT my knowledge or consent, my lifelong friend, Susan B. Anthony, who always seems to appreciate homage tendered to me more highly than even to herself, made arrangements for the celebration of my eightieth birthday, on the 12th day of November, 1895. She preferred that this celebration should be conducted by the National Council of Women, composed of a large number of organizations representing every department of woman's labor, though, as the enfranchisement of woman had been my special life work, it would have been more appropriate if the celebration had been under the auspices of the National Woman's Suffrage Association.

Mrs. Mary Lowe Dickinson, President of the National Council of Women, assumed the financial responsibility and the extensive correspondence involved, and with rare tact, perseverance, and executive ability made the celebration a complete success. In describing this occasion I cannot do better than to reproduce, in part, Mrs. Dickinson's account, published in *The Arena:*

" In the month of June, 1895, the National Council of Women issued the following invitation:

" ' Believing that the progress made by women in the last half century may be promoted by a more general notice of their achievements, we propose to hold, in

New York city, a convention for this purpose. As an appropriate time for such a celebration, the eightieth birthday of Elizabeth Cady Stanton has been chosen. Her half century of pioneer work for the rights of women makes her name an inspiration for such an occasion and her life a fitting object for the homage of all women.

" ' This National Council is composed of twenty organizations; these and all other societies interested are invited to co-operate in grateful recognition of the debt the present generation owes to the pioneers of the past. From their interest in the enfranchisement of women, the influence of Mrs. Stanton and her coadjutor, Miss Anthony, has permeated all departments of progress and made them a common center round which all interested in woman's higher development may gather.'

" To this invitation came responses, from the Old World and the New, expressing sympathy with the proposed celebration, which was intended to emphasize a great principle by showing the loftiness of character that had resulted from its embodiment in a unique personality. The world naturally thinks of the personality before it thinks of the principle. It has, at least, so much unconscious courtesy left as to honor a noble woman, even when failing to rightly apprehend a noble cause. To afford this feeling its proper expression, to render more tangible all vague sympathy, to crystallize the growing sentiment in favor of human freedom, to give youth the opportunity to reverence the glory of age, to give hearts their utterances in word and song was perhaps the most popular purpose of the reunion. In other words, it gave an opportunity for those who revered Mrs. Stanton as a queen among women to show their reverence, and to recognize the work her life had wrought, and to see in it an epitome of the progress of a century.

" The celebration was also an illustration of the distinctive idea of the National Council of Women, which aims to give recognition to all human effort without demanding uniformity of opinion as a basis of co-operation. It claims to act upon a unity of service, notwithstanding differences of creed and methods. The things that separate, shrank back into the shadows where they belong, and all hearts brave enough to think, and tender enough to feel, found it easy to unite in homage to a life which had known a half century of struggle to lift humanity from bondage and womanhood from shame.

" This reunion was the first general recognition of the debt the present owes to the past. It was the first effort to show the extent to which later development has been inspired and made possible by the freedom to think and work claimed in that earlier time by women like Lucretia Mott, Lucy Stone, Mrs. Stanton, and many others whose names stand as synonyms of noble service for the race. To those who looked at the reunion from this point of view it could not fail of inspiration.

" For the followers in lines of philanthropic work to look in the faces and hear the voices of women like Clara Barton and Mary Livermore; for the multitude enlisted in the crowded ranks of literature to feel in the living presence, what literature owes to women like Julia Ward Howe; for the white ribbon army to turn from its one great leader of to-day whose light, spreading to the horizon, does not obscure or dim the glory of the cru-

sade leaders of the past; for art lovers and art students
to call to mind sculptors like Harriet Hosmer and Anna
Whitney, and remember the days when art was a
sealed book to women; for the followers of the truly
divine art of healing to honor the Blackwell sisters and
the memory of Mme. Clemence Lozier; for the mercy
of surgery to reveal itself in the face of Dr. Cushier, who
has proved for us that heart of pity and hand of skill need
never be divorced; for women lifting their eyes to meet
the face of Phebe A. Hanaford and Anna Shaw and
other women who to-day in the pulpit, as well as out of
it, may use a woman's right to minister to needy souls;
for the ofttime sufferers from unrighteous law to welcome women lawyers; for the throng of working women
to read backward through the story of four hundred
industries to their beginning in the ' four,' and remember that each new door had opened because some
women toiled and strove; for all these the exercises were
a part of a great thanksgiving pæan, each phase of progress striking its own chord, and finding each its echo
in the hearts that held it dear.

"To the student of history, or to him who can read
the signs of the times, there was such a profound significance in this occasion as makes one shrink from
dwelling too much upon the external details. Yet as a
pageant only it was a most inspiring sight, and one truly
worthy of a queen. Indeed as we run the mind back
over the pages of history, what queen came to a more
triumphant throne in the hearts of a grateful people?
What woman ever before sat silver-crowned, canopied
with flowers, surrounded not by servile followers but by
men and women who brought to her court the grandest
service they had wrought, their best thought crystallized

in speech and song. Greater than any triumphal procession that ever marked a royal passage through a kingdom was it to know that in a score or more of cities, in many a village church on that same night festive fires were lighted, and the throng kept holiday, bringing for tribute not gold and gems but noblest aspirations, truest gratitude, and highest ideals for the nation and the race.

" The great meeting was but one link in a chain; yet with its thousands of welcoming faces, with its eloquence of words, with its offering of sweetest song from the children of a race that once was bound but now is free, with its pictured glimpses of the old time and the new flashing out upon the night, with the home voices offering welcome and gratitude and love, with numberless greetings, from the great, true, brave souls of many lands, it was indeed a wonderful tribute, worthy of the great warm heart of a nation that offered it, and worthy of the woman so revered.

" It seemed fitting that Mme. Antoinette Sterling, who, twenty years ago, took her wonderful voice away to England, where it won for her a unique place in the hearts of the nation, should, on returning to her country, give her first service to the womanhood of her native land. ' I am coming a week earlier,' so she had written, ' that my first work in my own beloved America may be done for women. I am coming as a woman and not as an artist, and because I so glory in that which the women of my country have achieved.' So when she sang out of her heart, ' O rest in the Lord; wait patiently for him!' no marvel that it seemed to lift all listening hearts to a recognition of the divine secret and source of power for all work.

" One charming feature of the entertainment was a series of pictures called ' Then and Now,' each illustrating the change in woman's condition during the last fifty years. And after this, upon the dimness there shone out, one after another, the names of noble women like Mary Lyon, Maria Mitchell, Emma Willard, and many others who have passed away. Upon the shadows and the silence broke Mme. Sterling's voice in Tennyson's ' Crossing the Bar.' And when this was over, as with one voice, the whole audience sang softly ' Auld Lang Syne.'

" And last but not least should be mentioned the greetings that poured in a shower of telegrams and letters from every section of the country, and many from over the sea. These expressions, not only of personal congratulation for Mrs. Stanton, but utterances of gladness for the progress in woman's life and thought, for the conditions, already so much better than in the past, and for the hope for the future, would make of themselves a most interesting and wonderful chapter. Among them may be mentioned letters from Lord and Lady Aberdeen, from Lady Henry Somerset and Frances E. Willard, from Canon Wilberforce, and many others, including an address from thirty members of the family of John Bright, headed by his brother, the Right Honorable Jacob Bright; a beautifully engrossed address, on parchment, from the National Woman Suffrage Society of Scotland, an address from the London Women's Franchise League, and a cablegram from the Bristol Women's Liberal Association; a letter from the Women's Rights Society of Finland, signed by its president, Baroness Gripenberg of Helsingfors; telegrams from the California Suffrage Pioneers; and others from the Chicago Woman's Club, from the Toledo and Ohio Woman's Suffrage Society, from the son of the Rev. Dr. William Ellery Channing, and a telegram and letter from citizens and societies of Seneca Falls, New York, accompanied with flowers and many handsome pieces of silver from the different societies. There were also letters from Hon. Oscar S. Strauss, ex-minister to Turkey, Miss Ellen Terry, and scores of others. An address was received from the Women's Association of Utah, accompanied by a beautiful onyx and silver ballot box; and from the Shaker women of Mount Lebanon came an ode; a solid silver loving cup from the New York City Suffrage League, presented on the platform with a few appropriate words by its President, Mrs. Devereux Blake.

"Hundreds of organizations and societies, both in this country and abroad, wished to have their names placed on record as in sympathy with the movement. Many organizations were present in a body, and one was reminded, by the variety and beauty of the decorations of their boxes, of the Venetian Carnival, as the occupants gazed down from amid the silken banners and the flowers, upon the throng below. The whole occasion was indeed a unique festival, unique in its presentation, as well as in its purpose, plan, character, and spirit. No woman present could fail to be impressed with what we owe to the women of the past, and especially to this one woman who was the honored guest of the occasion. And no young woman could desire to forget the picture of this aged form as, leaning upon her staff, Mrs. Stanton spoke to the great audience of over six thousand, as she had spoken hundreds of times before in legislative halls, and whenever her word could influence the popular sentiment in favor of justice for all mankind."

My birthday celebration, with all the testimonials of love and friendship I received, was an occasion of such serious thought and deep feeling as I had never before experienced. Having been accustomed for half a century to blame rather than praise, I was surprised with such a manifestation of approval; I could endure any amount of severe criticism with complacency, but such an outpouring of homage and affection stirred me profoundly. To calm myself during that week of excitement, I thought many times of Michelet's wise motto, " Let the weal and woe of humanity be everything to you, their praise and blame of no effect; be not puffed up with the one nor cast down with the other."

Naturally at such a time I reviewed my life, its march and battle on the highways of experience, and counted its defeats and victories. I remembered when a few women called the first convention to discuss their disabilities, that our conservative friends said: " You have made a great mistake, you will be laughed at from Maine to Texas and beyond the sea; God has set the bounds of woman's sphere and she should be satisfied with her position." Their prophecy was more than realized; we were unsparingly ridiculed by the press and pulpit both in England and America. But now many conventions are held each year in both countries to discuss the same ideas; social customs have changed; laws have been modified; municipal suffrage has been granted to women in England and some of her colonies; school suffrage has been granted to women in half of our States, municipal suffrage in Kansas, and full suffrage in four States of the Union. Thus the principle scouted in 1848 was accepted in England in 1870, and since then, year by year, it has slowly progressed in America until the fourth star shone out on our flag in 1896, and Idaho enfranchised her women! That first convention, considered a " grave mistake " in 1848, is now referred to as " a grand step in progress."

My next mistake was when, as president of the New York State Woman's Temperance Association, I demanded the passage of a statute allowing wives an absolute divorce for the brutality and intemperance of their husbands. I addressed the Legislature of New York a few years later when a similar bill was pending, and also large audiences in several of our chief cities, and for this I was severely denounced. To-day fugitives from such unholy ties can secure freedom in many of the Western States, and enlightened public sentiment sustains mothers in refusing to hand down an appetite fraught with so many evil consequences. This, also called a " mistake " in 1860, was regarded as a " step in progress " a few years later.

Again, I urged my coadjutors by speeches, letters, and resolutions, as a means of widespread agitation, to make the same demands of the Church that we had already made of the State. They objected, saying, " That is too revolutionary, an attack on the Church would injure the suffrage movement." But I steadily made the demand, as opportunity offered, that women be ordained to preach the Gospel and to fill the offices as elders, deacons, and trustees. A few years later some of these suggestions were accepted. Some churches did ordain women as pastors over congregations of their own, others elected women deaconesses, and a few churches allowed women, as delegates, to sit in their conferences.

Thus this demand was in a measure honored and another " step in progress " taken.

In 1882 I tried to organize a committee to consider the status of women in the Bible, and the claim that the Hebrew Writings were the result of divine inspiration. It was thought very presumptuous for women not learned in languages and ecclesiastical history to undertake such work. But as we merely proposed to comment on what was said of women in plain English, and found these texts composed only one-tenth of the Old and New Testaments, it did not seem to me a difficult or dangerous undertaking. However, when Part I. of " The Woman's Bible " was published, again there was a general disapproval by press and pulpit, and even by women themselves, expressed in resolutions in suffrage and temperance conventions. Like other " mistakes," this too, in due time, will be regarded as " a step in progress."

Such experiences have given me confidence in my judgment, and patience with the opposition of my coadjutors, with whom on so many points I disagree. It requires no courage now to demand the right of suffrage, temperance legislation, liberal divorce laws, or for women to fill church offices—these battles have been fought and won and the principle governing these demands conceded. But it still requires courage to question the divine inspiration of the Hebrew Writings as to the position of woman. Why should the myths, fables, and allegories of the Hebrews be held more sacred than those of the Assyrians and Egyptians, from whose literature most of them were derived? Seeing that the religious superstitions of women perpetuate their bondage more than all other adverse influences, I feel impelled to reiterate my demands for justice, liberty, and equality in the Church as well as in the State.

The birthday celebration was to me more than a beautiful pageant; more than a personal tribute. It was the dawn of a new day for the Mothers of the Race! The harmonious co-operation of so many different organizations, with divers interests and opinions, in one grand jubilee was, indeed, a heavenly vision of peace and hope; a prophecy that with the exaltation of Womanhood would come new Life, Light, and Liberty to all mankind.

AFTERWORD

"THE story of my private life . . . may amuse and benefit the reader." With that statement in her preface to *Eighty Years and More*, Elizabeth Cady Stanton confuses modern readers who understand her to mean an intimate look at personal relations but find in the book a political career. When the book appeared in 1898, reviewers responded differently. The New York *Evening Sun* called it "frankly personal," while the daytime *Sun* noted its omission of her public career in favor of "the story of her private life."[1] Some difference between the two reactions can be accounted for by changing perceptions about the personal in the lives of public figures. People accustomed to learning gritty details of a life deem Stanton's revelations about her love of good food, her acute memory for physical discomfort, and her well-timed naps insufficiently personal. But modern readers work at a disadvantage, too, because they know much less about Elizabeth Cady Stanton before reading her autobiography than did readers in the 1890s.

Stanton never intended that her reminiscences be *the* evidence for establishing her historical significance. Rather, she took advantage of how well known she was to the public after fifty years as a leader of women, successful lecturer, frequent writer, and historian. While her book avoids private life in modern terms, it also omits a record of much of her public life. The book merely

alludes to public and political events that Stanton takes
for granted as knowledge available to her audience, much
of it provided by the comprehensive record in three volumes of the *History of Woman Suffrage* that she published
between 1881 and 1886.[2] Within *Eighty Years* she adds
a new layer of interpretation, a personal dimension to
that public history.

Her chapter on the first women's rights convention in
Eighty Years is a good illustration of how she takes a
familiar public event and recasts it in personal terms. So
intent is Stanton on the psychological aspect of liberation
in this chapter, she omits to state the meeting's purpose,
the object of its resolutions, or her advocacy of suffrage
as a right of women. Her account roots the convention
in private experience and traces its effect on the dilemmas
of individuals. A more overtly political narrative would
proceed from the convention in July of 1848 to legal
reforms and more conventions, but here Stanton describes how daily expectations and small town relations
changed as a consequence of the birth of reform.

One can also read this chapter as being more about a
turning point in women's history than about Stanton
herself. As elsewhere in the book, Stanton avoids exploring her individuality for its own sake or detailing
what distinguished her from the group of women who
broke out of their solitude into political reform. Her habit
of generalizing from herself to her allies and friends in-
troduces a possible distinction between "individual" and
"personal," leaving it ambiguous whether she writes
about her own particular life or about how people, herself
included, experienced history on a personal level.

The same ambiguity can be found even in the early
chapters, where individual experience as a child in a

particular family seems to focus the story precisely on Elizabeth Cady and her unique personality. There she makes the struggle against religious orthodoxy central to her own emancipation, placing her earliest rebelliousness in the context of resistance to Scotch Presbyterianism (24). By the end of the book, however, readers learn that Stanton believes resistance to religious orthodoxy enabled the women's rights movement and informs its ongoing mission. This knowledge casts her story of childhood in a different light; the story illustrates her view of history at least as much as it accounts for her youthful experience. In her mind agitation for women's rights was predicated on the realization that "the religious superstitions of women perpetuate their bondage more than all other adverse influences" (467–68), as she writes in the book's penultimate paragraph. The rebelliousness she highlights in her childhood foretells the social change without necessarily vouching for a particular child's behavior.

Eighty Years and More is a carefully crafted culmination to a lifetime of writing. Unambiguously a woman's story, the book is shaped throughout by Stanton's intimate knowledge of the inequality she and other women have lived with. It is also agitational, consistent with her use of immediate experience to enliven political presentations, bridge the gap between leader and followers, and demonstrate how women's voices should be heard in discussions of public policy and government, indeed in any dialogue that defined the nation.

Stanton began to explore the potential of woman's experience as a basis for social and political commentary in her first articles, published in the *Lily* in the 1850s, while she was tied to home by small children and domestic responsibilities. Finding her material in daily life

— in conversations with children, domestic catastrophes, smells emanating from a local brewery, or chatter over-heard in the barber's shop — she took the measure of society from the vantage point of woman-working-in-the-household and drew conclusions of public impor-tance.[3] Within a few years, she had so well mastered this style of contributing to political dialogue while speaking as a woman that she published her work not only in the early women's newspapers but in the national press as well.

When she took up work as a lecturer after the Civil War, she continued to discover wisdom, principles, and even jokes in women's personal world to inform her contributions to political debate. While she agitated for a republic governed in the best interests of both sexes, she gave voice to women's experience, humor, and pain. She could shift with great wit from cookbooks to Con-gress in one breath and demystify men's power with jokes about their incompetence in the domestic realm. If every woman knew that boys and men could never find their own hats, how could women long endure the sheer silli-ness of men asserting they could govern for women? Personal stories and woman's perspective served neither to distinguish herself nor to separate the worlds of women and men. Supporting oneself as a lecturer, as Stanton did successfully for more than a decade, required attracting male audiences as well as female. Her stories bridged the gap created by inequality.

Even the decision to prepare the *History of Woman Suffrage* in the early eighties staked women's claim to a voice in defining the nation, in this case by seizing the turf of historical documentation and interpretation. The three volumes that Stanton coauthored reflect the nation's

sense of itself as a beacon to the world and a self-im-
proving polity. But because they document how hard
and against what odds women struggled to share the
benefits of that tradition, the volumes use women's per-
spectives to redefine the tradition, to rethink what Ellen
DuBois calls the "principle of America."

Stanton wrote most of the text in *Eighty Years* first as
newspaper articles that appeared from 1889 until 1892,
while she presided over the National Woman Suffrage
Association and its successor, the National-American
Woman Suffrage Association. In seventy-two articles
that appeared under the title "Reminiscences," she began
to construct a loosely chronological and comprehensive
narrative from her recollections of life, submitted against
deadlines to the leading woman suffrage newspaper
aligned with her organization, the *Woman's Tribune*.[4]
When the series stopped in the summer of 1892, she put
the project aside for several years before refining the
articles into a book.

Because Stanton had always considered her experience
a valid basis from which to speak out about the world,
many incidents in her life had been put into words and
assigned meanings long before she wrote her autobiography. The story about cutting laws from law books had
appeared in lectures since the sixties. For at least as long,
she had been called upon to write biographies of Susan B.
Anthony in which she explored the early years of their
friendship. She had also used the title "Reminiscences"
for a few chapters in the three volumes of the *History of
Woman Suffrage* that supplemented the documentary history.[5]

Though Stanton mined earlier writings for material to
include in her autobiography, she often rewrote her mem-

ories, sometimes turning familiar stories on their head, giving them nearly opposite meanings. In 1884 she had published some random recollections in general circulation newspapers. Only a few of the articles can be located now, but those few offer unusual insight into her notions of truth and storytelling.[6] An article called "A Lecturer's Trials" explored the working conditions of the lecturer by recounting how other people's mistakes could make the work harder. The trials of the title are caused by an absent-minded telegrapher, a thoughtlessly noisy audience, a mother who cannot keep her baby content and thus quiet, and people ignorant of the laws of health who endure bad ventilation. The lecturer is their victim; among her "sorest trials" are mothers who bring their babies to hear her; at Salt Lake City, the "effect of the occasion was destroyed by the babies" and the lecturer suffered "great humiliation." The episodes recur in "Reminiscences" and *Eighty Years*, and though the people make the same mistakes, Stanton reacts generously in the later telling. She casts the women and their need for child care sympathetically, concedes that lecturing over the sound of babies "was rather trying at first," but boasts that she learned to adapt to the distraction (285–86).

In this revision, Stanton presents herself more favorably as a woman empathetic about the differences between her expectations and those of the people she met, but she also makes herself less important to the incidents. They are no longer stories about her troubles but have become stories about the nation and its people.

Some revisions also occurred between the "Reminiscences," published from 1889 to 1892, and the text of *Eighty Years and More*, published six years later. The book's chapter "School Days," in which her brother's death is recounted, began as two articles in the *Woman's Tribune*.[7] In the earlier telling she had not yet realized the full potential of this moving story about learning the limits of being a daughter. Calling the first article "Church and Parsonage" and beginning it with an extended description of the church of her childhood, the Reverend Hosack, and her friendship with him, she put her brother's death at the close of the article, like an addendum to the main story. Studying Greek is part of the story of her closeness to Hosack, a privilege borne of the minister's own unhappiness; she revives her Greek studies only incidentally in relation to her brother's death and her decision to be like a boy. By reversing this article for the text of her book, Stanton made the study of Greek a powerful symbol in the more memorable symmetry of her brother's death and the change it wrought in her own aspirations.

Nothing seems fixed or final in these versions of a life. Was she or was she not humiliated at Salt Lake City? Had arrangements for Elizabeth to study Greek been made before her brother died, as she earlier implied? Stanton does not pin down episodes of what happened to her but explores their potential for illuminating history. Critical incidents in her relationship with her father were especially useful. In the interval between writing about him for the *Woman's Tribune* in 1889 and revising the text for the book, Stanton published, in 1894, a different version of the encounter over her address to the New York State legislature, one that enhances the story's emotional power but scrambles time and place and invents public occasions.[8] In this version Stanton dates the event, within the space of two paragraphs, as 1840, 1846, and 1848, but never as 1854. She sets the scene in 1840 when, as a new bride, she lived in her father's house while her husband studied law. Her character is naive about political news and plans to sneak off to Albany as if on a shopping trip, without letting father or husband know her intent. When an Albany newspaper announces her scheduled appearance before the legislature, her father confronts her. Although he helps her find laws to illustrate her points, he is harsher here than in other versions, using guilt ("I wish you had waited till my head was under the sod before you did this") and bribes ("I will give you that house if you won't do this thing") in an effort to stop her. The daughter resists him and speaks to the legislature in person with great effect. Something may have happened in one of the years to which she refers, but the first legislative speech was prepared in 1854, and only a printed text reached individual legislators because she was not invited into chambers to speak.

What matters ultimately to Stanton is not, apparently, whether she recalls events accurately, represents her father fairly, records details correctly, but whether she conveys to people the complicated tensions over fathers, husbands, law, and public behavior that accompanied the advent of women's rights. In *Eighty Years* she provided a useful metaphor for thinking about this style. She describes a lecture she improvised when faced with an audience expecting entertainment from the Christy Minstrels rather than education from Elizabeth Cady Stanton. To hold the restless crowd she made "a medley of anecdotes and stories, like a string of beads, held together by a fine thread of argument and illustration" (308). If learning Greek while a girl is one bead, her friend Hosack another bead, and the death of her brother a third bead, Stanton acknowledges no necessary or inherent relationship among them until she crafts jewelry

from the beads available to her. Her memories are elements of experience to be strung together for different
arguments; the meaning of things lies in the "fine thread"
by which she holds them together.

Stanton's imagery of a necklace offers, too, a way to
consider an obvious change in the structure of her book
that occurs at about 1880. A "fine thread" becomes more
difficult to discover. There are, no doubt, themes in the
later chapters, like the contrast, in chapter 21, between
nineteenth-century progress in the United States and an
ever-present past of "soldiers and priests" in France. But
it is difficult to believe that every anecdote contributes
to a theme. Stanton tempts her readers to remember her
age and associate the writing with the rambling of the
old.

The change coincides with Stanton's decision to keep
a diary beginning on her sixty-fifth birthday in 1880 (325).
On the page where she notes this commitment, a literal
chronology intrudes. Thereafter, the record retained in
the diary often drives the story.[9] One can almost see her
flipping the pages of a journal and selecting items to
incorporate in her new narrative. Its notations prod her
memory and detail the places she resided, the weather
she found there, the callers who came, and the books she
read. Up until this point in the narrative, chronology of
book and life alike is hazy. Though the chronological
order of a single year appears to govern the chapter
"Lyceums and Lecturers," for instance, in fact it lacks
clear pointers to a temporal sequence. Stanton constructs
an archetypal year, realistically limited by geography to
make the travel feasible but in fact selected from a decade
of memories. Stanton the artist, not a time line, provides
the chapter's coherence.

When Stanton clearly creates and controls the thread

in her chapters, she is allusive and unconventional in her methods. To some extent her success depends on her distance from events and the opportunities she has had to rewrite, revise, or rethink incidents from her life. But as the book progressed, real life began to catch up with the act of writing about it, allowing her less time to identify the most potent meaning in her memories. Stanton's last articles in the *Woman's Tribune* in 1892 described her visit with Anthony in Rochester only a few months earlier. The last event in *Eighty Years* occurred in 1895, six years *after* the year she began to publish her reminiscences in the *Woman's Tribune*.[10] Rarely can autobiographers find coherence in their later life to match what they have learned about their youth.

But Stanton had also relied on her historical sense to discover coherence in her story. A vision of American history permeates the book, as Ellen DuBois demonstrates in her introduction to this volume, and critical moments in the history of the woman suffrage movement are used throughout as elements of Stanton's own story. Her footing in history is less sure near the end of the book. When she selected the year 1876 as the focal point for writing about the politics of woman suffrage, she could string her beads into an elegant necklace that illustrated both the ideological bankruptcy of the nation at its Centennial and the readiness of women to seize the mantle of revolutionary ideals. That year in history produced the end of Reconstruction, Supreme Court decisions that restored states' rights over suffrage, and the beginning of woman suffragists' major nineteenth-century campaign for a federal amendment granting them the right to vote. Suffragists would turn for help to all those women Stanton describes at the fair as showing the advancement of their sex without yet grasping the crucial connection between the fight against political slavery and advancement in other realms. Within the chapter Stanton recaptures the mounting anger that she and her allies had felt at this turning point.

The book's last chapters are about beginnings. History had not revealed itself, and the book lacks finality. By the time Stanton wrote about the eighties and nineties, she could measure the suffrage movement's spread, its social acceptance, its rare but valuable successes, and its (by then) inevitability. But her new struggle, introduced in the chapter "Woman and Theology," had not yet reached a time for summing up. Chapters explore possibilities, introduce allies; they express her interests and aims and her faith in progress, her belief that these things will come to pass. She cannot, however, single out critical moments of change.

She may have hoped that *Eighty Years* would serve as a catalyst for reform, giving meaning to the "*and More*" of her title. The articles of "Reminiscences" stopped at about the same time that Stanton stepped down from the presidency of the National-American Woman Suffrage Association, and Stanton turned her attention to a new series of articles on the Bible, also published in the *Woman's Tribune*. Even while she served as president of the principal suffrage organization, she disagreed with new tendencies: an emphasis on campaigns for state suffrage rather than the federal amendment; the isolation of suffrage from other reforms needed for a new republic; the mobilization of women whose values, other than belief in their need for the vote, collided with hers; and, perhaps most important of all, a marriage between woman suffragism and religious conservatism. When she published

The Woman's Bible, Part I, in 1895, the small book provoked a rebellion within the suffrage association, led by women who claimed it obstructed their organizing by linking woman suffrage with irreligion. Stanton would not compromise. She pulled the ongoing Bible series from the *Woman's Tribune* and submitted it instead to the *Boston Investigator*, a newspaper for freethinkers predisposed to her conviction that organized religion obstructed reform. With that series complete in 1897, she prepared two books for publication; her son's publishing firm released both *Eighty Years and More* and *The Woman's Bible* within the space of months.

When Stanton's children wanted to document their mother's place in American history and particularly to establish her preeminence in the movement for woman suffrage, they revised her autobiography and reissued it in 1922, along with a volume of letters and excerpts from her diary.[11] Although they accounted for changes in the text by claiming that Stanton had herself revised it just before her death in 1902, a lot of circumstantial evidence points to the children, not the mother, as the perpetrators. Motivated by a sincere desire to secure their mother's reputation, Harriot Stanton Blatch and her brother Theodore Stanton needed to enhance the evidentiary value of the reminiscences and consequently worked against her inconclusive narrative. At one end of the political story, they restored the contextual history missing from the chapter on the Seneca Falls Convention, adding the Declaration of Sentiments and an account of Stanton's advocacy of women's right to vote. At the other end, they dropped the chapter on theology and eliminated the concluding paragraphs that sum up her religious goals. The results are a peculiar hybrid that juxtaposes sections retaining Stanton's metaphors with sections that seem to be better grounded in verifiable evidence.

They made a judgment, perhaps a cruel judgment, about their mother's role. By 1922 women had won the vote, and Stanton's children wanted to identify their mother with that victory and associate her forever with its history. Her accomplishment should be the theme. Furthermore, they knew that Stanton's vision about the next phase of emancipation had not yet happened, that women had not accepted her challenge to throw off the chains of orthodoxy. By limiting that part of her story, they polished her reputation, stressed her successful cause, and swept her errors of judgment under the rug. They took from the book many of the ways that make it radiate Stanton's youthfulness even at age eighty-five.

This, the 1898 edition of *Eighty Years and More*, came back into print twenty years ago, to recover something closer to Stanton's vision of herself, without the apologies of her children. It gives us a very strong individual whose sense of her power and leadership rarely falters. Although internally the story reminds readers time and again that the author is not yet free and awaits her equality, it avoids the suggestion that in their lack of freedom women are victims. To the contrary, it depicts enormous change wrought by women: breaking away from orthodoxy, rising above the need for paternal approval, making one's way through marriage and maternity to the adulthood of children, discovering the power of political action, reforming the legal code, transforming women's self-definition, bringing the question of women's civil equality into the mainstream of society and politics, even winning the vote in some places. It is not Stanton's story alone, but rather an exemplification of what women can accomplish and a celebration of their power. It survives in large part because a call to continued action permeates the book.

ANN D. GORDON

Notes

1. From "Press Comments" used in advertisement for *Eighty Years and More* in Elizabeth Cady Stanton, *The Woman's Bible* (New York: European Publishing Co., 1898).

2. Coauthored with Susan B. Anthony and Matilda Joslyn Gage, the first volume of the *History of Woman Suffrage* appeared in 1881, the second in 1882, and the third in 1886.

3. These and other articles by Stanton are available in *The Papers of Elizabeth Cady Stanton and Susan B. Anthony*, ed. Patricia G. Holland and Ann D. Gordon (Wilmington, Del.: Scholarly Resources, 1991, microfilm).

4. The articles appeared in the *Tribune* from April 1889 through July 1892. Manuscripts of some articles in this version and all the printed texts are included in the microfilm edition cited in note 3.

5. Some sections of *Eighty Years* can be traced directly to the chapters in the *History of Woman Suffrage*: for example, chapter 10 about Anthony, the portions of chapter 12 about addressing the legislature and of chapter 13 about the 1860 tour against slavery, come from volume 1; the chapter on British reformers is an abridged version of a chapter in volume 3 in the *History*.

6. Elizabeth Cady Stanton, "Lyceum Experiences," dated September 3, 1884, clipping from unidentified, undated newspaper, in Elizabeth Cady Stanton Papers, Library of Congress, and "A Lecturer's Trials," dated November 25, [1884], clipping from unidentified, undated newspaper, in scrapbook 2, the Papers of Elizabeth Cady Stanton, Vassar College, both in Holland and Gordon, *Papers of Stanton and Anthony*.

7. "Church and Parsonage" appeared on April 20, 1889, followed on May 4 by "A New Brother, With New Ideas," both in the *Woman's Tribune*.

8. "Reminiscences of Elizabeth Cady Stanton," undated typescript with corrections in Stanton's hand, in Political Equality Club of Minneapolis Papers, Minnesota Historical Society, and published in the *Mail and Express* (New York City), December 15, 1894.

9. Stanton's revisions of her diary cannot be judged because the original diary is lost. What her children published in 1922 as a diary is highly suspect as a text (see note 11).

10. On April 2, 1892, the *Woman's Tribune* published "My Home & Susan's. Reception — Co-Education. Mrs. Osborne and Her Knitting." After a pause the *Tribune* carried "Madam Willard and Her School Scholarships" on July 9, 1892. The text of her speech about Willard without any introductory matter carried an editorial note explaining that Stanton had asked that it appear as a part of her reminiscences.

11. *Elizabeth Cady Stanton As Revealed in Her Letters, Diary and Reminiscences*, ed. Harriot Stanton Blatch and Theodore Stanton (New York: Harper and Brothers, 1922), 2 vols.

INDEX OF NAMES.

[*Portions of Chapters X. and XI. of this book are taken by permission from an article written by Mrs. Stanton for " Our Famous Women," published by A. D. Worthington & Co.*]